Museums &Galleries
1998/99

The guide to over 1,800 museums and galleries in England, Northern Ireland, Scotland and Wales

In association with:

ENGLISH
TOURIST BOARD

Northern Ireland
Tourist Board

SCOTLAND

BWRDD CROESO CYMRU
WALES TOURIST BOARD

THE OFFICIAL GUIDES TO ACCOMMODATION IN BRITAIN

All entries graded and classified for quality under the National Tourist Board's grading and classification schemes.

Scotland: Hotels and Guesthouses 1998
Price: UK£8.99   US$17.95
The *Scottish Tourist Board*'s guide to over 1,500 places to stay from luxury hotels to budget priced accommodation. Full colour throughout.

Scotland: Bed and Breakfast 1998
Price: UK£5.99   US$11.95
Over 1,500 bed and breakfast establishments offering inexpensive friendly accommodation.

Scotland: Camping and Caravan Parks 1998
Price: UK£3.99   US$7.95
Over 2,000 parks, often situated in the most breathtaking settings. Also included are caravan holiday homes for hire.

Scotland: Self-Catering Accommodation 1998
Price: UK£5.99   US$11.95
Included in this full-colour guide are over 1,100 cottages, apartments and chalets, many in Scotland's finest scenic areas.

Where to Stay in Northern Ireland 1998
Price: UK£3.99   US$7.95
The official accommodation guide from the *Northern Ireland Tourist Board*, listing hotels, guesthouses, self-catering and bed & breakfast establishments, as well as youth hostels and camping parks.

Wales: Hotels and Guesthouses 1998
Price: UK£3.95 US$7.95
The official guide to Hotels and Guesthouses in Wales.

Wales: Bed and Breakfast 1998
Price: UK£3.50   US$6.99
Bed and Breakfast establishments throughout the Principality.

Wales: Self-Catering Accommodation 1998
Price: UK£3.75   US$7.50
Official guide to cottages, chalets and static caravans.

Wales Tourist Map
Price: UK£1.99   US$3.95
The official map of the *Wales Tourist Board* at 5 miles to 1 inch (1:300,000)

Where to Stay: Hotels and Guesthouses. England 1998
Price: UK£9.99   US$19.95
The *English Tourist Board*'s guide to 2,500 hotels and guesthouses, listed alphabetically by location under ten regional sections, each with an informative introduction and suggestions on attractions to visit.

Where to Stay: Bed and Breakfast, Farmhouses, Inns and Hostels. England 1998
Price: UK£8.99   US$17.95
Contains details of around 2,000 bed and breakfast establishments, farmhouses, inns and hostels in England. Entries are alphabetically listed by location under ten regional sections, each with an informative introduction and suggestions on attractions to visit.

Where to Stay: Families Welcome. England 1998
Price: UK£4.99   US$9.95
Annual guide to over 300 places to stay which both welcome and have a specific range of facilities for children. Includes both serviced and self-catering accommodation.

Where to Stay: Self-Catering Holiday Homes. England 1998
Price: UK£6.99   US$13.95
Contains details on around 1,500 self-catering homes for the visitor who enjoys the freedom and flexibility associated with self-catering holidays. Entries give a description of the establishment together with details of the facilities offered. Includes ideas for places to visit.

Where to Stay: Somewhere Special. England 1998
Price: UK£7.99   US$15.95
Full-colour guide to quality places to stay – all of which have been awarded a *Highly Commended* or *De Luxe* quality grading under the *English Tourist Board*'s Grading and Classification Scheme, reflecting a very high standard of service, furnishings and warmth of welcome.

Where to Stay in London 1998
Price: UK£2.99   US$5.95
The official guide of the *London Tourist Board* listing all types of accommodation from luxury hotels to bed and breakfast establishments.

ORDER THE GUIDES TO BRITAIN USING THE FORM BELOW AND HAVE THEM DELIVERED... ...DIRECT TO YOUR HOME OR OFFICE. ✂

			Quantity	Cost
ENGLAND — Where to Stay: Hotels and Guesthouses	£9.99	US$19.95		
— Where to Stay:Bed & Breakfast	£8.99	US$17.95		
— Where to Stay: Families Welcome	£4.99	US$9.95		
— Where to Stay: Self-Catering	£6.99	US$13.95		
— Where to Stay: Somewhere Special	£7.99	US$15.95		
SCOTLAND — Hotels and Guesthouses	£8.99	US$17.95		
— Bed & Breakfast	£5.99	US$11.95		
— Camping and Caravan Parks	£3.99	US$7.95		
— Self-Catering Accommodation	£5.99	US$11.95		
WALES — Hotels and Guesthouses	£3.95	US$7.95		
— Bed & Breakfast	£3.50	US$6.99		
— Self-Catering Accommodation	£3.75	US$7.50		
— Tourist Map	£1.99	US$3.95		
Where to Stay in **LONDON** 1998	£2.99	US$5.95		
Where to Stay in **NORTHERN IRELAND**	£3.99	US$7.95		
Total Cost of Guides UK£/US$				

Total Cost of Guides   UK£/US$

Postage and packing   UK£/US$

Total   UK£/US$

PLEASE PRINT   M&G98

Name

Address

Postcode

Credit Card details

☐ VISA   ☐ MASTERCARD   ☐ ACCESS   ☐ AMEX   ☐ SWITCH

Card number   Expiry Date

Signature

Postage & Packing
UK: If you are ordering 1 book please add UK£3.50 to cover postage and packaging, and a further 50p for every subsequent book.
USA: If you are ordering 1 book please add US$12.95 to cover postage and packaging, and a further US$2.95 for every subsequent book.
Payment can be made by credit card:
Visa, Mastercard, Access, Amex or Switch
You have three options of how to order.
1) Mail your order,**together with payment or credit card details** to: British Tourist Authority Publication Sales, Finance Department, Thames Tower, Black's Road, London W6 9EL. Please remit in Sterling(UK£) or US$ and make cheques/checks payable to *The British Tourist Authority*.
2) Fax this order form **with your credit card details** to +44 (0)181 563 3289.
3) Phone our **Credit Card Hotline** on +44 (0)181 563 3276.

Museum-going — a lifelong habit

Loyd Grossman. © WALKER PRINT LTD

Thanks to geographical accident and dedicated parents I got the museum-going habit early. I was lucky enough to grow up in the shadow of two great American museums: the Peabody Museum in Salem, Massachusetts, and the Museum of Fine Arts nearby in Boston.

The Peabody was the more old-fashioned establishment with a collection of marine antiquities and ethnographic curiosities brought home by eighteenth- and nineteenth-century sea captains. Although most of its displays were in glass cases it was a vivid and exciting place to visit: the Hawaiian war god there still frightens me. The Museum of Fine Arts conformed more to everyone's idea of a high-culture establishment – a building of severe neoclassical grandeur full of works by the big names of art history. It offered me the chance to come face to face with some of the most profound and beautiful examples of human creativity.

Today, in the United Kingdom, we are determined to make the museum-going habit as easy to get as possible. We are endowed with an extraordinary number of museums and galleries, so it isn't surprising that more people go to museums than to football matches, the cinema or the theatre. And our museums are not only full of artefacts, but they are also tremendously active and extrovert institutions.

For many people, museum-going starts with a school visit: not just a lively way of learning from real objects, but also a key way of meeting the requirements of the curriculum. Museum curators, designers and educators are working hard to develop educational programmes that stimulate and inspire new generations.

Our museums are a great educational and cultural resource for the nation as a whole. If we believe that our society should be one in which lifelong learning enriches all of us, museums are the first place we should turn to. And new technology is playing a vital role in providing museum visitors with more information than ever before, through wonderful interactive exhibits and via the internet.

Events and activities of all kinds feature regularly on museum calendars, especially during Museums Week, organised annually by the Campaign for Museums (see page 36). Visit a museum and you may find yourself dressing up, creating new artwork, making replicas, singing, dancing, music-making or taking part in an historical re-enactment. Such events also show just how much work goes on behind the scenes in looking after our great collections.

This Guide, published in association with the national tourist boards of England, Northern Ireland, Scotland and Wales, is an excellent introduction to the very wide range of museums and galleries throughout the United Kingdom. It will, I hope, encourage you to take advantage of one of the nation's greatest assets, to explore new subjects and new experiences, and to nurture your museum-going habit for life.

Loyd Grossman
Chairman of the Campaign for Museums

Brighton & Hove

Regency City by the Sea

Booth Museum of Natural History

The Heritage Collection

The Royal Pavilion

One of the premier royal palaces in Europe, painstakingly restored to its full Regency glory. This former home of King George IV is one of the most exotically beautiful buildings in the British Isles. Indian Mogul architecture contrasts with interiors inspired by the Orient. Magnificent collections of furniture and soft furnishings, decorative art, silver gilt and chinoiserie. Set in restored Regency gardens. Open daily. Admission fee payable.

Hove Museum & Art Gallery

Housed in an impressive Victorian villa, the Museum contains a superb collection of 20th-century paintings and drawings, 18th-century furniture and decorative art. The South East Arts collection of contemporary craft, 'Hove to Hollywood' film collection and the toy-filled 'Childhood Room', plus events and exhibitions. Open daily (except Mons). Free admission.

525,000 insects and animals, 50,000 fossils, minerals and rocks, 30,000 plants, 11,000 books and maps... just some of the specimens and data extending back over three centuries in this fascinating Museum. British birds displayed in recreated natural settings, together with butterflies and beetles, fossil fish and dinosaur bones, plus events and exhibitions programme. Open daily (except Thurs). Free admission.

Brighton Museum & Art Gallery

This outstanding Museum houses collections of national and local importance including the Art Nouveau and Art Deco collections of furniture, glass and ceramics, new non-western art galleries, and the acclaimed Willett ceramics collection. Plus fashion, fine art, local history including *My Brighton* interactive community history project, archaeology, costumes, events and exhibitions. Open daily (except Weds). Free admission.

Preston Manor

A delightful Manor House which powerfully evokes the atmosphere of an Edwardian gentry home both 'Upstairs' and 'Downstairs'. Explore more than twenty rooms over four floors from the servants' quarters, kitchens and butler's pantry in the basement to the attic bedrooms and nursery on the top floor. Walled gardens, pet cemetery, 13th-century parish church. Open daily. Admission fee payable.

West Blatchington Windmill

Dating from the 1820s, this Grade II listed building still has all the original mill workings in place over five floors. Discover how grain is turned into flour in a traditional windmill, and explore a fascinating display of historical milling and agricultural exhibits including a thresher and an oat crusher. Open Sundays and Bank Holidays only. Admission fee payable.

Foredown Tower

A disused Edwardian water tower is home to the countryside centre on the Sussex Downs and the only operational camera obscura in the South East. The viewing gallery gives outstanding views over the surrounding countryside and across the Channel. Plus weather station, interactive computers, countryside data, astronomy events. Open Sat & Sun; weekday opening subject to revision — call for details. Admission fee payable.

Telephone Visitor Services (01273 290900) for specific opening times, admission fees, exhibitions, events, guided tours and details on Portslade Old Manor, etc.

Brighton & Hove

Contents

Features

Attraction highlights

Geographical listings

Photo 98: the power of the image

SAMANTHA CLUTTEN, freelance writer and former curator at the Victoria and Albert Museum, looks at Photo 98, a celebration of the art of photography

Not everybody paints, not everybody sculpts, but everybody takes photographs. Why then is one of the most popular art forms, and one of the nation's favourite pastimes, so frequently overlooked in favour of the other two? Often marginalised by the creative community, photography is about to come into its own. A multitude of exciting exhibitions, installations and events all over the country are celebrating 1998 as the Year of Photography and the Electronic Image.

So what makes this 'year of' different from the numerous other celebratory year ofs that have recently inundated the British public? The sheer size of the £10 million programme of events certainly makes it noteworthy and the series of outdoor installations projected onto buildings makes it simply inescapable.

The event is part of an Arts Council initiative, Arts 2000, celebrating a different medium every year leading up to the millennium. Each year a different part of the country wins the right to host the arts celebration and Yorkshire is currently hosting Photo 98 on behalf of the nation.

Photo 98 is the biggest celebration of photography ever staged in Britain. As such,

it has attracted some high-profile patrons including David Puttnam. 'I am supporting this event because my father was a photographer,' he says. 'I was brought up with photography and it has sustained my interest throughout my life.' Puttnam hopes Photo 98 will 'encourage more people to develop an interest in photography that goes beyond taking snaps.' The aim of the year is, indeed, to raise the profile of creative photography given 'its low status as an art form in this country,' according to Photo 98's artistic director, Anne McNeill.

A commitment to new work

As well as an innovative exhibition programme, the commissioning of new work is an important aspect of the year. The result is the biggest ever programme of regional commissions – the Yorkshire Commissions. The scheme allows both established regional photographers and newcomers to showcase in venues throughout Yorkshire and Humberside. Entrants were encouraged to challenge traditional approaches in one of seven categories: architecture, fashion, image and text collaboration, landscape, photojournalism, sound/new media and open.

Stephen Cornell, winner of the £7,500 landscape commission, is touring Yorkshire seaside resorts by train during the out-of-season months and is recording his travels using his own handmade pinhole camera. With no lens, viewfinder or focusing apparatus, pinhole cameras were the first type of camera to be used. Consisting merely of a light-proof box, the device shows the image upside down which, Cornell remarks, produces 'strange, yet familiar colour images that resemble half forgotten memories'. Postcards produced by the artist will be available through local newsagents, shops and post offices in the towns and villages he visits. The end work will be shown at Sewerby Hall Museum and Art Gallery, Bridlington (5 September– 9 November), and at stations featured in his photojourney.

The photojournalism commission was won by Gavin Parry with his proposal for a series of large-scale colour photographs exploring car-boot sales. The project is divided into pictures of the objects bought and sold (especially those which are left at the end of the sale) and pictures of the buyers and sellers themselves. The finished commission will be exhibited at the Huddersfield Art Gallery (1 August–26 September).

Lee Miller wearing Yraíde saílcloth overalls by George Hoyningen-Huene (1930). COURTESY OF THE TRUSTEES OF THE V&A/GEORGE HOYNINGEN-HUENE

Photo 98 is a vast collaborative project with 96 partner organisations involved in over 200 projects. One of the biggest joint ventures is a series of new commissions, *10x98*, in which ten international artists explore what it is to be European. The ten exhibitions, which opened simultaneously on 18 April in venues across Yorkshire, come together on 3 October at an exhibition in the Fruitmarket Gallery, Edinburgh.

Reaching new audiences

In order to reach the widest possible audience, Photo 98 has organised National Photo Week (20–26 July) when high-street shops throughout the UK will run competitions, promotions and events, and hundreds of galleries will introduce photography, many for the first time. Unexpected art venues such as shops, cafés, bars and even homes are showing artist-organised exhibitions in fringe festivals in Hull, Huddersfield, Leeds and Sheffield. Café Society in Hull has created a series of photography exhibitions rotating around the city's bars and cafés. All this work can be seen on its virtual gallery on the internet (www.pulsemag.demon.co.uk).

Another attempt to bring artworks out of the gallery and into everyday life is made through a year-long programme of public artworks, involving over 400 contemporary artists in 120 new commissions. The *Public Sightings* project transforms hospitals, car parks, billboards and railway stations into living, accessible artists' canvases.

Reversing fields. © HEATHER ACKROYD AND DANIEL HARVEY

A series of imaginative temporary installations by contemporary artists opens between August and October in the city centre of Kingston upon Hull. The public sighting *Exposed* organised by Hull Time Based Arts celebrates the continual history of new technologies in photography. For *Photosynthesis* (1–31 August) artists Heather Ackroyd and Dan Harvey will grass over an entire building and create images over this canvas by projecting slides onto the walls. *Lumina* (7–11 October) by Andy Hazell also employs a rather unusual screen; a film projection of luggage and travel images will be shown against the side of a departing North Sea ferry bound for Rotterdam. Gillian Dyson, project manager for Hull Time Based Arts, enthuses, 'It is a fantastic opportunity to raise the profile of this medium on a regional and international platform.'

On-Line is another series of commissions which similarly explores the relationship between technology and the experience of journeying. It is being co-ordinated by the Impressions Gallery of Photography, York. Alert rail travellers using the East Coast main line between London, York and

A humorous image featured in the fringe festivals. © FFOTO FICTIONS

Edinburgh will see five site-specific installations along the route between June and December. One installation by Graham Gussin is a series of six large, temporary billboards with digitally created, futuristic landscapes and cityscapes situated in empty fields along the track. Exhibition curator Andrew Cross says the £180,000 scheme is only possible because of Photo 98. He adds, 'It provides a context for the project, and equally, although Photo 98 is geographically specific, *On-Line* extends the boundaries further.'

Electronic creations

The electronic image is as much a part of Photo 98 as photography. Many projects celebrate the information age as an alternative means to creating art. The arts project *Golem*, also organised by the Impressions Gallery of Photography in York, makes use of the widespread interest in the internet. Artist Anno Mitchell uses information about York, such as traffic flow, electricity usage and bank transactions, to map a three-dimensional image of the city as if it were a living body live on the internet (www.golem.org). This dynamic site will be running throughout Photo 98 displaying 150 constantly merging and layering images of 'invisible' data supplied by York Council. The information will also be fly posted in areas of the city as hard-copy graphic data. Curator Matt Lock sees this as guerrilla activity to show the city population, in a subversive way, the invisible world of computer information at work behind everyday activity.

Another project concentrating on networks is one of the biggest digital schemes established by Photo 98. *Indiginet* is a network of nine ISDN-linked multimedia workstations located at digital imaging and photographic organisations around Yorkshire. The pilot, initiated on general election day last year (1 May 1997), can be accessed on www.channel.org.uk/polling/ According to curator Peter Ride, 'The purpose of *Indiginet* is to allow museums, galleries, multimedia organisations and the public to communicate and participate.' The computerised project will create new art on the net, developing over the year with people sending in ideas, photographs and images, as well as artists creating solo work.

The year includes many electronic media-based exhibitions such as *Star Dot Star*, a major exhibition about the development of electronic arts within popular culture which includes many newly commissioned works. *Star Dot Star* opens on 27 June at the Site Gallery, Sheffield.

Celebrated artists

Traditional gallery-based exhibitions form an equally significant part of Photo 98. A series of blockbuster exhibitions celebrates Henri Cartier-Bresson's 90th birthday. Cartier-Bresson was a founder member of Magnum Photos and has had a prolific career spanning 60 years. The London venues include the Victoria and Albert Museum (26 November 1998–March 1999), the Hayward Gallery, and the National Portrait Gallery (both ending 7 June). The National Portrait Gallery exhibits 120 of Cartier-Bresson's self-selected works in the first ever retrospective of his portraits in this country: *Tête-à-tête*. The hanging includes portraits of Matisse, Marilyn Monroe, Tony Hancock, Harold Pinter and the 1997 portrait of painter Lucien Freud. The images differ from the photographer's usual 'decisive moment' technique of capturing sitters unaware, with all the head-to-head shots taking place in the subjects' own environment.

Another big-name exhibition of the renowned photographer Lee Miller is being staged at the newly opened Design Centre, Barnsley (1 September–31 December). Lee Miller had a prolific life being variously a fashion model, *Vogue* photographer, US armed forces war correspondent and writer. Miller worked as a fashion staff photographer for *Vogue* in 1940 and shortly after gained a war correspondent post. This exhibition juxtaposes Miller's unease about juggling what she considered frivolous fashion work with pictures of war-ravaged cities. Rita Britton, founder member of the Design Centre and patron of Photo 98, hopes the exhibition will reach a wide audience through the celebratory year: 'Photography is becoming more of an important art form than ever. We really are watching a quiet revolution take place as new digital art forms emerge. Gone are the days when photography meant simply a snapshot of the family. Things are much more exciting now.'

Featured in the Lee Miller exhibition at the Design Centre, Barnsley. © LEE MILLER ARCHIVES

Events and sightings are happening all over the country to celebrate the Year of Photography and the Electronic Image. So don't be alarmed if you see a grass-covered house showing photographic images or a train carriage with a cinema screen and no seats. After all, through the telescopic world of the camera lens, anything goes.

NATIONAL MUSEUM OF PHOTOGRAPHY, FILM AND TELEVISION

The National Museum of Photography, Film and Television (NMPFT), Bradford, will re-open in December after a £14 million redevelopment taking it into the digital age. The major restructuring will increase space by 25 per cent with a new entrance, five floors of updated galleries, including new digital imaging, interactive, science-based and temporary exhibition galleries, the addition of another cinema and multimedia theatre, and a new café and shop.

products company created by artist Alvar Gullichsen (2 May–28 June). *The Patient Planet* (13 June–30 August) covers 60 years of photojournalism. *Young Meteors: A Revolution in British Photography* (13 June–30 August) explores vintage British photography between 1959 and 1966 by names such as David Bailey, Don McCullin and Terence Donovan. *Sun Pictures to Cyberspace* (5 September– 1 November) completes the exhibition

line-up and draws from the museum's collection of three million objects to show virtuoso photographic techniques from the birth of photography to the present.

In November the temporary exhibitions end and work begins on moving the collections back to the main site. The refurbishment has seen the largest evacuation of a national collection since the Second World War. The objects were temporarily rehoused in the village of Queensbury, Yorkshire, and will be returned ready for the grand opening.

Museum in Exile, The Art Mill, Upper Parkgate, Little Germany, Bradford, West Yorkshire BD1 5BJ (tel: 01274 727488) OPEN: *Tues–Sun 10am–5pm, closed Mon;* ADMISSION FREE

National Museum of Photography, Film and Television, Pictureville, Bradford, West Yorkshire BD1 1NQ (tel: 01274 727488) internet: www.nmsi.ac.uk/nmpft/ OPEN: *Tues–Sun 10am–6pm, closed Mon (except main bank holidays);* ADMISSION FREE

The new look of the NMPFT. NATIONAL MUSEUM OF PHOTOGRAPHY, FILM AND TELEVISION

Ten million people have visited the NMPFT since it opened in 1983. Director Amanda Nevill says, 'We wanted to remain the most popular museum outside London and because we are a young museum people have higher expectations of us; we want to exceed those expectations.'

When the old museum closed in September 1997, a Museum in Exile took its place based in a Victorian textile mill in Bradford's Little Germany district. The Museum in Exile has three gallery spaces to show a wide range of temporary exhibitions as part of Photo 98. Martin Parr's *Ooh La La!* (closes 31 May) is a *10x98* commission. Parr travelled to European cities to document stereotypes and clichés associated with national characteristics. *Bonk Business Inc* is a humorous, fictitious exhibition history of 100 years of a Finnish anchovy

Featured in Martin Parr's *Ooh La La!* exhibition, a *10x98* commission. © MARTIN PARR

VICTORIA AND ALBERT MUSEUM

The Victoria and Albert Museum (V&A), London, opens its first ever photography gallery, appropriately, in the Year of Photography and the Electronic Image. Curator of photography, Mark Haworth-Booth, hopes the year 'will make people more aware of the possibilities of photography as an artistic medium than they were before'.

The £500,000 project, opening in May, converts an existing 350 square metres of temporary exhibition space into a state-of-the-art gallery. Even though the V&A was designated the national collection of photographs in 1977, it has never before had a dedicated gallery to display some of the 300,000 photographs in its collection. Haworth-Booth remarks: 'Britain has lacked a gallery of this kind for a long time; a place where you can see really great photographs, well displayed, with good lighting, in pleasant surroundings.'

The art gallery consists of three elements: a history of photography display (changed once yearly), a contemporary collection and a special show (both changed twice yearly). The opening special show,

Photography: An Independent Art, displays 100 V&A masterpieces from 1839–1996. This is replaced by 50 Henri Cartier-Bresson photographs, chosen by the artist himself, from the V&A's 400-strong archive of his work (26 November 1998–March 1999). Helen Chadwick's photographic installation *Oval Court* is the opening, contemporary collection.

Established in 1853, the photography collection is the oldest in the world. The V&A has always collected photographic prints for their aesthetic quality; the first art photographs were bought by Henry Cole, the museum's founding director, in 1856. The oldest object in the collection is a daguerreotype of Trafalgar Square. Dating from October 1839, only a few months after the discovery of photography, it is not surprising that this picture is the most expensive single photograph in the museum's collection. The V&A also has many fine contemporary works and this is one of the main areas of the collection which continues to grow, a recent purchase being photographs of the Autumn 1997 Prada campaign.

Rocker and Rosie going home, Lynemouth (1983).
COURTESY OF THE TRUSTEES OF THE V&A/PHOTOGRAPHER

Mick Jagger by David Bailey (1964).
COURTESY OF THE TRUSTEES OF THE V&A/DAVID BAILEY

Victoria and Albert Museum,
Cromwell Road, South Kensington,
London SW7 2RL (tel: 0171 938 8500)
OPEN: *Mon 12 noon–5.50pm, Tues–Sun 10am–5.50pm;* ADMISSION CHARGED

A roundup of the Photo 98 venues in this article

Design Centre, 11–11a Shambles Street, Barnsley, South Yorkshire S70 2SQ
(tel: 01226 771133)
OPEN: *Phone for opening times and admissions charges*

Fruitmarket Gallery,
45 Market Street, Edinburgh EH1 1DF
(tel: 0131 225 2383)
OPEN: *Tues–Sat 10.30am–5.30pm, Sun during Edinburgh Festival (Aug–Sept) 12pm–5pm;* ADMISSION FREE *(occasional charge for special exhibitions)*

Hayward Gallery, South Bank Centre, Belvedere Road, London SE1 8XZ
(tel: 0171 928 3144)
OPEN: *Daily 10am–6pm (extended opening Tues & Weds to 8pm);* ADMISSION CHARGED

Huddersfield Art Gallery,
Princess Alexandra Walk,
Huddersfield HD1 2SU
(tel: 01484 221964)
OPEN: *Mon–Fri 10am–5pm, Sat 10am–4pm;* ADMISSION FREE

Impressions Gallery of Photography,
29 Castlegate, Castle Walk, York YO1 1RN
(tel: 01904 654724)
OPEN: *Mon–Sat 9.30am–5.30pm, Sun 10am–5pm;* ADMISSION FREE

National Portrait Gallery,
St Martin's Place, London WC2H 0HE
(tel: 0171 306 0055)
OPEN: *Mon–Sat 10am–6pm, Sun 2pm–6pm;* ADMISSION FREE *(occasional charge for special exhibitions)*

Sewerby Hall Museum and Art Gallery, Church Lane, Sewerby, Bridlington YO15 1EA
(tel: 01262 677874)
OPEN: *10 April–1 Nov daily 10am–6pm, phone for opening at other times;* ADMISSION FREE *(small admission charge to grounds)*

Site Gallery, 1 Brown Street,
Sheffield S1 2BS (tel: 0114 281 2077)
OPEN: *Tues–Sat 11am–5pm;* ADMISSION FREE

Time Based Arts Ltd, 8 Posterngate,
Hull HU1 2JN (tel: 01482 216446)
E-mail: htba.demon.co.uk

For further details contact Photo 98 direct:

Photo 98, Kirklees Media Centre,
7 Northumberland Street,
Huddersfield HD1 1RL
(tel: 01484 531201)
E-mail: photo98@photo98.com;
internet: www.photo98.com

Mythical quest: on the trail of the Celts

Archaeologist **DR SIMON JAMES** is currently on secondment from the British Museum while undertaking a research fellowship in the Department of Archaeology at Durham University. He is the author of numerous works, including *Exploring the World of the Celts* and *Britain and the Celtic Iron Age*.

'Celtic' is a highly evocative term, conjuring some of the most romantic and mysterious images of the British and Irish past. For some, it may call to mind white robed figures in the dawn at stone circles, especially Avebury and Stonehenge. For others, it may be the vast brooding hillforts of the Iron Age, the deeds of warrior heroes such as Arthur or Cú Chulainn, the piety of early medieval Irish monks and the stunning manuscript gospels they created, or the wild clans of the Scottish Highlands before the battle at Culloden.

What links these images together is that they seem to be facets of an unbroken history. They tell of a people who dwelt in these islands before the coming of the Romans and the English, and who thrive here still. There is thought to be a seamlessness between the ancient Britons and Irish of the Iron Age (roughly the last six centuries BC), and the peoples of modern Wales, Scotland, Ireland and other areas like Cornwall.

All this is agreed to be a Celtic past, populated by societies who used related Celtic languages and shared common values, social organisation and, perhaps most notably, arts. To many people these common characteristics tell of a shared Celtic spirit

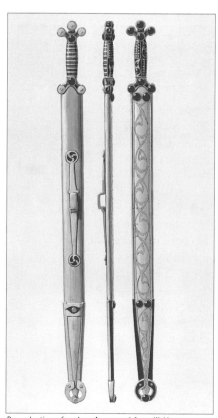

Reproduction of an Iron Age sword from Kirkburn, Yorkshire (c third century BC) – the original is housed in the British Museum. SIMON JAMES

and continuity from ancient to modern times, constituting an essentially timeless Celticness. It is the brilliant Celtic art in particular which epitomises this period of history in the minds of most. The beautiful and distinctive patterns, which swirl across Iron Age swords and shields from the fourth century BC, and illuminate the pages of early Christian manuscripts, such as the Lindisfarne Gospels, of the seventh century AD, still remain popular today.

The Celts, then, are a key part of the agreed common story of the British Isles – a thread running through a thousand history books and novels, films and television programmes. Indeed, this theme is so deeply entrenched that its historical accuracy has never really been questioned.

The shape of a Celtic history

For some people the story of the Celts is a strongly spiritual one, evoked especially by burial mounds and standing stones which

Opening of the Christmas Gospel, St Matthew, Chap I, V 18 – the beautiful and vivid illumination of the Lindisfarne Gospels. BY PERMISSION OF THE BRITISH LIBRARY

were actually erected a thousand years and more before the name Celt is recorded anywhere. But more often, the story of the insular Celts is thought to begin with their migration northwards into the British Isles. For the earliest recorded people named Celts lived in Continental Europe, north of the Alps, around the sixth century BC. Greeks and Romans recorded subsequent mass migrations of these Celts or Gauls southwards, into Northern Italy and towards Greece. But the north was still beyond history: no written records of the northern peoples or their activities survive from this, the Iron Age. It was only with the development of modern linguistics, and especially of archaeology, that some light was shone on the mysterious centuries before the Romans came.

In the nineteenth century archaeologists in Continental Europe found Iron Age cemeteries rich with grave goods. These artefacts, often decorated with the now famous artistic style which bears their name, seemed to be the physical

remains of Celtic societies. Discovery of such decorated artefacts in Britain and Ireland, including many of the pieces which are now displayed in the British Museum and other major galleries, encouraged the idea that the Celts had indeed migrated northwards as well as south. The earliest historical account, Julius Caesar's eyewitness description of his invasions of Britain in 55 and 54 BC, also suggested settlement by Continental migrants. The idea of Celtic invasions during the Iron Age became established, and for many people remains the basic understanding of the early histories of Britain and Ireland.

The twentieth century has seen the continued exploration of the Iron Age landscape, with increasingly sophisticated excavation of such important sites as the great hillforts of Maiden Castle, Dorset, and Danebury, Hampshire, and ritual centres like Navan, County Armagh. Iron Age life was underpinned by agriculture and stock-raising, and

exploitation of the natural resources of land and sea. An excellent impression of the skills of farming people may be gained among the Iron Age-style crops, livestock and reconstructed buildings at Butser Ancient Farm in Hampshire.

A turning point

Roman conquest of what would one day be England and Wales marked a turning point for the peoples of the British Isles. The existence of the Roman province from AD 43 to the early 400s had a considerable effect even on areas the Romans did not actually conquer.

In the contested zones and unconquered regions of the north and west the indigenous societies and their artistic traditions flourished through and beyond the Roman period. Beyond Hadrian's Wall, new states evolved, such as the Pictish kingdom, famed today for the extraordinary art in stone and silver which it produced once it had outlived the Roman Empire. In Western Scotland and the Isles some of the most remarkable buildings of our early history were produced, in the form of tall, dry-stone tower-houses. A fine example of such a 'broch' is to be seen at Dun Telve, Glenelg.

However, the same cannot be said for the main target of the Roman invaders, the peoples of the south and east. Among these Britons, the languages and traditions of their Iron Age forebears did not survive the Roman occupation. The various small states which emerged from the collapse of the Roman province consisted of mixed populations of Romano-Britons and Germanic immigrants from across the North Sea. These gradually merged to become the English.

The Iron Age hillfort at Maiden Castle, Dorset. ROYAL COMMISSION ON THE HISTORICAL MONUMENTS OF ENGLAND, © CROWN COPYRIGHT

Glenn Beigg broch at Dun Telve on the West Coast of Scotland. SIMON JAMES

An idea like common Celticness did not exist in the British Isles before 1700 because it simply did not need to. Indeed, it may have been literally unthinkable. Throughout history the British Isles have always been home to a rich multiplicity of societies. Britain and Ireland were patchworks of chiefdoms, petty kingdoms, or small states far into medieval times, and remained strongly regionalised much later still. These societies may have known little of each other. They were as likely to look outwards across the seas for contacts, trade and exchange, as inwards to the other side of their own island, which before canals and railways was often harder to reach anyway.

So how and why did the idea of a distinct Celtic identity in the British past appear at all? The idea of Celts in the Atlantic archipelago appears to be an invention, one of many national or ethnic identities which have been called into being over the last 2,000 years and more of our history. It involved the projection into the past of a recently created identity, born not of antiquity, but of modernity.

The centuries following the collapse of the Roman army, the so-called Dark Ages, seem dark to us only because we know so little of them. The enigma of Arthur encapsulates this, his legendary exploits associating him with Tintagel and many other sites the length of Britain. However, it is clear that although these were times of war and political instability, they were also times of great vitality and cultural achievement. This is particularly true for the Irish, who, as *Scotti* sea-raiders, established a new temporal kingdom in Britain, Scot-land.

It is, then, the peoples of the north and west, largely untouched by the Roman occupation, that are usually called Celtic today and are thought of as ancestral to the modern Scots, Welsh and Irish. But were they really Celtic?

Creating the Celts of the islands

The astonishing reality seems to be that no-one used the term Celt of anyone in the British Isles before about 1700.

A woman living at Maiden Castle in the fourth century BC, a pagan priest at Navan in the second century BC, a monk on Iona eight hundred years later, a child at the court of Hywel Dda in 950, or a Highland clansman driving cattle in sixteenth century Scotland – all would have been surprised to hear themselves called Celts.

Remains of Tintagel Castle, associated with the legend of King Arthur. ROYAL COMMISSION ON THE HISTORICAL MONUMENTS OF ENGLAND, © CROWN COPYRIGHT

A family of similar tongues

Creating the Celts in Britain started with linguistics. In his *Archaeologia Britannica*, published in 1707, the Welsh patriot Edward Lhwyd illustrated the connections between the languages of the non-English peoples of Britain and Ireland. From this he proposed the idea of their common ethnic origin. Drawing on other research which related Welsh, Irish, Scots Gaelic and other languages to that of the ancient Celtic Gauls of Continental Europe, he named this family of similar tongues Celtic.

It is perhaps the timing of the publication of Lhwyd's book which is most symbolic. In the same year, 1707, the Act of Union between England and Scotland saw the creation of a new political identity, the British. With the signing of the Act, the name Briton – previously used by those peoples of the island who saw themselves

The Desborough Mirror dating from the first century AD – found in Northamptonshire in 1908 and now housed in the British Museum.
© THE BRITISH MUSEUM

as other than English – was adopted for all subjects of the new English-dominated union. At that very moment Lhwyd was able to give the non-English peoples of the isles a new name and identity, Celtic. Like Britishness and many other national identities, Celticness claimed its roots deep in the past.

It appears that this state takeover of the name Briton was a key reason for the uptake of the name Celt during the eighteenth century, and its subsequent establishment in popular culture. Henry Rowlands, a friend and fellow-countryman of Lhwyd, was writing of 'We the Celtae...' by 1723, and the following year the famous antiquary William Stukeley was using it of ancient burial mounds in the British landscape. By 1773 Samuel Johnson and James Boswell could encounter a clergyman in the Hebrides who believed there had been ancient Celts from Asia Minor to Skye. By 1817, Sir Walter Scott, in *Rob Roy*, could refer to eighteenth-century Scottish Highlanders as Celts, without feeling any need to elaborate. The Celts had arrived.

Celticness provided the peoples of the west and north with a framework for understanding their origins. But unfortunately this has had a serious effect on our endeavours to understand the shape of the early history of these islands. For we have tended to project back into the past the dividing lines of more recent times, by thinking of all the peoples of the pre-Roman past as Celts, and all the post-Roman peoples as Celts or Germans (or other non-Celts). In doing so, we are undoubtedly obscuring the real, lost diversity of identities in these lands which have bestowed upon us such a rich and dramatic heritage. The peoples of the past did not think themselves Celts, but further, they may well not have thought of themselves as even Britons or Irish, but as Catuvellaunians, Picts, Dumnonii, Brigantes, People of Ulster, of Strathclyde, of Powys...

Lands with many peoples

But were all these societies not descendants of Iron Age Celtic invaders, and so Celts by ancestry? For a generation now, most archaeologists have ceased to believe that invasions were the primary means by which the societies of pre-Roman Britain were created. Traces of substantial migrations have been sought in vain. The overwhelming underlying pattern of settlements and artefacts, now they are better explored and understood, is of continuity from the Bronze Age. The peoples of the British and Irish Iron Age and after were largely descended from peoples already here; there were multiple, diverse societies as far back as we can see. It is perhaps the complexities of these societies that we should aim to explore and understand.

So how is it that there were such similarities across the Iron Age British Isles and much of Europe, for example in art, religion and social organisation? These do exist and it is certain that people were crossing the seas in all directions during this time. However, rather than mass migrations of people, it now seems that it was mostly ideas, artistic fashions and technologies which were moving.

The wealth of artefacts discovered throughout the British Isles bearing stunning Celtic designs is obviously testament to this. These represent important cultural connections – but not common ethnicity.

The ancient Celts of Britain and Ireland, then, at least as imagined in millions of modern minds, never really existed as a distinct and unified people – but a fascinating myriad of other, almost lost, societies did. The paradox is that

the shape of the past has been obscured by the very real aspirations of peoples in recent times. For the Celts exist *now* – today Celtic identity is at least as real as many other identities not least that of the British.

Celtic connections

The following are just a few of the wealth of sites, monuments and museums throughout the United Kingdom where you will discover more about this fascinating period of our history.

Avebury Stone Circles,
Avebury, Marlborough,
Wiltshire SN8 1RF
(tel: 01672 539250)
OPEN: *The stones are situated on an open site with free access at all times;*
ADMISSION FREE
Pre-Celtic site.

British Library,
96 Euston Road, London NW1 2DB
(tel: 0171 412 7332, visitor enquiries)
OPEN: *Library opening times Mon–Fri 9.30am–8pm, Sat 9.30am–5pm; Exhibition gallery opening times Mon–Thurs 9.30am–6pm, Fri & Sat 9.30am–5pm, Sun 11am–5pm;* ADMISSION FREE
Displaying the Lindisfarne Gospels in the exhibition galleries.

British Museum,
Great Russell Street, London WC1B 3DG
(tel: 0171 636 1555)
OPEN: *Mon–Sat 10am–5pm, Sun 2.30pm–6pm;* ADMISSION FREE
Celtic Europe Gallery (Iron Age) – Room 50; Early Medieval Europe – Room 41.

Butser Ancient Farm,
Bascomb Copse, near Chalton, Horndean,
Waterlooville, Hampshire PO8 0QE
(tel: 01705 598838)
OPEN: *March–Oct Daily 10am–5pm;*
ADMISSION CHARGED
Reconstructions of Iron Age buildings.

Celtica, Y Plas, Aberystwyth Road,
Machynlleth SY20 8ER
(tel: 01654 702702)
OPEN: *Daily 10am–6pm;*
ADMISSION CHARGED

Danebury Iron Age Hillfort,
Stockbridge, Hampshire
(tel: 01962 860948, Ranger's office)
OPEN: *The hillfort is situated on an open site with free access at all times;*
ADMISSION FREE

Dorset County Museum,
High West Street, Dorchester,
Dorset DT1 1XA (tel: 01305 262735)
OPEN: *Mon–Sat 10am–5pm, Sun 10am–5pm (July and Aug only);*
ADMISSION CHARGED
Housing a permanent exhibition on Maiden Castle hillfort.

Dun Telve Broch, Glenelg, Highland
OPEN: *The broch is situated on an open site with free access at all times;*
ADMISSION FREE

Iona Abbey, Iona, Argyll PA76 6SN
(tel: 01681 700404)
OPEN: *Free access daily to Abbey and Cloisters; nearby ruins of Benedictine nunnery on open site with free access;*
ADMISSION FREE
On the site of the former monastery founded by St Columba in the sixth century AD.

Maiden Castle Hillfort,
Dorchester, Dorset
OPEN: *The hillfort is situated on an open site with free access at all times;*
ADMISSION FREE

Museum of the Iron Age, 6 Church Close,
Andover, Hampshire SP10 1DP
(tel: 01264 366283)
OPEN: *Tues–Sat 10am–5pm, Sun & bank holidays 2pm–5pm (April–Sept only);*
ADMISSION CHARGED

National Museum & Gallery Cardiff,
Cathays Park, Cardiff CF1 3NP
(tel: 01222 397951)
OPEN: *Tues–Sun 10am–5pm;*
ADMISSION CHARGED

Navan Fort Centre, 81 Killylea Road,
Armagh BT60 4LD (tel: 01861 525550)
OPEN: *April–Sept Mon–Sat 10am–6pm, Sun 11am–6pm, Oct–March Mon–Sat 10am–5pm, Sun 11am–5pm;*
ADMISSION CHARGED *for exhibition tour within the centre (free access to Navan Fort itself and general facilities at the centre)*

Stonehenge, near Amesbury,
Wiltshire SP4 7DE (tel: 01980 623108)
OPEN: *Daily opening times 16 March–31 May 9.30am–6pm, 1 June–31 Aug 9am–7pm, 1 Sept–15 Oct 9.30am–6pm, 16 Oct–15 March 9.30am–4pm;*
ADMISSION CHARGED
Pre-Celtic site.

Tintagel Castle,
Tintagel, Cornwall PL34 0HE
(tel: 01840 770328)
OPEN: *Daily April–Oct 10am–6pm, Daily Nov–March 10am–4pm;*
ADMISSION CHARGED
Early British monastery, legendary Arthurian associations.

Ulster Museum,
Botanic Gardens, Stranmillis Road,
Belfast BT9 5AB
(tel: 01232 383000)
OPEN: *Mon–Fri 10am–5pm, Sat 1pm–5pm, Sun 2pm–5pm;*
ADMISSION FREE *(except for special exhibitions)*

East Anglia: coast, countryside and culture

MIRIAM STEAD, director of the Museum of East Anglian Life, takes a seasonal look at the wealth of museums and galleries in four of our most easterly counties

I have only worked in Suffolk for a year, but I have been seeking an opportunity to come and live here for more than a decade. East Anglia, in this case the counties of Cambridgeshire, Essex, Norfolk and Suffolk, is a region which, to me, has everything – wild lonely coasts, epitomised by the music of Benjamin Britten, a native of Suffolk, tranquil rivers, ideal for quiet sailing and contemplation, beautiful countryside including the Norfolk Broads, Constable

Country and the Stour Valley, and vibrant historic towns such as Bury St Edmunds, Norwich, Cambridge, Peterborough, and Colchester, the oldest recorded town in Britain. Lovers of architecture will find some of the finest churches in the land, built on the proceeds of the wool trade and featuring native flint in varied patterns, rich brick-built country houses, and timber-framed buildings second to none, as a visit to Lavenham in Suffolk or Cressing Temple Barns in Essex will prove.

With over 200 museums and galleries, ranging from nationally important collections to local, volunteer run displays, East Anglia has something to enlighten and entertain visitors throughout the seasons.

Spring

The basis of East Anglia's economy was, and still is, agriculture. In the Middle Ages wool dominated, but now wheat, barley and sugar beet are the main crops. Up to the post-war period, horse and steam power prevailed. The mechanisation of farming by steam gave rise to the main industrial concerns in the region: Charles Burrell & Sons of Thetford, Garrett of Leiston, Ransomes, Sims & Jeffries of Ipswich and Davey Paxman of Colchester. These became known internationally, exporting their products all over the world.

As one would expect, each county in East Anglia can boast a museum dedicated to displaying life and work on the land: Barleylands Farm in Essex, the Farmland Museum at Waterbeach in Cambridgeshire and Norfolk's Rural Life Museum at Gressenhall. However, the largest of these is the 70-acre open-air Museum of East

Flatford Mill on the River Stour was a subject for Constable's paintings. DAVID W COLLINS

Traction engine wheel bearing the maker's name. JOHN M CAPES

Anglian Life at Stowmarket in Suffolk. Here, there are displays of the domestic, industrial and agricultural life of the region, including a number of historic buildings which have been moved to the site. Suffolk rare farm breeds are kept, most notably the Suffolk Punch, Remus. Throughout the spring and summer there are demonstrations of old farming techniques, local crafts and steam engines at work.

Local life and industry in East Anglia can also be explored at the wealth of town and village museums such as at Burwell, March and Wisbech in Cambridgeshire, Braintree, Maldon and Saffron Walden in Essex, Thetford, Fakenham and Swaffham in Norfolk and Beccles, Leiston and Woolpit in Suffolk. These are to name but a few.

Summer

Summer means the seaside and along the length of the East Anglian coast there is something for every taste – sailing, fishing, long sandy beaches, quiet resorts, lively towns, and plenty of museums to tell the rich stories of the people who lived, worked and played in these attractive and sometimes bracing surroundings.

Traditionally, one of the great days out from London was a steamer trip down the Thames to Southend, boasting the longest pier in the world which now houses a museum about its history. The town museum is home to the only planetarium in the south-east outside the capital. Harwich and Felixstowe, which face each other across the mouth of the Orwell and Stour estuaries, are today both major passenger and freight ports. Accordingly each town has historical displays charting their maritime pasts. Harwich was once the headquarters of the navy in the days of Samuel Pepys, who served as the town's Member of Parliament. It was also the base for Trinity House and its network of coastal protections, including lighthouses and buoys.

The charming and elegant seaside resort of Southwold is home to three museums, including the Sailors

Reading Room, an historic building set on the cliff. It not only houses the town's maritime exhibits, but is also a club and reading room for retired seafarers. Lowestoft, Britain's most easterly town, is both a flourishing seaside resort and a fishing port. Its story is told at the Lowestoft and East Suffolk Maritime Museum. Newly opened in the town is the ISCA Maritime Museum, which displays a large collection of ethnographic boats, including a Chinese junk. Not far to the north is another major seaside destination on the east coast, Great Yarmouth, which is home

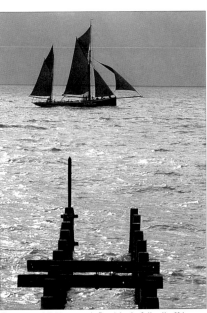

The restored fishing smack *Excelsior* in full sail off her home port of Lowestoft. DAVID W COLLINS

to five museums including a maritime museum. The latter focuses on the story of the Norfolk coast, encompassing the herring trade and the Norfolk Wherry, which used to ply the Norfolk Broads.

For those looking to explore inland, there is the Imperial War Museum at Duxford which presents a number of air shows throughout the summer. The museum houses an outstanding collection of over 140 historic aircraft, including Concorde. Newly opened on the site is the impressive American Air Museum in Britain.

Museum of East Anglian Life, Stowmarket. MUSEUM OF EAST ANGLIAN LIFE

Inside the American Air Museum. IMPERIAL WAR MUSEUM DUXFORD

in Cambridge is highlighted at Kettle's Yard, which houses a major permanent collection of twentieth-century paintings and sculpture, and also hosts temporary exhibitions.

Twentieth-century and contemporary art in Essex can be found in the Firstsite Gallery at the Minories, Colchester, and the Fry Public Gallery, Saffron Walden. The latter is home to works by Edward Bawden and Eric Ravilious.

Norwich Castle Museum has a large collection of art, most notably works by the Norwich School of Artists. For true tea lovers, there is also a fine and extensive collection of English teapots. On the outskirts of the city is the Sainsbury Centre for Visual Arts, housing the Robert and Lisa Sainsbury Collection. Some 700 paintings, sculptures and ceramics are on permanent display with works by Picasso, Henry Moore, Roger Bacon and Giacometti shown alongside art from Africa, the Pacific and the Americas.

Pleasant sunny days often bring thoughts of travel to mind. The East Anglian Railway Museum at Chappel near Colchester is based on a busy Victorian country station. Visitors can enjoy steam train rides and a miniature railway. Railways, trams and trolley buses are the main stars at the East Anglia Transport Museum in Carlton Colville near Lowestoft, and Bressingham Steam Museum in Norfolk combines working vintage steam engines with six acres of picturesque gardens.

Autumn

As the evenings draw in, why not enjoy the calm and relaxing atmosphere of one of East Anglia's many art galleries? The abundance of both traditional and

contemporary collections on display in the region include works of international significance.

Gainsborough's House in Sudbury is the birthplace of Thomas Gainsborough, the great eighteenth-century painter. Examples of his work, together with temporary exhibitions of arts and crafts, are shown in the house throughout the year. Nearby is Bury St Edmunds whose gallery is housed in Robert Adam's only public building in the east of England.

The Fitzwilliam Museum in Cambridge has a renowned collection of European paintings, drawings, prints and sculpture, as well as fine displays of ceramics, furniture, and clocks. Contemporary art

Winter

Short days and thoughts of festive preparations inevitably turn the mind towards towns and cities, and a trip to a museum will undoubtedly help to while away a pleasant day. East Anglia has a host of bustling communities whose stories are told in a variety of attractive and atmospheric settings.

Colchester Castle houses impressive displays about the Roman and later history of the town, including its destruction by Boudicca in AD 60. Visitors to the gaol can hear the interrogation of a suspected witch by Matthew Hopkins, the infamous Witchfinder General. There are plenty of

Thomas Gainsborough: Portrait of a boy and a girl (fragment). GAINSBOROUGH'S HOUSE SOCIETY

paintings. The town's museum and art gallery boasts a Victorian natural history gallery and Suffolk geology and wildlife galleries, as well as Roman and Saxon Suffolk displays. Newly opened is the Tudor Ipswich exhibition.

The vibrant city of Norwich has a broad selection of museums, including the Castle Museum housed in the twelfth-century keep, the Inspire Hands-on Science Centre, the Royal Norfolk Regimental Museum and the Mustard Shop, with displays illustrating the history of Colmans mustard. As an alternative, the historic town of King's Lynn has the Old Gaol House, the Lynn Museum and the Town House Museum. The latter concentrates on the merchants, tradesmen and families who, for 900 years, have made the town so prosperous.

The diversity of museums which grace the elegant streets of Cambridge reflect not only the interests of the town and county, but also the world-famous university. The Fitzwilliam Museum is much more than an art gallery; it houses important collections of Egyptian, Greek and Roman antiquities. Other university

hands-on exhibits for both adults and children. To complete a day's visit, there are three other museums in the town; the Tymperleys Clock Museum, Holytrees Local History Museum and the Natural History Museum.

Bury St Edmunds is home to the Moyse's Hall Museum and the Manor House, which has displays of local history (including the notorious Maria Marten red barn murder), as well as fine arts and decorative clocks. Christchurch Mansion in Ipswich is a handsome Tudor house with exhibitions of furniture, ceramics and

Norwich Castle Museum. JOHN M CAPES

collections open to the public are the Sedgwick Museum housing fossils from around the world, including mounted dinosaur skeletons, the Museum of Archaeology and Anthropology, and the Collection of Air Photographs.

The industry and folk life of the county are displayed at the Museum of Technology, set in a preserved Victorian pumping station, and at the Cambridge and County Folk Museum, housed in a former farmhouse and inn.

Coast, countryside and culture – the counties of East Anglia are indeed rich in character. All I can suggest is that you take the time to visit, whatever the season, and discover this charming and diverse region for yourself.

A selection of East Anglia's museums and galleries

Further details of the museums and galleries mentioned in the article, which represent only a small selection of the variety found throughout the region.

CAMBRIDGESHIRE

Cambridge museums and galleries: details from the Tourist Information Centre, Wheeler Street, Cambridge CB2 3QB (tel: 01223 322640)

Farmland Museum and Denny Abbey, Ely Road, Waterbeach, Cambridgeshire CB5 9PQ (tel: 01223 860988)
OPEN: *April–Oct daily 12 noon–5pm;* ADMISSION CHARGED

Imperial War Museum Duxford, Duxford Airfield, Duxford, Cambridge CB2 4QR (tel: 01223 835000)
OPEN: *mid-March–Oct 10am–6pm, Nov–mid-March 10am–4pm;* ADMISSION CHARGED

ESSEX

Barleylands Farm Museum & Visitor Centre, Barleylands Road, Billericay, Essex CM11 2UD (tel: 01268 282090)
OPEN: *Tues–Sun & bank holidays 10am–5pm;* ADMISSION CHARGED

Colchester museums and galleries: details from the Tourist Information Centre, 1 Queen Street, Colchester, Essex CO1 2PG (tel: 01206 282920)

East Anglian Railway Museum, Chappel & Wakes Colne Station, Colchester, Essex CO6 2DS (tel: 01206 242524)
OPEN: *Daily 10am–5.00pm;* ADMISSION CHARGED

Fry Public Art Gallery, Castle Street, Saffron Walden, Essex CB10 1BD (tel: 01799 513779)
OPEN: *April–Oct Sat, Sun & bank holidays 2.45pm–5.30pm;* ADMISSION CHARGED

Harwich Maritime Museum, Low Lighthouse, The Green, Harwich, Essex (tel: 01255 503429)
OPEN: *April & Sept Sun only 10am–12 noon & 2pm–5pm, May–Aug daily 10am–5pm;* ADMISSION CHARGED

Southend Pier Museum, Southend Pier, Marine Parade, Southend-on-Sea, Essex SS1 2EL (tel: 01702 611214)
OPEN: *May–Oct Fri–Mon 11am–5pm, school holidays 11am–6pm;* ADMISSION CHARGED

NORFOLK

Bressingham Steam Museum, Bressingham, Diss, Norfolk IP22 2AB (tel: 01379 687386)
OPEN: *Easter–Oct daily 10.30am–5.30pm;* ADMISSION CHARGED

King's Lynn museums: details from the Tourist Information Centre, The Old Gaol House, Saturday Market Place, King's Lynn, Norfolk PE30 5DQ (tel: 01553 763044)

Maritime Museum, Marine Parade, Great Yarmouth, Norfolk NR30 2EN (tel: 01493 842267)
OPEN: *Phone for opening hours;* ADMISSION CHARGED

Norfolk Rural Life Museum, Beech House, Gressenhall, Dereham, Norfolk NR20 4DR (tel: 01362 860563)
OPEN: *April–Oct Mon–Sat 10am–5pm, Sun 12 noon–5.30pm;* ADMISSION CHARGED

Norwich museums and galleries: details from the Tourist Information Centre, The Guildhall, Gaol Hill, Norwich, Norfolk NR1 4AP (tel: 01603 666071)

SUFFOLK

Bury St Edmunds museums and art gallery: details from the Tourist Information Centre, 6 Angel Hill, Bury St Edmunds, Suffolk IP33 1BT (tel: 01284 764667)

East Anglia Transport Museum, Chapel Road, Carlton Colville, Lowestoft, Suffolk NR33 8BL (tel: 01502 518459)
OPEN: *Phone for details of opening;* ADMISSION CHARGED

Gainsborough's House, 46 Gainsborough Street, Sudbury, Suffolk CO10 6EU (tel: 01787 372958)
OPEN: *Tues–Sat 10am–5pm, Sun & bank holidays 2pm–5pm (closes at 4pm during winter months);* ADMISSION CHARGED

Ipswich museums and galleries: details from the Tourist Information Centre, St Stephen's Church, St Stephen's Lane, Ipswich, Suffolk IP1 1BZ (tel: 01473 823824)

Lowestoft museums and galleries: details from the Tourist Information Centre, East Point Pavilion, Royal Plain, Lowestoft, Suffolk NR33 0QF (tel: 01502 523000)

Museum of East Anglian Life, Stowmarket, Suffolk IP14 1DL (tel: 01449 612229)
OPEN: *April–Oct Mon–Sat 10am–5pm, Sun 11am–5pm, Nov–March Mon–Sat 10am–3pm;* ADMISSION CHARGED

Southwold Sailors Reading Room, East Cliff, Southwold, Suffolk IP18 6EI (tel: 01502 723782)
OPEN: *Daily 9am–5.30pm;* ADMISSION FREE

From match day to museum exhibition

Whether player or spectator, sport is a part of our lives. Writer and photographer **CARL PENDLE** explains that it has a place in our museums too.

How many sports museums can you name? Two, maybe three? The MCC Museum at Lord's cricket ground, the Wimbledon Lawn Tennis Museum and the National Horseracing Museum in Newmarket. Then you may have to think a little harder. But all that is about to change – exciting times lie ahead for sports fans and museum-goers alike.

Few will dispute the fact that sport appeals to millions of people across gender, age and race. On the other hand, many people might think that the words sport and museum are a contradiction. After all, sporting activities are about excitement, drama, competition, speed and larger-than-life personalities. Surely a museum can't compete? That may have been true in the past, but today with the help of new interactive exhibits, sports museums can be much more than a testament to the history of the game. Match day excitement can live on in the museum exhibit.

The first sports museums, the bastions like the MCC and Wimbledon, to be followed by the Donington Grand Prix Collection and the National Horseracing Museum

at Newmarket, opened to lure the true enthusiasts, the pilgrims who worshipped their sport. While that remains true today, these museums are also enticing a broader range of visitors by continually updating and bringing in new and exciting hands-on exhibits to cater not just for the fanatics, but families too.

With the early sports museums providing the lead, other sporting bodies have now emulated their success. With all the benefits that the new gadgetry of the information age brings, the truly interactive, multimedia sports museum has arrived. The Museum of Rugby at Twickenham and the Science of Sport exhibition housed inside the Science Museum in London are two of the first of this new breed, and from their conception were designed with the idea of encouraging visitors to get involved.

But what of our towns and cities with celebrated sporting links, where community and sport have grown side by side? Here, the sport is part of a bigger picture, the essence of which must be seen as a whole. The River and Rowing Museum at Henley, due to open this summer, is a perfect example. It is dedicated to three inextricably

Meeting the rock face challenge at the Science of Sport exhibition. SCIENCE MUSEUM/ SCIENCE AND SOCIETY PICTURE LIBRARY

linked themes: rowing, the Thames and Henley. Paul Newman, the museum's commercial and marketing manager sums up the impetus for their project perfectly: 'Our three themes are so closely linked that you couldn't tell one of the stories without mentioning the others.' He also makes the more serious point that 'a rowing museum on its own wouldn't have been financially viable.'

Sports museums look set to boom. Plans are currently afoot for football museums in Carlisle and Preston and a National Museum of Hockey, possibly at the national hockey stadium in Milton Keynes. However, it will not only be the fast games that will benefit from the new technologies. Snooker, cricket and even swimming will all be winners from the information technology age.

Early sports museums: setting the trend

To keep the enthusiasts coming back for more, the early sports museums have had to continually expand and update their collections. This is exactly what has happened at the National Horseracing Museum in Newmarket since they opened in 1983. Located in the heart of the High Street, they have successfully grabbed the attention of the inquisitive passer-by. As the curator, Graham Snelling, points out, 'You don't have to have an interest in racing to enjoy the museum.'

Champion jockey Sir Gordon Richards on Sun Chariot by Alfred Munnings. NATIONAL HORSERACING MUSEUM, NEWMARKET

The story of racing unfolds inside the six galleries downstairs and two upstairs. The exhibition delves into the obvious racing paraphernalia like Frankie Dettori's silks worn when he won all seven races at Ascot. There's also a look at the crowd and social scene, the Royal connection and a wonderful collection of racing artwork.

The traditional exhibits mix well with the interactive experiences. The new have-a-go environment really gets visitors involved. 'We now have a practical gallery,' says Graham Snelling. 'There's a horse simulator as well as a life-size fibreglass horse so people can learn how to saddle-up. It is staffed by ex-jockeys and trainers and it is proving to be very

popular with the children.' There are plans for further interactive exhibits including a commentary box.

Newmarket also draws in the crowds with guided tours, including an introduction to racing tour. 'After a visit around the museum a guide takes the visitors to the meeting and gives advice on how to place a bet,' says Mr Snelling. 'The only thing we don't guarantee is a win,' he laughs.

At the Donington Grand Prix Collection understandably the most popular exhibits are the Formula One Grand Prix cars. Visitors can get up close to true classics which sit side by side: Ayrton Senna's McLaren next to Nigel Mansell's Williams and Nelson Piquet's Brabham. Then there's the authentic 1920s garage scene and an array of racing memorabilia from all the racing greats. In total the collection encompasses five halls covering a quarter of a mile with over 130 historic vehicles. It is the world's largest collection of single-seater racing cars.

This unique collection is the brainchild of the construction tycoon Tom Wheatcroft who bought the land in 1971 and opened the collection, then of around 50 cars, in 1973. Regular additions have been made since in parallel with the rapid evolution of this dynamic sport and manager of the collection, Rachel Brown, expects interactive videos and computers will be a part of the museum's future.

These early sports museums have set the standards. They are well aware that the challenge now is to keep up with the pace of new technologies, whilst retaining their original character. Experimenting with technology might sometimes be a gamble, but of course at Newmarket, they are used to that.

Two of the historic vehicles from the Donington Collection. DONINGTON GRAND PRIX COLLECTION

Jackie Stewart's Tyrrell lines up with other classic cars. DONINGTON GRAND PRIX COLLECTION

Alain Prost's McLaren. DONINGTON GRAND PRIX COLLECTION

**National Horseracing Museum,
99 High Street, Newmarket,
Suffolk CB8 8JL
(tel: 01638 667333)**
OPEN: *March–Oct Tue–Sun 10am–5pm
(also on Mon during July & Aug);*
ADMISSION CHARGED

**Donington Grand Prix Collection,
Donington Park,
Castle Donington,
Derby DE74 2RP
(tel: 01332 811027)**
OPEN: *Daily 10am–5pm;*
ADMISSION CHARGED

Part of a bigger picture

Sport touches most people in everyday life and in many of our towns and cities it is an integral part of a bigger picture. Here, to tell the story of the sport alone would be an impossible task.

The River and Rowing Museum at Henley, due to open this summer, is a perfect example, encompassing three distinct but interwoven themes: the international sport of rowing, the River Thames and the historic town of Henley. The impressive purpose-built home for the project was designed by the famous architect David Chipperfield and has already won international acclaim by being short-listed for an Award for European Architecture. The striking oak clad upper walls and turned steel roof encompasses over 2,900 square metres of display galleries with stunning views out over the Thames.

Baldersby Park cricket club from 1912. THIRSK MUSEUM

The rowing segment will illustrate the history of the sport. Interactive displays on the art of rowing and the search for speed will enable visitors to learn more about the techniques and skills involved. 'We will look at the hull shapes and show why one boat moves faster than another. We've been given the Pinsent and Redgrave Olympic boat that won Great Britain's only gold medal in 1996, and we've also been donated the oldest known competitive rowing boat in the world – The Royal Oak,' says the commercial and marketing manager, Paul Newman.

The Thirsk Museum in North Yorkshire is a very small museum but is comparable to the project currently unfolding in Henley in that it also encompasses three themes: local Thirsk history, industry and cricket. The building was once the home of Thomas Lord, the founder of Lord's cricket ground. The museum is run entirely by volunteers on a shoestring budget, but has successfully survived and fittingly celebrates its 21st anniversary this year.

Although both these museums operate on a different scale, here is further proof that sport has an important place in the museum environment.

River and Rowing Museum,
Mill Meadows, Henley-on-Thames,
Oxfordshire RG9 1BF (tel: 01491 415600)
OPEN: *Due to open summer 1998*

Thirsk Museum, 16 Kirkgate, Thirsk,
North Yorkshire YO7 1PQ (tel: 01845 524510)
OPEN: *Easter–Oct Mon–Sat 10am–4.30pm
(last admission), Sun 2pm–4pm;*
ADMISSION CHARGED

Artist's impression of exhibits and interactives at the new River and Rowing Museum. RIVER AND ROWING MUSEUM, HENLEY

The future of sporting museums

The Museum of Rugby at Twickenham and the Science of Sport exhibition within the Science Museum are obviously hitting the spot. These highly interactive museums are being copied. 'We've had the Gaelic Athletic Association from Ireland, the Manchester United Museum curator and a representative from Yorkshire cricket down to see what we are doing,' says Jed Smith at the Twickenham-based Museum of Rugby. 'It's the ultimate form of praise,' he adds. The approach of both is to actively engage visitors with all the ingredients of interactive technology. And the recipe seems to be working.

The Museum of Rugby is a private museum run by the Rugby Football Union which opened on 26 January 1996 to promote the game to the young and old. This is a real hands-on interactive museum; there are 14 individual rooms where the new technology is used to educate rather than to be used as a gimmick. The museum is arranged both chronologically and thematically. There is something for everyone.

Capturing the action – a large-scale line-out at the Museum of Rugby. MUSEUM OF RUGBY, TWICKENHAM

Once past the turnstiles visitors are confronted by crowd noises and a large-scale line-out. All the senses are aroused with noise, smells and film. 'No one is forced to stand and read anything. The nine touch-screen computers are the spine of the museum. Visitors can make up their own visit. If the 1975 Grand Slam matches interests them, that's what they can call up on the computer,' says Jed.

It is a similar experience at the Science of Sport exhibition inside the Science Museum. The exhibition is 150 metres long with lots of interactive displays mixed sensibly with a science element. Phil McCartney, the manager, is keen to give children an introduction into the science of sport that they wouldn't otherwise learn by watching television. The exhibition has been open since March 1997 with plans for it to continue until April 1999. After that it might tour as a travelling exhibition or be set as a stand-alone site.

According to Phil McCartney the most popular exhibit is called 'Get off the blocks'. It is a two-lane ten-metre stretch of track with a pair of starting blocks donated by running aces Linford Christie and Carl Lewis. Seiko have donated a stopwatch that records visitors' times to within one-thousandth of a second. Other favourites are a penalty shoot-out machine, a simulated rock face, and virtual reality golf, tennis and snowboarding. These exhibits delight adults and children alike: 'If you can combine technology and sport, you're always onto a winner,' says Phil enthusiastically.

Special events are another important aspect at these two venues. As part of Museums Week last year, Jed Smith organised for actors to play 1920s rugby captains, and craftsmen from one of the major rugby ball manufacturers demonstrated hand-stitching of rugby balls. Science of Sport holds special events on a weekly basis. When we spoke, footballing hero Gary Lineker was due to give a talk on the importance of exercise.

There is no doubt that by their very nature sporting activities lend themselves to the interactive experience. As Phil McCartney enthuses: 'Sport is a proactive pastime. Our museum is the future.'

The Museum of Rugby at Twickenham, Rugby Football Union, Rugby Road, Twickenham, Middlesex TW1 1DZ (tel: 0181 892 2000)
OPEN: *Non-match days Tues–Sat 10.30am–5pm, Sun 2pm–5pm, match days 11am to one hour prior to kick-off (match ticket holders only);* **ADMISSION CHARGED**

Science of Sport Exhibition at the Science Museum, Exhibition Road, London SW7 2DD (tel: 0171 938 8000)
OPEN: *Daily 10am–6pm;* **ADMISSION CHARGED**

Shooting a few hoops at the Science of Sport basketball exhibit.
SCIENCE MUSEUM/SCIENCE AND SOCIETY PICTURE LIBRARY

Win two free tickets to The Natural History Museum!
MUSEUMS & GALLERIES QUESTIONNAIRE

Hobsons Publishing is committed to ensuring that *Museums & Galleries* maintains its high level of quality and information. In order to do this we need your help. Please take a few minutes to fill in this questionnaire. All entries received by **1 July 1998** will be put into a draw and the winner will receive two free tickets to The Natural History Museum.

Please return to: The Editor, *Museums & Galleries*, Hobsons Publishing, FREEPOST CB264, Bateman Street, Cambridge CB2 1LZ

1) Name: ....
   Address: ....
   ....
   ....
   Job title: ....

2) Age:
   ❐ Under 25
   ❐ 25-45
   ❐ 45+

3) How did you obtain your copy of *Museums & Galleries* 1998/99?
   ....

4) On average, how long do you spend reading your copy of the Guide?
   ❐ 30 minutes
   ❐ 1 hour
   ❐ 2 hours or more

5) Approximately how often do you refer to this Guide during a year?
   ....

6) What do you use the Guide for?
   ❐ to obtain information on specific museums and galleries
   ❐ to find out about new events and exhibitions
   ❐ to find out about new museums and galleries

7) How long do you keep this Guide?
   ❐ less than 6 months
   ❐ 1 year
   ❐ more than 1 year

8) Which section of the Guide do you refer to most?
   ❐ the feature articles
   ❐ the attraction highlights
   ❐ the geographical listings

9) Do you find the book easy to use?
   ❐ Yes
   ❐ No
   If no, please state your reasons why:
   ....
   ....

10) How far do you usually travel to visit specific museums and galleries?
    ❐ less than 1 hour
    ❐ 1-3 hours
    ❐ more than 3 hours

11) What sort of information would you like to see in the next edition of *Museums & Galleries*?
    ❐ more articles on new events and exhibitions
    ❐ regional features
    ❐ detailed information on more museums and galleries
    ❐ anything else (please state below)
    ....
    ....

12) Approximately how many museums and galleries do you visit in a year?
    ❐ less than 5
    ❐ 5-15
    ❐ 15 or more

13) What other museum and gallery guides do you use?
    ....
    ....

14) Do you usually visit museums and galleries:
    ❐ on your own?
    ❐ with your family?
    ❐ In a group of ten or more?

15) Do you have any other comments?
    ....
    ....
    ....

A museum in the making

SARA GOODWINS, freelance writer and official photographer for the National Trust, follows the development of the new Museum of Scotland from concept to realisation

On St Andrew's Day, 30 November 1998, the Museum of Scotland will be formally opened to the public. The ceremony will mark the culmination of almost ten years of hard work by those involved with the project, which brings together in a unique setting information and exhibits about Scotland's past, peoples, culture and achievements. But how is such a vast project organised and what steps need to be taken to ensure success?

The trustees of the National Museums of Scotland have long been aware of the need for a new museum tracing the stories of Scotland's past. At the beginning of the project the board of trustees noted this fact

rather poignantly: 'Scotland stands alone among countries of its size in having nowhere to tell the full story of its peoples and to show properly its most treasured possessions.' A nation's heritage – especially three thousand million years of it – requires specially designed display areas to be fully appreciated and in 1989 the Secretary of State for Scotland announced backing for a new purpose-built home for the Scottish collections.

Edinburgh's existing Royal Museum now has a new and complementary neighbour. The building acts both as a foil and a pivot for the regular, classical geometry of the city's eighteenth- and nineteenth-century developments on its north side, and the

irregular street patterns and varied building forms of the medieval city to the south and west.

A design for the past and the future

Designed by Gordon Benson and Alan Forsyth, the new building has been praised as one of the finest examples of architectural design in Scotland in the second half of the twentieth century. As befits a museum for Scotland, the architects have used Scottish materials wherever possible. The main structure is steel-reinforced concrete, but the external walls are clad with almost 1,000 tonnes of Clashach sandstone. One of the hardest of the

Artist's impression of the new museum from the corner of George IV Bridge, by Carl Laubin. © TRUSTEES OF THE NATIONAL MUSEUMS OF SCOTLAND

Scottish sandstones, it is quarried near Elgin in Morayshire in north-east Scotland and is an attractive, almost marbled, buff colour.

Within the new building Clashach sandstone is also used in some of the internal walls and floors, and the inclusion of natural light wherever possible helps to provide an open and welcoming atmosphere. The architect's were asked specifically to maximise the use of natural light, but prevent direct sunlight falling into the exhibition areas. In this way the museum balances its two-fold nature – preservation and display – by ensuring that the exhibits are protected from rapid changes in temperature, humidity and light, but are also imaginatively presented for the million visitors per year expected to come and see them.

As well as creating fine exhibition spaces the building is also designed so that the visitor can look beyond it into the city of Edinburgh where many of the historical and topographical references within the museum originate, thus breathing life into the stories depicted within. The gallery housing the display dealing with the reformed church, for example, has a view to Greyfriars Kirk, reflecting the church's importance in the history of the Covenanting movement; the circular tower at the north-west corner of the building reflects the form of Edinburgh Castle's half-moon battery, which can be seen from the museum's tower rooms. Echoing the strong defensive system of its ancient counterpart, the museum tower's was inspired by castle architecture and designed to safeguard the special display of Scotland's national treasures it houses.

A place in history – design for the chain.
© TRUSTEES OF THE NATIONAL MUSEUMS OF SCOTLAND

Raising the funds

Such an ambitious project needs huge amounts of money to pay for it. The Government agreed to fund the construction of the building, which left the museum trust with the task of finding almost £15 million to pay for special exhibit areas, equipment, educational facilities and interactive resources. Appeals to the Heritage Lottery Fund secured half the sum required and Lord Rothschild, the fund's chairman, expressed his pleasure about the award: 'This is one of the great, great projects of the last decade and we are extremely proud to be able to help with the balance of the funding.' The trust is appealing to members of the public and businesses to raise the remainder of the funds required.

One of the novel ideas to encourage giving is the chain appeal. The chain in question has been designed in mellow brass and has been commissioned from Richard Kindersley, a leading contemporary letter cutter, whose work also appears elsewhere in the new building. The separate links carry the names of individuals, all of whom will make their own mark in history when the finished chain is set into the floor of Scottish sandstone in the main public concourse, the Hawthornden Court. Some people pay for their own names to be included; others commemorate someone special to them whom they wish to honour. Gavin Hastings, the former Scotland rugby captain, bought a link to commemorate the birth of his son, Adam, and is eager to show him his place in history: 'I'm really looking forward to taking him to the new museum... it'll be great for him to see his own name in there.'

In tandem with traditional craftsmen's skills, the fund-raising campaign is also harnessing the very latest technology in order to reach exiled Scots and their families throughout the world. The Museum of Scotland's web site is already accessible and carries details of the project so far, a brief history of the museum and an appeal for funds (see page 33). The campaign has been enormously successful, receiving e-mailed requests for information and pledges of help from places as far away as the United States, Australia and Japan.

Ivory chessmen dating from the twelfth century discovered on the island of Lewis.
© TRUSTEES OF THE NATIONAL MUSEUMS OF SCOTLAND

The Brecbennoch of St Columba, a portable house shrine dating from around 750 AD brought to the battle of Bannockburn in 1314. © TRUSTEES OF THE NATIONAL MUSEUMS OF SCOTLAND

A rich diversity of exhibits

The design of the museum was influenced by the exhibits which the trustees wish to display; consequently the new building is divided into five permanent galleries tracing Scotland's history from its geological beginnings to the Scotland of living memory:

- *Scotland's Geology and Natural History is located in the upper basement*

- *Scotland in Pre-history is in the lower basement*

- *Kingdom of the Scots 1100–1707 encompasses the ground floor*

- *Industry and Empire 1707–1914 takes up both the first and second floors*

- *Within Living Memory, Scotland in the Twentieth Century is on the third floor.*

These, together with the display of national treasures in the stronghold tower, make up the core of the museum's displays, although new temporary exhibitions are also planned.

The arrangement of the galleries and the themes to which they are to be devoted was decided very early in the project so that the design of the building could take particularly large objects or arrangements into account. Indeed, the largest exhibits are already in place and had to be installed a year before the building was completed around them. The majestic *Ellesmere* locomotive was the first exhibit to be brought in. Constructed from cast iron, wrought iron and wood, it is the oldest surviving Scottish locomotive and was built at Leith by Hawthorne & Co in 1861. The arrival of the locomotive was followed by a large whisky still, which was transported to the museum packaged as a giant whisky bottle.

Junior Board members. © TRUSTEES OF THE NATIONAL MUSEUMS OF SCOTLAND

More than 15,000 exhibits are to be displayed in total but the smaller exhibits must wait until the building is completed before being installed. The co-ordinators responsible for each of the galleries are already working with designers to plan the furnishings and displays to fully exploit the wealth of exhibition space. The gallery closest to the museum's main information desk is devoted to the Kingdom of the Scots and is planned around interwoven themes, each of which occupies a discrete area created by the structural features of the building.

A museum for all

From the outset the museum was designed to involve all ages and was the first organisation in Scotland to set up a Junior Board to ensure that the displays in the new museum are of interest to young people. So far the twelve members of the board have evaluated displays and conducted market research among their peers. Kieran Malcolmson is from Shetland and, despite feeling a bit nervous before his first time as chairman, was soon enjoying the job and getting down to business: 'I liked chairing the meeting and I had to ask people about the museums they had visited this summer.' Kieran and his fellow board members are also involved in the plans for celebrating the opening of the museum.

Visitors with special needs are also able to enjoy the new museum's exhibits to the full as exhibits, signs and facilities have all been designed accordingly. The main entrance is at pavement level, allowing easy access for wheelchair users and, although there are many floors and half landings, six lifts provide access to all visitor areas. Blind or partially-sighted visitors will be assisted by talking lifts and tactile displays, and audio and visual information will be available throughout the building to help all visitors with orientation.

Key dates in the Museum of Scotland's own history

1780 Society of Antiquaries of Scotland founded in Edinburgh

1858 Society's museum collections taken into the care of the nation

1951 Need for new home for Scottish collections agreed by Government

1971 Site in Chambers Street adjacent to Royal Museum cleared

1985 National Museums of Scotland formed by Act of Parliament

1989 Secretary of State for Scotland backs new home for Scottish collections

1990 Government agrees to fund purpose-built museum – eventual cost is £32.5 million

1991 International architectural competition won by Benson + Forsyth

1992 Additional funds of £15 million required for furnishing and exhibits – fund-raising campaign begins

1993 Work begins on site

1994 Her Majesty the Queen inaugurates the Museum of Scotland project

1995 Heritage Lottery Fund makes award of £7.25 million, £4 million raised by campaign

1996 First installation, the locomotive *Ellesmere*, moved to new building

1997 Main building completed, interior furnishing begins

1998 Installations completed, new Museum of Scotland opens

The construction site at dusk, early 1997. © TRUSTEES OF THE NATIONAL MUSEUMS OF SCOTLAND

Innovative features

From its conception, the aim of the museum was to create something more than just a suitable home for the exhibits and various special features help to achieve this. As well as landscaping the external areas of the museum, the roof of the highest part of the building is to be turned into a rooftop garden terrace. Visitors will be able to see Edinburgh laid out before them – a living map flanked by the towering hill of Arthur's Seat on one side and the distinctive silhouette of the Castle on the other.

Visitors on the ground floor will be able to enjoy an entirely different panorama. A special area housing several computer terminals will be linked to the Museum of Scotland's Advanced Interactive Computer System (MOSAICS). This multimedia encyclopaedia will enable visitors to find out more about the exhibitions and piece together their own understanding of Scotland's dramatic stories. Information will be available on-line and on CD-Rom so the museum's resources are not only available to people visiting the museum. Donald Dewar, Secretary of State for

Scotland, is particularly impressed by the planned extent of the computer facilities: 'Its imaginative use of new technologies to interact with the objects will serve to stimulate our senses and extend access to the vast intellectual resources.'

A fitting tribute

Such a world-class museum obviously requires a world-class opening ceremony and arrangements are well under way for the St Andrew's Day opening. The museum is planning to involve as many people as possible in the celebrations, not only in Scotland but throughout the world. A special children's event is planned, as well as a gala dinner for all those involved in the project. The opening will also be marked by specially commissioned musical and literary works from Scotland.

The new Museum of Scotland is being designed, built and developed as a monument to the Scottish people, their lives and history – an educational resource, an international attraction and an interactive experience. On St Andrew's Day 1998 the vision of the project, captured so dramatically by Magnus Magnusson, will undoubtedly be realised: 'Nothing would be a more fitting tribute to our past than to give it the future it deserves, in the kind of setting it deserves.'

> *Breathes there a man,*
> *with soul so dead,*
> *Who never to himself hath said,*
> *This is my own, my native land...*
>
> **The Lay of the Last Minstrel, VI, i–ii**
> **Sir Walter Scott**

Museum of Scotland,
Chambers Street, Edinburgh EH1 1JF
(tel: 0131 225 7534)
DUE TO OPEN: *30 November 1998*

A taste of what's new

While not exhaustive, the following list provides information on some of the new museums and galleries opening during 1998 and the early part of 1999, as well as a few of the exciting changes taking place at our established museums and galleries.

Captain Cook Birthplace Museum,
Stewart Park, Marton, Middlesbrough,
Cleveland TS7 6AS (tel: 01642 311211)
DUE TO OPEN: *early 1998 (official opening)*
Complete redevelopment of existing museum presenting Cook's life and work in a unique way using a range of interactive multimedia exhibits.

Crewkerne & District Museum,
Heritage Centre, Market Square,
Crewkerne, Somerset TA18 7JU
(tel: 01460 73441)
DUE TO OPEN: *late 1998/early 1999*
New museum based in a renovated sixteenth-century building with permanent and temporary exhibitions covering the history of the local area.

Cynon Valley Museum,
Depot Road, Gadlys, Aberdare,
Mid Glamorgan CF44 8DL
(tel: 01685 886729)
DUE TO OPEN: *winter 1998*
New social history museum based in an old iron-casting house focusing on the lives of the rich diversity of people living in the valley during the last 200 years.

The Heritage Centre, Queen Anne's Walk,
The Strand, Barnstaple, Devon EX31 1EU
(tel: 01271 373311)
DUE TO OPEN: *spring 1998*
New interactive experience of Barnstaple from Saxon times through to the eighteenth century based in the old merchant's meeting house.

Quarry Bank Mill, Styal, Wilmslow,
Cheshire SK9 4LA (tel: 01625 527468)
DUE TO OPEN: *spring 1998*
Second phase of the ongoing power project involving restoration of the steam power system and the creation of four major new galleries with interactive displays.

Milton Keynes Museum,
Stacey Hill Farm,
Wolverton, Milton Keynes,
Buckinghamshire MK12 5EJ
(tel: 01908 316222)
DUE TO OPEN: *spring 1998*
(first phase of ongoing project)
Complete refurbishment of local community museum after serious fire in 1996.

Sunderland Museum & Art Gallery,
Borough Road,
Sunderland SR1 1PP
(tel: 0191 565 0723)
DUE TO OPEN: *autumn 1998*
(first phase of ongoing project)
Major five-year redevelopment to improve and expand the oldest public museum outside London, including the creation of several new permanent galleries exploring different local themes.

River and Rowing Museum,
Mill Meadows, Henley-on-Thames,
Oxfordshire RG9 1BF
(tel: 01491 415600)
DUE TO OPEN: *summer 1998*
New museum celebrating the history and tradition of the River Thames, the international sport of rowing and the riverside community of Henley-on-Thames.

Vale and Downland Museum,
The Old Surgery, Church Street,
Wantage, Oxfordshire OX12 8BL
(tel: 01235 771447)
DUE TO OPEN: *summer 1998*
Major refurbishment and modernisation of museum covering local history, archaeology, arts and crafts including the introduction of new permanent galleries and interactive exhibits.

Victoria and Albert Museum,
Cromwell Road,
South Kensington,
London SW7 2RL
(tel: 0171 938 8500)
DUE TO OPEN: *May 1998*
New photography gallery housing changing exhibitions of the museum's national collection of photographs and displays charting the history of the medium from 1839 to the present day.

Web of intrigue

ROBERT MASON, editor with LineOne and former deputy editor of the *Museums Journal*, explores the fascinating world of museums and galleries on the internet

Surfing the net. THE EXPLORATORY HANDS-ON SCIENCE CENTRE, BRISTOL

As little as three years ago many people had never even heard of the internet. At the same time most people would have been totally unaware that a new independent museum was opening in remote rural Scotland.

Today, things have changed dramatically; the internet is increasingly becoming a part of everyday life. We all want to travel the information superhighway and for Kilmartin House in Argyll, which launched its web site back in September 1995, it has been an enormously successful vehicle for raising awareness and local support for the project. The trust's web pages, full of striking images which reflect the area's rich archaeological heritage, have put the new museum and the whole area firmly on the map.

Making a hit

Kilmartin House, being a small-scale venture, is at one end of the enormous spectrum of museum web sites now available with a total of about 10,000 visits, or 'hits', to date. At the other end is one of the nation's most popular museums, the British Museum, which launched its web site almost exactly a year after Kilmartin House. At the end of 1997 it could boast around 350,000 hits a week (70,000 real visits per week were made during the same period).

Whether big or small, most museum web sites have been launched with one main aim – to promote the museum and inspire people to visit the real-life version. At the very least web sites can provide, at the press of a button or two, all the up-to-date practical information visitors might want to know. Most sites contain the basics: details on the museum and its collections, previews of forthcoming events and special exhibitions, floor plans and, of course, details of how to get there. The two-way nature of the internet means that it is also a good vehicle for gathering feedback from people after a visit. E-mail is a quick and convenient way for people to record their comments and ideas and this information can help curators to enhance the visitor experience.

However, many museums have gone much further than this. The Kilmartin House site includes an excellent interactive map of the whole of the Kilmartin Valley, where clicking on any site or monument brings up specific information and accompanying photographs. Some of the Museum of London's pages can be viewed in Spanish, French or German, as well as English, by simply clicking the language button on the side of the home page, and at the Museum of the History of Science site

an electronic mailing list provides space for an online discussion about the history of scientific instruments. Many sites, including the stylish web pages of the Museum of Costume in Bath, have a feature of the month which takes a special in-depth look at one of the museum's exhibits.

Galleries of modern art by their nature aim to be trendy, innovative and eye-catching. Glasgow's Gallery of Modern Art web site gives a taste of the future of animation on the web, using flash and quicktime plug-ins (software which gives the user the ability to play audio or video samples) to create a visually stunning effect. The pioneering Natural History Museum, Britain's first museum to go online, is never afraid to try new technology. In the past its web site has been home to interactive fossils and currently boasts interactive three-dimensional surround videos of the Life and Earth Galleries. This allows the viewer to 'virtually' stand and turn 360 degrees within the gallery spaces while zooming in and out.

The virtual museum

Taking the whole concept a stage further, the internet also offers the possibility of the 'virtual museum'. At one level this allows new museums to have a presence on the internet and grab the attention of potential visitors even before they open. The River and Rowing Museum in Henley-on-Thames (see page 25) has had a presence on the internet charting the progress of the project since 1994, even though it only opens this year. The Museum of Scotland project (see page 27) is also on the internet, as is the Transport and Technology Museum that is planned for Basingstoke. There are even web sites for museums that will never open like the Virtual Museum of Computing which intends to remain just that – a virtual museum.

It is not only the large, national museums that are making the most of the new technology. David Saywell, IT manager at the National Portrait Gallery, makes the key point that creating a web site is 'a relatively cheap and easy thing to do,' which is particularly significant for smaller, less well known museums. They are attracting many visitors via their web sites: 'Some people have recorded in the visitors' book that they saw us on the internet,' says Martin Sach, web master of the London Canal Museum. The international scope of the net also means the message is spread worldwide; 'We've even gained a small booking from an American university through the internet site,' he adds.

WHERE TO LOOK

Some museum web sites have stunning graphics, others have imaginative gimmicks, but when it comes down to it, the best sites have interesting and informative content that is always up to date.

The larger museums like the Natural History Museum, the Museum of London and the Science Museum show the benefits of their greater IT budgets with stylish web pages.

But museums don't necessarily have to have big budgets to have interesting web sites. Smaller museums like the Museum of the History of Science, Oxford, or Museum of Antiquities, Newcastle upon Tyne, do a great job with online exhibitions. Your own local museum may already be online.

In the rapidly changing world of the internet, new web sites are always popping up and established ones are being enhanced and updated. For a taste of the variety currently on offer why not try some of the 20 sites listed here? You never know where they might take you...

Armagh Planetarium
http://www.star.arm.ac.uk/planet/planet.html

Ashmolean Museum, Oxford
http://www.ashmol.ox.ac.uk/

British Museum
http://www.british-museum.ac.uk/

Gallery of Modern Art, Glasgow
http://www.goma.glasgow.gov.uk/

Hampshire County Council
Museums Service
http://www.hants.gov.uk/museums/index.html

Kilmartin House Museum, Argyll
http://www.kht.org.uk/

London Canal Museum
http://www.charitynet.org/~LCanalMus/

Marischal Museum, Aberdeen
http://www.abdn.ac.uk/~ant010/

Mary Rose Maritime Museum, Portsmouth
http://www.maryrose.org/

Museum of Antiquities,
Newcastle upon Tyne
http://www.ncl.ac.uk/~nantiq/

Museum of Costume, Bath
http://www.museumofcostume.co.uk/

Museum of the History of Science, Oxford
http://www.mhs.ox.ac.uk/

Museum of London
http://www.museum-london.org.uk/

Museum of Scotland, Edinburgh
http://www.museum.scotland.net/

National Museums and Galleries of Wales
http://www.cardiff.ac.uk/nmgw/overv.html

Natural History Museum, London
http://www.nhm.ac.uk/

River and Rowing Museum,
Henley-on-Thames
http://www.comlab.ox.ac.uk/archive/other/museums/rowing.html

Science Museum, London
http://www.nmsi.ac.uk/welcome.html

Ulster Folk and Transport Museum
http://www.nidex.com/uftm/

Virtual Museum of Computing
http://www.comlab.ox.ac.uk/archive/other/museums/computing.html

Sites for inquisitive eyes – a selection of pages from museum web sites. COURTESY OF KILMARTIN HOUSE, MUSEUM OF THE HISTORY OF SCIENCE AND MUSEUM OF ANTIQUITIES

The Earth Galleries can be explored in the 3D virtual tour on the Natural History Museum's web site.
© THE NATURAL HISTORY MUSEUM

It is actually quite easy for museums to make archival information available on the internet as computer documentation is a key part of what they do as a matter of course. The step to make this information available on the web is a relatively simple one. Indeed, in 1996 Hampshire County Museums Service put 80,000 object records on the web with minimal extra work and at no extra expense.

The future

It is still early days for museum web sites which are continuing to learn how to make the internet work for them and their visitors, whether they are families, students or academics. Few have yet explored the possibilities of online shopping or ticket sales. Ann Steedman, of Bath's Museum of Costume, would like to develop her site to include internet shopping from her museum gift shop, resource packs for teachers to use in preparation for a visit, distance purchase of tickets, and group bookings by e-mail. All these facilities are likely to become more and more commonplace as more people gain access to the internet.

Initial scepticism that web sites and virtual reality might stop people visiting museums and galleries is rapidly diminishing as the benefits of having an online presence become clear. If there is one person who can allay any fears it is computer science lecturer Jonathan Bowen. He manages the Virtual Library of Museums and has been monitoring the growth of museum web sites since their appearance. 'The internet is never going to replace real museums,' he says emphatically. 'It will merely be supplementary.'

Academic links

Many of the first wave of museum web sites came about from academic links. Universities have been using the internet for a number of years, so university museums (like the Ashmolean in Oxford or the Marischal Museum in Aberdeen) or those like the Natural History Museum (which happens to be next to Imperial College) were the first to be hooked up to the web.

Now museums are keen to explore the educational potential of their internet connections to offer easier access for researchers in those universities and many more around the world. Nowhere is this more apparent than at the Natural History Museum. Home to a unique collection of a staggering 68 million specimens, of which 28 million alone are insects, there is no way that the museum could put all these items on general display. There are simply too many and a large number have only scientific value. The delicate nature of the collections means that many of the specimens must be kept under carefully controlled environmental conditions. The internet is the perfect answer. As well as promoting museums in a popular sense, it can make a wealth of specialised information easily available to academics or private researchers.

The internet can even do away with the need for researchers to visit archives in person, leaving staff more time to concentrate on improving the experience for people who make real visits. The National Army Museum, which receives many genealogical inquiries from people as far away as Canada, Australia and New Zealand, has found the web particularly useful in dealing with research requests. Chris Drake, the museum's head of computer services remarks, 'The site has taken over 36,000 hits which has given us the incentive to develop it into a more informative and researcher-friendly site.'

HOW TO GET ON THE NET – A BEGINNER'S GUIDE

'An internet connection is like the telephone; soon everyone will have one.' This is the view of Ann Steedman of Bath's Museum of Costume. She is absolutely right and there is no time like the present to get acquainted with the internet.

Novices need not be daunted by this new technology. It has never been easier to go surfing as more and more libraries get linked to the world wide web and internet cafés spring up in towns and cities all over the country. So, check out what is available locally and have a go.

If you want to get online at home you will need three things: a computer, a modem (which links the computer to the telephone network) and an account with an internet service provider (ISP). It is worth bearing in mind that the more powerful the computer and modem you have, the quicker the surfing.

There are a number of ISPs currently advertising in the national press and most offer a free month's trial. For less than £10 a month, ISPs like LineOne, Compuserve, Demon or Virgin Net will give you access to the internet (and personal e-mail); the only other costs you are likely to incur are local telephone charges for the time you are online.

Once online, you'll want find the pages that interest you. With literally millions of web pages on offer, targeting the right information can sometimes be a bit tricky at first, unless you know exactly what you are looking for. And the choice is only going to get bigger – in 1996 alone the number of sites on the web increased six-fold.

If you know the address of a web page, in other words all those odd little letters, symbols and numbers which now frequently accompany museum postal addresses, you're already half way there. Known in the business as a uniform resource locator, or URL, you simply have to type it into the address box at the top of your browser. You can then navigate from the page that appears by clicking on underlined text or graphics.

However, quite often you will not know the URL of the site you are looking for. In this case you need to try a search engine, which allows you to type in keywords and then presents you with a number of possible web pages to explore. There are several enticingly entitled search engines available; for starters you could try Yahoo or Excite. Don't be disheartened if it takes a little while to find what you want; searching can sometimes be a hit-and-miss affair.

Help is also at hand from the number of web sites that conveniently collect links to museum sites – a web site of web sites. The oldest and probably the best of these launch-pads is the Virtual Library of Museums. Since 1994 computer science lecturer Jonathan Bowen has been gathering a comprehensive list of museum URLs worldwide. For British museums alone, a good starting point is the Museums Association's pages. The Museums Association is a membership organisation for UK museums and the people who work in them and so has the latest information on the web sites of its members.

Using the internet is extremely easy, so if you haven't had a go yet there is no time like the present to start. The following information should help you on your way.

INTERNET SERVICE PROVIDERS

LineOne (tel: 0800 111 210)
Compuserve (tel: 0990 000 030)
Demon (tel: 0345 666222)
Virgin Net (tel: 0500 558800)

LAUNCH PADS WITH LINKS TO MUSEUM WEB SITES

Museums Association
http://www.museumsassociation.org

Virtual Library of Museums
http://www.icom.org/vlmp

SEARCH ENGINES

Yahoo   http://www.yahoo.co.uk/
Excite   http://www.excite.co.uk/

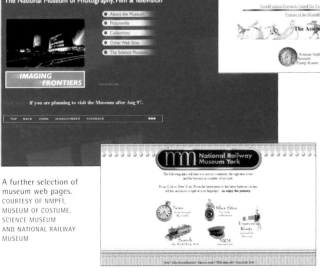

A further selection of museum web pages.
COURTESY OF NMPFT, MUSEUM OF COSTUME, SCIENCE MUSEUM AND NATIONAL RAILWAY MUSEUM

Museums Week 1998

Following our interview with Loyd Grossman in *Museums & Galleries* 1997, we once again turn the spotlight on Museums Week as this truly national event goes from strength to strength

Since its conception in 1995 Museums Week has achieved enormous success. In just four years it has become the best known and largest museums promotion in the United Kingdom and is now a regular springtime fixture on the cultural calendar. This week-long programme of events, organised by the Campaign for Museums, is certainly achieving its aims of increasing visitor numbers, broadening public support and raising the profile of museums and galleries throughout the UK. However, the event's organisers are setting their sights even higher for 1998.

Due to run from 16 to 24 May, and a designated event of the UK's six-month Presidency of the European Union, Museums Week 1998 will undoubtedly be the best yet. The aim is for over 1,000 participating museums and galleries. This year's patron is the Rt Hon Chris Smith, Secretary of State for Culture, Media and Sport, and Vauxhall Motors are sponsoring the event for a second year.

Building success year on year

The ambitious targets set for this year stem from the record-breaking figures achieved during Museums Week 1997.

■ A grand total of 889 museums throughout the United Kingdom participated in some way and between them organised over 2,000 special events.

■ A third of museums reported an increase in visitors during Museums Week 1997, one-quarter of whom said they were visiting as a direct result of the event.

■ Despite the general election, over 60 MPs visited their local museums and many more who were unable to participate wrote to pledge their support.

■ In addition to lots of national media coverage, Museums Week 1997 was covered in almost 600 local and regional newspaper and radio features.

Themes for 1998

Every museum taking part in Museums Week 1998 will be running at least one event or special offer. This year there are three themes to help museums plan and develop their own ideas.

Events based around *Museums in the community* will draw inspiration from the local area and the wider community of

East Coast by LNER (Tom Purvis, 1925) from the V&A's *Power of the poster* – a major new exhibition running during Museums Week. COURTESY OF THE TRUSTEES OF THE V&A

Europe to tie in with the UK's Presidency of the European Union in the first half of the year. Kent County Council has already organised a joint programme with museums in Nord Pas de Calais, and other museums are working to forge similar links.

Behind-the-scenes secrets will be revealed during *Conservation*-themed events. Visitors will have the opportunity to see 'before and after' conservation exhibits, or to take along their own objects for a conservation clinic with museum curators.

Hidden treasures will see museums displaying some of their more unusual objects or setting up treasure trails within the museum or around the local area. This theme is intimately tied to the British Tourist Authority's year-long campaign promoting the wealth of secret treasures in our museums and galleries to overseas visitors.

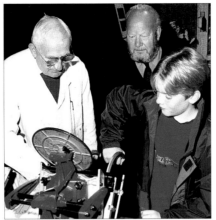

A young visitor lends a hand during Museums Week at the Museum of Science and Industry in Manchester.
© JEAN HORSFALL

Getting involved

Museums Week is all about getting involved and these are just a few of the events organised for this year which allow you to do just that:

- On Sunday 17 May the Brighton Fishing Museum will be hosting the annual Mackerel fair. A blessing of the nets ceremony will celebrate the landing of the first mackerel by the town's fishing boats.

- Visitors to the Museum of Childhood in Edinburgh on Monday 18 May will be invited to take part in a toy conservation clinic and visit the new exhibition of ethnic dolls.

- The Rydedale Folk Museum in York is holding a working weekend on 23 and 24 May when visitors will be invited to handle all the exhibits on display.

- The Elmbridge Museum in Weybridge will be inviting visitors to put their best foot forward in a special exhibition of historic shoes and boots running through and beyond Museums Week.

Major exhibitions

A number of new long-running exhibitions will be on during Museums Week 1998:

- The Cheltenham Art Gallery and Museum is holding *Fainting for fashion*, an exhibition looking at some of the more uncomfortable garments worn by Victorian women (1840–1900). Opening on 2 May, the collection includes corsets, crinolines, underwear and outwear. Call 01242 237431 for further details.

- Celebrating the 50th anniversary of the first Porsche sports car the Design Museum in London is hosting *Ferdinand Porsche: design dynasty* from 9 April.

The electric Lohner-Porsche Chaise (1900) and the much-loved Volkswagen Beetle are just two of the cars on show. Call 0171 403 6933 for further details.

- The *Power of the poster* is running from 2 April to 26 July at the Victoria and Albert Museum. Taken from the museum's own collection, the 300 exhibits – some full hoarding size – will look at the evolution of the pictorial poster over the last 120 years. Call 0171 938 8500 for further details.

WHERE TO FIND OUT MORE

- Get online and check out the Museums Week web site at **www.museumsweek.co.uk**

- Look out for posters and news-letters in and around museums and at tourist information centres in your local area

- Check out the *Radio Times* in the run up to Museums Week for competitions and special offers

- Tune-in to national and regional radio and television for up-to-the-minute information during the event

Museums Week is there to remind everyone just how important our museums are on a national and an international scale. So take this opportunity to visit somewhere new or find out what's happening at your favourite museum.

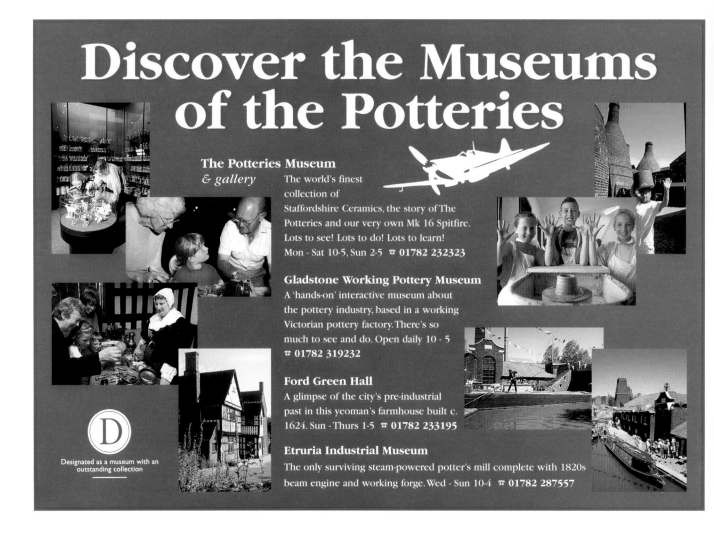

Discover the Museums of the Potteries

The Potteries Museum
& gallery

The world's finest collection of Staffordshire Ceramics, the story of The Potteries and our very own Mk 16 Spitfire. Lots to see! Lots to do! Lots to learn! Mon - Sat 10-5, Sun 2-5 ☎ 01782 232323

Gladstone Working Pottery Museum

A 'hands-on' interactive museum about the pottery industry, based in a working Victorian pottery factory. There's so much to see and do. Open daily 10 - 5 ☎ 01782 319232

Ford Green Hall

A glimpse of the city's pre-industrial past in this yeoman's farmhouse built c. 1624. Sun - Thurs 1-5 ☎ 01782 233195

Etruria Industrial Museum

The only surviving steam-powered potter's mill complete with 1820s beam engine and working forge. Wed - Sun 10-4 ☎ 01782 287557

D
Designated as a museum with an outstanding collection

NATIONAL MARITIME MUSEUM

THE OLD ROYAL OBSERVATORY AND QUEEN'S HOUSE, GREENWICH, LONDON SE10 9NF
TELEPHONE: 0181 858 4422

NATIONAL MARITIME MUSEUM

These three dramatic buildings set in the midst of beautiful parkland with panoramic views across London house collections including globes, clocks, telescopes and paintings, which together explain the history of Britain and the sea and the story of time itself.

The Old Royal Observatory is home of Greenwich Mean Time and Longitude O'. Here visitors can stand astride the Prime Meridian which marks the beginning of all time and space on earth. Try the hands-on science stations and examine the largest refracting telescope in the UK. A recent addition to the Observatory is the Accurist Millennium Countdown Clock, which positioned on the Prime Meridian, is counting down the remaining days, hours, minutes, seconds and hundredths of seconds to the start of the year 2000.

The National Maritime Museum, is the largest and most important maritime museum in the world, covering every aspect of ships and seafaring, in peace and at war, from pre-history to today. Visitors can explore the galleries of 20th Century Sea Power, Nelson, The Ship of War and the 'All Hands' interactive galleries. The museum is currently undergoing a major redevelopment programme which will effectively create a new museum for the 21st century, opening in Spring 1999. As a result, not all of the galleries are currently accessible.

The Queen's House is a unique 17th century royal villa, designed by Inigo Jones. Originally begun for Anne of Denmark, consort of King James I, it was completed for Henrietta Maria, wife of King Charles I. It has been faithfully restored to its 1660's splendour, where the Queen's apartments can be viewed, along with a rich collection of fine royal portraits, early scenes of Greenwich and 17th century Dutch marine painting.

EVENTS – A programme of special events covering each holiday period. It includes live planetarium shows, story-telling, workshops, dance, drama and song.
OPENING TIMES – Open Daily 10am–5pm (Closed 24–26 December)
ADMISSION – By ticket to all sites, for details telephone: 0181 858 4422.
BRITISH RAIL – Greenwich

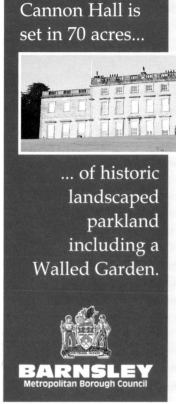

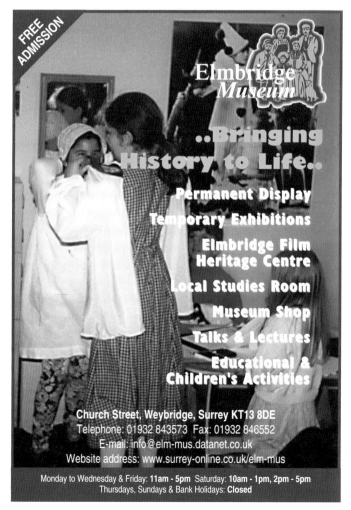

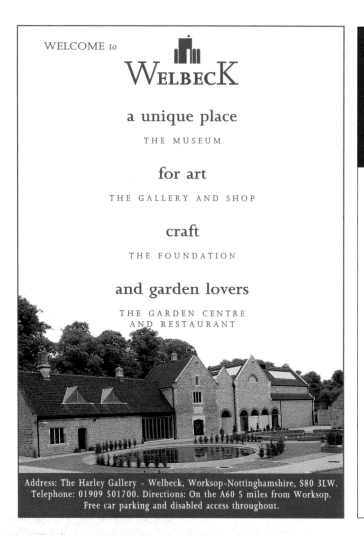
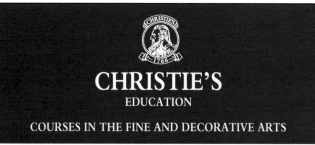

Attraction highlights

Detailed profiles of a selection of museums and galleries arranged alphabetically by country and county.

American Museum in Britain

The American Museum in Britain

Claverton Manor, Bath BA2 7BD. Tel: 01225 460503

The American Museum shows, in 18 authentically recreated rooms, how Americans lived in the 17th to 19th centuries. The rooms depict life from the early colonies of New England to New Orleans on the eve of the Civil War. In addition there are galleries devoted to the Native Americans, Shakers, Pennsylvanian Germans, and the Spanish colonists of New Mexico. The grounds include an American Arboretum.

EXHIBITIONS/EVENTS

This year's exhibition 16 May–18 October – SHAKER: The Art of Craftsmanship. Nearly 100 objects characterising the traditional Shaker values of simplicity, utility, order and fine craftsmanship will be displayed, some within room settings, in the New Gallery of the American Museum. Items on display include large cupboards for storage, counters for tailoring, chairs, tools, textiles, boxes and herb labels. The special events programme includes Native American Dancing (13/14 June), French and Indian War re-enactment (15/16 August) and the American Civil War Battle (19/20 September).

ADMISSION

Adults £5.00. Seniors £4.50. Children £3.00.

OPENING TIMES

21 March–1 November 1998
Tuesday–Friday
Gardens 1–6pm. Museum 2–5pm.
Saturday–Sunday
Gardens 12–6pm. Museum 2–5pm.

The Holburne Museum and Crafts Study Centre

Great Pulteney Street, Bath BA2 4DB
Tel: 01225 466669. Fax: 01225 333121

Henrietta Laura Pulteney
by Angelica Kauffmann

This historical Georgian building, a jewel in Bath's Crown, is set in gardens chronicled by Jane Austen and contains treasures of national importance. The nucleus of the 17th/18th century fine and decorative art on display was made by two inspired Bath collectors, Sir William Holburne (1793–1874), and Ernest E. Cook, who died in 1955. Galleries show outstanding silver, porcelain, maiolica, bronzes and paintings by Old Masters including Gainsborough, Turner, Raeburn, Stubbs and Zoffany. The collections have been enhanced over the years, with the addition in 1977 of the Crafts Study Centre containing ceramics, woven and printed textiles, calligraphy and furniture by leading 20th century artist-craftspeople, including Bernard Leach.

EXHIBITIONS 1998

6 March–4 May
Travelling Companions – *Madame de Pompadour* by Drouais & *Queen Charlotte* by Lawrence
Important paintings toured by the National Gallery.
12 May–5 July
The Collector's Eye: From Romney to Renoir
A Private Collection Revealed.
20 June–6 September
Heritage Regained: Arthur Gilbert's Spectacular Silver
21 July–13 September
An Indian Summer, Watercolours by Charlotte, Viscountess Canning in India 1856–61. Lent by the Earl of Harewood.
3 October–11 December
Peter Collingwood – Master Weaver. A major exhibition toured by firstsite.

ADMISSION

£3.50 with concessions.

OPENING TIMES

Monday–Saturday 11am–5pm. Sunday 2.30–5.30pm.
(Closed Mondays November to Easter.)

Licensed Teahouse in garden setting. Free parking. Disabled Access. Museum Shop. Group bookings and Study Facilities by appointment.

The Museum of East Asian Art

12 Bennett Street, Bath BA1 2QL. Tel: 01225 464640

Based in a restored Georgian building, this unique Museum houses a fine collection of Chinese, Japanese, Korean and Southeast Asian artefacts. The objects on display range in date from c.5000 BC to the twentieth century and reveal the finest achievements in East Asian craftsmanship. Exhibits include Jades, Ceramics and Metals.

EXHIBITIONS/EVENTS

The exhibition programme is supported by an active events calendar including: tours, lectures, object identification clinics, storytelling and workshops.

EDUCATIONAL FACILITIES

The Museum represents an excellent resource for schools by helping to develop visual awareness, deduction and practical skills across a broad range of topics. By visiting the Museum pupils are able to learn through seeing and handling artefacts, and involvement in practical activities which relate to various aspects of the National Curriculum.

ADMISSION

Adults £3.50. Concessions. Groups welcome, rates on application.

OPENING TIMES

April–October:
Monday to Saturday 10am–6pm, Sunday 10am–5pm.
November–March:
Monday–Saturday 10am–5pm, Sunday 12 noon–5pm.

Octagon Galleries

The Octagon
Milsom Street
Bath BA1 1DN
Tel: 01225 462841
Fax: 01225 448688

Bungee jump, Brighton. Photograph by Ben Dray, bronze medal winner of the RPS 141 Annual International Print Exhibition 1998.

The Octagon Galleries is the second largest photographic exhibition space in the UK attracting some of the world's greatest photographers: names like Don McCullin, Sebastiao Salgado and David Bailey.

There are four galleries of constantly changing, contemporary and historical photographic exhibitions plus a museum of photography, a fascinating holography gallery and a permanent display of rare photography and equipment from the Royal Photographic Society's acclaimed Collection.

The Octagon Cafe provides welcome refreshment in artistic surroundings with gentle jazz music and Zwemmer's bookshop offers an opportunity to purchase a momento. All of this is housed in one of Bath's most notable 18th century buildings.

ADMISSION

Adults £2.50. BANES residents £1.75. Family ticket £5. OAP, UB40, NUS £1.75. Disabled/children under 7 free.

OPENING TIMES

Open every day 9.30am–5.30pm (last admission 4.45pm) except Christmas day and Boxing day.

LOCATION

The Octagon Galleries is located half way up the high street in the centre of Bath. Visitors can park in the public car parks signposted.

The Royal Photographic Society

BATH AND NORTH EAST SOMERSET

BEDFORDSHIRE

Number 1 Royal Crescent

Bath BA1 2LR
Tel: 01225 428126
Fax: 01225 481850

A Georgian Town House in Bath's most magnificent crescent; redecorated and furnished to show the visitor how it might have appeared in the late 18th century.

Number One was the first house to be built in the Royal Crescent in 1767. It is a fine example of John Wood the Younger's Palladian architecture. Visitors can see a grand town house of the late 18th century with authentic furniture, paintings and carpets.

ADMISSION

Adults £3.80. Concessions £3.00. Groups £2.50. Family £8.00.

OPENING TIMES

10 February–25 October Tuesday–Sunday and Bank Holiday Mondays 10.30am–5pm.
29 October–1 December Tuesday–Sunday 10.30am–4pm (last admission half an hour before closing). Closed Good Friday.

Museum shop.

Private tours out of hours by arrangement with the Administrator.

Victoria Art Gallery

[Bath and North East Somerset Council]

Bridge Street
Bath BA2 4AT
Tel: 01225 477233
Fax: 01225 477231

Located next to shop-lined Pulteney Bridge, the Gallery has a plush top-lit room on the first floor with pictures by Gainsborough, Zoffany, Farrington, Lawrence and others, capturing the elegance of the Georgian period. Downstairs, two modern temporary exhibition galleries show art, craft and photography from the region, plus work by artists of national and international importance. New shop with everything from cards to works of art and craft. Wheelchair access to ground floor only, via side entrance.

EXHIBITIONS/EVENTS

Please 'phone for full details of the programmes. Highlights include:
Sea Dreams: Art Salutes the Boat, until 14 June;
Flexible Furniture, 20 June–31 July;
Head First: Portraits from the Arts Council Collection, 6 March–18 April 1999.

ADMISSION

Currently free (under review)

OPENING TIMES

Tuesday to Friday 10am–5.30pm.
Saturday 10am–5pm,
Sunday 2–5pm.

Cecil Higgins Art Gallery

Castle Lane, Bedford MK40 3RP. Tel: 01234 211222

Housed in an elegantly converted and extended Victorian mansion, original home of the Higgins family of wealthy Bedford brewers, the Cecil Higgins Art Gallery is home to one of the most outstanding fine and decorative art collections outside London.

The gallery offers:
- a remarkable collection of British and European watercolours from the 18th to the 20th centuries and international prints from Impressionism to the present. It includes works by Rembrandt, Turner, Blake, Cotman, Rossetti, Burne-Jones, Whistler, Renoir, Picasso, Dali, Moore, Warhol, Hockney. The exhibition changes regularly.
- a distinguished group of ceramics and glass from the Renaissance to the 20th century, with particular focus on 18th century porcelain, Whitefriars glass and ceramics of the Arts and Crafts movement.
- authentically reconstructed Victorian room settings in the Victorian mansion, suggesting the life of a prosperous 1880's household.
- The William Burges room: a complete Arts and Crafts experience, with Burges' own furniture in a full decorative setting, inspired by his designs.
- hands-on activities for children and workshops for all ages.
- changing exhibitions from the collection and elsewhere.
- programme of events, lectures, performances, concerts and more.
- fully guided tours available for groups on request (charges vary).

ADMISSION

Free.

OPENING TIMES

Tues–Sat 11am–5pm. Sun and Bank Holiday Mon 2–5pm.
Closed Mondays, Good Friday, 25 and 26 December.

Reading Museum Service

Blagrave Street
Reading
Berkshire RG1 1QH
Tel: 0118 939 9800

Reading
BOROUGH COUNCIL

The Museum of Reading features a wealth of reconstructions and artefacts from Reading's past and present. Displays include Britain's only full-size replica of the Bayeaux Tapestry, the Story of Reading Gallery tracing the development of the town from Saxon times to the present day and The Silchester Gallery, featuring a selection of artefacts from the Roman site of Calleva Atrebatum.

Housed in a Victorian pumping station on the banks of the River Kennet, **Blake's Lock Museum** traces the industrial life of Reading during the 19th and early 20th centuries. Displays include reconstructions of Victorian shops, a restored gypsy caravan and turbines dating from the 1920's.

EXHIBITIONS/EVENTS

Annual programme of temporary exhibitions, children's activities and special events at both museums. Free events leaflet available from the above address.

ADMISSION

Free.

OPENING TIMES

Museum of Reading:
Tues–Sat 10.00am–5.00pm;
Sun and Bank Holidays
2.00pm–5.00pm.
Blake's Lock Museum:
Tues–Fri 10.00am–5.00pm;
Sat, Sun and Bank Holidays
2.00pm–5.00pm.

University of Reading

Whiteknights, PO Box 217
Reading RG6 6AH
http://www.reading.ac.uk

The Museum of English Rural Life
Tel: 0118 931 8661

The Museum exhibitions depict farming, crafts and village life of the last 200 years. Special facilities are available for school groups.

ADMISSION

Adults £1. Children free.

OPENING TIMES

Tuesday–Saturday 10am–1pm;
2–4.30pm.

The Ure Museum of Greek Archaeology
Tel: 0118 931 8420

Small museum housing the fourth most important collection of Greek ceramics in Britain. Study trail available for teachers and students.

ADMISSION

No charge for individuals.

OPENING TIMES

Weekdays 9am–5pm when not in use for teaching. Please telephone before visiting.

The Cole Museum of Zoology
Tel: 0118 931 8903

Contains over 4,000 items illustrating comparative anatomy although only a selection are on display in the foyer of the School of Animal and Microbial Sciences.

ADMISSION

No charge. Please give prior notice of group visits.

OPENING TIMES

Weekdays 9am–5pm.

Bristol City Museums and Art Gallery

Queen's Road, Bristol BS8 1RL. Tel: 0117 922 3571

Explore a fascinating building full of wonderful objects. Beautiful Victorian paintings rub shoulders with fossil 'Sea Dragons'. Encounter the mysteries of ancient Egypt and learn about the plants and animals of south-west England. Gaze at the outstanding collection of oriental art, and closer to home, the Bristol ceramics. In addition there is a regular programme of temporary exhibitions and events covering a wide variety of topics.

Whether a Bristolian or a visitor to our city, you will find something to interest you here. Our shop and café complete the visit.

ADMISSION

Admission charge, children free. Free admission on Sundays.

OPENING TIMES

Open daily 10am–5pm. Open some Bank Holidays. Disabled access.

Blaise Castle House Museum
Henbury Road, Henbury, Bristol BS10 7QS. Tel: 0117 950 6789

Bristol's museum of everyday life. Opening Hours – 1 Apr to 31 Oct inclusive 10am–5pm Sat to Wed. Open most Bank Holidays within those months.

Bristol Industrial Museum
Princes Wharf, Wapping Road, Bristol BS1 4RN
Tel: 0117 925 1470

The fascinating museum of Bristol at Work. Opening Hours – 1 Apr to 31 Oct inclusive 10am–5pm Sat–Wed. Open most Bank Holidays within those months. 1 Nov to 31 Mar inclusive 10am–5pm Sat and Sun.

The Georgian House
7 Great George Street, Bristol BS1 5RR. Tel: 0117 921 1362

A West India merchant's town house of 1791. Opening Hours – 1 Apr to 31 Oct inclusive 10am–5pm Sat–Wed. Open some Bank Holidays within those months.

The Red Lodge
Park Row, Bristol BS1 5LJ. Tel: 0117 921 1360

The only surviving Tudor domestic interior in Bristol. Opening Hours – 1 Apr–31 Oct inclusive 10am–5pm Sat–Wed. Open some Bank Holidays within those months.

Arnolfini

**16 Narrow Quay
Bristol BS1 4QA
Tel: 0117 929 9191
Fax: 0117 925 3876
e-mail arnolfini@arnolfini.
demon.co.uk
www.channel.org.uk/
arnolfini**

Arnolfini is one of Europe's leading centres for the contemporary arts with a national and international reputation for presenting new and innovative work in the visual arts, performance, film and music. Ten to twelve exhibitions are mounted annually and recent showings have included Dominique Blain, Jan Fabre, ACE!, Rhapsodies in Black – Art of the Harlem Renaissance and Nick Stewart.

Situated in the heart of Bristol's historic docks Arnolfini welcomes over 450,000 visitors a year. Its facilities include a 231 seat auditorium, 3 galleries, education room, specialist art bookshop and a Café/Bar, uniquely designed by artist Bruce Mclean and architect David Chipperfield in 1987.

EXHIBITIONS/EVENTS

Voiceover – 31 Jan–22 Mar
Select – 28 Mar–10 May
Kenny Hunter – 16 May–
28 June
John Hilliard – 24 Oct–6 Dec

ADMISSION

Free to exhibitions
Other events contact Box
Office for details

OPENING TIMES

Galleries open
Mon–Sat 10am–7pm
Sun 12 noon–6pm

Buckingham-shire County Museum

**Church Street, Aylesbury
Bucks HP20 2QP
Tel: 01296 331441
Fax: 01296 334884**

Award-winning, hands-on museum. The county's heritage is represented in a range of galleries combined with a splendid Art Gallery and the Roald Dahl Children's Gallery. Housed in 15th century buildings in a garden setting, with cafe, shop and meeting rooms.

Step into the magical world of Roald Dahl with a visit to this unique Gallery. Enter the Giant Peach, discover Willy Wonka's inventions, crawl through Fantastic Mr Fox's tunnel – let your imagination run wild!

EXHIBITIONS/EVENTS

For events and changing exhibitions please telephone the Museum.

OPENING TIMES

Main Galleries: Mon–Sat 10am–5pm, Sun and Bank Hols 2–5pm. Please call for details of charges, group bookings and opening times for the Dahl Gallery.

LOCATION

An hour by train from London Marylebone or 25 minutes off the M25 via the A41. Near St Mary's Church (five minutes' walk from station).

EDUCATIONAL SERVICES

A full programme of teaching sessions and workshops for both young and old is available. Contact David Erskine or Ros Castling for details.

Wycombe Museum

[Wycombe District Council]

**Priory Avenue
High Wycombe
Buckinghamshire
HP13 6PX
Tel: 01494 421895
Fax: 01494 421897
Email: enquiries@
wycombemuseum.
demon.uk**

Wycombe Museum is full of surprises. Its home is historic Castle Hill House, an eighteenth century building set in attractive grounds. Inside, the displays explore the history of the Wycombe area, especially the chairs and chair making for which the town is famous. There are interactive displays, changing exhibitions, historic films, a computer quiz and much more. In fact . . . something for everyone. There is a car park on site and ramped access to the ground floor. The gift shop specialises in local crafts and there are indoor and outdoor picnic areas.

ADMISSION

Free. School parties and large groups are asked to book in advance.

OPENING TIMES

Monday–Friday 10am–5pm. Closed Sundays and Bank Holidays except for special events.

WYCOMBE
•MUSEUM•

Cromwell Museum

**Grammar School Walk
Huntingdon PE18 6PH
Tel: 01480 375830**

Oliver Cromwell went to school in the building, which dates from the late 12th century, and is now the Cromwell Museum. From his birth in Huntingdon in 1599 he rose to become the Head of State, the Lord Protector, from 1653 until his death in 1658. The collection explains his life and legacy through portraits, documents and personal items.

The Museum has many objects known to have been owned by Cromwell which have been passed down through his descendants. As well as contemporary portraits of himself and his family and colleagues, the Museum has material illustrating the progress of the English Civil Wars, including arms and armour, and James Ward's interpretation of the Battle of Marston Moor.

ADMISSION

Free.

OPENING TIMES

April–October
Tues–Fri 11am–1pm, 2–5pm.
Sat and Sun 11am–1pm, 2–4pm.
November–March
Tues–Fri 1–4pm.
Sat 11am–1pm, 2–4pm.
Sun 2–4pm.

Peterborough Museum and Art Gallery

Priestgate
Peterborough PE1 1LF
Tel: 01733 343329
Fax: 01733 341928

Classic Jurassic Age collection of Pleisiosaurs, Pliosaurs and Ichthyosaurus, some of the best dinosaur specimens in Britain.

The history of Peterborough and the surrounding area from the bronze age to the present day.

An excellent art collection including works by Turner, Sickert and Elizabeth Frink. Rareties include the most comprehensive Napoleonic prisoner of war work collection from the Norman Cross Depot.

EXHIBITIONS/EVENTS

Art Exhibitions including painting photography and craft. Exhibition celebrating 50 years of the National Health services from April 28.

ADMISSION

Free.

OPENING TIMES

Tuesday–Saturday 10am–5pm. Closed 24 December 1998– 2 January 1999.

St Neots Museum

The Old Court
8 New Street
St Neots
Cambs PE19 1AE
Tel: 01480 388788/388921
Fax: 01480 388791

This new local history museum was highly commended in the 1997 Gulbenkian awards. Housed in the town's former magistrates court/police station building, complete with its 1907 cell block in near-original condition, the museum tells the story of the St Neots area from prehistoric times to the present day.

The four main display galleries appeal to all ages and cover the Story of St Neots, local crafts and trades, home and community life.

EXHIBITIONS/EVENTS

Regular programme of exhibitions, usually changing monthly. Holiday activities for children, monthly lacemaking demonstrations, occasional workshops and living history events.

May to August '98 – exhibition and events to commemorate 350th Anniversary of the Battle of St Neots.

ADMISSION

Adults £1.50. Children and OAPs 75p.

OPENING TIMES

Weds–Sat 10.30am–4.30pm all year.

Chester Museums

[Chester City Council]

Grosvenor Museum
27 Grosvenor Street
Chester CH1 2DD
Tel: 01244 402008
Fax: 01244 347587
Website:
www.chestercc.gov.uk

Something for Everyone – in this award-winning Museum you will find interactives to entice you, exhibitions to intrigue you, and displays to absorb you!

* Walk through a Roman Graveyard and gaze at the larger-than-life mural
* hear about life in Deva from a Roman soldier and try out the hands-on computer
* be dazzled by the gleam of Chester-made silver
* contemplate artists' views of the city's past
* see a dinosaur's footprints
* listen as a Victorian Naturalist works in his study
* relive past times as you explore the Period House – a Tudor dining room, Georgian drawing room, and Victorian life above and below stairs
* take refreshments in the panelled splendour of the Kings Arms Kitchen
* browse for special gifts and souvenirs in the Museum Shop.

EXHIBITIONS/EVENTS

April 4–July 19
'Two Faces of Rome' – experience the virtual reality of the Roman fortress of Deva.
August 1–October 11
'Pastimes: a Century of Entertainment'

ADMISSION

Free.

OPENING TIMES

Mon–Sat 10am–5pm. Sun 2–5pm.
Closed Good Friday, Christmas, Boxing and New Year's days.
* Disabled access with assistance • baby changing facilities
* Museum shop • light refreshments • parking nearby
* coach dropping-off point.

Chester Heritage Centre and King Charles Tower
Call 01244 402008 for opening times in 1998.

Warrington Museum & Art Gallery

Bold Street
Warrington WA1 1JG
Tel: 01925 442392
Fax: 01925 442399

Broad-based collections housed within authentic Victorian galleries. Visit the Sarcophagus and rich art collections including a 'Still Life' by Van Os. Natural History, Geology, Ethnology and Egyptology, Bronze Age and Roman collections of interest to specialists. Local history is well represented. See the rare Roman actor's mask. Social history is featured in the 'Time Tunnel' including fire engine, Gibbet iron and stocks.

EXHIBITIONS/EVENTS

Exhibition programme in a superb refurbished Art Gallery satisfying interests from Fine Art to Popular Culture. Community Gallery supports local interest groups and Artists. Lively Education Department with programmes covering many topics linked to the National Curriculum. Children's holiday activities.

ADMISSION

Free.

OPENING TIMES

Mon–Fri 10.00am–5.30pm.
Sat 10.00am–5.00pm.
Closed Sunday and Bank Holidays.

Jamaica Inn and Museums

Jamaica Inn, Bolventor, Launceston, Cornwall PL15 7TS
Tel: 01566 86250. Fax: 01566 86177
Mr Potter's Museum Tel:/Fax: 01566 86838
Smugglers at Jamaica Inn Tel:/Fax: 01566 86025

Made immortal by Dame Daphne du Maurier's novel, come and visit Jamaica Inn and Museums.

Daphne du Maurier's Smugglers at Jamaica Inn
★★★ New for 98 ★★★

At Daphne du Maurier's Smugglers at Jamaica Inn, we introduce you to the life and works of Daphne du Maurier, and our arch Villain Demon Davey, the Vicar of Altarnun, invites you to enter an exciting presentation of the story of Jamaica Inn told in tableaux, sound and light. Finally, on to see probably the finest collection of smuggling relics, dating from today back into the mists of time.

Meet our arch villain Demon Davey.

Mr Potter's Museum of Curiosity

One of the last truly Victorian Museums in England, consisting of assembled items of curiosity worldwide.

Come and browse around our fascinating Victorian Museum, founded in 1861, by the famous taxidermist, Walter Potter, containing his humorous tableaux, 'The Death of Cock Robin', 'House that Jack Built', 'Kitten's Wedding', 'Guinea Pigs Cricket Match' and many others. Packed also with over 10,000 unusual and rare curios world-wide – General Gordon's autograph, 2 headed pig sought by witches, ancient Egyptian mummified crocodile, native whistle made with human arm bone, 3 legged chicken, postillion boots, a church made of feathers etc.

These two attractions, including gift shops, open all year except January. Refreshments available from the Inn.

Penlee House Gallery and Museum

Morrab Road
Penzance
Cornwall TR18 4HE
Tel: 01736 363625
Fax: 01736 361312

Housed in the former home of wealthy Penzance miller and merchant, J. R. Branwell, the Gallery and Museum was originally founded in 1839 and is the home of the town's and district's historic collections. Re-opened in November 1997 after major refurbishment, Penlee House now includes the Orangery café, baby changing facilities, full access to the disabled including limited parking and a well stocked gift shop.

TEMPORARY EXHIBITIONS

16 May 1998–30 Aug 1998
'Walter Langley – Pioneer of the Newlyn Art Colony'
14 Sept 1998–14 Nov 1998
'Do You Remember the Thirties?'
15 Nov 1998–9 Jan 1999
'Rustic Simplicity – Scenes of Cottage Life in 19C Britain'.
Mar and Apr 1999
'Prints and Printmaking'

ADMISSION

Adults £2. Concessions £1. Children Free. Saturdays Free.

OPENING TIMES

All Year Mon–Sat 10.30am–4.30pm including Bank Holidays.
July and Aug 1998 only, open Sun 12.30pm–4.30pm.
Closed Christmas Day, Boxing Day, New Year's Day and Good Friday.

Tate Gallery St Ives

Porthmeor Beach
St Ives
Cornwall TR26 1TG
Tel: 01736 796226

Tate Gallery St Ives opened in 1993 and offers a unique introduction to modern art, where many works can be seen in the surroundings and atmosphere which inspired them. The gallery presents changing displays from the Tate Gallery's collections, focusing on the post-war modern movement St Ives is so famous for. Tate Gallery St Ives also runs the Barbara Hepworth museum in St Ives.

EXHIBITIONS

Works by artists including Ben Nicholson, Barbara Hepworth, Piet Mondrian, John Wells, Patrick Heron, Roger Hilton, Serge Poliakoff and Pierre Soulages will be on show during 1998. The displays are complemented by temporary exhibitions and contemporary artists' projects and residencies.

ADMISSION

£3.50. Concessions £2.

OPENING TIMES

Apr to Sept – Mon–Sat 11am–7pm. Sun 11am–5pm. Oct to Mar – Tues–Sun 11am–5pm.

FACILITIES

Rooftop café, Gallery shop, education services, guided tours, events and activities, disabled access.

Trevarno Estate Gardening Museum

Trevarno Estate
Helston
Cornwall TR13 0RU
Tel: 01326 574274
Fax: 01326 574282

The recently opened gardens and grounds at the heart of the historic Trevarno Estate provide a magical and atmospheric backdrop to a new and fascinating gardening museum housing what is believed to be the largest and most comprehensive collection of implements, requisites, ephemera and related gardening items in the country.

Hundreds of exhibits including many rare and unique items reflect the numerous aspects and influences of gardening for young and old alike.

Of added interest the Museum houses a separate collection of children's antique barrows, tools and miniature garden items.

Visitors of all ages will find the themed and informal layout an entertaining, intriguing and informative insight into the head gardener's kingdom of a bygone era.

ADMISSION

Museum:
Adults £2. OAPs £1.50.
U14s £1. U5s Free.
Gardens:
Adults: £3. OAPs £2.50.
U14s £1.25. U5s Free.
Groups: Welcome, prior booking helpful.

OPENING TIMES

All Year except Christmas Day 10.30am–5pm.

Cumbria's Western Lakes and Coast Museums

Maryport Maritime Museum
1 Senhouse Street, Maryport CA15 6AB
Tel: **01900 813738**

This fascinating Museum houses a range of objects, pictures, models and paintings.

ADMISSION

Free.

OPENING TIMES

Easter–Oct: Mon–Thurs 10am–5pm, Fri/Sat 10am–1pm & 2–5pm, Sun 2–5pm. Nov–Easter: Mon–Sat 10am–1pm & 2–4.30pm

Workington Hall
c/o Tourism Section, Allerdale
Borough Council, Allerdale House
Workington, Cumbria CA14 3YJ
Tel: **01900 735408**

ADMISSION

Adults 90p. Children/OAP 60p. Family £2.30.

OPENING TIMES

Easter–Oct Tues–Fri: 10am–1pm & 2–5pm, Sat–Sun 2–5pm. Bank Holiday Mondays: 10am–1pm & 2–5pm.

Helena Thompson Museum
Park End Road, Workington
Cumbria, CA14 4DE
Tel: **01900 62598**

A fine, listed mid-Georgian building, displays include costumes, pottery and local history.

ADMISSION

Free.

OPENING TIMES

Easter–Oct: 10.30am–4pm. Nov–Easter: 11am–3pm.

Keswick Museum & Art Gallery
Station Road, Fitz Park, Keswick
Cumbria CA12 4NF
Tel: **017687 73263**

ADMISSION

Adults £1.00. Children 50p. Concessions 50p. Group Rates.

OPENING TIMES

Easter–Oct: Mon–Sun 10am–4pm. Open Bank Holidays.

CUMBRIA

Abbot Hall Art Gallery and Museum of Lakeland Life

Kendal, Cumbria LA9 5AL
Tel: 01539 722 464
Fax: 01539 722 494

This elegant Georgian building provides a superb setting for its collection of fine art. Paintings include work by George Romney. Touring exhibitions complement the permanent collection of 18th, 19th and 20th century British art.

SELECTED TEMPORARY
EXHIBITIONS 1998

10 June–13 September
Head First – Portraits from the Arts Council Collection
22 September–1 November
Kitty North – Landscapes
10 November 1998–
31 January 1999
Bridget Riley – A Retrospective

The adjacent Museum of Lakeland Life looks at local history over the past 200 years. Also nearby is Kendal Museum of Natural History on Station Road.

ADMISSION
Adult £2.80. Senior Citizen £2.50. Child/Student £1.25. Family £6.90. Season Tickets start from £3.80.

OPENING TIMES
Daily: 12 February 1998–31 January 1999
10.30am–5pm (reduced hours in winter).

FACILITIES
Disabled Access, Coffee Shop. Gift Shop. Free Parking.

DERBYSHIRE

The National Tramway Museum

Crich, Matlock
Derbyshire DE4 5DP
Tel: 01773 852565
Fax: 01773 852326

The National Tramway Museum . . . the most delightfully different 'Action Attraction' you'll probably ever find!
You can ride and compare these historic vehicles with the new trams now appearing in various towns and cities. If you can't remember the originals, this is a fantastic opportunity to discover the experience. The indoor attractions are equally inviting! There's a vast exhibition hall, video theatre and tram depots to explore. Special rates and offers are available for group bookings and schools. Wheelchair ramps to all facilities. Braille guide books, and a newly-converted tram is in service, specially imported and converted to lift and carry wheelchairs.

ADMISSION
Please ring for details.

OPENING TIMES
Please ring for details.

Sir Richard Arkwright's Cromford Mills

[The world's first successful Water Cotton Spinning Mill – one of the great historic industrial monuments of the world]

The Arkwright Society
Mill Lane
Cromford
Derbyshire DE4 3RQ
Tel: 01629 824297

Guided tours • exhibition • clothing at factory prices • cards and gifts • books • wholefood restaurant • free parking • friendly staff.

There is an on-going restoration programme and a guide will explain the history and plans for the future.

You will find us at Cromford, Derbyshire, just off the A6. Look out for the brown signs.

ADMISSION
Free. Guided tours: Adults £2.00, Concessions £1.50.

OPENING TIMES
Open daily 9.00am–5.00pm.

The Arkwright Society is a Registered Charity. Reference No: 515526.

DEVON

The Museum of Dartmoor Life

3 West Street
Okehampton
Devon EX20 1HQ
Tel: 01837 52295

Housed in an early 19th century Agricultural Mill: the Museum tells the story of how the people of Dartmoor have lived, worked and played throughout the centuries.

Book and Gift Shop; Tea Rooms and Devon Crafts Shop are all situated within the Museum Courtyard, which is a rare example of a Medieval Burgage Plot.

The Museum is a starting point for walking on Dartmoor. It is also a Devon Record Office Service Point for research into family history.

EXHIBITIONS
Temporary exhibitions presented in the Cranmere Gallery.

ADMISSION
Adults £1.90. Over 60's £1.60. Children/Students 90p. Family Ticket £5. School parties 60p per head. Reduction for groups of 10 and over.

OPENING TIMES
10am–5pm. Daily All Year, plus Saturdays Easter to end of September and 7 days a week June to end of September.

PARKING
There is a small car park at the rear of the museum off George Street, where you will find a large, working waterwheel.

Plymouth City Museum & Art Gallery

Drake Circus
Plymouth PL4 8AJ
Tel: 01752 304774
Fax: 01752 304775

The City Museum & Art Gallery opened in its present location at Drake Circus, Plymouth in 1910, and is home to fine and decorative art collections of paintings, prints and Reynolds family portraits, silver, and Plymouth porcelain. The Cottonian Collection of prints, drawings, bronzes and a libarary is also on view.

The Museum's collections include entomology, geology, natural history and social history. In addition to the exhibitions and permanent collections there are a number of children's workshops, lunchtime talks and concerts taking place during the year.

The Museum's facilities include: access for the disabled, gift shop and refreshment area. There is no parking available.

EVENTS

For further details about current exhibitions and events and information about the Merchants House, the Elizabethan House and other branch museums please call 01752 304774.

ADMISSION

Free.

OPENING TIMES

Tuesday–Friday 10am–5.30pm, Saturdays & Bank Holiday Mondays 10am–5pm.

Waterfront Museum

[Borough of Poole]

4 High Street
Poole BH15 1BW
Tel: 01202 683138
Fax: 01202 660896

The Waterfront Museum is housed in buildings dating from the Medieval period adjacent to Poole Quay. It tells of the history of the town and of its connections with the sea. The Museum makes use of modern audio visual techniques, hands on and traditional museum displays. There is something for everyone in this Museum. There is a School Education Service with opportunities for school parties to take part in many educational activities. The Museum has a lift, craft shop and facilities for the disabled.

EXHIBITIONS/EVENTS

There is a changing programme of temporary exhibitions and a programme of holiday activities for children.

ADMISSION

Admission charge made.

OPENING TIMES

Easter to October
Monday to Saturday
10am–5pm
Sundays 12 noon–5pm.
November to Easter
Monday to Saturday
10am–3pm
Sundays 12 noon to 3pm.

Beverley Art Gallery

[East Riding of Yorkshire Museums Service]

Champney Road
Beverley
HU17 9BQ
Tel: 01482 883903/884266
Fax: 01482 885136

The gallery holds the largest public collection of paintings by Beverley-born artist, Fred Elwell (1870–1958), Victorian and Edwardian pictures, and an excellent topographical collection, including views of Beverley Minster.

EXHIBITIONS

An exciting programme of changing exhibitions featuring both contemporary art and crafts and the selections from the gallery's collections. Highlights for 1998 include: *A Hard Day's Night: Fred Elwell's Beverley at Work* (7 February– 5 April 1998); *Domestic Spill: Andrea Roe Installation & Sculpture* (14 March–12 April 1998); *Town and Country*, a Photo 98 exhibition (18 April– 10 May 1998); *Robert Horne Printmaking Exhibition* (16 May–12 July 1998); *Sea Dreams: Art Salutes the Boat* (18 July–6 September 1998); *Life Below Stairs* (17 October– 6 December 1998).

Central Beverley, 5 mins from Railway Station.
Car park near.
Limited access for disabled.
Coffee available.

ADMISSION

Free.

OPENING TIMES

Wednesday–Sunday 10am–5pm (closed 12.30–1.30pm Saturday and Sunday). Closed Bank Holidays, Christmas and New Year.

The Waterways Museum and Adventure Centre

The Sobriety Project
Dutch River Side
Goole
East Yorkshire DN14 5TB
Tel: 01405 768730
Fax: 01405 769868

The Waterways Museum contains interactives, model boats, walk-in displays, interchangeable photographs and contemporary art exhibitions. A café, gift shop, nature trail and day boat make the museum a good day out for all.

OPENING TIMES

Weekdays 9am–4pm.
April–October
Sat/Sun 12 noon–5pm.

ENGLAND

The British Engineerium

off Nevill Road
Hove
East Sussex
Tel: 01273 559583

A beautifully restored 19th century Victorian Pumping Station crammed with full size and model road, agricultural, locomotive and marine steam engines, hot air engines, and hand and domestic tools.

The huge, elegant 1876 Eastons and Anderson original beam engine and the magnificent 16 ton Corliss engine are IN STEAM on the first Sunday in the month and Sunday and Monday of public holidays.

EXHIBITIONS

The Giant's Toolbox hands-on exhibition for children is both great fun and instructive.

ADMISSION

Adults £3.50, concessionary tickets £2.50. Family ticket £10. Telephone for information about school visits and hiring the museum for events.

OPENING TIMES

Open seven days a week 10am–5pm; closed the week prior to Christmas; last admission 4pm.

Disabled visitors please ask for help on arrival.

Free car parking on site.

Beautiful garden with a pond, ideal for a picnic.

Buckleys Yesterday's World

Next to Battle Abbey
High Street
Battle, between Eastbourne and Hastings
East Sussex TN33 0AQ
Tel: 01424 774269
Fax/Voicemail: 01424 775174

Experience a sparkling celebration of shopping and history at Yesterday's World. Walk through a charming medieval hall-house and be captivated by thousands of exhibits dating from 1850. Commentaries, smells and hands-on activities enhance the displays including a Victorian Kitchen, Edwardian chemists, a 1930's wireless shop, photographers studio.

Enter the Royalty Room and come face to face with a life-size figure of Queen Victoria. Here, you will see Victoria's lace nightdress and other royal memorabilia. Outside, you can taste the delights of the Terrace Café in the Country Garden or explore the play village, toddlers activity area and miniature golf course.

EXHIBITIONS/EVENTS

Below are some of the events.
June 21st Sunday – 'CHEESY' MUSIC DAY
August 16th Sunday – COLLECTORS DAY. Do you have a collection to show?
Entry is free.
October 11th Sunday & October 14th Wednesday – HAROLD DAY. A celebration of everything *Anglo-Saxon*. Participants required.
October 25th Sunday to 31st. HALLOWEEN WEEK.

ADMISSION

Museum & Garden Entry:
Adults £3.95. Concessions £3.75. Child (4–15) £2.85.
Family Ticket £11.95. Garden Only Entry £1.50 all ages.
All Prices subject to change.

OPENING TIMES

Open all year. 7 days a week, from 10am. 1st November to 31st March times are subject to change.

FACILITIES

Group visit prices from £1. Education packs, talks and video are available.
Disabled access is limited. Disabled toilet on-site.
Car Parking is down a road at the side of Battle Abbey.

The Sussex Toy and Model Museum

52–55 Trafalgar Street
Brighton
Sussex BN1 4EB
Tel: 01273 749494

One of the finest and most exceptional toy and model exhibitions in the world. On exhibition are examples and collections from the world's top toy makers over the last 100 years. Over 10,000 spectacular items on display!

FEATURES

Priceless toy and model train collection.
Extensive 'O' gauge and 'OO' gauge working layout.
Beautiful Victorian and modern dolls.
Evocative Military Dioramas.
Rare dolls house furniture.
Farm and country scene settings.
Tin plate toys, cars and buses.
Extensive diecast toy range.
Period ships and aeroplanes.
Meccano and other construction sets.

ADMISSION

Adults £3.00.
Children (Under 16) £1.50.
Family (2+2) £7.
Students/OAP £1.50.

OPENING TIMES

Mon–Fri 10am–5pm
Sat 11am–5pm
Closed 1–2pm for lunch
Also closed Sunday, Christmas day and Boxing day.

School and group visit rates on application.

LOCATION

Underneath Brighton Railway Station Forecourt.

Sponsored by Christies

Southend-on-Sea Museums

[Southend-on-Sea Borough Council]

**Central Museum, Victoria Avenue, Southend-on-Sea
Essex SS2 6EW. Tel: 01702 215130**

Central Museum & Planetarium
Victoria Avenue, Southend-on-Sea

Archaeology, history and wildlife of south-east Essex, plus temporary exhibitions and the Planetarium – regular programmes about the night sky.

Opening Times Mon–Sat 10am–5pm (Planetarium Wed–Sat) Tel: 01702 215131. *Admission to museum Free. Admission charge for planetarium.*

Prittlewell Priory
Priory Park, Southend-on-Sea

12th century Cluniac Priory set in a delightful park. With displays of the Priory's history, Essex wildlife and history of radio.

Opening Times Tue–Sat, 10am–1pm, 2–5pm. Tel: 01702 342878. *Admission Free.*

Southchurch Hall
Southchurch Hall Close, Southend-on-Sea

13th century moated manor house in lovely park.

Opening Times Tue–Sat, 10am–1pm, 2–5pm. Tel: 01702 467671. *Admission Free.* Pre-booked school parties have priority, term-time am.

Beecroft Art Gallery
Station Road, Westcliff-on-Sea (opposite Cliffs Pavilion)

Changing exhibitions throughout the year, plus a selection from the fine permanent collections.

Opening Times Tue–Sat, 9.30am–1pm, 2–5pm. Tel: 01702 347418. *Admission Free.* All branches closed Sundays and Bank Holidays.

Hedingham Castle

**Bayley Street
Castle Hedingham
Nr Halstead
Essex CO9 3DJ
Tel: 01787 460261
Fax: 01787 461473**

EXHIBITIONS/EVENTS

24th & 25th May – Medieval Festival. Dancing, minstrels, jugglers, archery, drama and Knights in Combat. *Presented by 'The Lion Rampant'.*

25th & 26th July – Re-creation of the Visit of King Henry VII in 1498, on the occasion of the 500th anniversary. *Presented by the 'The White Company'.*

1st/2nd, 8th/9th, 22nd/23rd, 25th/26th August – Comedy Entertainment for a fun family day out. Tales of Robin Hood and Maid Marion, Legends of King Arthur and lots more. *Presented by 'Brouhaha'.*

30th & 31st August – Jousting Tournament. Two lively days of entertainment with mounted knights in full regalia. Exciting displays of jousting skills. *Presented by the Knights of Royal England'.*

OPENING TIMES

Easter to the end of October, 10am–5pm daily. Family tickets available. Coach parties and schools are welcome all the year round by appointment with the Curator.

For all details and admission prices please telephone 01787 460261.

Cheltenham Art Gallery & Museum

**Clarence Street
Cheltenham GL50 3JT
Tel: 01242 237431
Fax: 01242 262334**

A world-renowned collection relating to the Arts & Crafts Movement, including fine furniture and exquisite metalwork, made by Cotswold craftsmen – inspired by William Morris. Rare Chinese and English pottery. 300 years of painting by Dutch and British artists. The story of Edward Wilson, Cheltenham's Antarctic explorer. Also discover the town's history – Britain's most complete Regency town as it used to be, and archaeological treasures from the neighbouring Cotswolds. Special exhibitions throughout the year.

Café Museum and museum shop.

Galleries, café and shop totally accessible for disabled visitors (lift, ramps, wheelchair available). Handling tables for partially sighted visitors. Baby changing facilities.

ADMISSION
Admission free, donations welcome

OPENING TIMES
Mon–Sat 10am–5.20pm Closed Bank Holidays.

Cotswold Museums

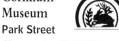

Corinium Museum
Park Street
Cirencester GL7 2BX
Tel: 01285 655611
Fax: 01285 643286

Roman Cirencester comes to life in a museum with one of the finest collections of Roman antiquities from Britain. Other local history displays plus a shop and café. Full disabled access.

ADMISSION

Adults £2.50. Concessions £2.00. Students £1.00. Children £0.80. Family (2+2) £5.00.

OPENING TIMES

April to October
Monday to Saturday
10am–5pm, Sunday 2–5pm.
Closed Mondays November to March.

Cotswold Countryside Collection

Fosseway
Northleach GL54 3JH
Tel: 01451 860715
Fax: 01451 860091

Cotswold rural life is displayed in a former House of Correction. The museum also has restored cells, a courtroom and displays on Victorian life. Exhibitions and events, tourist information, shop, café and picnic area make this a great visit.

ADMISSION

Adults £2.50. Concessions £2.00. Students £1.00. Children £0.80. Family (2+2) £5.00.

OPENING TIMES

April to October: Monday to Saturday 10am–5pm.
Sunday 2–5pm. Bank Holidays 10am–5pm.

Keith Harding's World of Mechanical Music

Oak House, High Street, Northleach
Nr Cheltenham GL54 3ET.
Tel: 01451 860181. Fax: 01451 861133

The World of Mechanical Music is a living museum of the various kinds of self-playing musical instruments which were the pride and joy of our Great Grandparents and the only kind of 'canned' music available in the home before regular broadcasting started up in 1924. The instruments are maintained in the most perfect possible order in our world famous workshops on the premises and introduced and played by our guides in the form of a live entertainment in a period setting. Musical boxes, barrel organs, polyphons, orchestrions, electric reproducing pianos, musical automata are heard at their best.

ADMISSION

Adults £5. Students/OAPs £4. Children £2.50.
Family (2 adults + 2 children) £12.50. Adults in charge of children or caring for disabled free. Every tenth admission free for booked parties. Children welcomed.

OPENING TIMES

Every day except Christmas and Boxing Day 10am–6pm.

LOCATION

High Street corner of A40 and A429 (Fosse Way).

REFRESHMENTS

Corner Green restaurant opposite, Red Lion 50 yds, both recommended, also the Wheatsheaf and the Sherborne nearby. All parts accessible to wheelchairs, toilets for disabled. Ample car parking. Free estimates by our restoration/conservation workshop.

Jet Age Museum

[Gloucestershire Aviation Collection]

Hangar 7, West Camp
Gloucestershire Airport
Cheltenham Road East
Gloucestershire GL2 9QY
Tel: 01452 715100

Britain's first jet aircraft was designed, built and first flew from an airfield near Gloucester on 8th April 1941. The Gloster Meteor quickly followed to become the first jet aircraft to enter RAF service.

The Meteor and Javelin can be seen under restoration at the museum.

Our museum, in temporary premises at the moment, offers a rare opportunity to get close to aircraft and even sit in some of the cockpits.

SPECIAL ATTRACTION

A full-size 1920's Gloster Gamecock replica under construction. Plus a working Link Trainer, a 'Battle of Britain' film Hurricane replica and approx. 600 aircraft models on display.

EVENTS DURING 1998

September 20th – Gloster Aircraft Company Reunion

The Gloucestershire Aviation Collection, is a registered charity staffed completely by volunteers to preserve the aviation heritage of Gloucestershire. Registered Charity No. 297818.

ADMISSION

Adults £3. Concessions £1.50.

OPENING TIMES

We are open most days 11am–4pm, special group visits can be arranged.

Free parking, Refreshments

Imperial War Museum

The Imperial War Museum
Lambeth Road, London SE1 6HZ.   Tel: 0171 416 5321

The Imperial War Museum is a site that should not be missed. It covers 20th century conflict, that involved Britain and the Commonwealth, both in the front line and on the home front. Housed in a former lunatic asylum, Bedlam, the museum offers a dramatic illuminated atrium which holds a wonderful collection of aircraft and tanks. There are permanent displays on the First and Second World Wars, Secret War and conflicts since 1945. Special features include: interactive videos, the walk through trench experience with soldiers going over the top, the dramatic Blitz experience complete with the sound, smell and other effects of London during a bombing raid. Special exhibitions and events throughout the year. Café, shop, baby changing facilities. Nearest station: Waterloo Underground, Lambeth North Underground.
Admission charge. Open daily 10am–6pm

Duxford Airfield
Duxford, near Cambridge CB2 4QR.   Tel: 01223 835000

Situated off junction 10 of the M11 this famous RAF station which played a vital role in the Battle of Britain, is now home to Britain's finest collection of military and civil aircraft. The legendary Spitfire is one of over 140 aircraft on show and you can even climb aboard Concorde. Military vehicles, artillery, naval exhibits and supporting exhibitions complement the aviation collection. The preserved hangars, control tower and operation room retain their wartime atmosphere and historic aircraft regularly take to the air. Restaurant, picnic areas, souvenir shops, ample free parking. See the stunning new American Air Museum and experience history in the air at Duxford's airshows. Admission charge. Open daily 10am.

HMS *Belfast*
Morgans Lane, Tooley Street, London SE1 2JH.   Tel: 0171 407 6434

For a day out on the river, why not visit HMS *Belfast*? Once onboard, you can experience how sailors lived, worked and fought during the Second World War. Permanently moored in the Thames, close to Tower Bridge, HMS *Belfast* was commissioned into the Royal Navy in 1939. In late 1942 she was assigned for duty in the North Atlantic where she played a key role in the battle of North Cape which ended in the sinking of the German battlecruiser *Scharnhorst*. In June 1944, HMS *Belfast* led the naval bombardment off Normandy in support of the Allied landing of D-Day. She last fired her guns in anger during the Korean War. A tour of the ship takes approximately two hours, giving visitors the opportunity to discover all seven decks, from the Captains Bridge all the way down to the massive boiler and engine rooms well below the waterline. Visitors can also explore the crew's messdecks, galley, operations room, six-inch-gun turrets and the punishment cells. Nearest station: London Bridge or Tower Hill Underground. Admission charge. Open daily 10am.

Cabinet War Rooms
Clive Steps, King Charles Street, London SW1A.   Tel: 0171 930 6961

In 1940, as the bombs fell on London, Winston Churchill, his Cabinet, his Chiefs of Staff and his Intelligence Chiefs met below ground in a fortified basement in Whitehall known as the Cabinet War Rooms. When the war ended, the lights which had burned constantly for six years were switched out, the staff went home and the site was silent once more. Today visitors can see it just as it looked during the war, with several of the most important rooms, including Churchill's bedroom, the Cabinet Room and the Map Room, undisturbed for over 50 years. The Rooms are situated on Horse Guards Road, opposite the beautifully landscaped St. James's Park. The Cabinet War Rooms welcomes groups and offers generous discounts to parties comprising 10 or more people. Complementary sound guides to the site are available in English, French, German and Spanish. Nearest station: St James's Park or Westminster Underground. Admission Charge. Open daily 10am.

Bromley Museum

The Priory, Church Hill,
Orpington BR6 0HH
Tel: 01689 873826

Housed in an interesting medieval building situated in attractive gardens • Find out about the archaeology of the London Borough of Bromley from earliest times to Domesday • Learn about Sir John Lubbock, 1st Lord Avebury, the eminent Victorian responsible for giving this country its Bank Holidays • See how people lived before World War II.

EXHIBITIONS EVENTS

• Changing exhibitions throughout the year.

• Free school and adult education service.

ADMISSION

Free.

OPENING TIMES

All year: Monday to Friday 1–5pm. Saturday 10am–5pm.
1 April to 31 October: Sundays and Bank Holidays 1–5pm.

Visit the remains of

Crofton Roman Villa

Crofton Road, Orpington (adj. Orpington BR Station)

• The only Roman Villa in Greater London which is open to the public • Ten rooms of a villa-house protected inside a public viewing building • Conducted tours • Schools service • Graphic displays • Access for people with disabilities.

ADMISSION

Adults 80p. Children 50p.

OPENING TIMES

1 April–30 October 1998.
Wednesdays, Fridays and Bank Holiday Mondays 10am–1pm and 2–5pm. Sundays 2–5pm.
Other days by arrangement with Bromley Museum

FURTHER INFORMATION

Bromley Museum, Orpington. Tel: 01689 873826.
Kent Archaeological Rescue Unit. Tel: 0181 462 4737.

THE LONDON BOROUGH

KARU

Design Museum

28 Shad Thames, London SE1 2YD
Tel: 0171 403 6933. Fax: 0171 378 6540

Desigmuseum
South Bank by Tower Bridge

Visitors of all ages can rediscover one hundred years of design history, view state-of-the-art innovations from around the globe and enjoy an extensive programme of critically acclaimed exhibitions on design and architecture.

EXHIBITIONS/EVENTS

Bike:Cycles – a tour of bicycle design from 1825–2000 (until March 1998).
Ferdinand Porsche – Design Dynasty (9 Apr–31 Aug 1998).
Bosch – 100 years of innovation (25 Apr–16 Aug 1998).
The work of Charles and Ray Eames (15 Sept–3 Jan 1999).
The Real David Mellor (29 Sept–24 Nov 1998).
Modern Britain 1927–1939 (20 Jan–18 Jul 1999).

ADMISSION

Adults £5.25. Concessions £4.00. Family £12.00. Groups of +10 from £3.00 per person, tours on request, book in advance.

OPENING TIMES

Weekdays 11.30am–6pm. Weekends 12 noon–6pm.

LOCATION

Situated on the South Bank, East of Tower Bridge. The nearest stations are the Tower Hill and London Bridge. Parking in the area is limited.

GIFT SHOP

The gift shop offers a wide selection of design related merchandise including gifts, home accessories and design books.

REFRESHMENTS

Visitors can relax in our river-side cafe and enjoy a wide selection of freshly made savouries and cakes, a variety of teas, freshly ground coffee and ice cold drinks.

EDUCATIONAL SERVICES

The Design Museum offers teacher training courses, outreach activities, workshops and lectures. Prices range from £2.00–£4.00.

DISABLED PROVISION

All areas are accessible to wheelchair users.

Spencer House

27 St James's Place, London SW1A 1NR
Tel: 0171 499 8620

Spencer House, built in 1756–66 for the first Earl Spencer, an ancestor of Diana, Princess of Wales (1961–97), is London's finest surviving 18th-century town house. This magnificent private palace has regained the full splendour of its late 18th-century appearance, after a painstaking 10-year restoration undertaken by RIT Capital Partners plc. Eight state rooms are open to the public for viewing on Sundays, and are available for private and corporate entertaining during the rest of the week.

Designed by John Vardy and James 'Athenian' Stuart, these rooms were amongst the first neo-classical interiors in Europe. Vardy's Palm Room, with its spectacular screen of gilded palm trees and arched fronds, is a unique Palladian setpiece, while the elegant mural decorations of Stuart's Painted Room reflect the 18th-century passion for classical Greece and Rome. Stuart's superb gilded furniture has been returned to its original location in the Painted Room, courtesy of the Victoria & Albert Museum and English Heritage. Visitors can also see a fine collection of 18th-century paintings and furniture, including five major Benjamin West paintings graciously lent by Her Majesty The Queen. The house has full disabled access.

ADMISSION

Adults £6. Concessions £5: students, Friends of the V&A, Tate Gallery and Royal Academy (all with cards), children under 16 (no children under 10 admitted).

OPENING TIMES

Sundays 10.30am–5.30pm (last tour 4.45pm).
Closed January and August.

The Wallace Collection

Hertford House, Manchester Square, London W1M 6BN
Tel: 0171 935 0687. Fax: 0171 224 2155

The Wallace Collection, a national museum, displays superb works of art in probably the most sumptuous interiors of any museum in London. Many people regard it as their favourite place in the capital.

Acquired principally in the nineteenth century by the third and fourth Marquesses of Hertford and Sir Richard Wallace, the illegitimate son of the fourth Marquess, the collection was bequeathed to the nation by Sir Richard's widow in 1897 and is displayed on the ground and first floors of Hertford House, the family's main London residence.

There you can see unsurpassed collections of French eighteenth-century painting, furniture and porcelain together with Old Master paintings by, among others, Titian, Canaletto, Rembrandt, Hals, Rubens, Velázquez and Gainsborough. The finest collection of princely arms and armour in Britain is shown in four galleries and there are further displays of gold boxes, miniatures, French and Italian sculpture and Medieval and Renaissance works of art including Limoges enamels, maiolica, glass, silver and illuminated manuscripts.

ADMISSION

Free.

OPENING TIMES

Monday to Saturday 10am–5pm. Sunday 2–5pm.

UNDERGROUND

Bond Street.

EVENTS AND EDUCATION

For information on exhibitions and special events contact the publicity department. Details on school tours, holiday events for children and adult education are available from the education department.

FACILITIES

Disabled access. Museum shop.

Wandsworth Museum

[Wandsworth Borough Council]

The Courthouse, 11 Garratt Lane (opposite the Arndale)
Wandsworth, London SW18 4AQ
Tel: 0181 871 7074. Fax: 0181 871 4602

Come and meet the lady who *is* a lamp! She was made in Wandsworth and used to stand on a TV bought by a Tooting family in 1953 for watching the Coronation. There is lots more to see and do at Wandsworth Museum. Our exciting interactive displays tell the story of Wandsworth from prehistoric times to the present. You can discover how Battersea, Balham, Putney, Tooting, Earlsfield, Wandsworth and Southfields grew from a scatter of rural and riverside villages into a bustling London suburb.

Meet the woolly rhino from Battersea, try on a Roman helmet, light up the Wandle mills and find out how the waggons rolled on Britain's first public railway. See portraits of local residents such as William Brodrick, Court Embroiderer to King James 1st and Battersea's John Burns, one of the founders of the Labour movement. Room displays include a Victorian parlour, chemist's shop and a wartime shelter.

EXHIBITIONS/EVENTS

Temporary exhibitions, holiday activities and talks.

ADMISSION

Free.

OPENING TIMES

Tuesday–Saturday 10am–5pm, Sunday 2–5pm.
Closed Mondays and Bank Holidays.

FACILITIES

Education and Outreach Service. Gift Shop. Toilets. Lift.

DISABLED PROVISION

Accessible to wheelchair users. Tactile floor plans. Adapted toilet. Hearing loop.

Age Exchange Reminiscence Centre

age exchange theatre trust

11 Blackheath Village
London SE3 9LA
Tel: 0181 318 9105
Fax: 0181 318 0060
Email: age-exchange@
lewisham.gov.uk

Unique hands-on museum and visitor centre. Changing exhibitions on various aspects of 20th century life, plus a permanent display of everyday objects from the 1920's, 30's and 40's and a restored period shop.

EVENTS

Exciting programme of cultural and educational events, with themed exhibitions, training courses in Reminiscence, visits arranged for schools and residential homes, touring theatre productions.

MUSEUM SHOP sells Age Exchange publications and local history books. Postcards, greeting cards and nostalgia gift selection.

ADMISSION

Free. A small charge is made for Group visits, bookable in advance. Disabled access.

OPENING TIMES

Mon to Sat 10am–5.30pm.

CAFÉ serving tea, coffee, homemade cakes and sandwiches.

Bankside Gallery

BANKSIDE GALLERY

48 Hopton Street
London SE1 9JH
Tel: 0171 928 7521
Fax: 0171 928 2820

Suffolk Landscape
Charles Bartlett PPRWS RE

Bankside Gallery is the home of the Royal Watercolour Society and the Royal Society of Painter-Printmakers. This friendly gallery runs a changing programme of exhibitions of contemporary watercolours and artists' prints.

Members of the two Societies are elected by their peers and represent a tradition of excellence reaching back two hundred years. Their work embraces both established and experimental practices and the exhibitions balance these different approaches. Please call the gallery for a programme of exhibitions.

EVENTS

Informal *Artists Perspectives* take place every Tuesday evening during the course of an exhibition and are free upon admission. A range of practical courses and tutorials are held every year by artist members of the two societies. Full details are available from the Gallery.

ADMISSION

£3.50. Concessions £2. Free admission to Friends.

OPENING TIMES

During exhibitions:
Tues 10am–8pm, Wed to Fri 10am–5pm, Sat & Sun 1–5pm.
Closed Mon.

Bexley Museum

[Bexley London Borough]

**Hall Place
Bourne Road
Bexley
Kent DA5 1PQ
Tel: 01322 526574**

The local history museum of the Bexley area, housed in part of a Tudor mansion set in gardens open to the public. Permanent archaeology and natural history displays, temporary exhibitions mainly social history.

Other exhibitions and events also in the house. Guided tours of the house by appointment. Visitor Centre with local history displays open in summer. Refreshments available on site.

ADMISSION
Free.

OPENING TIMES
Mon–Sat 10am–5pm (4.15pm in winter) Sunday in British Summer Time 2–6pm.

DISABLED ACCESS
Disabled parking. Wheelchair access to gardens, Visitor Centre and part of house but not yet to Museum.

The British Library

**96 Euston Road
London NW1 2DB
Tel: 0171 412 7332**

The British Library is the national library of the United Kingdom and one of the world's great libraries. In its new flagship building at St Pancras, London, three exhibition galleries are open free of charge. In the Treasures Gallery are displayed some of the world's most famous written and printed items: Magna Carta, Shakespeare's First Folio, Lindisfarne Gospels, Tyndale's 1526 New Testament, Handel's Messiah and the Diamond Sutra.

The Pearson Gallery explores the History of Science, Children's Books, the History of Writing, the Art of the Book and Images of Britain.

The Workshop offers displays of and hands on experience of calligraphy, bookbinding and designing with type.

To compliment its exhibitions, the Library offers talks, lectures, films and other events for visitors. Tours of the St Pancras building are also available.

For more information please call:
Visitor Services:
0171 412 7332
Events and Box Office:
0171 412 7222

Church Farmhouse Museum

**Greyhound Hill, Hendon
London NW4 4JR
Tel: 0181 203 0130**

One of the oldest surviving dwelling houses in the London Borough of Barnet. Built about 1660, it was the centre of a busy dairy and hay making farm until the 1930s. The house was opened as a museum in 1955.

Church Farmhouse Museum has three period furnished rooms to give you a glimpse of 19th century life. The 1820s kitchen has a huge open fireplace and a large display of Victorian kitchen utensils. The laundry room is full of washing bygones and the dining room is furnished as it would have been in the 1850s.

EXHIBITIONS/EVENTS
Temporary exhibitions throughout the year. School and group visits by prior arrangement. Outreach service to schools. Teachers' notes and pupils' worksheets. Artefact loan boxes. Museum shop.

ADMISSION
Free.

OPENING TIMES
Mon–Thurs 10am–12.30pm and 1.30–5pm.
Fri Closed. Sat 10am–1pm and 2–5.30pm. Sun 2–5.30pm.

LOCATION
Nearest Tube station Hendon Central (Northern Line). By car, just 200 yards from A41 (Watford Way).

The De Morgan Foundation

**Old Battersea House
30 Vicarage Crescent
Battersea SW11 3LD
Tel: 0181 785 6450**

A substantial part of The De Morgan Foundation collection of ceramics by William De Morgan and paintings by Evelyn De Morgan (*neé* Pickering), her uncle Roddam Spencer Stanhope, J. M. Strudwick, and Cadogan Cowper, are displayed in the ground floor rooms of elegantly restored Old Battersea House – a Wren-style building which is privately occupied. Works from the Foundation's collection may also be seen at Cardiff Castle, Cragside (Northumberland), and Knightshayes (Tiverton). The St John portraits are at Lydiard Park, Swindon.

ADMISSION
£2.00.

OPENING TIMES
By appointment only (usually Wednesday afternoons only). All visits are guided. Parties limited to groups of 15.

ENGLAND

Dulwich Picture Gallery

College Road
Dulwich Village
London SE21 7AD
Tel: 0181 693 5254
Fax: 0181 693 0923

 Described as London's most perfect gallery. The dazzling collection of Old Masters includes Rembrandt's *Girl at a Window*, important works by Poussin and Claude, Rubens, Van Dyck, Murillo, Watteau, Hogarth, Gainsborough and Reynolds. The Gallery – the oldest public gallery in England – was designed in 1811 by Sir John Soane.

EXHIBITIONS

4 March–24 May
Italy in the Age of Turner.
17 June–19 July
Paulo Rego.
3 September–15 November
Pieter de Hooch.

ADMISSION

£3. Concessions £1.50. Children, Unemployed and Disabled free (disabled access).

OPENING TIMES

Tuesday–Friday 10am–5pm. Saturday and Bank Holiday Mondays 11am–5pm. Sundays 2–5pm.

TRANSPORT

BR Victoria to West Dulwich or London Bridge to North Dulwich. The Gallery lies just off the A205, The South Circular. Free parking.

GROUPS

For guided tours @ £4 a head ring 0181 693 5254 and ask for Francesco Nevola.

SCHOOLS

Award winning Education Department. To book school groups ring 0181 693 6911.

Forty Hall Museum

[Enfield Arts and Museums]

Forty Hill, Enfield
Middlesex EN2 9HA
Tel: 0181 363 8196
Fax: 0181 367 9098

Forty Hall is on London's northern edge, close to the junction of the M25 and A10. The house is a very fine Grade 1 listed building set in rolling parkland. It was originally constructed in 1629 for Sir Nicholas Raynton, a wealthy haberdasher and Lord Mayor of London. Although the house has undergone numerous alterations, much of the original plasterwork and carved woodwork can still be seen. Forty Hall remained a family home until the 1950s, its last private owners being the Parker Bowles's. Today it is a museum exhibiting collections related to the London Borough of Enfield. It is also an important venue for local artists and art groups. The ground floor of the museum, including the reception desk, sales desk and temporary exhibition galleries has easy access for everyone, the first floor can only be reached by stairs.

EXHIBITIONS/EVENTS

Exhibitions and events throughout the year.

ADMISSION

Free.

OPENING TIMES

Thursday–Sunday 11am–5pm.

Freud Museum

20 Maresfield Gardens
London NW3 5SX
Tel: 0171 435 2002
Fax: 0171 431 5452

The Freud Museum was the home of Sigmund Freud and his family when they fled Nazi persecution in 1938. They brought all their possessions with them and Freud's study and library were preserved with his remarkable collection of antiquities. Archaeology fascinated Freud, and collecting was a passion. His collections include Egyptian, Greek, Roman and Oriental antiquities; bronzes, terracotta figures, ceramic and glass vessels, a personal museum ranging over five thousand years. The most famous item is Freud's psychoanalytic couch covered with a Persian rug. Home movies are shown of the family.

Education visits by appointment.

Limited wheelchair access. Shop.

Underground: Finchley Road.

ADMISSION

£3 and £1.50 (Concessions) Under 12 Free.

OPENING TIMES

Wednesday to Sunday 12 noon–5pm.

Geffrye Museum

[English Domestic Interiors]

Kingsland Road
London E2 8EA
Tel: 0171 739 9893
Fax: 0171 729 5647

The Geffrye Museum presents the changing style of the English domestic interior from 1600 to the present day through a series of period room settings. The displays lead the visitor on a walk through time, from the 17th century with oak furniture and panelling, past the refined elegance of the Georgian rooms and the ornate style of the Victorian parlour, to 20th century art deco and modern style.

One of London's most friendly and enjoyable museums, the Geffrye is set in elegant 18th century almshouses with attractive gardens just north of the City. Walled herb garden, shop, coffee bar and reference library.

EXHIBITIONS/EVENTS

The museum and gardens are regularly brought to life through drama, music, workshops and seminars, with special holiday activities for families and children. Temporary exhibitions are mounted throughout the year.

ADMISSION

Free.

Gunnersbury Park Museum

London W3 8LQ
Tel: 0181 992 1612 or 2247
Fax: 0181 752 0686

This lively community museum presents the Heritage of Ealing and Hounslow through changing displays featuring plenty of hands-on activities for children. Its wide ranging collections include costume and toys, archaeology and carriages. The museum has fine interiors and its original kitchens are on show on summer weekends. It is surrounded by 198 acres of beautiful parkland with many historic follies and ruins.

EXHIBITIONS/EVENTS

Fashion in Hogarth's Century
– *until August 1998*
Hogarth prints and Georgian dress.
Rothschilds at Gunnersbury
– *until 1999.*
Remembering the 1930's
20th July 1998–17 January 1999
Residents recalling life in the thirties.
Apples!
– *until July 1998*
Their history and cultural importance.

ADMISSION

Free. Donation welcome.

OPENING TIMES

Nov–Mar daily 1–4pm.
April–Oct daily 1–5pm.
(6pm w/e and Bank Hols).

LOCATION

Acton Town Underground.
Bus:E3 (daily). Café in the park, open daily in the summer.

Hayward Gallery

Belvedere Road
London SE1 8XX
Tel: 0171 928 3144

Exhibitions of international stature are the hallmark of the Hayward Gallery with a programme featuring the works of modern masters, thought-provoking historical shows and the most exciting names in contemporary art.

EXHIBITIONS

Exhibitions for 1998:
Francis Bacon:
The Human Body
5 February–5 April 1998
The first major London showing for ten years of Britain's greatest 20th-century painter.
Henri Cartier-Bresson:
Europeans
5 February–5 April 1998
Cartier-Bresson captures a changing Europe from the 1930s to the 1970s.

Also in 1998:
Anish Kapoor 30 April–
14 June 1998
Bruce Nauman 16 July–
6 September 1998
Art and Fashion 8 October
1998–4 January 1999

ADMISSION

Tickets £5. Concessions £3.50. Group rates available.

OPENING TIMES

Open daily 10am–6pm.
Late nights Tuesday and Wednesday until 8pm. Closed between exhibitions.

LOCATION

Situated on the South Bank of the Thames. Nearest stations Waterloo and Embankment.

Leighton House Museum

12 Holland Park Road
London W14 8LZ
Tel: 0171 602 3316

Leighton House was the home of Frederic, Lord Leighton (1830–1896), the great classical painter and President of the Royal Academy. Built between 1867 and 1879 to designs by George Aitchison, it expresses Leighton's vision of a private palace devoted to art. The Arab Hall is the centrepiece of the House, evoking the world of the Arabian Nights, with dazzling gilt mosaics and authentic Isnik tiles. This opulent fantasy extends throughout the House culminating in Leighton's Studio. Paintings by Leighton, Burne-Jones, Millais and their contemporaries are on display.

EXHIBITIONS/EVENTS

The temporary exhibition galleries feature a wide-ranging programme throughout the year.

ADMISSION

Free.
Guided tours Wednesday and Thursday at 12 noon – £1.50 per person.

OPENING TIMES

Monday–Saturday 11am–5.30pm. Closed Sundays and Bank Holidays.

Merton Heritage Centre

[Merton Education, Leisure & Libraries]

MERTON HERITAGE CENTRE

The Canons
Madeira Road
Mitcham CR4 4HD
Tel: 0181 640 9387

Based at The Canons, a beautiful historic house in Mitcham, the Heritage Centre tells the story of Merton and its people, through a changing programme of exhibitions and special events.

Merton Heritage Centre is committed to making local history accessible for people of all ages and exhibitions have frequently included 'hands-on' displays, from period costume and natural dyeing, to Roman artefacts and a Tudor Stocks.

EXHIBITIONS/EVENTS

Four temporary exhibitions per year plus associated events and seasonal children's activities.
School/group visits by prior arrangement.
Education outreach services for schools – loan boxes, craft workshops, etc.
Accessible for disabled visitors.
Museum shop.
Nearest Tube station –
Morden (Northern Line)
Wimbledon (District Line)

ADMISSION

Free, parking nearby.

OPENING TIMES

Fri/Sat, 10am–5pm.
Last Admission at 4.30pm.

ENGLAND

Museum of Artillery in the Rotunda

Repository Road
Woolwich
SE18 4DN
Tel: 0181 781 3127

The Rotunda, designed and brought to Woolwich by Regency architect John Nash, provides the stunning setting for a unique collection. Begun in 1778 at the Royal Military Repository in Woolwich, it was used originally for training the men of the Royal Artillery.

Spanning 600 years, ornately decorated pieces from the Indian sub-continent and the Orient rub shoulders with early European cannon. Heavy ordnance of the 1st and 2nd World Wars and more modern equipment are displayed in the grounds.

ADMISSION
Free.

OPENING TIMES
Mon–Fri only 1–4pm.
Closed Bank holidays.

School parties and groups welcome by prior arrangement.

Wheelchair accessible.

Parking free.

Museum of Garden History

Lambeth Palace Road
London SE1 7LB
Tel: 0171 401 8865
Fax: 0171 401 8869
Internet:
http://www.compulink.
co.uk/~museumgh

Fascinating permanent exhibition of the history of gardens, collection of ancient tools and re-created 17th century knot garden displaying flowers and shrubs of the period – seeds of which may be purchased in the Garden Shop. Tombs of the Tradescants and Captain Bligh of the Bounty also in the grounds. Plus knowledgeable staff, attractively stocked gift shop and café serving tea, coffee, snacks and light lunches. Lectures, courses, concerts and art exhibitions held regularly throughout the year – full details available on request.

ADMISSION
Free (donations appreciated).

OPENING TIMES
Mon–Fri 10.30am–4pm. Sun 10.30am–5pm. Closed Sat. Closed 2nd Sun in Dec to 1st Sun in Mar.

BECOMING A FRIEND
From only £15 per year you can become a Friend and enjoy many benefits. For further details and an application form, please contact The Membership Secretary.

LOCATION
Lambeth Palace Road. Station(s): Waterloo or Victoria, then 507 Red Arrow bus, alight Lambeth Palace.

Parties catered for but prior booking essential.

The Musical Museum

368 High Street
Brentford
Middlesex TW8 0BD
Tel: 0181 560 8108

Enjoy the sight and sounds of one of the country's finest collections of historic automatic musical instruments.

Step back in time as sounds from the past fill the air – the sweet tones musical box – the grandeur of the Mighty Wurlitzer theatre organ – the subtle sounds of the concert pianist and the racy rhythms of ragtime.

Experience this fascinating world during a visit including a continuous demonstration in which the instruments are explained and played.

ADMISSION
Admission from £2.50 (OAP's, children, UB40). Adults £3.50.
Party bookings by arrangement.

OPENING TIMES
Open Saturday and Sunday 2.00pm–5.00pm April to October inclusive and Wednesday 2.00pm–4.00pm in July and August plus series of summer concerts.

A registered charity no: 802011.

National Portrait Gallery

St Martin's Place
London WC2H 0HE
Tel: 0171 306 0055
Fax: 0171 306 0058
Internet:
http://www.npg.org.uk

The National Portrait Gallery has the largest collection (9,000 in total) of portraits of British men and women in the world with over 1,000 paintings, photographs and caricatures on display of leading figures in history. Exciting programme of special exhibitions throughout the year. Gift Shop. Café from Autumn 1998.

EVENTS
A changing programme of exhibitions, free lectures and educational events take place throughout the year.

ADMISSION
Free except certain exhibitions.

OPENING TIMES
Monday–Saturday 10am–6pm.
Sunday 12 noon–6pm.
Closed Good Friday, May Day Bank Holiday, 24th–26th December, 1st January.

SCHOOLS & GROUPS
Group and School discounts available for special exhibitions when pre-booked through education department.

NATIONAL
PORTRAIT
GALLERY

National Postal Museum

King Edward Street
London EC1A 1LP
Tel: 0171 776 3636
Fax: 0171 776 3637

The story of the world's first postage stamps and the history of the British Post Office are told through the finest stamp and postal artefact collection in the country. It features all British postage stamps from the Penny Black to the present day; postal history letters from 1635 and world stamps from 1878. Postal artefacts include blunderbusses, vehicles and pillar boxes amongst many others. There are special exhibitions every year.

Researchers to collections of artwork, stamps or artefacts not on view are welcome, but by appointment only.

ADMISSION
Free.

OPENING TIMES
Open Monday–Friday 9.30am–4.30pm. Closed weekends. Bank Holidays and Public Holidays.

FACILITIES
No parking; limited access for disabled; sales point; Friends' organisation.

GOVERNING BODY
The Post Office.

STAFF
Director: Christine Jones; *Head of Administration:* Sam Kelly; *Curator, Philately:* Douglas N. Muir; *Paper Conservator:* Krystyna Koscia.

The Natural History Museum

Cromwell Road
London SW7 5BD
Tel: 0171 938 9123

The world's finest museum of nature and one of London's most beautiful landmarks. The Natural History Museum is home to a wide range of exhibitions certain to appeal to anyone with an interest in their world. Highlights include the popular *Dinosaurs* exhibition, *Creepy – crawlies* and *The power within*. In summer 1998 four major new exhibitions open: *From the beginning* will tell the story of the Earth from its formation to the present day, *The Earth for today and tomorrow* will explore the management of our demand on the environment, *Earth lab* will offer opportunities to investigate, hands-on, the geology of the British Isles and *Earth's treasury* will display specimens from the Museum's famous collection of gems and minerals.

Myths & Monsters, an exciting new special exhibition open from Easter to September 1998, examines the links between tales of yetis, mermaids and sea serpents and their roots in the natural world.

ADMISSION
An admission charge is made.

OPENING TIMES
Mon–Sat 10am–5.50pm.
Sun 11am–5.50pm.

New Academy Gallery and Business Art Galleries

34 Windmill Street
Fitzrovia, London W1P 1HH
Tel: 0171 323 4700
Fax: 0171 436 3059

'Dancer' by Clare Bigger who has just completed a commission for the new Jigsaw store in Edinburgh.

The New Academy Gallery was founded in 1978 by the Royal Academy of Arts. Now an independent company, we exhibit a wide range of painting, sculpture and original prints by leading and emerging British artists including Barry Atherton, Clive Blackmore, Roger Cecil, Jane Corsellis, Peter Dover, Bernard Dunstan RA, Frederick Gore RA, Alistair Grant ARA, Donald Hamilton Fraser RA, Brenda Hartill, Susan-Jayne Hocking, Sarah Holliday, Andrew Macara, Padraig Macmiadhachain, Jacqueline Rizvi, Hans Schwarz, Keith Roberts, Richard Walker and Peter Wray.

Business Art Galleries offers a comprehensive art service to companies including free consultancy, a flexible hire scheme, on-site presentations and special commissions (including portraits).

ADMISSION
Free.

OPENING TIMES
Mon–Fri 10am–6pm (Thurs 10am–8pm) Sat 11am–5pm.

LOCATION
Nearest Tube: Goodge St.

Museum of the Order of St John ❉

[St John's Gate]

St John's Lane
London EC1M 4DA
Tel: 0171 253 6644

From Crusade to First-Aid, and a whole lot more!

Fascinating insight into the religious, military and medical history of the Order of St John, from the Crusades to St John Ambulance today. Set in Tudor Gatehouse, Priory Church and 12th century Crypt.

Includes arms and armour, Maltese silver and furniture, paintings and prints of the Hospitaller Knights, and historic medical equipment from St John Ambulance and the Order's Ophthalmic Hospital in Jerusalem.

Also Hogarth's childhood home, Dr Johnson's workplace and associated with Shakespeare.

ADMISSION
By donation.

OPENING TIMES
Museum
Mon–Fri 10am–5pm
Saturday 10am–4pm
Tours of Gate, Church and Crypt
11am and 2.30pm Tues, Fri, Sat (Groups pre-book).

Farringdon and Barbican Underground.

Orleans House Gallery

**Riverside
Twickenham TW1 3DJ
Tel: 0181 892 0221
Fax: 0181 744 0501**

Overlooking the Thames, Orleans House Gallery resides in preserved natural woodland less than half an hour from central London. The Gallery comprises the 18th century Octagon Room and two surviving wings of the former Orleans House, and is responsible for the prestigious Richmond Borough art collection, containing works by Peter Tillemans, Lord Leighton and J.B.C. Corot. Exhibitions for 1998 include work by the sculptor William Tucker, a look at the life of 19th century explorer Sir Richard Burton and an exhibition on Contemporary Ceramics and the written word.

OPENING TIMES
April–September
Tuesday–Saturday 1–5.30pm.
Sunday 2–5.30pm.
October–March
Tuesday–Saturday 1–4.30pm
Sunday 2–4.30pm.

St Margarets/Twickenham stations from Waterloo.

The Percival David Foundation of Chinese Art

**53 Gordon Square
London WC1H 0PD
Tel: 0171 387 3909**

The Percival David Foundation houses the finest collection of imperial Chinese ceramics outside China, presented to the University of London in 1950 by the late Sir Percival David.

The collection comprises approximately 1,700 ceramic items reflecting Chinese court taste and dating mainly the period 10th–18th century.

ADMISSION
Admission is free of charge but donations are appreciated.

OPENING TIMES
Monday–Friday
10.30am–5pm. Closed weekends and Bank Holidays.

Special exhibitions are held in the ground floor Lady David Gallery.

The Tate Gallery

**Millbank
London SW1P 4RG
Tel: 0171 887 8008
Fax: 0171 887 8007**

The Tate Gallery houses the national collections of modern and British art, including work by Hogarth, Blake, Constable, Turner, Picasso, Matisse, Mondrian, Rothko, Giacometti, Pollock, Dubuffet, Bacon, Moore and Freud.

Displays are regularly re-arranged to show new acquisitions, bring works out of storage and explore new themes. There are also three major exhibitions each year, with loans from public and private collections from around the world.

EXHIBITIONS/EVENTS
Pierre Bonnard
12 February–17 May 1998.
Patrick Heron
25 June–6 September 1998.
John Singer Sargent
15 October 1998–17 January 1999.
Jackson Pollock
4 March–31 May 1999.

There is also a full programme of talks, seminars, courses, films and guided tours, many of which are free.

ADMISSION
Free, with a charge for major exhibitions.

OPENING TIMES
Daily 10am–5.50pm.
Closed 24, 25, 26 December.

The Tower Bridge Experience

**Tower Bridge
London SE1 2UP
Tel: 0891 600 210
Fax: 0171 357 7935**

Interactive computers, model characters, holograms and an unbeatable view of London all form part of The Tower Bridge Experience, which brings the story of London's most internationally famous landmark to life. The Experience transports visitors back in time to the 1890's to discover how and why the bridge came to be built and gives them a chance to visit the original Victorian engine rooms and to see the London skyline from on top of the Thames.

SPECIAL EVENTS
16–20 Feb – Half Term Quiz for Children.
21–22 Feb – Scouts 90th Birthday Celebrations.
5–8 and 12–15 Mar – Twilight Tours – enjoy the lights and views of London at sunset.
19–21 Mar – Engineers' Evening Tours.

ADMISSION
Adults £5.95. Children/ Seniors/Students £3.95. Family (2+2) £14.95. Group & Education discounts available.

OPENING TIMES
Open Daily except 1 and 28 Jan, 24–26 Dec 1998.
Mar–Oct 10am–6.30pm.
Nov–Apr 9.30am–6pm.

Victoria and Albert Museum

[The National Museum of Art and Design]

Cromwell Road
South Kensington
London SW7 2RL
Tel: 0171 938 8500
http://www.vam.ac.uk

The V&A is the world's greatest museum of art and design. Founded in 1852, the 146 galleries of furniture, fashion, textiles, paintings, silver, glass, ceramics, sculpture, jewellery, books, prints and photographs, reflect centuries of artistic achievement from all over the world.

EXHIBITIONS/EVENTS

The Power of the Poster, 2 April–26 July; Aubrey Beardsley, 8 October–10 January 1999; Grinling Gibbons and the Art of Carving, 22 October–24 January 1999; and The Canon Photography Gallery, a superb new gallery opening 21 May.

ADMISSION

Full £5, senior citizens £3. V&A annual season ticket £15, senior citizens £9. Admission is free for those under 18, students, pre-booked educational groups, disabled people with carer, ES40 holders, V&A Friends, Patrons and American and International Friends and season ticket holders. Entry is free daily between 4.30–5.45pm.

OPENING TIMES

Mon 12 noon–5.45pm. Tues–Sun 10am–5.45pm. Wed Late View (seasonal) 6.30–9.30pm. Open every day except 24, 25 and 26 December.

Nearest Station:
South Kensington

The Manchester Museum

The University of Manchester, Oxford Road
Manchester M13 9PL
Tel: 0161 275 2634. Fax: 0161 275 2676

The Manchester Museum is an outstanding example of a Victorian purpose-built museum. This listed building was designed by Alfred Waterhouse, renowned architect of the Natural History Museum in London. Over the years the Museum has won many awards for the quality of its exhibitions and displays, including the Museum of Year Award 1980, 1987 and the Royal Mail North West Award 1994 and 1996.

There are four floors with fifteen galleries showing displays of Archaeology, Archery, Botany, Egyptology, Entomology, Ethnology, Geology, Mineralogy, Numismatics and Zoology. Highlights include animals and plants from across the world. Whatever your age or interests, you'll find The Manchester Museum a rich storehouse of treasures.

TEMPORARY EXHIBITION PROGRAMME FOR 1998

16 June–19 September 1998. The Birth of the Baby: Manchester and the Modern Computer 1948–98
A celebration marking the development of the first stored programme computer in 1948.
12 October 1998–January 1999. 'Living on the Edge'
An exhibition illustrating the Museum's on-going research project at Alderley Edge which features the impact of mining on the area.

ADMISSION

Free.

OPENING TIMES

Monday–Friday 10am–5pm. Closed Sundays, Good Friday, Christmas, Boxing and New Year's Day. Telephone for details of openings between Christmas and New Year.

FACILITIES

Disabled access with assistance by prior arrangement • Baby changing facilities • Disabled toilet • Museum shop • No café at present, but refreshments available nearby • Parking nearby in The University of Manchester car parks.

Bury Art Gallery and Museum

Moss Street, Bury
Lancashire BL9 0DR
Tel: 0161 253 5878
Fax: 0161 253 5915

The Gallery opened in 1901 and is the home of the Wrigley collection of Victorian oil and watercolour paintings including works by Turner, Constable and Landseer. The 20th century collection features Lowry, Burra and Pasmore. There is a lively programme of temporary exhibitions.

The Museum opened in 1907 and now takes the form of a street showing Bury as it was around 1953, with a working model railway.

There is limited access for disabled visitors by ramp and lift via Silver Street, next to Textile Hall. Attendant staff will be pleased to assist – there is a toilet for the disabled at Gallery level.

The Art Gallery and Museum is centrally located – only a short walk from both bus and metrolink stations. By car Bury is within easy reach of the M66 and M62 and the rest of the motorway network.

ADMISSION

Free.

OPENING TIMES

Tuesday–Saturday 10am–5pm. (Closed Sunday and Monday).

Manchester Jewish Museum

**190 Cheetham Hill Road
Manchester M8 8LW
Tel: 0161 834 9879
Fax: 0161 832 7353**

Formerly the synagogue of the Manchester Congregation of Spanish and Portuguese Jews which opened in 1874, this architectural gem is now a Grade II★ Listed Building. A permanent display charts the history of the Jewish community in the Greater Manchester region, and is supported by a temporary exhibition gallery.

The Museum's exceptional Education and Outreach programme attracts schools and colleges nationwide. The Museum Shop stocks a wide range of products, which can be purchased through mail order.

EXHIBITIONS/EVENTS

An exhibition celebrating Jewish Weddings (until 21 June 1998) is followed by one marking the 50th anniversary of the State of Israel. Live events are planned throughout the year – please ring for details.

ADMISSION

Adults £2.75. Concessions £1.95. Family £6.95.

OPENING TIMES

Mondays–Thursdays 10.30am–4pm.
Sundays 10.30am–5pm.
Closed Fridays (except for educational parties, by arrangement), Saturdays and Jewish Holidays.

The Museum of Science and Industry in Manchester

**Liverpool Road, Castlefield
Manchester M3 4FP
Tel: (enquiries)
0161 832 2244/(24 hour
info. line) 0161 832 1830
Fax: 0161 833 2184**

One of the world's largest science museums, full of working exhibits and action-packed galleries. Follow the thread of Manchester's textile industry, past and present, in Fibres, Fabrics and Fashion. Discover how the pioneers of the sky made flying history in the Air and Space Gallery. Follow the fascinating story of the world's first industrial city in the Making of Manchester. In the Power Hall you can experience the sight, sound and smell of working steam mill engines – the largest collection in the world. Get your hands on a different perspective in Xperiment! the mind-binding science centre.

EXHIBITIONS/EVENTS

Stunning programme of special exhibitions and events. Ring the Marketing Department for details.

ADMISSION

(until 31 March 1999)
Adults £5, Concessions £3, Under 5s Free.
Group Rate (min. 10 people): Adults £4, Concessions £2.

OPENING TIMES

Open daily 10am–5pm (except 24–26 December).

FACILITIES FOR PEOPLE WITH DISABILITIES

Wheelchair access to 90% of the Museum. Accessible toilets. Sympathetic hearing scheme.

Oldham Art Gallery, Museum and Local Studies Library

[Oldham M.B.C. Education & Leisure Services: Galleries and Museums]

**Union Street,
Oldham OL1 1DN
Tel: 0161 911 4657/4654**

200 years of British Art and Craft. The natural and human history of Oldham and its multicultural communities, prehistory to present. Exhibitions from near and far. Interactive education programmes for schools, teachers and other groups delivering high quality, challenging, life-long learning experiences. Oral and family history, wildlife surveys, publishing, archives, enquiries and advice services. Shop and café. We are innovative, lively and ever keen to involve our visitors.

Access for people with disabilities.
Toilets and car parking.

ADMISSION

Free. Full programme on request.

OPENING TIMES

Tues 10am–1pm; Wed–Sat 10am–5pm; Closed Sun and Mon. (Local Studies Library & Archives: Mon and Thurs 10am–7pm; Tues 10am–2pm; Wed, Fri and Sat 10am–5pm.) Closed Christmas, Boxing and New Year's Day and Good Friday.

Museum of Army Flying

**Middle Wallop
Stockbridge
Hants SO20 8DY
Tel: 01980 674421/8
Fax: 01264 781694**

Award winning Museum depicts the role of Army flying since the late 19th century. History brought to life through vivid dioramas. Helicopters, Aircraft and Gliders.

Restaurant/Coffee Shop overlooking the operational airfield of the Army Air Corps, watch the pilots of tomorrow go through their rigorous training. Souvenir Gift Shop. Free Parking. Full facilities for the disabled.
Plus . . .
EXPLORERS' WORLD
Interactive Science Centre
Sensory Trail.
Hall of Mirrors.
Camera Obscura.
State Rooms.
Computer Suite with Internet and much, much more . . .

EVENTS 1998

'Music in The Air' – 11 June evening concert featuring the London Philharmonic Youth Orchestra plus synchronised flying including the **RED ARROWS.** Bring along your own picnic supper.
International Air Show: 13 & 14 June
Daily 6 hour flying display from the old favourites such as the Spitfire, Lancaster and Catalina up to the very latest jets.

ADMISSION

Adults £3.90. OAPs £3. Child £2.60. Family (2+2) £11. Groups welcome, please phone for details of group rates.

OPENING TIMES

Museum and Explorers' World open daily throughout the year (closed week prior to Xmas).

Hampshire County Council Museums Service

 Hampshire County Council
MUSEUMS SERVICE

Chilcomb House, Chilcomb Lane, Winchester SO23 8RD
Tel: 01962 846304. Fax: 01962 869836

Rockbourne Roman Villa

We manage a county-wide network of 24 museums and historic sites for the enjoyment of local people and visitors to Hampshire.

A wealth of collections representing Hampshire's archaeology, history, art and environment have been preserved in a rich diversity of museums and sites, ranging from Rockbourne Roman Villa in Fordingbridge to our military museum in Aldershot.

EXHIBITIONS/EVENTS

An exciting and varied programme of over 70 temporary exhibitions each year caters for a wide range of interests, from costume and textiles, art and craft to photography and local history. Facilities for groups and disabled people. Gift shops and refreshments.

Our exciting new museum, Milestones, in Basingstoke, opens its doors to the public at Easter 2000.

Hampshire's living history museum

EDUCATIONAL SERVICES

Facilities for handling collections, interactive exhibitions and workshops for all age groups. The award-winning, hands-on centre for history and natural history, SEARCH, at Gosport, provides superb facilities for schools.

Please refer to the individual listings for details of our museums. For opening times, admission charges and facilities contact the museums direct or telephone (01962) 846315.

Hampshire's history on your doorstep

Winchester Museums Service

(Winchester City Council – Leisure Department)

75 Hyde Street
Winchester SO23 7DW
Tel: 01962 848269
Fax: 01962 848299

The City Museum

Located between the High Street and the cathedral, the City Museum includes important exhibits illustrating the archaeology and history of Winchester.

ADMISSION
Free.

The Westgate

This fortified medieval gateway houses the city's unique collection of standard weights and measures, and provides fine views of the High Street from the roof.

ADMISSION
Adults 30p, Concessions 20p. Booked parties free.

The Guildhall Gallery

Changing exhibitions of sculpture, ceramics, modern works and topographical art are presented in part of Winchester's Victorian Guildhall.

ADMISSION
Free.

Historic Resources Centre

The museum's headquarters is the base for the education service and houses collections of old photographs, and the sites and monuments record for the area. Access by appointment.

Hartlepool Museums Service

Sir William Gray House
Clarence Road
Hartlepool TS24 8BT
Tel: 01429 523438

Hartlepool Art Gallery
Church Square, Hartlepool

Opened in 1996, this stunning restoration and conversion of a town centre church includes permanent galleries, a craft and book shop, café, 100ft viewing tower and tourist information services. It also has 3000 square feet of temporary exhibition space which shows a wide variety of contemporary and historical fine art and craft exhibitions.

ADMISSION
Free.

OPENING TIMES
Tuesday to Saturday 10am–5.30pm.
Sunday 2–5pm.

Museum of Hartlepool
Jackson Dock, Hartlepool

This multi award winning museum opened to the public in 1995 in the new Marina development. The Museum tells the story of Hartlepool from prehistory to the present day through a lively mix of traditional museum displays and hands on interactives. The Museum won the BT Favourite Children's Visit in its first year and was also recognised as the most popular new tourist attraction in England. Moored alongside the Museum is the fully restored Hartlepool built paddle steamer, Wingfield Castle which also houses the museum café. Ample free parking.

ADMISSION
Free.

OPENING TIMES
Daily 10am–6pm.

Bewdley Museum

**Load Street, Bewdley
Worcestershire DY12 2AE
Tel: 01299 403573**

Situated in the picturesque riverside town of Bewdley, the museum provides a fascinating insight into the past trades of the Wyre Forest area and the lives of its people. Displays feature woodland industries, brass founding and pewtering with daily demonstrations of clay pipe and rope making.

EXHIBITIONS/EVENTS

Annual programmes of special exhibitions, craft courses from basket making to stick dressing, and family events.

FACILITIES

Education service, group bookings welcome, museum shop, delightful herb garden and picnic area. Most of the museum is on ground level and accessible. Incorporated T.I.C.

ADMISSION

Adults £2.00. Senior Citizens, Unemployed, Unaccompanied Children £1.00. Accompanied Children free.

OPENING TIMES

10 April–30 September, Daily 11am–5pm.
1–31 October Daily 11am–4pm.
Inclusive of Bank Holidays.

LOCATION

Bewdley is situated on the edge of the Wyre Forest, four miles to the west of Kidderminster off the A456 Leominster Road, on the B4190.

Hereford City Museums and Art Galleries

**The City Museum and Art Gallery
Broad Street
Hereford HR4 9AU
Tel: 01432 364691
Fax: 01432 342492**

Museum Gallery

'Get in Touch' is an exciting hands-on exhibition which is running from April 1998 to April 1999. It offers opportunities for visitors to touch and handle some of the Museum's objects.

Art Gallery

The Art Gallery has regularly changing exhibitions of fine art, photography, decorative art and crafts.

The Old House
**High Town
Hereford HR1 2AA
Tel: 01432 364598
Fax: 01432 342492**

The Old House is one of the county's most famous 'black and white' houses. Built in 1621, the whole house is furnished in 17th century style.

ADMISSION

Free.

OPENING TIMES

Tues to Sat 10am–5pm all year. Sun and Bank Holiday Mondays including Easter, 10am–4pm Apr to Sept.

Verulamium Museum

 **St Michaels, St Albans AL3 4SW
Tel: 01727 819339**

Set in 100 acres of parkland the award–winning Verulamium is the museum of everyday life in Roman Britain. Re–displayed galleries include recreated Roman rooms, hands–on Discovery Areas, touch screen databases and a video presentation that brings archaeology alive. The Museum houses some of the finest Roman mosaics and wall plasters outside the mediterranean. Situated nearby in the park are the remains of Roman Walls and a well–preserved Hypocaust. On the second weekend of every month the galleries are occupied by Legion XIIII who demonstrate the tactics of the Roman army. Regular talks and walks are held by the Honorary Guides at weekends. Free newsletter available from the above address.

ADMISSION

Adults £2.80, Children/Concessions £1.60, Family (2+2) £7.00.

OPENING TIMES

Mon–Sat 10.00–5.00pm. Sun 2.00–5.00pm.
Car park, gift shop, full disabled access.

The Museum of St Albans

 **Hatfield Road, St Albans AL1 3RR
Tel: 01727 819340**

At the Museum of St Albans you can discover the fascinating story of our historic cathedral city. The rise of St Albans from a market town and coaching centre to a modern commuter city is told through lively displays using the Museum's collections. A new gallery is home to the famous Salaman collection of trade and craft tools. Outside is a wildlife garden with pond, picnic area and small woodland trail. Temporary exhibitions which range from the Egyptians, to textiles, to natural history, are held throughout the year. Regular activities and events are organised to coincide with these. Please telephone for details. Free newsletter is available from the above address.

ADMISSION

Free.

OPENING TIMES

Mon–Sat 10.00–5.00pm. Sun 2.00–5.00pm.
Car park, gift shop, toilets, disabled access ground floor only.

ENGLAND

Mill Green Museum and Mill

Mill Green
Hatfield AL9 5PD
Tel: 01707 271362
Fax: 01707 272511

Fully restored 18th century watermill, producing organic wholemeal flour every week, and local history museum.

EXHIBITIONS/EVENTS

There is a small temporary exhibitions gallery and a programme of craft demonstrations and special events at summer weekends. Special for 1998, an Egyptian Fair on Sunday 6th September 1998.

ADMISSION

Free. Donations welcome.

OPENING TIMES

Tuesday–Friday 10am–5pm. Saturday, Sunday and Bank Holidays 2–5pm. Closed Mondays except Bank Holidays.

MILLING HOURS

Tuesday, Wednesday 10.30am–12.30pm. 1.30–3.30pm. Sunday 2.30–4.30pm.

Sales Point Souvenirs, local history publications and freshly ground Mill Green Flour available.

The Walter Rothschild Zoological Museum

Akeman Street
Tring HP23 6AP
Tel: 01442 824181
Fax: 01442 890693

Once the private collection of Lionel Walter, 2nd Baron Rothschild, more than 4000 animal and bird specimens on display in a unique Victorian setting.

Whales to fleas, Butterflies to tigers, humming birds and a collection of domestic dogs. Mounted specimens of animals from all parts of the world.

REFRESHMENTS

Picnic shelter and garden picnic area.

OPENING TIMES

Monday–Saturday 10–5pm. Sunday 2–5pm. Closed December 24–26. Booked school parties free.

Welwyn Roman Baths

Welwyn By-Pass
Welwyn Village
Tel: 01707 271362
all correspondence to
Mill Green Museum
and Mill

A 3rd century bathing suite, the one surviving feature of a villa, ingeniously preserved within the embankment of the A1(M).

ADMISSION

Adults £1. Children free.

OPENING TIMES

January–November Saturday, Sunday and Bank Holidays 2–5pm or dusk when earlier. School half terms and holidays Monday–Sunday 2–5pm or dusk when earlier. Closed December. Pre-booked parties any time. Small charge per head.

SALES POINT

Souvenirs and local archaeology publications on sale.

Canterbury Museums

Canterbury Roman Museum

Butchery Lane, Canterbury
Tel: 01227 785575

A new museum around remains of a Roman house with fine mosaics. Walk through fascinating reconstructions. See amazing objects rescued by excavation, including 2000 year old swords and silver spoon hoard. And be an archaeological detective in the hands-on area.

Canterbury Heritage Museum

Stour Street, Canterbury
Tel: 01227 452747

Rupert Bear TM & © Express
Newspapers plc

An enthralling time-walk linking the great events, famous people, and precious objects from Canterbury's 2000 year story. From the building of the Roman town to the delights of the Rupert Bear gallery.

OTHER ATTRACTIONS

Canterbury West Gate Museum.
Canterbury Royal Museum & Art Gallery.
For excellent value, enquire about the museum passport!

Powell-Cotton Museum, Quex House and Gardens

Quex Park, Birchington, Kent CT7 0BH
Tel: 01843 842168. Fax: 01843 846661

Quex House is one of Kent's loveliest Regency houses and home to five generations of the Powell and Cotton families. The house is set in a large estate, 15 acres of which is open to the public.

Quex was the birthplace of a most remarkable man: Major P. H. G. Powell-Cotton. Explorer, hunter, naturalist, author and philanthropist, he spent much of his lifetime travelling to remote corners of Africa and Asia, learning about the peoples and their customs and observing wildlife in its natural environment. A vast collection of treasures gathered by Powell-Cotton and his family on 28 expeditions has been assembled at Quex making this an exciting place to visit and an important centre of academic study.

At Quex you'll find the finest dioramas in the world! Major Powell-Cotton was fascinated by the exotic animals he saw on his travels and set about preserving representative specimens for others to enjoy. He built a museum at Quex to house dioramas in which over 500 animals have been arranged against backdrops of savannah, forest and swamp, giving a wonderful impression of the teeming wildlife of Africa and Asia. The displays – some of which are over 70 feet long – have been carefully maintained just as Powell-Cotton created them at the end of the last century and are of great historical and scientific significance. The animals were all mounted by Rowland Ward's, one of the world's leading taxidermy companies.

In addition to the natural history and ethnography displays there are galleries of local archaeology, decorative arts and porcelain, as well as rooms in Quex House which are open to the public in the afternoon. The Museum and House is now supported by a large restaurant and a museum shop and the whole site has disabled access.

OPENING TIMES

April–October
Tuesday, Wednesday, Thursday, Sunday plus Bank Holidays 11am–6pm.
March, November and December
Sundays only 11am–5pm.
All party visits must be pre-booked.
House closed.

Dickens House Museum Broadstairs

[On the main seafront]

Victoria Parade
Broadstairs CT10 1QS
Tel: 01843 862853

"The house on the cliffs" immortalised by Dickens as the home of Miss Betsey Trotwood, "David Copperfield's" aunt.

The parlour where Dickens and his son, Charles Jnr, had tea with Miss Mary Strong, has been restored as he described it in his novel "David Copperfield."

His letters from Broadstairs, written during his many holidays in the town that he was to call "Our English Watering Place," with other memorabilia, fill the ground floor rooms. The first floor features Costume and Victoriana.

OPENING TIMES

Open daily: April to mid October 2.00pm–5.00pm. Parties by arrangement with the Hon. Curator.

Finchcocks Living Museum of Music

Goudhurst, Kent
TN17 1HH
Tel: 01580 211702
Fax: 01580 211007
Director/founder:
Richard Burnett

Magnificent collection of historical keyboard instruments, many fully restored, housed in fine 18th century manor in beautiful garden and parkland. Demonstration tours and music whenever house is open. Also exhibition of pictures, prints and costumes.

SPECIAL EVENTS

Include Music Festival, September weekends. Educational events: workshops, courses. Fairs in May and October.

Available for functions and licensed for civil marriages.

ADMISSION

Adults £5.50. Children £3.80 (house, garden and music) £2.00 garden only.

OPENING TIMES

Easter to end September Sundays, Bank Holiday Mondays, Wednesdays and Thursdays in August. 2–6 pm. Teas.

BY APPOINTMENT

For Groups and Individuals: most days, April to end October. Morning, afternoon and evening. Musical tours. Full catering.

KENT

Maidstone Museum and Art Gallery

MAIDSTONE

MUSEUM
& Art Gallery

**St Faith's Street
Maidstone
Kent ME14 1LH
Tel: 01622 745597
Fax: 01622 602193**

This exceptionally fine regional museum housed in Chillington Manor, a delightful Elizabethan manor house, boasts a rich and impressive variety of historical objects, fine art and natural history. These include Continental and English paintings, sculpture, costume and textiles, an extensive archaeological collection with artefacts from the Prehistoric, Roman, Anglo-Saxon and Medieval periods, and an Egyptian collection including our own Mummy. The Japanese collection is internationally recognised and there are also beautiful examples of Victoriana and Ceramics. The Natural History Galleries exhibit fascinating displays of British birds, bees and plants, butterflies and moths, fish, shells, nature conservation, skeletons and fossils including a whale, mammoth and Maidstone's very own dinosaur – *the Iguanodon.*

ADMISSION
Free

OPENING TIMES
Monday – Saturday
10.00 hrs–17.15 hrs.
Sunday 11.00 hrs–16.00 hrs.

LANCASHIRE

Blackburn Museum and Art Gallery

**Museum Street
Blackburn BB1 7AJ
Tel: 01254 667130
Fax: 01254 695370**

Right in the middle of Blackburn town centre and one more good reason to pay a visit to Lancashire's Hill Country, Blackburn Museum and Art Gallery has something for all the family to enjoy from fine art to our feathered friends. Paintings and fine pottery, manuscripts and a mummy, coins and collectables are all on show in a friendly and welcoming listed building. Whether you know your Poussin from your Picasso or you just like to browse, we guarantee you'll find what you're looking for. Lively programme of changing exhibitions and children's quizzes and activities for all ages – phone us for the latest details. Completely accessible for pushchairs or wheelchairs on all floors.

EXHIBITIONS/EVENTS
Telephone 01254 667130 for details.

ADMISSION
Free.

OPENING TIMES
Tuesday–Friday
12.00 noon–4.45pm.
Saturday
9.45am–4.45pm.

Educational visits and group visits by arrangement.

Wheelchair access to all areas.

LEICESTERSHIRE

Bosworth Battlefield

LEICESTERSHIRE

**Bosworth Battlefield Visitor Centre and Country Park
Sutton Cheney, Market Bosworth
Leicestershire CV13 0AD Tel: 01455 290429**

The famous historic site of the Battle of Bosworth Field 1485, where King Richard III was defeated by the future Henry VII. Award-winning interpretation of the Battle with the Visitor Centre giving a complete insight into medieval times • Film theatre, book and gift shop. • Tourist Information Centre. • Country Park with Picnic Areas and Battle Trails • Medieval Events July–September. Telephone for details.
• *Parking:* cars £1, coaches £5.
• *Disabled Visitors:* visitor centre and battle trail accessible.
• *Catering:* Bosworth Buttery cafeteria.

ADMISSION
Visitor Centre: Adults £2.30. Children (under 16) and Senior Citizens £1.50. *Group rates:* pre-booked 20 or more: adults £1.90 per head, children and senior citizens £1.20 per head.

OPENING TIMES
Visitor Centre April 1st to October 31st Monday–Friday 1–5pm. Saturday, Sunday and Bank Holidays 11am–6pm (early opening 11am from July 1st to August 31st). Pre-booked parties taken all year.

Car parks and footpaths open all year in daylight hours.

Charges and opening times subject to review.

COUNTRY PARKS SERVICE
DEPARTMENT OF PROPERTY
LEICESTERSHIRE
COUNTY COUNCIL

Snibston Discovery Park

 Ashby Road, Coalville, Leicestershire LE67 3LN
Tel: 01530 510851. Fax: 01530 813301

Where miners once spent long gruelling hours underground at the former Snibston Colliery, visitors of all ages can now have hours of fun unravelling the mysteries of science and technology, delving into Leicestershire's rich industrial heritage and exploring the big outdoors.

Built on a 100-acre site, Snibston Discovery Park has at its centre a huge exhibition hall where visitors can get their 'hands-on' over 30 experiments in the popular Science Alive! Gallery. Explore a variety of transport methods from 18th century packhorses to a 1960s Auster aircraft in the Transport Gallery, and step back in time and discover the working conditions of men, women and children at a 19th century coalface in the Extractives Gallery. In the Engineering Gallery see how a beam engine drew water for a local reservoir and explore the fashions of yesteryear in the Textile and Fashion Gallery.

Outside, join ex-miners in a lively surface tour of Snibston's colliery buildings, or let off steam in Science Play with its 15 Big experiments. Have gallons more fun in Wild Water – Snibston's new water playground.

ADMISSION

Adults £4.75. Children £2.95. Concessions £3.25.
Family Ticket (2 Adults and 3 Children) £13.50.

OPENING TIMES

Open daily 10am–6pm, April–September.
10am–5pm, October–March.
Closed 25/26 December.

Boston Guildhall Museum

South Street, Boston PE21 6HT
Tel: 01205 365954. Fax: 01205 359401

Boston Guildhall Museum is a fascinating 'time capsule' of history from the 1400's onwards. The building has been used for various roles in its 550 year history including even a WWI soup kitchen and WWII 'British Restaurant'.

Originally a religious hall catering for the Guild of St Mary, the great wooden frame structure became the Town Hall of Boston in 1546. It gained notoriety in 1607 when used as the courthouse and gaol where the original Pilgrim Fathers were tried and imprisoned. You can still see the cells today and be locked inside!

There is also an Australia connection. Joseph Banks, who sailed with Captain Cook on 'Endeavour' later became the Recorder of Boston. His famous portrait now hangs in the Council Chamber, a room where he worked and where every mayor was elected until 1887.

Other features of the Guildhall include the medieval Banqueting Hall with its minstrel gallery, fine stained glass window and William Etty paintings; the  Sixteenth Century Kitchens complete with roasting spits ingeniously turned by hot air; and the Maritime Room.

ADMISSION

Entrance is just £1.20 for adults (80p concessions). This includes a free audio tour. Admission is free on Thursdays.

OPENING TIMES

Monday–Saturday: 10am to 5pm throughout the year.
Sundays: April–September 1pm to 5pm. Gift Shop.

Atkinson Art Gallery

[Metropolitan Borough of Sefton Arts and Cultural Services]

Lord Street
Southport PR8 1DH
Tel: 01704 533133 ext 2110
Fax: 0151 934 2109

Established in 1878 the main strengths of the permanent collection lie in substantial holdings of 18th and 19th Century English watercolours, Victorian painting and academic British painting of the turn of the Century. A small but rapidly expanding collection of contemporary painting, sculpture and prints extends the scope of the collection to the present day.

EXHIBITIONS/EVENTS

Throughout the year there is an everchanging programme of temporary exhibitions covering all aspects of painting, sculpture and print-making.

OPENING TIMES

Mon & Tues 10am–5pm
Wed & Fri 10am–5pm
Thurs & Sat 10am–1pm
Closed Sun & Bank Holidays.

THE LOCATION

The Atkinson Art Gallery is situated in the main shopping area on Lord Street between the Library and the Arts Centre. It is easily reached by car and by public transport. The nearest railway station is situated on Chapel Street only five minutes' walk from the Gallery.

National Museums and Galleries on Merseyside

PO Box 33
127 Dale Street
Liverpool L69 3LA
Tel: 0151 207 0001

National Museums and Galleries on Merseyside (NMGM) holds outstanding collections made up of 1.2m objects covering art, history and science. Many of these collections are displayed in our eight museums and galleries: Liverpool Museum, Merseyside Maritime Museum (incorporating Anything to Declare? HM Customs and Excise National Museum), the Museum of Liverpool Life, Walker Art Gallery, Lady Lever Art Gallery, Sudley House and The Conservation Centre.

NMGM offers special services for schools, programmes of temporary exhibitions, public events, lectures and courses linked to its collections of fine and decorative art, archaeology and ethnology, natural sciences, social, industrial and maritime history.

ADMISSION

The NMGM Eight Pass gives 12 months' unlimited visits to all venues.
Standard £3.00
Concessions £1.50
Family £7.50
Admission charge for schools from September 1998
Annual Pass:
less than 500 pupils £30
more than 500 pupils £60

OPENING TIMES

Monday–Saturday 10am–5pm.
Sunday 12 noon–5pm.
(Maritime Museum and Museum of Liverpool Life open daily 10am–5pm).

Port Sunlight Heritage Centre

95 Greendale Road
Port Sunlight, Wirral
Merseyside L62 4XE
Tel: 0151 644 6466

Visit Port Sunlight village the picturesque 19th century garden village on the Wirral, built by William Hesketh Lever for his soap factory workers. It was named after Lever's famous Sunlight Soap.

EXHIBITIONS/EVENTS

Port Sunlight is a conservation area and is still within its original boundaries. The history of the village and its community is explored in Port Sunlight Heritage Centre, where there is a scale model of the village and of a Victorian house, the original plans for the buildings, a video of early film footage, and displays of period advertising and soap packaging.

The Village Trail leaflet, available at the Heritage Centre, shows you the village's attractions, including the Lady Lever Art Gallery which contains Leverhulme's world-famous collection of pre-Raphaelite paintings and Wedgwood.

ADMISSION

Adults 40p. Children 20p.
Educational Parties Free.

OPENING TIMES

1st April or Easter (whichever is the sooner) to the end of October every day 10am–4pm.
Rest of the year
Monday–Friday 10am–4pm.

PROVISION FOR GROUPS

Guided tours of the village can be booked (in advance) for coach parties by arrangement.

Tate Gallery Liverpool

Albert Dock
Liverpool L3 4BB
Tel: 0151 709 3223
Recorded Information Line:
0151 709 0507

Wyndham Lewis Workshop c.1914–15
Credit: Tate Gallery

Experience the National Collection of Modern Art on four floors of galleries with stunning views across the River Mersey. The Gallery is housed in a converted warehouse, which is part of the historic Albert Dock. There is a regular programme of events, workshops and talks.

The Gallery re-opens on 23 May 1998. A £6.96 million development scheme has transformed previously undeveloped spaces into new top floor galleries allowing more art to be shown.

EXHIBITIONS

Art Transpennine 98
23 May–16 Aug 1998
Modern British Art
23 May 1998 onwards
Urban
23 May 1998–Apr 1999
The Spirit of Cubism
23 May 1998–Apr 1999
Willie Doherty
29 Aug–4 Oct 1998
Salvador Dalí: A Mythology
24 Oct 1998–31 Jan 1999

ADMISSION

Free, with a charge for exhibitions.

OPENING TIMES

Tues–Sun, Bank Hol Mon 10am–6pm. Closed Mon, Good Fri, 24–26 Dec, 1 Jan.

NORFOLK

Norwich Castle Museum

Norwich NR1 3JU
Tel: 01603 493648
Fax: 01603 765651

The ancient Norman Keep of Norwich Castle dominates the city and is one of the most important buildings of its kind in Europe. Once a royal castle, it now houses one of England's finest regional collections of archaeology, natural history and art, including the work of the Norwich School of Painters and regular exhibitions from the Tate Gallery collection. Also on display is the world's largest collection of teapots. Guided tours of the battlements and dungeons offer the chance to discover the darker secrets of this 900 year-old castle.

EXHIBITIONS/EVENTS

A lively programme of exhibitions, children's events, trails and holiday activities, gallery and evening talks take place throughout the year.

ADMISSION

July–September:
Adults £3.20. Concessions £2.20. Children £1.60.
Family £8.00.
October to June:
Adults £2.40. Concessions £1.60. Children £1.10.
Family £5.90.

OPENING TIMES

Monday–Saturday 10am–5pm.
Sundays 2–5pm.

Cafeteria and shop available.

N E LINCOLNSHIRE

Normanby Hall Country Park

NORTH LINCOLNSHIRE
COUNCIL

Normanby
Scunthorpe
North Lincolnshire
DN15 9HU
Tel: 01724 720588
Fax: 01724 721248

Regency Mansion, once the home of the Sheffield family, former owners of Buckingham Palace. Rooms decorated in period style, costume galleries, ice house, servants' trail, sculpture trail, farming museum, over 300 acres of parkland, deer herds, ducks and peacocks. Also a fully restored and working Victorian Kitchen Garden. Special events, held on summer Sundays throughout the season. Gift shop and café open all year round.

ADMISSION

Adult £2.50. Concessions £1.50. (50% discount to North Lincolnshire residents).

OPENING TIMES

Park – all year round
9am until dusk.
Walled Garden –
all year round 11am–5pm
(4pm in Winter).
Hall and Farming Museum
30 March–4 October 1998,
1–5pm daily.

NORTH YORKSHIRE

Royal Pump Room Museum

Crown Place, Harrogate HG1 2RY. Tel: 01423 503340

The Royal Pump Room Museum tells the story of Harrogate's history as England's only truly European spa. Housed over the famous sulphur wells, displays show why visitors from around the world came to take the cure, enjoy the culture and the social whirl, and tour the surrounding beauty spots in Yorkshire's Dales, such as Knaresborough Castle. No visit is complete without sampling the water that made Harrogate famous – the strongest sulphur water in Europe! A programme of changing exhibitions draws on highlights from the collections. 'Collectors' Corner' runs until June 1998 and is a treasure trove of collections, large and small, on loan from local people.

ADMISSION

Adults £1.75, under 14's and over 60's £1.00.

OPENING TIMES

Monday to Saturday 10am–5pm. Sunday 2–5pm, closes at 4pm November to March.

Knaresborough Castle

Visit the King's Tower, the secret underground sallyport and the Old Courthouse Museum with its new Civil War Gallery. The Castle site overlooks one of the most picturesque views in North Yorkshire, over the spectacular Nidd Gorge.

ADMISSION

Adults £1.75, under 14's and over 60's £1.00.

OPENING TIMES

Easter–September 30, 1998 10.30am–5pm.

NORTHAMPTON

Northampton Museums & Art Gallery

Central Museum & Art Gallery
Guildhall Road
Northampton NN1 1DP
Tel: 01604 39415

Fascinating footwear worn throughout the ages is just one of the attractions in the museum. Also on display **Northampton's History**: objects, sound and film combined to tell the history of the town from the Stone age to the present • **Decorative Arts**: outstanding oriental and British ceramics • The art galleries have a fine collection of Italian 15th–18th century paintings, and British art • **The Leathercraft Gallery**: historic leathercraft from around the world.

OPENING TIMES
Mon–Sat 10am–5pm.
Sun 2–5pm.

Abington Museum
Abington Park
Northampton
Tel: 01604 31454

Set in a 15th century manor house, displays include a room with 16th century oak panelling • a Victorian cabinet of curiosities • Northamptonshire's military history – at home and abroad • A 19th century fashion gallery • Northampton life – from the cradle to the grave.

ADMISSION
Temporary exhibitions, free admission.

OPENING TIMES
Tues–Sun 1–5pm. Bank Holiday Mondays 1–5pm.

NOTTINGHAMSHIRE

The Harley Gallery & Museum

Welbeck, Nr Worksop
Nottinghamshire S80 3LW
Tel: 01909 501700

This unique gallery is set in an elegant water garden. The design reflects the industrial origins of the original structure by using a combination of traditional and modern materials and methods. The Gallery incorporates an exhibition area showing the finest arts and crafts. A changing exhibition of art and artefacts from the past are displayed in the adjoining Harley Museum. Our unique workshops open their doors to visitors this year. You will see renowned crafts people specialising in tapestry, weaving and textile restoration, musical instrument building, ceramics and other traditional and modern crafts. (Open days on request.)

EXHIBITIONS/EVENTS
Until 14 June
'Landscapes and Lives'
27 June–31 August
British Tapestry Exhibition
12 September–1 November
Ceramics by Phil Rogers
14 November–20 December
Schools Art Exhibition

ADMISSION
£1.50 (concessions 50p).

OPENING TIMES
Thurs–Sun 11.30am–5pm.

Free Parking. Disabled access. Gallery shop.

OXFORDSHIRE

Oxfordshire Museums Service

Oxfordshire County Museum
Fletcher's House, Park Street, Woodstock OX20 1SN
Tel: 01993 811456

Discover the people, buildings and landscapes of Oxfordshire in this fine 17th–18th century town house.

Temporary exhibitions. Shop. Coffee shop.

ADMISSION
Adults £1.50. Concessions £1.00. Children 50p.

OPENING TIMES
May–September: Tuesday–Saturday 10am–5pm. Sunday 2–5pm.
October–April: Tuesday–Friday 10am–4pm.
Saturday 10am–5pm, Sunday 2–5pm.

Cogges Manor Farm Museum
Church Lane, Witney OX8 6LA. Tel: 01993 772602

A working museum with an historic manor house and original Cotswold stone farm buildings. 20 acre farm stocked with traditional Victorian breeds of farm animals. Cooking on the range and regular demonstrations of farm and dairy work, as well as traditional craft activities and special weekend events.

Gift shop. Cafe. Picnic area.

ADMISSION
Adults £3.25. Concessions £2.00. Children 3–16 £1.75. Family ticket £9.00. Season tickets available.

OPENING TIMES
31 March–1 November: Tuesday–Friday 10.30am–5.30pm★
Saturday and Sunday 12 noon–5.30pm★. Bank Holiday Mondays 10.30am–5.30pm. (★4.30 after BST ends).

Museum of Oxford
St Aldates, Oxford OX1 1DZ. Tel: 01865 815559

The story of the City and University, archaeological treasures, outstanding medieval collection and period room settings. Temporary exhibitions. Summer Exhibition: 'Looking for Alice – Lewis Carroll and Alice in Oxford' 6 July–3 October 1998.

ADMISSION
Adults £1.50. Concessions £1.00. Children 50p. Family ticket £3.50.

OPENING TIMES
Tuesday–Friday 10am–4pm. Saturday 10am–5pm.

University of Oxford

The Ashmolean Museum of Art and Archaeology
Beaumont Street, Oxford OX1 2PH
Tel: 01865 278000. Fax: 01865 278018

British, European, Mediterranean, Egyptian and Near Eastern archaeology. European paintings, Old Master and modern drawings, watercolours and prints; miniatures; European ceramics; sculpture and bronzes; English silver, objects of applied art. Coins and medals of all countries and periods. Chinese and Japanese porcelain, painting and lacquer. Tibetan, Indian and Islamic applied arts. Free admission. Café and Shop.

OPENING TIMES

Tuesday–Saturday 10am–4pm. Closed Mondays, St Giles Fair in Sept and a period over Christmas, the New Year and Easter. Open Bank Holiday Mondays and Easter Monday.

Oxford University Museum of Natural History
Parks Road, Oxford OX1 3PW. Tel: 01865 272950.
Fax: 01865 272970. Information Line: 01865 270949

The museum displays the University's very extensive natural history collections, which include the remains of the Dodo, fossil dinosaur material and the historic collections donated by scientists such as Darwin, Burchall and Hope. The wrought-iron arches and carved stone capitals depicting birds, animals and plants of the glass-roofed museum court, show the influence of John Ruskin. Free admission.

OPENING TIMES

Monday–Saturday 12 noon–5pm.
(Opening times change at Easter and Christmas)

The Pitt Rivers Museum
Parks Road, Oxford OX1 3PW
(entrance through University Museum)
Tel: 01865 270949. Fax: 01865 270943

One of the world's great ethnographic museums. The display cases are crowded with collections of masks, jewellery, weaponry, textiles, toys, tools and much more in a setting now famous for its period atmosphere. Audio guide presented by Sir David Attenborough. From June to Christmas 1998 the Museum may be closed at certain times. Please ring for detailed information. The Balfour Building, a modern annexe nearby, offers displays on archaeology, Hunter Gatherer societies, and musical instruments with audio guide facility. All group visits should be booked tel: 01865 270931.

OPENING TIMES

Monday–Saturday 1–4.30pm. Closed for a period over Christmas, the New Year and Easter. Free admission.

The Museum of Modern Art Oxford

30 Pembroke Street
Oxford OX1 1BP
Tel: 01865 722733
Fax: 01865 722573
Recorded information:
01865 728608

The Museum is a venue for temporary exhibitions of modern and contemporary art from all over the world and also provides a variety of related activities: talks, music, film and events.

OPENING TIMES

Museum:
Tuesday–Sunday 11am–6pm.
Thursday 11am–9pm. Closed Monday.

Full access is provided to disabled visitors.

ADMISSION

Adults £2.50. Concessions £1.50. Children under 16 free. (Group booking discounts available, please ring 01865 813815).

The Café at MOMA serves a variety of freshly prepared foods: breakfasts, lunches, teas, wines and spirits are available throughout the day.
Open: Tuesday–Saturday 9.30am–5pm, Thursday 9am–9pm, Sunday 11am–5pm. Closed Monday.
The Book House stocks books on contemporary art and literature, and a range of gifts, posters, calendars and postcards.

Aerospace Museum

Cosford, Shifnal
Shropshire TF11 8UP
Tel: 01902 374872/374112
Fax: 01902 374813

The Aerospace Museum is located at Cosford on the A41, one mile from junction 3 of the M54.

This is one of the largest aviation collections in the UK. Exhibits include the Victor and Vulcan bombers, the Hastings, York and British Airways airliners, the Belfast freighter and the last airworthy Britannia. World War II aircraft, including the Spitfire, Mosquito and Hurricane.

The Research & Development Collection includes the notable TSR2, Fairy Delta, Bristol 188 and many more important aircraft. There is a British Airways Exhibition Hall and a comprehensive missile and aero engine display.

Shop, restaurant, picnic area, large car park, all in a large parkland setting on an active airfield.

EVENTS

Summer 1998 sees the opening of a purpose built Aviation Heritage and Training Centre, housing a Restaurant, Souvenir Shop, Conference Centre along with enhanced visitor facilities.

Royal Air Force Cosford Air Show is on 14 June 1998.

ADMISSION

Adult £5.00. Child £3.00.
Senior Citizens £4.00.
Family £13.00.
Reduced rates for groups and educational visits.

Ironbridge Gorge

Ironbridge Gorge Museum Trust Ironbridge, Telford Shropshire TF8 7AW Tel: 01952 433522 Fax: 01952 432204

The Ironbridge Gorge is a World Heritage Site, in beautiful Shropshire countryside. The world's first Iron Bridge, cast in 1779 by Abraham Darby III, is the centrepiece of the Museums and Monuments of the Ironbridge Gorge. Here the Industrial Revolution was born over 250 years ago, and the Museums bring it to life:

The Ironbridge **VISITOR CENTRE** is the ideal place to start your visit.

Jackfield **TILE MUSEUM**: kaleidoscope displays of tiles and demonstrations of tile making.

Other attractions and monuments are: **the Tar Tunnel, the Ironmaster's Homes, The Ironbridge Tollhouse and the Pipeworks Museum at Broseley.**

ADMISSION

Adult £9.50. Senior (60) £8.50. Child/Student £5.50. Family (2 adults+5 Children) £29. Telephone – Freephone 0800 590258 for **free** Visitor Guide. Prices valid 4 April 98– 26 March 99.

OPENING TIMES

Daily all year 10am–5pm with Seasonal variations. Major Sites remain open in the winter. Telephone (for daily details) – 01952 432166 or 433522.

Somerset County Museums Service

Somerset Rural Life Museum
Glastonbury
Tel: 01458 831197

The magnificent 14th century Abbey Barn is the centrepiece of the Somerset Rural Life Museum. The barn and the farm buildings contain displays illustrating the tools and techniques of farming in Victorian Somerset. Traditional local activities, like willow growing, peat digging and cider making are included. Museum shop, tea room, facilities for the disabled, baby-changing area and free car park.

OPENING TIMES

Open Easter to 31 Oct Tues to Fri, 10am–5pm. Weekends 2–6pm. Closed Good Friday. Please telephone for winter opening hours.

Somerset County Museum
Taunton. Tel: 01823 320201

There is a rich variety of objects on show at the museum relating to the County of Somerset to intrigue and stir the imagination. There are toys and dolls, fossils, fine silver, pottery, archaeological items and the Somerset Light Infantry Museum. Facilities for the disabled.

OPENING TIMES

Open Easter to 31 Oct. Tues to Sat, 10am–5pm. For winter opening hours from 1 Nov please telephone or visit our web site http://www.somerset.gov.uk

ADMISSION

Both Museums: Adults £2.20. OAP's £1.65. Children between 5–18, 50p.

Rotherham Museums and Arts Service

Clifton Park Museum Clifton Lane Rotherham S65 2AA Tel: 01709 823635 Fax: 01709 823631

The Museum, set in a delightful 18th century house, once the home of the Rotherham iron magnate, Joshua Walker, displays the UK's finest collection of Rockingham porcelain. There are also displays of glass, furniture, local and social history.

EXHIBITIONS/EVENTS

There is a programme of temporary exhibitions throughout the year, and special events for children.

ADMISSION

Free to all.

OPENING TIMES

Mon–Thurs and Sat 10am–5pm. Sun 2.30–4.30pm. Closed on Fridays.

York and Lancaster Regimental Museum
The Arts Centre, Rotherham S65 1JH. Tel: 01709 382121

The displays cover the story of the regiment and of the men who served during its 200 year history. The extensive regimental archive is housed at the Museum and can be visited by appointment.

ADMISSION

Free to all.

OPENING TIMES

Mon–Sat 10am–5pm. Closed Sundays and Bank Holidays.

Rotherham Art Gallery
The Arts Centre, Rotherham S65 1JH. Tel: 01709 382121

A continuous programme of temporary exhibitions of contemporary arts and crafts, with an emphasis on photography for Photo '98.

ADMISSION

Free to all.

OPENING TIMES

Mon–Sat 10am–6pm. Closed Sundays and Bank Holidays. Please 'phone for further details.

ROTHERHAM
MUSEUMS
&ARTS

Sheffield Galleries and Museums Trust

The Millennium Gallery will be opening in 2000 as part of the Heart of the City regeneration of the city centre. Funded by the Millennium Commission.

Bishops' House
Norton Lees Lane S8 9BE
Tel: 0114 255 7701
A 16th century timber framed farmhouse.
Admission charge.
Wed–Sat 10am–4.30pm.
Sun 11am–4.30pm.

City Museum and Mappin Art Gallery
Weston Park S10 2TP
Tel: 0114 276 8588
Sheffield's major museum collections and the Mappin Art Gallery.
Exciting exhibitions and educational programmes.
Free admission.
Wed–Sat 10am–5pm.
Sun 11am–5pm.

Graves Art Gallery
Surrey Street S1 23E
Tel: 0114 273 5158
City centre gallery situated above the Central Library.
Exhibition programme.
Free admission.
Tues–Sat 10am–5pm.

Ruskin Gallery and the Ruskin Craft Gallery
101 Norfolk Street S1 2JE
Tel: 0114 273 5299
Founded by John Ruskin in 1875 with the addition of the Ruskin Craft Gallery since 1988.
Exhibition programme.
Free admission.
Tues–Sat 10am–5pm.

The Museums of the Potteries

Designated as a museum with an outstanding collection

The Potteries Museum
(formerly known as City Museum & Art Gallery)
Bethesda Street, Hanley, Stoke-on-Trent ST1 3DW
Tel: 01782 232323
See the world's finest collection of Staffordshire ceramics. Exhibitions, and events for all the family. Lots to See! Lots to Do! Lots to Learn! Access for disabled people. Admission: Free.

OPENING TIMES
Monday–Saturday 10am–5pm. Sunday 2–5pm.

Gladstone Pottery Museum
Uttoxeter Road, Longton, Stoke-on-Trent ST3 1PQ
Tel: 01782 319232 and 311378
A typical Victorian pottery factory preserved from the days of coal-fired kilns. Exciting opportunities for 'hands-on' experience with clay.

OPENING TIMES
Daily 10am–5pm.

Ford Green Hall
Ford Green Road, Smallthorne, Stoke-on-Trent ST6 1NG
Tel: 01782 233195
A furnished farmer's house, built in 1624. Period garden. Regular special events.

OPENING TIMES
Sunday–Thursday 1–5pm.

Etruria Industrial Museum
Lower Bedford Street, Etruria, Stoke-on-Trent ST4 7AF
Tel: 01782 287557
See how they put the bone into china at Britain's sole surviving steam-powered potters mill. 1820's beam engine. Working blacksmith's forge.

OPENING TIMES
Wednesday–Sunday 10am–4pm.

ADMISSION
Gladstone Pottery Museum, Ford Green Hall, Etruria Industrial Museum: Please phone for details.

Stafford Borough Council

The Ancient High House
Greengate Street, Stafford ST16 2HS
Tel: 01785 240204

The Ancient High House is England's largest timber-framed town house. It is a registered museum with rooms set out to show the house's 400 year history. The top floor contains the Museum of the Staffordshire Yeomanry. There is an attractive gift shop on the first floor and Stafford's Tourist Information Centre on the ground floor.

Stafford Castle and Visitor Centre
Newport Road, Stafford ST16 1DJ
Tel: 01785 257698

Stafford Castle is the site of a Norman fortress. The visitor centre tells the story of the site through archaeological artefacts discovered during extensive excavations. A video presentation and a 'hands-on' display provide extra fun for the family.

Izaak Walton's Cottage
Worston Lane, Shallowfield, Stafford ST15 0PA
Tel: 01785 760278

Izaak Walton, author of the 'Compleat Angler' bequeathed this cottage to Stafford. It is set out as a registered museum of fishing and the interior includes rooms in the style of the 17th century.

ADMISSION
Admission per museum:
Adults £1.75. Children/Concessions £1.10.

For further information please telephone Stafford Tourist Information Centre on 01785 240204.

The Bass Museum

The Perfect Day in Every Way

the
BASS MUSEUM

PO Box 220
Horninglow Street
Burton upon Trent
Staffordshire
Tel: 01283 511000

If you want a great family day out, visit The Bass Museum. Based in Burton – at the heart of Britain's brewing capital – this fascinating experience brings brewing history bang up–to–date.

With award–winning exhibitions, guided brewery tours, nostalgic working model brewery vehicles and the famous Bass Shire Horses, this is the perfect day out for all the family – whatever the weather! And don't forget the gifts you can buy from The Museum Shop.

There's no better way to round off your trip than to sample the beers and enjoy a bite to eat in the restaurant. So why not treat yourself and your family soon?

Shire Hall Gallery

The **SHIRE HALL** *Gallery*

Market Square
Stafford, ST16 2LD
Tel: 01785 278345
Fax: 01785 278327

The 1798 Crown Court building was vacated in 1991, with the Shire Hall Gallery opening in 1993. It is now an important visual arts venue for Staffordshire.

EXHIBITIONS/EVENTS
The Gallery has a varied programme of temporary exhibitions, including Fine Art, Contemporary Craft, Photography & Textiles. Educational opportunities for groups can be arranged throughout the year, including creative workshops and exhibition related events. The Great Hall and Courtrooms are available for hire for business and social functions. Courtrooms are open to the public and can be used for a wide range of social and educational functions. Guided tours are available on request. "The Balcony" coffee bar serves speciality tea, coffee and a selection of homemade cakes. The craft shop is selected for quality by the Crafts Council and stocks a wide range of contemporary craft by leading British makers.

ADMISSION
Free.

OPENING TIMES
Monday-Saturday 10.00am-5.00pm (may close for exhibition changes – please ring for details).
Closed Bank Holidays.

STAFFORDSHIRE

Tamworth Castle Museum

[Tamworth Borough Council]

**The Holloway
Tamworth
Staffordshire B79 7LR
Tel: 01827 63563
Fax: 01827 56567**

The oldest parts of the Grade I listed building date from the late 12th century. The intact apartments contain 15 public rooms spanning 800 years of history. There are two permanent exhibitions: one on Norman castle life, the other on Tamworth's history from Roman times. The latter has interactive elements for adults and children. Other features include a slide show on local transport history, battlemented wall-walks, a dungeon, a haunted bedroom and a unique giftshop.

EXHIBITIONS/EVENTS

Special events take place at Bank Holidays and during the school holidays. 'Castle by Candlelight' is on 15, 16, 17, 22, 23 and 24 October this year.

ADMISSION

Adults £3.40. Concessions £1.75. Family ticket £8.55. Children under 5 free.

OPENING TIMES

Mon–Sat 10am–5.30pm. Sun 2–5.30pm. Last admission 4.30pm. Closed 24, 25 and 26 December.

SUFFOLK

The Museums of Bury St Edmunds and Beyond

Take a glimpse into the fascinating past of West Suffolk . . .

Manor House Museum

The Museum is a Georgian Mansion which has been restored to its 18th century glory. The sparkling collections of costume, fine and decorative art and horology are displayed in superb surroundings and interpreted through touch screen computers.

There is a full range of permanent and temporary exhibitions throughout the year and the museum offers a quality gift shop and cafeteria. Schools and groups are particularly welcome.

Opening times: Tues–Sun 10am–5pm. Closed Mondays except Bank Holidays. Tel: 01284 757072.

Moyse's Hall Museum

The collections are housed in one of England's rare surviving Norman townhouses where the original features are still clearly visible. The Nationally important archaeological collection and local history artefacts are complemented by a lively programme of changing exhibitions.

Educational visits are a speciality of Moyse's Hall as are holiday workshops for youngsters. Moyse's Hall also boasts a fine shop where quality traditional gifts can be bought.

Opening times: Mon–Sat 10am–5pm. Sun 2–5pm.
Tel: 01284 757488.

Abbey Visitor Centre

The Visitor Centre is situated in Samson's Tower, part of the West Front of the now ruined Abbey of St Edmund. The Abbey at Bury St Edmunds was one of the most important in medieval Europe and dedicated to St Edmund, once Patron Saint of England.

'Hands-on' activities and walkman tours of the ruins ensure that there is something to interest everyone.

Opening times: Open daily 10am–5pm Easter until end of October. Tel: 01284 763110.

St Edmundsbury
BOROUGH COUNCIL

Leisure Services

Christchurch Mansion

**Christchurch Park
Ipswich IP4 2BE
Tel: 01473 253246
Fax: 01473 210328**

At the heart of Ipswich for 400 years:

A fine Tudor house set in beautiful parkland. Period rooms are furnished in styles from 16th–19th century, including the Victorian Parlour, the Tudor rooms, the State bedroom and the Saloon; there are outstanding collections of china, clocks and furniture.

The **Suffolk Artists Gallery** shows paintings by Gainsborough, Constable and other prominent local artists. The attached **Wolsey Art Gallery** has a lively temporary exhibition programme ranging from touring contemporary exhibitions, local Open Submission shows to exhibitions of historical works.

There is an active education programme supporting the displays in the gallery and around the house.

ADMISSION

Free.

OPENING TIMES

Tuesday–Saturday 10am–5pm
Sundays 2.30–4.30pm (November–January closes 4.15pm).
Open most Bank Holiday Mondays 10am–5pm.

Gainsborough's House

46 Gainsborough Street, Sudbury, Suffolk CO10 6EU
Tel: 01787 372958. Fax: 01787 376991

Gainsborough's House is the birthplace of Thomas Gainsborough RA (1727–88).

The Georgian fronted town house, with an attractive walled garden, displays more of the artist's work than any other gallery. The collection is shown together with 18th century furniture and memorabilia.

Commitment to contemporary art is reflected in a varied programme of exhibitions throughout the year. These include fine art, craft, photography, printmaking, sculpture and highlights in particular the work of East Anglian artists.

EXHIBITIONS IN 1998 INCLUDE

A Talent to Amuse: Henry William Bunbury (1750–1811)
30 May to 26 July.

Sculpture for the garden selected by Tony Venison
30 May to 27 September.

Drawings for All '98: biennial open drawing competition
1 August to 27 September.

Drawings by Thomas Gainsborough
3 October to 22 November.

ADMISSION

Adults £2.80. OAPs £2.20. Children and Students £1.50. Group rates are available on request.

OPENING TIMES

Tuesday–Saturday 10am–5pm.
Sunday 2–5pm.
Closes 4pm 1 November–31 March.
Closed Mondays, Good Friday and between Christmas and the New Year.

Ipswich Museum

High Street
Ipswich IP1 3QH
Tel: 01473 213761
Fax: 01473 281274

There's something for everyone at Ipswich Museum:

The Anglo-Saxons come to Ipswich – vivid and realistic displays of everyday life with treasures from the Sutton Hoo burials, video and touch screen discovery point; life, death, work and worship in **Roman Suffolk**; the foundations of Suffolk shown in the **Geology galleries** – rocks, fossils, and minerals; the best collection of **British birds** in the country; the **Suffolk Wildlife** gallery with its massive reconstruction of a woolly mammoth; the **Victorian Natural History** gallery, including the familiar and much-loved rhinoceros and giraffe; the **Mankind** galleries showing rare and fascinating objects from Africa, Asia, the Pacific and Americas; and new for 1998 an exhibition featuring the carved timber houses of **Tudor and Stuart Ipswich.**

ADMISSION

Free.

OPENING TIMES

Tuesday–Saturday 10am–5pm.

The National Horseracing Museum and Tours

99 High Street, Newmarket
Suffolk CB8 8JL
Tel: 01638 667333

Newmarket, set in beautiful countryside about 30 minutes from Cambridge, is world-famous for its horseracing. Behind the High Street is a magical world of studs and stables which you can only visit on a Museum minibus tour. Meet the horses, mares, foals and stable staff, watch the horses on the historic gallops and in their pool, or go racing with us. In the Museum, find out about the people and horses involved in racing from its Royal origins to Frankie Dettori. Retired jockeys answer your questions and let you ride the horse simulator. New this year – record your own racing commentary.

EVENTS

Please telephone for a list of special tours and inaugurations to the Hall of Fame.

ADMISSION

Museum – Adults £3.50. Over 60s £2.50. Children £1.50. Tours – £20. Concessions £16. Booking for tours essential.

OPENING TIMES

3rd March–31st October, 10am–5pm, daily. Closed Mondays except July and August.
Tours depart 9.25am.

Gift shop and café open all year round. Teachers' packs.

The Sue Ryder Museum

Sue Ryder Home
Cavendish
Sudbury
Suffolk CO10 8AY
Tel: 01787 280252
Fax: 01787 280258

This small museum is set in beautiful surroundings here at the headquarters of this International Foundation. It depicts the remarkable story of how the Foundation was established, its works today and its hopes for the future.

The museum is located on the A1092 Long Melford – Cambridge road (Long Melford 4 miles: Sudbury 8 miles: Bury St Edmunds 16 miles: Cambridge 29 miles).

The gift and coffee shop provides lunches and light meals. Parties welcome, menu on request. For special bookings please write to Trinda Baxter at the above address.

ADMISSION
Adults 80p. Children 12 and under and OAPs 40p.

OPENING TIMES
Open daily 10.00am–5.30pm. Closed Christmas Day.

Guildford House Gallery

[Guildford Borough Council, Department of Leisure Services]

155 High Street, Guildford, Surrey GU1 3AJ
Tel: 01483 444740 Fax: 01483 444742

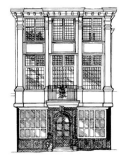

Fascinating Grade I Listed town house dating from 1660. Finely decorated plaster ceilings, panelled rooms, wrought iron work and richly carved staircase. A wide range of changing exhibitions. Includes occasional exhibitions of selections from Guildford Borough's art collection, which includes several fine pastel and oil portraits by Guildford-born artist John Russell and paintings, drawings and prints of Guildford and the surrounding countryside.

EXHIBITIONS/EVENTS
6–30 May
Drawling, Stretching and Fainting in Coils
Looking at the influence of Lewis Carroll's work
6 June–11 July
Looking in Wonderland
Tenniel's illustrations for the 'Alice' books
18 July–29 August
The Magic of Paper Sculpture
Children are invited to a FREE drop-in 'Help make a paper dragon' workshop for national Gallery Week on 24 July, 10am–4pm.

ADMISSION
Free.

OPENING TIMES
Tuesday–Saturday 10am–4.45pm (not Bank Holidays)

LOCATION
Top of Guildford's cobbled High Street (opposite Sainsbury's).

FACILITIES
Toilets – on lower ground floor.
Gift Shop – Cards, crafts, prints and publications.
Provision for groups – Tours available. Pre-booked groups only.
Disabled provision – Difficult access – many stairs and steps.
Carvings and wrought-ironwork can be touched.
Parking – No parking on-site. Nearby public car parks off pedestrianised High Street.
Education Services – Lecture programme. School sessions.

Bede's World

Church Bank
Jarrow
Tyne & Wear NE32 3DY
Tel: 0191 489 2106
Fax: 0191 428 2361

Bede's World explores early Northumbria and the life and work of the Venerable Bede. *Gyrwe*, an 11-acre re-created Anglo-Saxon farm has field systems, rare breeds of animals and replica timber buildings. Exhibitions in a new Museum and 18th century Jarrow Hall contain archaeological material, including Anglo-Saxon coloured window glass and stone sculpture. Church of St Paul and ruins of the monastery where Bede lived date from 7th century. Audio-Visual, Herb garden, Gift/Craft Shop and Cafe.

EXHIBITIONS/EVENTS
Programme of visiting exhibitions, Living History displays, concerts, feasts and special activities.

ADMISSION
Adults £3.00. Concessions £1.50. Family £7.20.

OPENING TIMES
Apr–Oct:
Tues–Sat 10am–5.30pm,
Sun 2.30–5.30pm.
(May–Sept:
Sun 12 noon–5.30pm).
Nov–Mar:
Tues–Sat 10am–4.30pm,
Sun 1.30–4.30pm.
Closed Mondays except Bank Holidays. Christmas to New Year opening times vary.

The Shakespeare Houses in and around Stratford-upon-Avon

Five beautifully preserved Tudor homes all associated with William Shakespeare and his family.

In Town:
Shakespeare's Birthplace
Nash's House and New Place
Hall's Croft

Out of Town:
Anne Hathaway's Cottage
Mary Arden's House and the Shakespeare Countryside Museum

Open every day, all year except 23–26 December.

ADMISSION

Combined ticket available for three in-town or all five properties.

For further information
Tel: 01789 204016
The Shakespeare Birthplace Trust
The Shakespeare Centre Henley Street Stratford-upon-Avon Warwickshire CV37 6QW

The Shakespeare Birthplace Trust is a Registered Charity, No. 209302.

Black Country Living Museum

Tipton Road, Dudley, West Midlands DY1 4SQ
Tel: 0121 557 9643. Fax: 0121 557 4242

A Museum with a difference: friendly costumed demonstrators bring original shops, cottages and workshops to life on a 26 acre site. Features include the reconstructed turn-of-the-century village beside the canal, underground 1850s coalmine tours, 1920s working cinema and electric tramcar rides. Live demonstrations including glass-cutting, chain-making and sweet-making. Refreshments available from 1930s Fried Fish Shop, Bottle and Glass Inn and Stables Restaurant.

ACTIVITIES AND EVENTS

Throughout the year the Museum operates a changing programme of working activities including brass-casting, cooking and baking demonstrations and engine-steaming. Trolleybuses run most Sundays and Bank Holiday Mondays. 1998 events: Museums Week 16th–24th May; Father's Day Special 21st June; Vehicle Rally 20th September; Traditional Bonfire Night 5th November; Christmas Evenings 18th and 19th December (pre-book only).

ADMISSION

1998: Adults £6.95; Children £4.50; Senior Citizens £5.95; Family ticket (2 adults and 3 children) £19.50. Group rates are available for booked parties of 10 or more.

OPENING TIMES

Open all year: March to October, every day 10am–5pm; November to February, Wednesday to Sunday, 10am–4pm. Closed 21st to 25th December 1998 inclusive.

Barber Institute of Fine Arts

University of Birmingham, Edgbaston, Birmingham B15 2TS
Tel: 0121 414 7333
Fax: 0121 414 3370

One of the finest small picture galleries in the world housing an outstanding permanent collection of Old Master and modern paintings, drawings and sculpture including masterpieces by Bellini, Rubens, Poussin, Murillo, Gainsborough, Rossetti, Whistler, Monet, Degas and Magritte.

EXHIBITIONS/EVENTS

Series of temporary displays and exhibitions to be launched in 1998. Varied events programme includes lectures, gallery talks, study days, children's holiday workshops and annual Open Day (6 June 1998). For details about activities for schools, please contact the Education Officer on 0121 414 7335.

ADMISSION

Free.

OPENING TIMES

Monday to Saturday 10am–5pm.
Sunday 2–5pm.
Closed 1 January, Good Friday, Easter Monday, 25 December, 26 December.

FACILITIES

For details about the gallery shop, guided tours for groups and disabled access, please call the Visitor Services Officer on 0121 414 6985.

Discover Birmingham's Heritage

Birmingham boasts some of the finest collections in the country. To find out more, telephone 0121 303 2834 for our leaflet, 'Discover Birmingham's Heritage', quoting Ref: MG98.

Birmingham Museum and Art Gallery
Chamberlain Square
Birmingham B3 3DH
Tel: 0121 303 2834
Please quote Ref: MG98
This magnificent Victorian building houses one of the world's finest collections of Pre-Raphaelite art. The highlight of this year's programme is the Burne-Jones centenary exhibition.

ADMISSION

Free. Voluntary contributions welcome.

OPENING TIMES

Open all year.

Jewellery Quarter Discovery Centre
75–79 Vyse Street. Tel: 0121 554 3598
Please quote Ref: MG98
This award winning museum built around a real jewellery workshop has been perfectly preserved since it opened almost a century ago. Guided tours and demonstrations.

OPENING TIMES

Open all year – closed Sundays.

Soho House
Soho Avenue (off Soho Road),
Handsworth, Birmingham B18 5LB
Tel: 0121 554 9122. Please quote Ref: MG98
The former home of industrialist Matthew Boulton, James Watt's business partner, is the city's newest museum, and already an award-winner.

OPENING TIMES

Open all year – closed Mondays except Bank Holidays.

Admission to either museum is £2.00 (concessions £1.50). Family (2 adults + 3 children) £5.00.
Discounts for groups of 10 or more pre-booked.

Museum of British Road Transport

MUSEUM OF·BRITISH·ROAD TRANSPORT
St AGNES LANE · HALES STREET
COVENTRY
POST CODE : CV1 1PN
Telephone 01203 832425. FAX 01203 832465

St Agnes Lane
Hales Street
Coventry CV1 1PN
Tel: 01203 832425
Fax: 01203 832465

Take a free tour through Britain's road transport heritage. At the home of the nation's motor industry, our new entrance foyer shop and additional display areas, known as Revolutions, makes the Museum one of the largest displays of its kind – from the earliest cycles to the latest high-tech developments in the motor industry. You can step back through time to the elegance of Edwardian motoring and the glamour of the 30s. You'll see how Royalty rode in style, and reflect on family cars of the 50s and 60s, then marvel at today's high-tech advances and follow the fascinating story of Thrust 2 – on it's record breaking 633mph run in 1983. You'll also see how the Blitz Experience recreates the devastating air raid on Coventry.

ADMISSION

Free of charge.

Walsall Museum and Art Gallery

Lichfield Street
Walsall WS1 1TR
Tel: 01922 653116/653196

Situated in the heart of the West Midlands, Walsall Museum and Art Gallery is home to the renowned Garman Ryan Collection – an 'A to Z of European art'. Given to the Gallery in 1974 by Kathleen Garman, wife of the artist Sir Jacob Epstein, the Collection contains an impressive array of famous artists from Monet and Turner through to Van Gogh and Picasso.

Our other permanent display is the Community History Gallery 'Walsall Inside Out' which presents the histories of Walsall and its people from medieval origins to 1990s popular culture.

EXHIBITIONS/EVENTS

Walsall has a national reputation for innovative and high quality temporary exhibitions and events. In September 1999 Walsall's amazing New Art Gallery will open, providing a new home for the Garman Ryan Collection and improved facilities and services for all our visitors.

ADMISSION

Free.

OPENING TIMES

Tuesday–Saturday 10am–5pm.
Sunday 2–5pm.

Wolverhampton Art Gallery and Museum

Lichfield Street
Wolverhampton WV1 1DU
Tel: 01902 552055

At Wolverhampton you can see the largest collection of contemporary art in the region. Beautifully restored galleries show an excellent collection of 18th and 19th century paintings. We also house an outstanding collection of British and American Pop Art. The 'Ways of Seeing' Gallery offers hands-on ways of looking at art for adults and children alike. Throughout the year we stage exciting temporary exhibitions of visual arts and crafts – please phone for the current exhibition leaflet. Don't miss our well-appointed tea room and enticing gallery shop. The Gallery is proud to have won the 1997 Interpret Britain Award for Access for Visitors with Disabilities.

ADMISSION
Free.

OPENING TIMES
Mon–Sat 10am–5pm. Closed Bank Holidays.

Bilston Art Gallery and Museum
Mount Pleasant
Bilston WV14 7LU
Tel: 01902 552507

Just 3 miles from Wolverhampton you can see the fine collection of exquisite Bilston enamels. The 'Out of the Smoke' display tells the story of Bilston from 1600 to the present day. On a fine day enjoy the magical sculpture garden with Amber the Firebreather.

ADMISSION
Free.

OPENING TIMES
Mon–Thurs 11am–4pm.
Sat 11am–4pm. Closed Bank Hols.

Amberley Museum

Amberley, Arundel
West Sussex BN18 9LT
Tel: 01798 831370
Fax: 01798 831831
http://www.fastnet.co.uk/amberley.museum/

Amberley Museum brings to life the working heritage of the South-East. Craftsmen can be seen at work each day, using traditional materials and tools to produce a range of fine wares, keeping their trades alive. Visitors can ride on a workmen's train on the narrow gauge railway, or on one of the Museum's fleet of vintage motor buses. Other major exhibitions include Seeboard electricity hall, and the Paviors' museum of roads and roadmaking, while there are many other fascinating displays and exhibits to enjoy within this unique 36-acre site.

ADMISSION
Adults £5.20. Over 60s £4.70. Children £2.70. Family £14.

OPENING TIMES
Open 14 March–1 November 1998, Wednesdays–Sundays, 10am–5pm. Open daily during local school holidays.

LOCATION
Amberley Museum is situated in the South-West of Sussex, on the B2139, mid-way between Arundel and Storrington, adjacent to Amberley railway station. Free car and coach parking is provided for Museum visitors.

Henfield Museum

(Henfield Parish Council)
Village Hall
Henfield, West Sussex
BN5 9DB
Tel: 01273 492546
Fax: 01273 494898

Henfield is only a few miles north of the South Downs, on high ground overlooking the valley of the River Adur. It is an ancient village, its earliest known settlement being of Anglo Saxon date. It has many old farmhouses and much of the High Street is of Tudor age.

Henfield Museum is a local history museum giving a glimpse of life in a Sussex village from Tudor times. Domestic objects are mostly of Victorian and Edwardian age as are agricultural tools and dresses. The local uniforms are of the Sussex Rifle Volunteer Regiment. There is a large collection of local paintings and photographs.

This fine penny farthing bicycle is on show having been made by a local craftsman in 1887.

EXHIBITIONS/EVENTS
Temporary exhibitions three times a year.

ADMISSION
Free.

OPENING TIMES
All the year Mon, Tues, Thurs and Sat 10am–12 noon. Weds and Sat 2.30–4.30pm. Other times by appointment. Not open Bank Holidays.

LOCATION
On A281 Horsham to Brighton Road.
Car parking.
Access for disabled.

Worthing Museum and Art Gallery

Chapel Road, Worthing
West Sussex BN11 1HP
Tel: (Sat) 01903 204229
(Mon–Fri)
01903 239999 – ext 2528
Fax: 01903 236277

'Friendly', 'amazing' and 'fascinating' are just some of the remarks we overhear around the Museum. The story of the Worthing area from earliest times is told through geology, archaeology and history displays that include reconstructions of a Downland cottage kitchen and a Victorian nursery. The stunning costumes have inspired many of the clothes seen in historical television dramas. The toys, dolls, teddy bears and art displays are also well worth a visit.

The 1998 programme of temporary exhibitions, indoors, includes British Watercolours, Sculptures by Philip Jackson, Weddings, Archaeology, and Textile T'arts. *Touch Day* (18 April), *Museums Week* (16–23 May), *Gallery Week* (18–25 July) and *Archaeology Fun Day* (12 September) are just some of our special events.

Shop, toilets, parking for disabled visitors, good wheelchair access. Wheelchair available on request.

ADMISSION
Free.

OPENING TIMES
Monday–Saturday 10am–6pm (October–March 10am–5pm). Closed some Bank Holidays.

Leeds Museums and Galleries

Armley Mills
Canal Road, Armley,
Leeds LS12 2QF
Tel: 0113 263 7861

Once the world's largest woollen mills, housed on an island site on the River Aire. Adults £2.00. Concessionary £1.00. Children 50p.
Open Tues–Sat 10am–5pm. Sun 1–5pm.

Kirkstall Abbey and Abbey House Museum
Kirkstall Road, Leeds LS5 3EH. Tel: 0113 275 5821

Britain's finest monastic ruin, founded by Cistercian monks in 1152. Free Admission. **Open** daily, dawn to dusk. **Abbey House Museum,** will be closed from 19 April 1998 for major new display work. The new exhibitions, cafeteria and shop are scheduled to re-open in April 2000.

Leeds City Art Gallery
The Headrow, Leeds LS1 3AA. Tel: 0113 247 8248
Fax: 0113 244 9689

Collection of Victorian paintings, early English watercolours, 20th century British paintings and sculpture. Henry Moore Study Centre, Gallery cafe. Temporary exhibition programme. Free admission. **Open** Mon–Sat 10am–5pm (Wed until 8pm), Sun 1–5pm.

Leeds City Museum
Municipal Buildings, The Headrow, Leeds LS1 3AA
Tel: 0113 247 8275

Collections are shown in natural history, multicultural and archaeology galleries with a particular emphasis on the Yorkshire region. Free admission. **Open** Tues–Sat 10am–5pm. Closed Sun.

Thwaite Mills
Thwaite Lane, Stourton, Leeds LS10 1RP
Tel: 0113 249 6453

A working water-powered mill situated on a small island between the River Aire and the Aire and Calder Navigation. Adults £2.00. Concessionary £1.00. Children 50p.
Open Tues–Sat 10am–5pm. Sun 1–5pm. Closed Jan–Feb.

Leeds Museums and Galleries also run Historic Houses, **Temple Newsam House, Tel: 0113 264 7321** and **Lotherton Hall, Tel: 0113 281 3259.** Please ring for details.

The Colour Museum

Perkin House, PO Box 244
Providence Street
Bradford, West Yorkshire
BD1 2PW
Tel: 01274 390955

The Colour Museum is Britain's only museum of colour. It consists of two galleries both of which are packed with visitor operated exhibits.

The *World of Colour* gallery looks at the concept of colour, how it is perceived and its importance. You can mix coloured lights and experience colour illusions.

In the *Colour and Textiles* gallery you can discover the fascinating story of dyeing and textile printing from ancient Egypt to the present day. You can also use computerised technology to take charge of a dye making factory or to try your hand at interior design.

EXHIBITIONS/EVENTS

In addition to the permanent displays there is an annual programme of changing exhibitions, lectures and workshops. Free programme available.

ADMISSION

Adults £1.50. Concessions £1. Families (2+3) £3.75.

OPENING TIMES

Tuesday to Friday 2–5pm. Saturday 10am–4pm.

An Educational Activity of The Society of Dyers and Colourists

Thackray Medical Museum

Interpret Britain Award Winner

THACKRAY
MEDICAL MUSEUM
NEXT TO JIMMY'S IN LEEDS

Beckett Street,
LEEDS LS9 7LN
Information Line:
0113 245 7084
Minicom: 0113 245 7082
Other Enquiries:
0113 244 4343

You don't need years of training to visit the Thackray Medical Museum. Award winning interactive displays bring the history of medicine to life for visitors of all ages. Discover for yourselves how much fun you can have exploring how the past, present and future of medicine affect our lives today.

ADMISSION

£3.95. Concessions available. Special rates for groups and schools.

OPENING TIMES

Tuesday–Sunday 10am –5.30pm.

- Café and shop
- Car park
- Study and research centre
- Conference facilities
- All areas accessible by wheelchair users

WEST YORKSHIRE

Wakefield Museums, Galleries and Castles

Wakefield Art Gallery
Wentworth Terrace
Wakefield
Tel: 01924 305796

Significant early sculptures by Henry Moore and Barbara Hepworth. Important work by other major British modern artists, European schools and other periods.

OPENING TIMES

Tues–Sat 10.30am–4.30pm, Sun 2–4.30pm.

Wakefield Museum
Wood Street
Wakefield
Tel: 01924 305351

The story of Wakefield and its complex history. Also the exotic and eccentric natural history collections of Victorian explorer, Charles Waterton.

OPENING TIMES

Mon–Sat 10.30am–4.30pm. Improvement works in 1998 may disrupt opening – please telephone to check.
Sorry – the Gallery and Museum are inaccessible to wheelchair users.

Sandal Castle
Manygates Lane
Wakefield

Ruins of 13th century stone castle of the Warenne family. Excavation finds displayed in Wakefield Museum. Open dawn to dusk all year. Access for wheelchair users.

EXHIBITIONS/EVENTS

Changing temporary exhibition programme. Children's activities, education service. Please telephone for details

ADMISSION

Free.

WILTSHIRE

Devizes Museum

[The Wiltshire Archaeological and Natural History Society]

Founded in 1853

41 Long Street, Devizes
Wiltshire SN10 1NS
Tel: 01380 727369
Fax: 01380 722150

Designated as having a pre-eminent collection Devizes Museum has artefacts of international renown. Neolithic, Bronze Age, Iron Age, Roman, Saxon and Medieval Galleries reflect Wiltshire's rich heritage including Bronze Age Gold from Stonehenge burials, the Celtic Marlborough bucket and Saxon jewellery. The hands-on Recent History Gallery shows aspects of Wiltshire life over the last three centuries. The Natural History Gallery explores the geology of Wiltshire, then looks at individual wildlife habitats including the unique chalk downland through a series of displays and dioramas.

EXHIBITIONS/EVENTS

Art Gallery with changing exhibitions programme, temporary exhibitions gallery and educational children's holiday activities. For a wide range of other education services please contact the Education Officer.

ADMISSION

Free Day Monday. Adults £2.00. Concession £1.50. Children 50p. Family ticket (2 adults, 4 children) £4.50. Special rates for organised parties.

OPENING TIMES

Mon–Sat 10am–5pm. Closed Bank Holidays.

CO LONDONDERRY

Tower Museum

Tower
MUSEUM

Union Hall Place
Derry
Tel: 01504 372411

The Tower Museum was opened in 1992 to tell the fascinating but turbulent story of the city of Derry or Londonderry. The two names reflect the dual origins of the city as a Celtic ritual oakgrove and (from the 6th century) early Christian monastery which was refounded in the early 17th century as a colony of the city of London. The museum uses a wide range of theatrical and audio-visual devices as well as archaeological and historical objects of all periods from the Mesolithic to the present day. The museum has the unique distinction of winning both Irish and British 'Museum of the Year' awards. It is located in a pedestrian area in the centre of the old city just inside the 17th century town walls and close to many other important historic monuments and buildings.

ADMISSION

Adult £3.25
Children/Concessionary £1
Family £6.50

OPENING TIMES

Tue–Sat 10am–5pm (last admission 4.30pm) Open all bank holiday Mondays. Full access for the disabled, souvenir shop, city centre parking and restaurants/cafés/bars nearby but not exclusive to Museum.

CO TYRONE

Ulster-American Folk Park

Omagh
County Tyrone BT78 5QY
Tel: 01662 243292
Fax: 01662 242241

The Ulster-American Folk Park is an outdoor museum of emigration, which tells the story of the millions of people who emigrated from these shores throughout the 18th and 19th centuries. The Old World and the New World layout of the Park illustrates the various aspects of emigrant life on both sides of the Atlantic. Traditional thatched buildings, American log houses and a full-scale replica emigrant ship help to bring a bygone era back to life.

EVENTS

Special events programme.
Residential Accommodation.

ADMISSION

(General Public/Individuals)
Adults £3.50. Children/Senior Citizens £1.70. Children under 5 Free. Family £10. Group rates available.

OPENING TIMES

Easter to September
Mon–Sat 11am–6.30pm.
Sun/Public Holidays
11.30am–7pm.
October to Easter
Mon–Fri 10.30am–5pm.
Last admission 1½ hours before closing.

Aberdeen Art Gallery

Schoolhill, Aberdeen AB10 1FQ. Tel: 01224 646333

With its excellent collections of 17th, 18th and 19th century art and in particular its impressive 20th century British art collection, Aberdeen Art Gallery attracts in excess of 300,000 visitors each year. Situated in the heart of the city the Gallery hosts a lively selection of temporary exhibitions featuring cutting edge contemporary art from home and abroad as well as historic work. Open Mon–Sat 10am–5pm. Sun 2–5pm. Gallery Shop and Café.

Aberdeen Museums

The Tolbooth
Castle Street, Aberdeen. Tel: 01224 621167

The Tolbooth brings to life the story of Aberdeen and tells how the witches, debtors, criminals and felons incarcerated there, spent their days.
Open Apr–Sept. Tues–Sat 10am–5pm. Closed Mon.

Provost Skene's House
Guest Row, Aberdeen. Tel: 01224 641086

Provost Skene's House recreates the atmosphere of the 17th and 18th centuries with splendid room settings in period style.
Open Mon–Sat 10am–5pm. Coffee Shop.

Aberdeen Maritime Museum
Shiprow, Aberdeen. Tel: 01224 337700

Aberdeen Maritime Museum tells the story of Aberdeen's long association with the North Sea through fabulous exhibits and reconstructions and using state of the art presentation techniques.
Open Mon–Sat 10am–5pm. Sun 11am–5pm.
Museum Shop. Licensed café.

ABERDEEN
CITY COUNCIL
ARTS & RECREATION

Royal Museum

Chambers Street, Edinburgh EH1 1JF. Tel: 0131 225 7534

Situated in the heart of Edinburgh's historic Old Town, the Royal Museum is the flagship of the National Museums of Scotland. Here the international collections are housed in an imposing Victorian building with a soaring, glass-topped hall of extraordinary elegance. There are galleries devoted to Western decorative art, Middle Eastern culture, China and Japan, Ancient Egypt, African and American ethnography; Science, Industry and 20th century Design; and the Natural World – mammals, fish and birds, geology and the environment. A new Crafts Gallery opens in August 1998. The Royal Museum has a full programme of exhibitions, talks, tours and activities for children.

In December 1998 the Museum of Scotland will open adjacent to the Royal Museum. This will house the Scottish collections, presenting a unique portrait of the nation through a rich variety of objects.

ADMISSION

Adults £3, season ticket £5. Children free. Concessions £1.50, season ticket £2.50. Family season ticket £9. Admission free on Tuesday evenings, 5pm–8pm. (Season tickets offer unlimited access to all NMS sites during one calendar year.)

OPENING TIMES

Monday to Saturday 10–5pm, Sunday 12 noon–5pm, late opening on Tuesdays to 8pm. Closed 25 December only.

The National Museums of Scotland also comprise:
Museum of Flight, East Fortune Airfield, East Lothian;
Shambellie House Museum of Costume, Dumfriesshire;
Scottish Agricultural Museum, Ingliston, by Edinburgh;
Scottish United Services Museum, Edinburgh Castle;
Museum of Piping, Glasgow. For details please call NMS Enquiries on 0131 247 4219.

National Galleries of Scotland

[Comprising four distinctive galleries set right in the heart of Edinburgh]

The National Gallery of Scotland
The Mound, Edinburgh EH2 2EL
Tel: 0131 624 6200 Information Fax: 0131 343 3250

The National Gallery of Scotland houses Scotland's greatest collection of European paintings, drawings and prints dating from the early Renaissance to the late 19th century. The collection includes works by Raphael, Titian, Velazquez, Vermeer, El Greco, Poussin, Rembrandt, Rubens, Turner and the Impressionists. Also houses the national collection of Scottish art with works by Ramsay, Raeburn, Wilkie and McTaggart. The Gallery was designed by William Henry Playfair in the 1850s and has a striking neo-classical facade. It stands on the Mound, adjacent to the Royal Scottish Academy, which is also used by the Galleries to house major exhibitions over the summer.

The Scottish National Portrait Gallery
1 Queen Street, Edinburgh EH2 1JD
Tel: 0131 624 6200 Information Fax: 0131 343 3250

The Scottish National Portrait Gallery provides a visual history of Scotland from the 16th century to the present day, told through portraits of the people who shaped it: royals and rebels, poets and philosophers, heroes and villains. The collection includes masterpieces of European and American portraiture as well as some of the greatest portraits by Scottish artists. The Gallery also houses the national photography collection, the core of which is its vast holding of work by Hill and Adamson, the Scottish pioneers of photography. Most of the best known figures of Scottish history are represented, including such luminaries as Mary, Queen of Scots, Bonnie Prince Charlie and Robert Burns. Contemporaries include the novelist Irvine Welsh, actor Sean Connery, and the footballer Danny McGrain. Almost as remarkable as the collection itself is the distinctive neo-gothic building, purpose designed by Sir Robert Rowand Anderson in the 1880s.

The Scottish National Gallery of Modern Art
Belford Road, Edinburgh EH4 3DR
Tel: 0131 624 6200 Information Fax: 0131 343 3250

The Scottish National Gallery of Modern Art houses Scotland's finest collection of 20th century paintings, sculpture and graphic art and includes works by Picasso, Matisse, Miro, Kirchner, Giacometti, Bacon and Hockney. It also has an unrivalled collection of 20th century Scottish art, from the Colourists right up to the contemporary scene. Within the international collection, the greatest strengths are its holdings of Dada and Surrealist masterpieces from the Penrose and Keiller Collections, as well as German Expressionism and French Art. Magnificent grounds surrounding the Gallery provide the ideal setting for sculptures by Henry Moore, Barbara Hepworth and Sir Eduardo Paolozzi.

The Dean Gallery: The Paolozzi Collection
Belford Road, Edinburgh EH4 3DR
Tel: 0131 624 6200 Information Fax: 0131 343 3250

Opening in the Spring of 1999, the new Dean Gallery will provide much-needed space for temporary exhibitions of modern and contemporary art. It will also house the library and archives of the Gallery of Modern Art, particularly rich in Dada and Surrealist material, along with the Sir Eduardo Paolozzi gift of sculpture and graphic art which he generously wished to present to Edinburgh, the city of his birth. With special landscaping, joining up the grounds of the Dean with those of the Gallery of Modern Art directly across the road, the new site will also provide a unique and extensive parkland setting for sculpture.

GENERAL INFORMATION

The Galleries are open Monday–Saturday 10am–5pm and Sunday 2–5pm with extended hours during the Edinburgh Festival. Holiday closure on 25 and 26 December. Admission to all the permanent collections is free. On occasion, entrance charges are made for special exhibitions. Information: 0131 624 6200.

Glasgow Museums

Glasgow Museums is the largest municipal collection in Britain. Each venue has its own emphasis and personality. There are eleven separate museums attracting three million visitors each year. Admission to the permanent collections is free although there may be a charge for temporary exhibitions.

Art Gallery and Museum, Kelvingrove

One of the finest civic art collections in Britain including works by Giorgione, Rembrandt, Van Gogh and Whistler. The red sandstone façade is one of the city's most imposing landmarks. It is Scotland's second most visited building.

The Burrell Collection

One of the most important museum buildings of the 20th century. Representing the life's passion of just one man, wealthy Glaswegian shipowner Sir William Burrell, the collection covers an astounding range of more than 8,000 items.

Pollok House

Set in formal gardens and rolling parkland. Pollok House is Glasgow's major example of 18th century domestic architecture. It contains one of the finest collections of Spanish paintings in Britain, with works by El Greco and Goya.
Open summer season only.

The Gallery of Modern Art

A magnificent 18th century landmark building. The main galleries are named after the four elements, Earth, Fire, Water and Air, and the most exciting and innovative aspects of modern art are on display.

Museum of Transport

The museum boasts a reconstruction of a 1938 Glasgow Street, an authentic car showroom and a railway station as the focal point for a display of Scottish railway locomotives.

The Saint Mungo Museum of Religious Life and Art

The first museum in the world to look at all the major religions together. It has the first permanent authentic Buddhist Zen Garden in Britain and it houses the most important religious painting of the 20th century, 'Christ of St John of the Cross' by Salvador Dali.

McLellan Galleries

This fine 19th century building is the largest exhibition venue in Britain outside London. The Charles Rennie Mackintosh exhibition in 1996 attracted over 200,000 visitors and established the McLellan Galleries as a world class temporary exhibition space. Opening dates and times vary.

The People's Palace

Celebrating its centenary in 1998, the totally refurbished and redisplayed 'Palace' tells the story of Glasgow's social and political history.

Provand's Lordship

The oldest house in Glasgow set in the heart of the most ancient part of the city. Dating from 1471, it was originally built as the Manse for St Nicholas Hospital and features period displays. Closed throughout 1998, from 30 March.

Fossil Grove

Glasgow's oldest tourist attraction. Set in tranquil Victoria Park, the building shelters fossilised trees and rocks over 330 million years old. It is the only preserved forest of its kind in the world. Open summer season only.

Scotland Street School Museum

The history of education in Scotland from 1872 to 1972 with Victorian, Second World War, 1950s and 60s classrooms. Building designed in 1904 by Charles Rennie Mackintosh.

For more details and opening times contact:
Glasgow Museums Marketing Department on 0141 331 1854

Strathnaver Museum

Clachan
Bettyhill (by Thurso)
Sutherland KW14 7SS
Tel: 01641 521 418/330

The Museum was founded in the 1950's by local people under the guidance of Dr Ian Grimble, the well-known historian.

The main theme of the museum is the Strathnaver Clearances of the early 19th century. The displayed collection includes references to both the domestic and working life of the local people, the oldest items including a 4,000 year old beaker.

The area is Clan Mackay country and this is reflected in the Clan Mackay Room.

In the surrounding graveyard, the Farr Stone with its richly patterned ornamentation and dating from the late 8th century can also be viewed. The museum holds a large collection of Scottish History books.

A small sales area selling books, pamphlets, postcards etc. is also available.

ADMISSION

Charges – including concessions.

OPENING HOURS

Summer: 10am–1pm. 2–5pm. Closed Sundays April–October. Winter: By appointment.

LOCATION

The museum can be found on the A836 along the north coast of Sutherland and is at the eastern outskirts of the crofting village of Bettyhill, halfway between John O'Groats and Cape Wrath. Housed in the former Parish Church of St Columba, 1710, the museum is close to the Tourist Office, café and a craft shop. Parking.

North Ayrshire Museums Service

North Ayrshire Museum
Manse Street,
Saltcoats KA21 5AA
Tel: 01294 464174
Fax: 01294 464234

The **North Ayrshire Museum** traces the history of North Ayrshire with displays on archaeology, costume, transport and popular culture.

The museum also includes a section showing the maritime history of the port of Ardrossan and a reconstruction of an Ayrshire cottage interior. Accompanied children can play in the children's activity area.

Glasgow Vennel Art Gallery

10 Glasgow Vennel
Irvine KA12 0BD
Tel: 01294 275059
Fax: 01294 275059

The **Glasgow Vennel Art Gallery** in Irvine has an exciting, changing programme of contemporary arts and crafts exhibitions. The Gallery includes the 'Heckling Shop' where Robert Burns worked and the Lodging House where he lived in 1781.

EXHIBITIONS/EVENTS

For details of exhibitions and events, contact either of the two museums above.

OPENING TIMES

North Ayrshire Museum
Mon, Tue, Thu, Fri and Sat. 10am–1pm. 2–5pm.

Glasgow Vennel Art Gallery
Tue, Thu, Fri and Sat. 10am–1pm. 2–5pm.
June–September:
Mon–Sat 10am–1pm.
Sun 2–5pm (closed Wed).

ADMISSION

Free.

Scottish Maritime Museum – Harbourside Irvine

Laird Forge
Gottries Road
Irvine KA12 8QE
Tel: 01294 278283
Fax: 01294 313211

With over 3,400 miles of coastline and 50 inhabited islands, Scotland is a country with a rich maritime history. The Scottish Maritime Museum presents its history through the exhibition of vessels, from small to large, and of the boat building and ship building industries that are so important a part of that history. People's lives are covered in a recreated shipyard worker's tenement flat and in an annual themed exhibition. This year's topic is 'Moorings'. The largest and most spectacular exhibit is the world's oldest clipper ship, the *City of Adelaide*, built in 1864 for transport of emigrants to southern Australia. She is under restoration and visitors may go on board.

Tea room, car parking, access for disabled (we do not provide wheelchairs).

ADMISSION

Adults £2.
Children/concessions £1.
Family £4. Special rates for schools and organised parties.

OPENING TIMES

April 1st–October 31st daily, 10am–5pm, other times by appointment.

The Pier Arts Centre

Stromness
Orkney KW16 3AA
Tel: 01856 850209
Fax: 01856 851462
Director: Neil Firth

The Pier Arts Centre opened in July 1979, as the result of a gift by Margaret Gardiner to Orkney of a remarkable collection of 20th century painting and sculpture. Among the artists represented are Ben Nicholson, Barbara Hepworth, Patrick Heron, Eduardo Paolozzi, John Wells, Peter Lanyon, Roger Hilton, Alfred Wallis, Naum Gabo.

The integration of innovative modern design within the traditionally constructed buildings creates a fine gallery space, domestic and intimate in scale and flooded with natural and reflected light. In the Pier Gallery, young Orkneymen once came to enlist for service in the Hudson's Bay Company.

The Centre hosts a year-round programme of contemporary art exhibitions based on local, national and international values and is an important focus for the arts in Orkney.

ADMISSION

Free.

OPENING TIMES

All year. Tuesday–Saturday 10.30am–12.30pm/1.30–5pm. 10.30am–5pm during July and August

Wheelchair access ground floors only.

Pay and display car park 100 metres.

SCOTLAND • WALES

PERTH & KINROSS

Blair Castle

Blair Atholl, Pitlochry
Perthshire PH18 5TA
Tel: 01796 481207
Fax: 01796 481487

The ancient home and fortress of the Earls and Dukes of Atholl for over 725 years. The Castle's strategic central location makes it easily accessible from all major Scottish Centres in less than two hours.

On display are 32 rooms of infinite variety: beautiful furniture, paintings, armour, china, lace, embroidery and other unique treasures.

The castle also offers Self-service Restaurant facilities a gift shop and is surrounded by grounds and parkland which are open to visitors.

PARKING

Large car and Coach Park £2 per car, £10 per coach (unless pre-booked).

CASTLE ADMISSION

Adults £5.50.
Family £17.
Group concessions.

OPENING

Open every day from Wednesday 1st April to Friday 30th October 1998 10am–6pm (last entry to Castle 5pm)

FACILITIES

• Gift shop
• Picnic areas, Nature trails
• 18th century wall garden restoration project
• Pony trekking

SOUTH AYRSHIRE

Rozelle House Galleries

[Rozelle House Galleries is owned and operated by South Ayrshire Council.]

Rozelle Park
Monument Road
Ayr KA7 4NQ
Tel: 01292 445447
Fax: 01292 442065

Set within beautiful woodland and park; Rozelle House Galleries houses South Ayrshire Council's Art Collections, selections of which are carefully chosen and displayed throughout the year. In addition the galleries host a range of touring exhibitions; with the adjacent Maclaurin Galleries renowned for displays of contemporary art.

Crafts at Rozelle features unique and individual items for sale by local craftspeople.

Adjacent coffee shop/restaurant; free car parking.

EVENTS

Varied programme of events and workshops throughout the year. Call for details.

ADMISSION

Free.

OPENING TIMES

Monday to Saturday from 10am–5pm. (Sundays during Summer period 2–5pm.)

DIRECTIONS

From A77 Glasgow–Stranraer: follow signs for Burns Cottage then continue approx. half a mile past the cottage to Rozelle Park.

S LANARKSHIRE

New Lanark Visitor Centre

[New Lanark Conservation Trust]

New Lanark Mills
Lanark ML11 9DB
Tel: 01555 661345
Fax: 01555 665738

Award-winning Visitor Centre in 200 year old conservation village, made famous by social pioneer Robert Owen. The Visitor Centre interprets the history of the village in a series of exhibitions such as the Millworkers' House, the Village Store, Robert Owen's House and "The Annie McLeod Experience", a dramatic dark ride in which a ten year old mill girl gives you a glimpse of her daily life. The Centre has large gift and coffee shops, and the spectacular setting, in beautiful countryside by the Falls of Clyde, makes New Lannark an ideal place for those who wish to capture the essence of Scotland's heritage while enjoying a relaxing day out.

EVENTS

There is a varied programme of events throughout the year. Please send for details.

ADMISSION

Adults £3.75 Concessions £2.75 Family [2+2] £9.95 Family [2+4] £12.50

OPENING TIMES

11am – 5pm daily, except 25 Dec and 1/2 Jan.

CARDIFF

National Museum & Gallery Cardiff

Cathays Park
Cardiff CF1 3NP
Tel: 01222 397951
Fax: 01222 373219

No other British museum claims such a dazzling range of displays on art, natural history and science as you find gathered under one roof at the National Museum & Gallery Cardiff. Visit the spectacular exhibition on the creation of Wales, complete with animated Ice Age creatures and simulated Big Bang; discover one of the finest collections of art treasures in Europe, with work from Canaletto to Cezanne; experience the natural history galleries, with woodland and wildlife displays to enthral all ages.

EXHIBITIONS/EVENTS

The National Museum & Gallery Cardiff sets the stage for a constantly changing programme of exhibitions, theatre, events and workshops, against a background of magnificent permanent displays.

ADMISSION

Admission charge.

OPENING TIMES

Tuesday–Sunday: 10am–5pm. Closed Mondays, except Bank Holidays, Christmas Eve and Christmas Day.

OTHER BRANCHES

South Wales
Museum of Welsh Life, Turner House, Roman Legionary Museum.

West and North Wales
Museums of the Welsh Woollen Industry, Welsh Slate Museum, Segontium Roman Museum.

CARDIGANSHIRE

Aberystwyth Arts Centre

Penglais Hill, Aberystwyth, Ceredigion, Wales SY23 3DE
Exhibitions: Tel: 01970 622887/621903
Gallery: Tel: 01970 622895 Education/courses:
Tel: 01970 622888/621903 Fax: 01970 622883

Aberystwyth Arts Centre was purpose-built in 1972 on the University Campus overlooking Cardigan Bay. It comprises a theatre, concert hall, 4 gallery spaces, community arts workshops, craftshop, cafe and bookshop. The Centre houses the University's extensive Ceramics Collection. A recently awarded Lottery grant of £2.5 million from the Arts Council of Wales will enhance the facilities even more. Plans include new dance, music, art and drama workshop spaces, better access (including a lift), a new art cinema, studio theatre and art gallery and a refurbishment of the theatre and theatre foyer. Work is due to be complete by Spring 1999. Disabled Access and wheelchair stairlift to mezzanine level.

EXHIBITIONS/EVENTS

The exhibitions programme explores the diversity of contemporary art, craft and photography with around 40 changing exhibitions throughout the year. It promotes the best of work from Wales as well as showing significant British and International work, regularly touring exhibitions to other major visual arts venues in the UK. There is a regular Ceramic Series of exhibitions which feature the best in contemporary British ceramics with special occasional shows of European work. The exhibitions programme is complemented by an Education Service offering a range of talks, residencies, events and courses to local schools/groups/adults.

ADMISSION

Free.

OPENING TIMES

Monday–Saturday 10am–8pm. Main Gallery and Craft shop 10am–5pm and 6.45pm–end of the interval on performance nights. Closed Good Friday and Christmas week.

REFRESHMENTS

Cafe Monday–Saturday 10am–8pm. Bar facilities for events.

CRAFTSHOP

A Crafts Council selected shop which stocks a wide range of work by leading British makers.

DENBIGHSHIRE

Ruthin Craft Centre

Park Road, Ruthin
Denbighshire LL15 1BB
Tel: 01824 704774
Fax: 01824 702060

North Wales' premier centre for the applied arts. A Crafts Council selected Gallery housed within a purpose built craft centre in the picturesque Vale of Clwyd. The Gallery shows the best of fine crafts by contemporary designer-makers from all over the British Isles. The Centre also houses a restaurant and 10 Independent Craft Studios where Designer Craftsmen make a wide range of artefacts ranging from fine art prints, designer jewellery and bench glass blowing to folk art and domestic ceramics.

EXHIBITIONS/EVENTS

Annual programme of temporary exhibitions which aim to show the breadth of excellence in the field of applied arts, through a stimulating and diverse view of contemporary work. The Centre also runs educational craft workshops for adults and children. Programmes are available from the above address.

ADMISSION

Free parking and admission.

OPENING TIMES

Winter:
Mon–Sat 10am–5pm.
Sun 12 noon–5pm.
Summer:
Daily 10am–5.30pm.

POWYS

W.H. Smith

24 High Street
Newtown
Powys SY16 2NP
Tel: 01686 626280

This is a unique combination of a W.H. Smith branch and the company museum.

The shop, which is open for business as usual, has in most part been restored to its original state when it first opened 70 years ago in 1927. It has a solid oak shop front, fascinating decorative tiling, plaster reliefs and many other details.

Upstairs, on the 1st floor, the small museum traces the history of W.H. Smith, Newsagents & Booksellers, from its humble beginnings in 1792. When Henry Walton Smith and his wife Anna then started a news walk – or paper round – they created a family business which has flourished for over two centuries to become one of today's biggest British retailers and a household name. Displays, models and memorabilia chart this progress and provide a graphic account of the many changes that have taken place in the world of newspapers, Smith station bookstalls, libraries and shops.

ADMISSION

Free.

OPENING TIMES

Mon–Sat 9.00am–5.30pm. Closed Sundays and Bank Holidays.

MOST LIFEFORMS HAVE MADE THEIR WAY HERE OVER THE YEARS.

WHEN'S YOUR TURN?

THE NATURAL HISTORY MUSEUM

Monday-Saturday 10am-5.50pm   Sunday 11am-5.50pm

Cromwell Road, London SW7.   Nearest Underground: South Kensington.

Geographical listings

Listings of over 1,800 museums and galleries arranged alphabetically by country and county.

ENGLAND

BATH AND NORTH EAST SOMERSET

AMERICAN MUSEUM IN BRITAIN
Claverton Manor, Bath
BA2 7BD
Tel: 01225 460503
Fax: 01225 480726
American home life during 17th–19thC, including Native American Indian galleries, tours, object-handling, costume sessions and videos.
For further details see page 42

BATH INDUSTRIAL HERITAGE CENTRE
Camden Works, Julian Road, Bath BA1 2RH
Tel: 01225 318348
Fax: 01225 318348
Re-creation of a Victorian engineering brass-foundry and mineral-water business. Café, shop, temporary exhibitions throughout the year.

BATH POSTAL MUSEUM
8 Broad Street, Bath BA1 5LJ
Tel: 01225 460333
History of the Post and its Bath connections.

THE BOOK MUSEUM
Manvers Street, Bath BA1 1JW
Tel: 01225 466055
Fax: 01225 482122
The craft of bookbinding and Bath in literature featuring Jane Austen and Charles Dickens among others.

BUILDING OF BATH MUSEUM – THE COUNTESS OF HUNTINGDON'S CHAPEL
The Vineyards, The Paragon, Bath BA1 5NA
Tel: 01225 333895
Fax: 01225 445473
The Building of Bath Museum tells the story of how Georgian Bath was built.

FASHION RESEARCH CENTRE
4 Circus, Bath BA1 2EW
Tel: 01225 477752
Fax: 01225 444793
The centre contains a library and study collection of costume and accessories for use of students and members of the public near to the Museum of Costume.

HERSCHEL HOUSE MUSEUM
19 New King Street, Bath BA1 2BL
Tel: 01225 311342
The 18thC house of distinguished astronomer, scientist, musician and composer William Herschel.

HOLBORNE MUSEUM & CRAFTS STUDY CENTRE
Great Pulteney Street, Bath BA2 4DB
Tel: 01225 466669
Fax: 01225 333121
Fine collection of silver, porcelain, Old Master paintings, portrait miniatures, furniture and majolica; also 20thC crafts by British artists. Temporary exhibitions.
For further details see page 42

MUSEUM OF COSTUME
Assembly Rooms, Bennett Street, Bath BA1 2QH
Tel: 01225 477789
Fax: 01225 444793
Outstanding display of fashionable dress for men, women and children from 16thC to present day, including 'dress of the year' contemporary fashion.

MUSEUM OF EAST ASIAN ART
12 Bennett Street, Bath BA1 2QL
Tel: 01225 464640
Fax: 01225 461718
This unique museum houses a fine collection of Chinese, Japanese, Korean and South East Asian artefacts dating from c50000 BC
For further details see page 43

NO. 1 ROYAL CRESCENT
Bath BA1 2LR
Tel: 01225 428126
Fax: 01225 481850
A Georgian Town House in Bath's most magnificent crescent; redecorated and furnished to show the visitor how it might have appeared in the late 18th century.
For further details see page 44

OCTAGON GALLERIES
The Octagon, Milsom Street, Bath BA1 1DN
Tel: 01225 462841
Fax: 01225 448688
The second largest photographic exhibition space in the UK attracting some of the world's greatest photographers; names like Don McCullin, Sebastiao Salgado and David Bailey.
For further details see page 43

RADSTOCK MIDSOMER NORTON & DISTRICT MUSEUM
Barton Meade House, Haydon, Radstock, Bath BA3 3QS
Tel: 01761 437722
Features reconstructed coal face, miner's cottage, Victorian schoolroom, 1930s Co-op shop, joiner's shop, blacksmiths, John Wesley Room, geology and chapel china.

ROMAN BATHS & MUSEUM
Pump Room, Stall Street, Bath BA1 1LZ
Tel: 01225 477774
Fax: 01225 477743
Roman baths and temple precinct, hot springs and Roman temple.

THE ROYAL PHOTOGRAPHIC SOCIETY
Milsom Street, Bath BA1 1DN
Tel: 01225 462841
Fax: 01225 448688
This octagonal houses four large galleries devoted to constantly changing photographic exhibitions, a museum and a holography display. Café.
For further details see page 43

SALLY LUNN'S HOUSE
4 North Parade Passage, Bath BA1 1NX
Tel: 01225 461634
Fax: 01225 447090
The oldest house in Bath.

VICTORIA ART GALLERY
Pulteney Bridge, Bridge Street, Bath BA2 4AT
Tel: 01225 477233
Fax: 01225 477231
Permanent collection includes British and European fine art from 17–20thC and decorative arts.
For further details see page 44

BEDFORDSHIRE

BEDFORD MUSEUM
Castle Lane, Bedford, Bedfordshire MK40 3XD
Tel: 01234 353323
Fax: 01234 273401
Interesting displays of local archaeology, social and natural history and geology.

CECIL HIGGINS ART GALLERY
Castle Lane, Bedford, Bedfordshire MK40 3RP
Tel: 01234 211222
Victorian mansion built in 1846 and furnished late 19thC style.
For further details see page 44

JOHN DONY FIELD CENTRE
Hancock Drive, Bushmead, Luton LU2 7SF
Tel: 01582 486983
Fax: 01582 422805
Natural history site.

LUTON MUSEUM & ART GALLERY
Wardown Park, Luton, Bedfordshire LU2 7HA
Tel: 01582 746739
Fax: 01582 746763
Victorian mansion in 50 acres of parkland.

THE MOSSMAN COLLECTION
Stockwood Country Park, Farley Hill, Luton LU4 4BH
Tel: 01582 738714
Fax: 01582 746763
The Mossman Collection is Britain's largest collection of horse-drawn carriages and is displayed in a new purpose-built building.

SHUTTLEWORTH COLLECTION
Old Warden Aerodrome, Biggleswade, Bedfordshire SG18 9EP
Tel: 0891 323310
Fax: 01767 627745
Unique historic collection of aircraft from a 1909 Bleriot to a 1942 Spitfire in flying condition, plus cars dating from an 1898 Panhard in running order.

STOCKWOOD CRAFT MUSEUM & GARDENS
Stockwood Country Park, Farley Hill, Luton LU4 4BH
Tel: 01582 38714
Fax: 01582 746763
Bedfordshire craft displays and workshops – including blacksmith, wheelwright, saddler, shoemaker and thatcher – housed in an 18thC stable block.

STONDON MUSEUM
Station Road, Lower Stondon, Henlow, Bedfordshire SG16 6JN
Tel: 01462 850339
Fax: 01462 850824
Transport exhibits from the early 1900s to the 1980s.

BERKSHIRE

BLAKE'S LOCK MUSEUM
Gasworks Road, off Kenavon Drive, Reading, Berkshire RG1 3DH
Tel: 0118 939 0918
Fax: 01734 590630
Exhibitions of Reading's waterways, trades and industries.
For further details see page 45

CLEWER HISTORY MUSEUM & CHURCH
Church Lodge Mill Lane, Clewer, Windsor, Berkshire SL4 5JQ
Tel: 01753 865185
Small museum created by the Rev D Shaw of Clewer: including artefacts, domestic items, pictures and photos.

COLE MUSEUM OF ZOOLOGY
University of Reading, Whiteknights, Reading, Berkshire RG6 6AJ
Tel: 0118 987 5123
Fax: 0118 931 6671
A teaching museum concerned with comparative anatomy and relationships between animals.
For further details see page 45

DISCOVERY OUTPOST
The Look Out Discovery Park, Nine Mile Ride, Bracknell, Berkshire RG12 7QW
Tel: 01344 868222
Fax: 01344 869343
An interactive hands-on science and nature centre set in 2,600 acres of woodland. Adventure play area, coffee shop and gift shop.

DOUGLAS CLOCKS
30 Parkview Drive South, Charvil, Reading RG10 9QX
Tel: 0118 934 5192
Private house with a unique collection of pre-1930 battery-driven electric clocks and master clocks including a grandfather clock powered by the earth.

HOUSEHOLD CAVALRY MUSEUM
Combermere Barracks, Windsor, Berkshire SL4 3DN
Tel: 01753 755203
Collection of ancient firearms, swords, uniforms and horse furniture dating back to 1660.

MUSEUM OF ANCIENT WIRELESS
Datchet Cottage, 138 Horton Road, Datchet, Slough
Tel: 01753 542242

THE MUSEUM OF BERKSHIRE AVIATION
Woodley RG5 4UE
Tel: 01734 403038
Aircraft archives, photographs, related aviation items, uniforms, etc housed in historic hangar.

MUSEUM OF ENGLISH RURAL LIFE
University of Reading, Whiteknights, Reading, Berkshire RG6 6AG
Tel: 0118 931 8660
Fax: 0118 975 1264
A national collection of material relating to the history of the English countryside.
For further details see page 45

MUSEUM OF READING
The Town Hall, Blagrave Street, Reading, Berkshire RG1 1QH
Tel: 0118 939 9800
Fax: 0118 956 6719
The museum houses the story of Reading and Britain's Bayeux Tapestry plus the Silchester Gallery, a permanant display of finds from the Roman town of Calleva Atrebatum.
For further details see page 45

NEWBURY DISTRICT MUSEUM
The Wharf, Newbury, Berkshire RG14 5AS
Tel: 01635 30511
Displays include local history, archaeology, natural history, jewellery, costume, rural crafts, ballooning, K&A canal and 17thC civil war battles.

REME MUSEUM OF TECHNOLOGY
Isaac Newton Road, Arborfield, Reading RG2 9NJ
Tel: 0118 976 3567
Fax: 0118 976 3563
The museum houses displays and collections illustrating military technology and REME's part in developing and maintaining the Army's equipment.

SLOUGH MUSEUM
278-286 High Street, Slough SL1 3UF
Tel: 01753 526422
Slough Museum has local history displays and a programme of temporary exhibitions.

STANLEY SPENCER GALLERY
Kings Hall, High Street, Cookham on Thames SL6 9SJ
Tel: 01628 520890
Paintings and drawings by Spencer and memorabilia associated with the artist.

THE URE MUSEUM OF GREEK ARCHAEOLOGY
Department of Classics, Faculty of Letters, The University, Whiteknights, Reading, Berkshire RG6 2AA
Tel: 0118 931 8420
Fax: 0118 931 6661
The museum is contained in one large room at the end of the classics department corridor. Ideal for school visits.
For further details see page 45

BRISTOL

ARNOLFINI GALLERY
16 Narrow Quay, Bristol BS1 4QA
Tel: 0117 929 9191
Fax: 0117 925 3876
Exhibitions of contemporary visual art with visual arts education programme.
For further details see page 46

BLAGDON PUMPING STATION & VISITOR CENTRE
Blagdon Lake, Blagdon, Bristol
Tel: 0117 953 6470
Fax: 0117 953 6471
Working giant beam engine, exhibitions on water and the environment, hands-on displays, nature trail, trout-feeding sessions.

BLAISE CASTLE HOUSE MUSEUM
Henbury Road, Bristol BS10 7QS
Tel: 0117 950 6789
Late 18thC house in 400 acres of parkland, housing museum of everyday life.
For further details see page 45

BRISTOL CITY MUSEUMS & ART GALLERY
Queen's Road, Clifton, Bristol BS8 1RL
Tel: 0117 922 3571
Fax: 0117 922 2047
Collection representing applied oriental and fine art, archaeology, geology, natural history, ethnography and Egyptology.
For further details see page 45

BRISTOL INDUSTRIAL MUSEUM
Prince's Wharf, Wapping Road, Bristol BS1 4RN
Tel: 0117 925 1470
Fax: 0117 929 7318
Comprehensive range of exhibits relating to industrial history of Bristol and region.
For further details see page 45

THE EXPLORATORY HANDS-ON SCIENCE CENTRE
Bristol Old Station, Temple Meads, Bristol BS1 6QU
Tel: 0117 907 9000
Fax: 0117 907 8000
Exhibition of lights, lenses, lasers, bubbles, bridges, illusions, gyroscopes and much more all housed in Brunel's original engine shed and drawing office. Science you can handle. There are over 150 experiments.

THE GEORGIAN HOUSE
7 Great George Street, Bristol BS1 5RR
Tel: 0117 921 1362
An elegant town house of 1791.
For further details see page 45

HARVEYS WINE MUSEUM
12 Denmark Street, Bristol BS1 5DQ
Tel: 0117 927 5036
Fax: 0117 927 5001
Wine museum in original 13thC cellars displaying artefacts connected with production and enjoyment of wines especially glass, silver and corkscrews.

MONTY'S MUSEUM
46 Alpha Road, Southville, Bristol BS3 1DH
Tel: 0117 966 5693
Exhibits include old maps, newspapers, postcards, sheet music, fashion plates, pictures and prints.

THE RED LODGE
Park Row, Bristol S1 5LJ
Tel: 0117 921 1360
The only surviving Tudor domestic interior in Bristol.
For further details see page 45

BUCKINGHAMSHIRE

AMERSHAM MUSEUM
49 High Street, Amersham, Buckinghamshire HP7 0DP
Tel: 01494 725754
Fax: 01494 725754
Small but expanding collection relating to Amersham and district from Roman times to the present day in the restored part of a 15thC house.

BUCKINGHAMSHIRE COUNTY MUSEUM
Church Street, Aylesbury, Buckinghamshire HP20 2QP
Tel: 01296 331441
Fax: 01296 334884
Award-winning lively, hands-on, innovative museum complex consisting of county heritage displays, regional art gallery and Roald Dahl Children's gallery.
For further details see page 46

CHILTERN OPEN AIR MUSEUM
Newland Park, Gorelands Lane, Chalfont St Giles, Buckinghamshire HP8 4AD
Tel: 01494 872163
Historic buildings rescued from demolition and re-erected at Newland Park with displays and exhibitions showing rural life from Iron Age to 1940s.

COWPER & NEWTON MUSEUM
Orchard Side, Market Place, Olney, Buckinghamshire MK46 4AJ
Tel: 01234 711516
Three-storey Georgian home of poet and hymn-composer William Cowper.

FENNY LODGE GALLERY
Simpson Road, Fenny Stratford, Bletchley, Milton Keynes MK1 1BD
Tel: 01908 642207
Fax: 01908 647840
18thC house on the Grand Union Canal showing an extensive range of paintings, ceramics, glass and jewellery.

MILTON KEYNES MUSEUM
Stacey Hill Farm, Wolverton, Milton Keynes, Buckinghamshire MK12 5EJ
Tel: 01908 316222
Extensive display of agricultural and industrial machinery, domestic printing and photographic artefacts, tracing 100 years of local North Buckinghamshire life.

OLD GAOL MUSEUM
Market Hill, Buckingham, Buckinghamshire MK18 1JX
Tel: 01280 823020

PITSTONE GREEN FARM MUSEUM
Vicarage Road, Pitstone, Leighton Buzzard, Bedfordshire LU7 9EY
Tel: 01296 668223
Major collection of historical farm implements, local rural crafts and domestic bygones housed in listed farm buildings.

ROALD DAHL CHILDREN'S GALLERY
Buckinghamshire County Museum, Church Street, Aylesbury, Buckinghamshire HP20 2QP
Tel: 01296 331441
Fax: 01296 334884
Unique hands-on gallery for children where exhibits will boggle the eyes and baffle the brain! Winner of the 1997 Gulbenkian Award for education.
For further details see page 46

WYCOMBE LOCAL HISTORY & CHAIR MUSEUM
Castle Hill House, Priory Avenue, High Wycombe, Buckinghamshire HP13 6PX
Tel: 01494 421895
Fax: 01494 421897
The museum looks at the crafts and history of the local area, highlighting the importance of the furniture industry with a collection of Windsor chairs.
For further details see page 46

CAMBRIDGESHIRE

BURWELL MUSEUM TRUST
Mill Close, Burwell, Cambridge, Cambridgeshire CB5 0HJ
Tel: 01638 741512
Rural village museum housed in re-erected 18thC timber-framed barn.

CAMBRIDGE & COUNTY FOLK MUSEUM
2–3 Castle Street, Cambridge, Cambridgeshire CB3 0AQ
Tel: 01223 355159
18th–20thC collection illustrating life and work of the county's people.

CAMBRIDGE UNIVERSITY COLLECTION OF AIR PHOTOGRAPHS
The Mond Building, Free School Lane, Cambridge, Cambridgeshire CB2 3RF
Tel: 01223 334578
Fax: 01223 334400
Display of photos in entrance hall; otherwise catering for special enquiries only.

CROMWELL MUSEUM
Grammar School Walk, Huntingdon, Cambridgeshire PE18 6HP
Tel: 01480 425830
Fax: 01480 459563
Portraits, signed documents and other articles belonging to Cromwell and his family.
For further details see page 46

ELY MUSEUM
28c High Street, Ely, Cambridgeshire CB7 4HL
Tel: 01353 666655
A chronological account of the history of Ely and the Isle, from prehistory to the present day.

FARMLAND MUSEUM AND DENNY ABBEY
Ely Road, Waterbeach, Cambridgeshire CB5 9PQ
Tel: 01223 860988
Local museum dedicated to displaying life on the land.

FITZWILLIAM MUSEUM
Trumpington Street, Cambridge, Cambridgeshire CB2 1RB
Tel: 01223 332900
Fax: 01223 332923
Large internationally renowned collection of antiquities, applied arts and fine arts.

IMPERIAL WAR MUSEUM DUXFORD
Duxford Airfield, Duxford, Cambridge, Cambridgeshire CB2 4QR
Tel: 01223 835000
Fax: 01223 837267
Over 140 aircraft on display plus tanks, vehicles and guns.
For further details see page 55

KETTLE'S YARD
Castle Street, Cambridge, Cambridgeshire CB3 0AQ
Tel: 01223 352124
Fax: 01223 324377
Major collection of 20thC paintings and sculpture exhibited in a house of unique character.

MARCH & DISTRICT MUSEUM
High Street, March, Cambridgeshire PE15 9JJ
Tel: 01354 655300
General collection of artefacts relating to social history, especially local history and local records.

MUSEUM OF TECHNOLOGY
The Old Pumping Station, Cheddars Lane, Cambridge, Cambridgeshire CB5 8HN
Tel: 01223 368650
Victorian pumping station housing unique Hawthorn Davey steam pumping engines and electrical equipment.

NORRIS MUSEUM
The Broadway, St Ives, Huntingdon, Cambridgeshire PE17 4BX
Tel: 01480 465101
The history of Huntingdonshire from earliest times to the present day.

OCTAVIA HILL BIRTHPLACE MUSEUM
1 South Brink Place, Wisbech, Cambridgeshire PE13 1JE
Tel: 01945 476358
Fax: 01945 467358
Museum in the grade 2 Georgian building in which Octavia Hill, social reformer and co-founder of the National Trust, was born.

OLIVER CROMWELL'S HOUSE
29 St Marys Street, Ely, Cambridgeshire CB7 4HF
Tel: 01353 662062
Fax: 01353 668518
Family home of Oliver Cromwell.

PETERBOROUGH MUSEUM & ART GALLERY
Priestgate, Peterborough, Cambridgeshire PE1 1LF
Tel: 01733 343329
Fax: 01733 391428
Classic Jurassic Age collection of some of the best dinosaur specimens in Britain. The history of Peterborough and the surrounding area from the bronze age to the present day. An excellent art collection including works by Turner, Sickert and Elizabeth Frink.
For further details see page 47

PRICKWILLOW ENGINE MUSEUM
Main Street, Prickwillow, Ely, Cambridgeshire CB7 4UN
Tel: 01353 688360
Fax: 01353 723456
Mirrlees Bickerton and Day diesel engine, plus four other diesel engines. Café for light refreshments. Free car park.

RAMSEY RURAL MUSEUM
The Wood Yard, Cemetery Road, Ramsey, Huntingdon, Cambridgeshire PE17
Tel: 01487 815715
Rebuilt farm buildings housing a collection of old farm implements of the Fens and exhibition of Victorian life in the home.

ST NEOTS MUSEUM
The Old Court, 8 New Street, St Neots, Huntingdon, Cambridgeshire PE19 1RE
Tel: 01480 388788
A new local history museum in former police station/court building. Attractive displays tell the story of St Neots area.
For further details see page 47

SEDGWICK MUSEUM
Department of Earth Sciences, Downing Street, Cambridge, Cambridgeshire CB2 3EQ
Tel: 01223 333456
Large collection of fossils from all over the world, both invertebrate and vertebrate.

STAINED GLASS MUSEUM
The Cathedral, Ely, Cambridgeshire CB7 4DN
Tel: 01353 667735/6
Fax: 01223 327367
Examples of stained glass from 13thC to present day in specially lit display boxes.

THORNEY HERITAGE MUSEUM
Station Road, Thorney, Peterborough, Cambridgeshire PE6 0QE
Tel: 01733 270908
Models development from monastic days, Walloon Fleming influence after Vermuydens drainage installed.

UNIVERSITY MUSEUM OF ARCHAEOLOGY & ANTHROPOLOGY
Downing Street, Cambridge, Cambridgeshire CB2 3DZ
Tel: 01223 337733
Displays relating to world pre-history, anthropology and local archaeology.

WHIPPLE MUSEUM OF THE HISTORY OF SCIENCE
Free School Lane, Cambridge, Cambridgeshire CB2 3RH
Tel: 01223 334540
Fax: 01223 334545
Extensive collection of scientific instruments.

WHITTLESEY MUSEUM
Town Hall, Market Street, Whittlesey, Peterborough, Cambridgeshire PE7 1BD
Tel: 01733 840968
Archaeology, agriculture, hand tools, brickmaking and local photos. Local history.

WISBECH & FENLAND MUSEUM
Museum Square, Wisbech, Cambridgeshire PE13 1ES
Tel: 01945 583817
Purpose-built Victorian local history museum.

CHESHIRE

BOAT MUSEUM
South Pier Road, Ellesmere Port, Cheshire L65 4FW
Tel: 0151 355 5017
Fax: 0151 355 4079
Over 50 historic craft housed in the largest floating collection in the world, with restored buildings, traditional cottages, workshops, steam engines, boat trips, shop and café.

CATALYST – THE MUSEUM OF THE CHEMICAL INDUSTRY
Mersey Road, Widnes, Cheshire WA8 0DF
Tel: 0151 420 1121
Fax: 0151 495 2030
Catalyst offers a unique award-winning formula of interactive exhibits and historical displays.

CHESHIRE MILITARY MUSEUM
The Castle, Chester CH1 2DN
Tel: 01244 327617
Fax: 01244 327617
Regimentalia of four Regiments: the 5th Royal Inniskilling Dragoon Guards, the 3rd Carabiniers, the Cheshire Yeomanry and the 22nd (Cheshire) Regiment.

CHESTER HERITAGE CENTRE
St Michael's Church, Bridge Street Row, Chester, Cheshire
Tel: 01244 402008
Fax: 01244 347587
Displays, models and video footage illustrating Chester's history and architecture.
For further details see page 47

CHESTER TOY & DOLL MUSEUM
13a Lower Bridge Street, Chester CH1 1RS
Tel: 01244 346297
Fax: 01244 340437
Boys' and girls' toys through the ages.

DEVA ROMAN EXPERIENCE
Pierpoint Lane, Bridge Street, Chester, Cheshire CH1 1NL
Tel: 01244 343407
Fax: 01244 343407
Roman galley and typical Roman street with museum display area, hands-on area and souvenir shop.

GRIFFIN TRUST
Hooton Park, North Road, Ellesmere Port, South Wirral L65 1BQ
Tel: 0151 350 2598
World War I grade II listed buildings (being renovated at present) housing vintage vehicles of all descriptions.

GROSVENOR MUSEUM
27 Grosvenor Street, Chester, Cheshire CH1 2DD
Tel: 01244 402008
Fax: 01244 347587
Internationally renowned Roman collections with displays illustrating the organisation of the Roman army.
For further details see page 47

KING CHARLES TOWER
City Wall, Chester, Cheshire
Tel: 01244 402008
Exhibition telling the story of Chester in the Civil War.
For further details see page 47

MACCLESFIELD SILK MUSEUM
The Heritage Centre, Roe Street, Macclesfield, Cheshire SK11 6UT
Tel: 01625 613210
Fax: 01625 617880
Silk trail, award-winning silk museum and guided tours of paradise mill, a working silk mill until 1981.

MOULDSWORTH MOTOR MUSEUM
Smithy Lane, Mouldsworth, Chester CH3 8AR
Tel: 01928 731781
Over 60 veteran vintage, postvintage and classic cars and motorcycles. Museum is directed by a qualified lecturer/teacher.

NANTWICH MUSEUM
Pillory Street, Nantwich, Cheshire CW5 5BQ
Tel: 01270 627104
Local history and dairy exhibition and temporary monthly exhibitions.

NORTON PRIORY MUSEUM & GARDENS
Tudor Road, Runcorn, Cheshire WA7 1SX
Tel: 01928 569895
Excavated Augustinian priory, remains of church cloister, chapter house. Museum gallery. Two and a half acre walled garden, woodland, sculpture trail.

ON THE AIR – THE BROADCAST MUSEUM
42 Bridge Street Row, Chester, Cheshire CH1 1NN
Tel: 01244 348468
Museum of radio and television broadcasting.

PARADISE MILL
Park Lane, Macclesfield, Cheshire SK11 6UT
Tel: 01625 618228
Fax: 01625 617880
Twenty-six Jacquard hand looms.

QUARRY BANK MILL
Styal, Wilmslow, Cheshire SK9 4LA
Tel: 01625 527468
Fax: 01625 539267
Georgian water-powered cotton spinning mill with four floors of displays and demonstrations in 284 acres of parkland.

SALT MUSEUM
162 London Road, Northwich, Cheshire CW9 8AB
Tel: 01606 41331
Fax: 01606 350420
Museum deals with history and development of salt making in Cheshire from early times to the present day.

TABLEY CUCKOO CLOCK COLLECTION
Old School House, Chester Road, Tabley, Knutsford, Cheshire WA16 0HL
Tel: 01565 633039
Fax: 01565 750462
The largest collection on display of Black Forest cuckoo clocks in the world. Also fair ground organs, street organ.

WARRINGTON MUSEUM & ART GALLERY
Bold Street, Warrington, Cheshire WA1 1JG
Tel: 01925 442392
Fax: 01925 442399
Display of local and natural history, geology, ethnology, Egyptology, 19thC oils, watercolours, local glass and clocks.
For further details see page 48

WEST PARK MUSEUM
(c/o Macclesfield Museums), Prestbury Road, Macclesfield, Cheshire SK11 6UT
Tel: 01625 613210
Fax: 01625 617880
Paintings by C F Tunnicliffe and others, Egyptian antiquities, items of local historical interest.

CORNWALL

AUTOMOBILIA – CORNWALL'S MOTOR MUSEUM
The Old Mill, St Stephen, St Austell, Cornwall PL26 7RX
Tel: 01726 823092
Fax: 01726 823092
Over 50 vehicles dating from 1904–1960s including motor cycles and commercial vehicles.

BARBARA HEPWORTH MUSEUM & SCULPTURE GARDEN
Barnoon Hill, St Ives, Cornwall TR26 1AD
Tel: 01736 796226
Fax: 01736 794480
Home of the late Dame Barbara Hepworth from 1949–75. Permanent exhibition of sculpture, tools and archive material.

BODMIN MUSEUM
Mount Folly Square, Bodmin, Cornwall PL31 2DQ
Tel: 01208 74159
Fax: 01208 79268
Items connected with local history, natural history, geological and folk customs.

BRITISH CYCLING MUSEUM
The Old Station, Camelford, Cornwall PL32 9TZ
Tel: 01840 212811
A history of cycles plus cycling memorabilia from 1818 to modern times. The nation's foremost museum of cycling history.

BUDE-STRATTON MUSEUM
The Wharf, Bude, Cornwall EX23 8LG
Tel: 01288 353576
Fax: 01288 353576
The development of town and canal traced through photographs.

CAMBORNE MUSEUM
Public Library, The Cross, Camborne, Cornwall TR14 8HA
Tel: 01209 713544
Exhibits relating to mining and the life of Richard Trevithick.

CAMBORNE SCHOOL OF MINES GEOLOGICAL MUSEUM & ART GALLERY
University of Exeter, Redruth, Cornwall TR15 3SE
Tel: 01209 714866
Fax: 01209 716977
Collection of rocks and minerals from all over the world. Monthly art shows by local artists.

COPELAND CHINA COLLECTION
Trelissick Mansion, Feock, Truro, Cornwall TR3 6QL
Tel: 01872 862248
Collection of bone china manufactured by Spode and Copeland (1770–1970).

CORNWALL MARITIME MUSEUM
2 Bell's Court, Market Street, Falmouth, Cornwall TR11 2AZ
Tel: 01736 368890
Historic listed building, with displays of models, artefacts, pictures and photographs, on the maritime history of Cornwall.

DUKE OF CORNWALL'S INFANTRY MUSEUM
The Keep, Lostwithiel Road, Bodmin, Cornwall PL31 1EG
Tel: 01208 72810
Fax: 01208 72810
Military museum containing weapons, medals, uniforms and battle relics, covering the regiment's history from 1702 to the present day.

FALMOUTH ART GALLERY
Municipal Buildings, The Moor, Falmouth, Cornwall TR11 2RT
Tel: 01326 313863
Fax: 01326 312662
Regularly changing exhibitions of contemporary artists, travelling exhibitions, topics of local interest.

GEEVOR TIN MINE
Pendeen, Penzance, Cornwall TR19 7EW
Tel: 01736 788662
Fax: 01736 786059
Cornish mining museum, tours of surface plant and video film. Underground visits, shop and panoramic café.

HELSTON FOLK MUSEUM
The Old Butter Market, Church Street, Helston, Cornwall TR13 8TA
Tel: 01326 564027
Folk museum covering the history of the town and surroundings.

HOLOGRAMA
43 Bank Street, Newquay, Cornwall TR7 5PD
Tel: 01637 877531
Fax: 01637 877531
Permanent exhibition of holography and illusion.

ISLES OF SCILLY MUSEUM
Church Street, St Mary's, Isles of Scilly TR21 0JT
Tel: 01720 422337
Fax: 01720 422337
All items dealing with the geology, archaeology, history and natural history of the Isles of Scilly.

JAMAICA INN MUSEUMS (POTTERS MUSEUM OF CURIOSITY)
Jamaica Inn Courtyard, Bolventor, Launceston, Cornwall PL15 7TS
Tel: 01566 86250/86838
Museum containing lifetime's work of Walter Potter, a Victorian taxidermist. Also Daphne Du Maurier's smugglers at Jamaica Inn.
For further details see pages IFC & 48

LANREATH FOLK & FARM MUSEUM
Churchtown, Lanreath-by-Looe, Looe, Cornwall PL13 2NX
Tel: 01503 220321
Tithe barn in which mill workings are assembled.

LAWRENCE HOUSE
9 Castle Street, Launceston, Cornwall PL15 8BA
Tel: 01566 773277
Local history museum housed in elegant Georgian house built in 1753, situated in Castle Street, close to the remains of the great Norman keep of Launceston Castle.

LEVANT STEAM ENGINE
Trewellard, Pendeen, Nr St Just, Cornwall
Tel: 01736 88662
Fax: 01736 786059

LOOK 3D
The Bridge, Boscastle, Cornwall PL35 0HE
Tel: 01840 250248
Fax: 01840 250248
Exhibition containing around 100 holograms on a 'cave' theme plus several large purpose-built exhibits.

MARITIME MUSEUM
19 Chapel Street, Penzance, Cornwall TR18 4AF
Tel: 01736 68890
Main exhibit is an exhibition section of an 18thC man-o-war with four decks of men and guns to full scale.

MEVAGISSEY FOLK MUSEUM
East Quay, Mevagissey, St Austell, Cornwall PL26 6QQ
Tel: 01726 843568
Local domestic fishing and agricultural exhibits.

NEWLYN ART GALLERY
New Road, Newlyn, Penzance, Cornwall TR18 5PZ
Tel: 01736 363715
Fax: 01736 331578
Changing exhibitions of contemporary art by leading local, national and international artists.

NORTH CORNWALL MUSEUM & GALLERY
The Clease, Camelford, Cornwall PL32 9PL
Tel: 01840 212954
Fax: 01840 212954
Reconstruction of the upstairs and downstairs of a Cornish cottage.

OLD GUILDHALL MUSEUM
Higher Market Street, East Looe, Looe, Cornwall PL13 1BP
Tel: 01503 263709
Artefacts and photographs, chiefly on the history of Looe, housed in former 16thC courthouse.

PADSTOW MUSEUM
The Institute, Market Place, Padstow, Cornwall PL28 8AD
Tel: 01841 532574
Local museum exhibiting material relating to Padstow and its environs including 'Obby 'Oss custom lifeboat, railway tools, domestic artefacts, photographs, shipwrecks.

PAUL CORIN'S MAGNIFICENT MUSIC MACHINES
St Keyne Station, St Keyne, Liskeard, Cornwall PL14 4SH
Tel: 01579 43108
Collection includes carousel organs, café organs, orchestrions, American Wurlitzer theatre pipe organ. Mechanical music of the 1890–1930 era.

PENLEE HOUSE GALLERY & MUSEUM
Morrab Road, Penzance, Cornwall TR18 4HE
Tel: 01736 363625
Fax: 01736 361312
Social history of man in the Land's End peninsula. Painting by the Newlyn school of artists.
For further details see page 48

PENWITH GALLERIES
Back Road West, St Ives, Cornwall TR26 1NL
Tel: 01736 795579
Continuous exhibitions of paintings, sculpture, pottery. Print and poster shop.

PERRANZABULOE FOLK MUSEUM
Ponsmere Road, Perranporth, Cornwall TR6 0BW
Tel: 01872 573368
Museum housed on first floor of 19thC Oddfellows Hall.

PLEASE REMEMBER – DON'T FORGET
34 Fore Street, Fowey, Cornwall PL23 1AQ
A celebration of collecting and in particular the varied work of world-famous artist Mabel Lucie Attwell, who spent the last 20 years of her lively life in Fowey.

PORTHCURNO MUSEUM OF SUBMARINE TELEGRAPHY
Porthcurno, Penzance, Cornwall TR19 6JX
Tel: 01209 612142
Fax: 01209 612142
A secret underground World War II tunnel system now houses the best museum of communications in the world.

ROYAL CORNWALL MUSEUM
River Street, Truro, Cornwall TR1 2SJ
Tel: 01872 72205
Fax: 01872 40514
World famous mineral collection, Old Master drawings, ceramics and oil paintings by the Newlyn School and others including John Opie and Hogarth.

ROYAL GEOLOGICAL SOCIETY OF CORNWALL MUSEUM
Alverton Street, Penzance, Cornwall TR18 2QR
A representative collection mainly of Cornish rocks, minerals and fossils related to main extractive industries of County.

ST IVES MUSEUM
Wheal Dream, St Ives, Cornwall TR26 1JN
Tel: 01736 796005
Cornish heritage displays covering fishing, the Great Western Railway and maritime connections.

ST IVES SOCIETY OF ARTISTS OLD MARINERS CHURCH
Norway Square, St Ives, Cornwall TR26 1NA
Tel: 01736 795582
Fax: 01736 731823
Oil paintings, water colours, sculptures, wood carvings and etchings, mostly in representational style.

TATE GALLERY ST IVES
Porthmeor Beach, St Ives, Cornwall TR26 1TG
Tel: 01736 796226
Fax: 01736 794480
A major new gallery showing changing groups of work from the Tate Gallery's pre-eminent collection of St Ives painting and sculpture.
For further details see page 49

TREVARNO HOUSE MUSEUM
Trevarno Estate, Helston, Cornwall TR13 0RU
Tel: 01326 574274
Fax: 01326 574282
The recently opened gardens and grounds provide a magical and atmospheric backdrop to a new and fascinating gardening museum housing what is believed to be the largest and most comprehensive collection of implements, requisites, ephemera and related gardening items in the country.
For further details see page 49

TRINITY HOUSE NATIONAL LIGHTHOUSE CENTRE
Wharf Road, Penzance, Cornwall TR18 4BN
Tel: 01736 60077
The national collection of lighthouse and vessel equipment development during the last 400 years.

TUNNELS THROUGH TIME
St Michael's Road, Newquay, Cornwall TR7 1RA
Tel: 01637 873379
Exhibition of over 70 full-sized characters portraying Cornish stories and legends.

WAYSIDE FOLK MUSEUM
Old Mill House, Zennor, St Ives, Cornwall TR26 3DA
Tel: 01736 796945
Artefacts of very local origin – farming, tin mining, mill, domestic forge, wheelwright's shop.

WHEAL MARTYN CHINA CLAY HERITAGE CENTRE
Carthew, St Austell, Cornwall PL26 8XG
Tel: 01726 850362
Fax: 01726 850362
Restored 19thC clay works. Historic and nature trails, working water wheels.

COUNTY DURHAM

THE ANKER'S HOUSE MUSEUM
The Parish Centre, Church Chare, Chester Le Street, County Durham DH3 3QB
Tel: 0191 388 3295
An anchorage attached to the church, with displays on Roman, Saxon and Medieval times.

BEAMISH
The North of England Open Air Museum, Beamish, County Durham DH9 0RG
Tel: 01207 231811
Fax: 01207 290933
Visit a town colliery, village farm and railway station all re-created to show life in the north of England early this century.

DARLINGTON RAILWAY CENTRE & MUSEUM
North Road Station, Darlington, County Durham DL3 6ST
Tel: 01325 460532
Restored 1842 station housing a collection of exhibits relating to railways in the north east of England, including Stephenson's Locomotion.

DURHAM LIGHT INFANTRY MUSEUM & DURHAM ART GALLERY
Aykley Heads, Durham DH1 5TU
Tel: 0191 384 2214
Fax: 0191 386 1770
Museum houses a collection tracing 200 years of the DLI county regiment, including medals and uniforms.

DURHAM UNIVERSITY ORIENTAL MUSEUM
Elvet Hill (Off South Road), Durham DH1 3TH
Tel: 0191 374 7911
Fax: 0191 374 3242
Exhibits on ancient Egypt, Eastern religion, Japanese arts and crafts, Chinese ceramics and jade, and the development of writing.

JOSEPHINE & JOHN BOWES MUSEUM
Barnard Castle, County Durham DL12 8NP
Tel: 01833 690606
Fax: 01833 637163
French-style chateau housing art collections of national importance and archaeology of south west Durham

KILLHOPE LEAD MINING CENTRE
Cowshill, County Durham DL13 1AR
Tel: 01388 537505
Fax: 01388 537617
Experience the life and work of Victorian leadmining families, including guided tours of park level mine.

MONKS DORMITORY
Durham Cathedral, The College, Durham DH1 3EH
Tel: 0191 386 4266
Anglo-Saxon stones, medieval timbered roof, items of local interest.

MUSEUM OF ARCHAEOLOGY
The Old Fulling Mill, The Banks, Durham DH1 3EB
Tel: 0191 374 3623
Exhibitions on archaeology of Durham city and county.

TIMOTHY HACKWORTH VICTORIAN & RAILWAY MUSEUM
Soho Cottages, Shildon, County Durham DL4 2QX
Tel: 01388 777999
Former home of Timothy Hackworth (1786–1850), railway pioneer. Museum houses artefacts, memorabilia and rolling stock to tell the story of Stockton and Darlington railway, Hackworth's genius and the effect Shildon had on the industrial world.

THE WEARDALE MUSEUM OF HIGH HOUSE CHAPEL
Ireshopeburn, Bishop Auckland, County Durham
Tel: 01388 537417
Formerly manse to the High House Chapel.

CUMBRIA

ABBOT HALL ART GALLERY
Abbot Hall, Kirkland, Kendal, Cumbria LA9 5AL
Tel: 01539 722464
Fax: 01539 722494
18thC mansion house.
For further details see page 50

ASPECTS OF MOTORING
The Maltings, Brewery Lane, Cockermouth, Cumbria CA13 9NE
Tel: 01900 824448
Museum exhibiting cars and motorcycles from the worlds of sport and leisure.

BEATRIX POTTER GALLERY
Main Street, Hawkshead, Ambleside, Cumbria LA22 0NS
Tel: 015394 36355
Award-winning exhibition of a selection of Beatrix Potter's original drawings and children's story book illustrations.

BECKSTONES ART GALLERY
Greystoke Ghyll, Penrith, Cumbria CA11 0UQ
Tel: 017684 83601
Specialist art gallery exhibiting original paintings by more than 30 leading artists.

BORDER REGIMENT & KINGS OWN ROYAL BORDER REGIMENT MUSEUM
Queen Mary's Tower, The Castle, Carlisle, Cumbria CA3 8UR
Tel: 01228 32774
Fax: 01228 21275
300 years of Cumbria's County Infantry Regiment: weapons, uniforms, trophies, medals, silver, paintings, model dioramas, archives and photographs.

CARLISLE CATHEDRAL TREASURY MUSEUM
Carlisle Cathedral, Castle Street, Carlisle CA3 8TZ
Tel: 01228 35169
The underground treasury contains a fine display of cathedral and diocesan silver and treasures illustrating the story of Christians in Cumbria through the centuries.

CARS OF THE STARS MOTOR MUSEUM
Standish Street, Keswick, Cumbria CA12 5LS
Tel: 017687 73757
Fax: 017687 72810
Features TV and film vehicles, including the Batmobile, Chitty Chitty Bang Bang, the James Bond collection, Herbie, FAB 1, plus many other famous cars and motorcycles.

CASTLEGATE HOUSE GALLERY
Castlegate, Cockermouth, Cumbria CA13 9HA
Tel: 01900 822149
Fax: 01900 822149
A listed Georgian house built in 1739 opposite Cockermouth Castle, containing original paintings, ceramics, sculpture and glass.

CUMBERLAND PENCIL MUSEUM
Southey Works, Keswick, Cumbria CA12 5NG
Tel: 017687 73626
Fax: 017687 74679
The pencil story from the discovery of graphite to present methods.

CUMBERLAND TOY & MODEL MUSEUM
Banks Court, Market Place, Cockermouth, Cumbria CA13 9NG
Tel: 01900 827606
A century of toys with visitor operated exhibits.

DOCK MUSEUM
North Road, Barrow-in-Furness, Cumbria LA14 2PW
Tel: 01229 870871
Fax: 01229 811361
The museum that presents the story of steel shipbuilding, for which Barrow is famous, straddles a Victorian graving dock.

THE DOLLS' HOUSE MAN AT FURNESS GALLERIES
1 Theatre Street, Ulverston, Cumbria LA12 7AQ
Tel: 01229 587657
Wooden dolls' houses made and displayed along with prints and paintings by local artists.

FLORENCE MINE HERITAGE CENTRE
Florence Mine, Egremont, Cumbria CA22 2NR
Tel: 01946 820683
Fax: 01946 820683
Mine museum with simulated underground workings, geology display, souvenir and coffee shop.

GOSSIPGATE GALLERY
The Butts, Alston, Cumbria CA9 3JU
Tel: 01434 381806
Exhibitions and a permanent collection of northern art, craft and food from Cumbria, Durham and Northumberland.

THE GUILD HALL MUSEUM
Greenmarket, Carlisle
Tel: 01228 34781
Fax: 01228 810249
Only remaining restored medieval half-timbered building in Carlisle, housing objects from the city's eight trade guilds.

HELENA THOMPSON MUSEUM
Park End Road, Workington, Cumbria CA14 4DE
Tel: 01900 62598
Costume and embroidery collection, jewellery, applied art, local, social and industrial history.
For further details see page 49

K VILLAGE HERITAGE CENTRE
Lound Road, Netherfield, Kendal, Cumbria LA9 7DA
Tel: 01539 732363

KENDAL MUSEUM
Station Road, Kendal, Cumbria LA9 6BT
Tel: 01539 721374
An outstanding natural history gallery with reconstructions of Lake District habitats. Archaeology and local history including interactive Kendal castle displays.

KESWICK MUSEUM & ART GALLERY
Fitz Park, Station Road, Keswick, Cumbria CA12 4NF
Tel: 017687 73263
Collection of manuscripts from the Romantic poets, centred on Robert Southey, also Hugh Walpole. Geology and archaeology.
For further details see page 48

LABURNUM CERAMICS
Yanwath, Nr Penrith, Cumbria CA10 2LF
Tel: 01768 864842
Small rural studio/gallery devoted to individually-made high-quality ceramics and glass. Eighty artist-craftsmen, Cumbrian, British and overseas.

LAKELAND MOTOR MUSEUM
Holker Hall, Cark in Cartmel, Grange-over-Sands, Cumbria LA11 7PL
Tel: 015395 58509
Fax: 015395 58509
Over 150 historic cars, motorcycles, bicycles and engines, including rare motoring automobilia and the Campbell legend Bluebird exhibition.

LAUREL & HARDY MUSEUM
4c Upper Brook Street, Ulverston, Cumbria LA12 7BQ
Tel: 01229 582292
Fax: 01229 582292
This world famous museum contains the largest collection of Laurel and Hardy memorabilia known, includes a free cinema showing films.

LOWES COURT GALLERY
12 Main Street, Egremont, Cumbria CA22 2DW
Tel: 01946 820693
An 18thC building restored by locals to promote appreciation of the arts.

MARYPORT MARITIME MUSEUM
1 Senhouse Street, Maryport, Cumbria CA15 6AB
Tel: 01900 813738
Local history collection emphasising Maryport's maritime tradition, including Fletcher Christian and the ill-fated Titanic.
For further details see page 49

MILLOM FOLK MUSEUM
St Georges Road, Millom, Cumbria LA18 4DQ
Tel: 01229 772555
Reconstruction of iron-ore mine with cage miner's cottage and blacksmith's forge.

MUSEUM OF LAKELAND LIFE & INDUSTRY
Abbot Hall, Kendal, Cumbria LA9 5AL
Tel: 01539 722464
Fax: 01539 722494
Reconstructions of workshops/farmhouse rooms.
For further details see page 50

NENTHEAD MINES HERITAGE CENTRE
Nenthead, Cumbria CA9 3PD
Tel: 01434 382037

PENRITH MUSEUM
Robinson's School, Middlegate, Penrith, Cumbria CA11 7PT
Tel: 01768 64671
Fax: 01768 890732
Local history museum for Penrith and the Eden district, housed in a former 17thC girls' charity school.

PRINTING HOUSE MUSEUM
102 Main Street, Cockermouth, Cumbria CA13 9LX
Tel: 01900 824984
Fax: 01900 823124
Preserve and conserve a representative collection of printing machinery to illustrate the history and evoloution of printing by guided tour.

RAVENGLASS RAILWAY MUSEUM
Ravenglass and Eskdale Railway Co Ltd, Ravenglass, Cumbria CA18 1SW
Tel: 01229 717171
History of the Ravenglass and Eskdale Railway with relics, models, photographs and a slide show.

SENHOUSE ROMAN MUSEUM
The Battery, Sea Brows, Maryport, Cumbria CA15 6JD
Tel: 01900 816168
Once the headquarters of Hadrian's coastal defence system.

THORNTHWAITE GALLERIES
Thornthwaite, Keswick, Cumbria CA12 5SA
Tel: 017687 78248
This charming 200 year-old building houses a splendid selection of oils and watercolours by lake artists.

THRELKELD QUARRY & MINING MUSEUM
Threlkeld Quarry, Threlkeld, Keswick, Cumbria CA12 4TT
Tel: 017687 79747
Building containing unique collection of mining/quarrying artefacts, memorabilia, minerals.

TULLIE HOUSE MUSEUM & ART GALLERY
Castle Street, Carlisle, Cumbria CA3 8TP
Tel: 01228 34781
Fax: 01228 810249
Major tourist complex housing museum, art gallery, education facility, lecture theatre, shop, herb garden, restaurant and terrace bars.

ULVERSTON HERITAGE CENTRE
Lower Brook Street, Ulverston, Cumbria LA12 7EE
Tel: 01229 580820

WINDERMERE STEAMBOAT MUSEUM
Rayrigg Road, Bowness-on-Windermere, Windermere, Cumbria LA23 1BN
Tel: 015394 45565
Fax: 015394 48769
A wealth of interest and information about life on bygone Windermere. Including classic steam and motor boat exhibits and cruises.

WORKINGTON HALL
c/o Tourism Section, Allerdale Borough Council, Workington, Cumbria CA14 3YJ
Tel: 01900 735408
Fax: 01900 735346
Built around the 14thC pele tower this striking ruin was once one of the finest manor houses in the region. Mary Queen of Scots spent her last night of freedom here in 1568. Guided and taped tours available.
For further details see page 49

THE WORLD OF BEATRIX POTTER ATTRACTION
The Old Laundry, Crag Brow, Bowness-on-Windermere, Windermere, Cumbria LA23 3BX
Tel: 015394 88444
Fax: 015394 88444
The life and works of Beatrix Potter presented on 9-screen video wall, film on her life and 3-dimensional re-creations of some of the scenes from her popular tales.

DERBYSHIRE

BAKEWELL OLD HOUSE MUSEUM
Cunningham Place, Bakewell, Derbyshire DE45 1DD
Tel: 01629 813165
Tudor house with varied collection of social life exhibits.

BLUE JOHN MUSEUM OLLERENSHAW COLLECTION
Cross Street, Castleton, Sheffield S30 2WP
Tel: 01433 620642
One of the finest collections of Blue John in the world, including clock columns, urns, tazzas, vases.

THE BOTTLE KILN
High Lane West, West Hallam, Derby DE7 6HP
Tel: 0115 932 9442
Listed building with fine art gallery paintings and prints by East Midlands artists. Also café, gift shop and crafts.

BUXTON MUSEUM & ART GALLERY
Terrace Road, Buxton, Derbyshire SK17 6DU
Tel: 01298 24658
Ground floor temporary exhibition space and reproduction late Victorian study. Archaeological and geological displays. Permanent fine art collection.

CARRIAGE MUSEUM
Red House Stables, Old Road, Darley Dale, Matlock, Derbyshire DE4 2ER
Tel: 01629 733583
Fax: 01629 733583
Collection of harnesses, collars, liveries.

CHESTERFIELD MUSEUM & ART GALLERY
St Mary's Gate, Chesterfield, Derbyshire S41 7TY
Tel: 01246 345727
Fax: 01246 345720
Museum depicting the story of Chesterfield from Roman times until present day.

DERBY CITY MUSEUM & ART GALLERY
The Strand, Derby DE1 1BS
Tel: 01332 255586
Joseph Wright paintings, Derby porcelain, antiquities, natural history, archaeology and militaria.

DERBY INDUSTRIAL MUSEUM
Silk Mill Lane, off Full Street, Derby, Derbyshire DE1 3AR
Tel: 01332 255308
Fax: 01332 255804
Displays on industries of Derbyshire, Rolls-Royce aeroplane engines, power sources, railway engineering and research.

EREWASH MUSEUM
High Street, Ilkeston, Derbyshire DE7 5JA
Tel: 0115 944 0440
Small local museum housed in late Georgian/Victorian building.

EYAM MUSEUM LTD
Hawk Hill Road, Eyam, Hope Valley, Sheffield, Derbyshire S32 5QP
Tel: 01433 631371
Fax: 01433 630777
Story of the Plague in Eyam (1666), and the village heroism in quarantine.

THE JOHN KING WORKSHOP MUSEUM
Victoria Road, Pinxton, Nottingham NG16 6LR
Tel: 01773 860103
John King Mine Cage Detaching Hook Invention (full size) and models of old railway lines, mining tools and head gear.

MEASHAM MUSEUM
56 High Street, Measham, Swadlincote, Derbyshire DE12 7HZ
Tel: 01530 273956
Artefacts, memorabilia, documents of Measham history.

MONTAGE GALLERY
35/36 Queen Street, Derby DE1 3DS
Tel: 01332 295858
Fax: 01332 295859
Specialist photography gallery with best of local, national and international photographic culture. Established education programme offered tailored cross curriculum activities.

THE NATIONAL TRAMWAY MUSEUM
Crich, Matlock, Derbyshire DE4 5DP
Tel: 01773 852565
Fax: 01773 852326
Collection of over 70 trams from Britain and overseas, built 1873–1957. Nearly 100 working, vintage trams, indoor and outdoor. Unlimited vintage tram rides, special rates/offers for groups.
For further details see page 50

THE NATIONAL TRUST MUSEUM OF CHILDHOOD
Sudbury Hall, Sudbury, Ashbourne, Derbyshire DE6 5HT
Tel: 01283 585305
Fax: 01283 585139
Museum of Childhood, depicts lives of children from the past and included room settings and fine toy and doll collections.

PEAK DISTRICT MINING MUSEUM
The Pavilion, Matlock Bath, Matlock, Derbyshire DE4 3NR
Tel: 01629 583834
Large exhibition on 2,500 years of lead mining, with displays on geology, the mines, the miners, their tools and engines.

PICKFORD'S HOUSE MUSEUM
41 Friar Gate, Derby DE1 1DA
Tel: 01332 255363
Built 1769 by architect Joseph Pickford.

POLLYANNA PICKERING
Brookvale House, Oker, Matlock, Derbyshire DE4 2JJ
Tel: 01629 55851
Fax: 01629 55851
Gallery displaying original paintings by Pollyanna Pickering as well as a selection of prints, limited editions, etc.

REVOLUTION HOUSE
High Street, Old Whittington, Chesterfield, Derbyshire S41 9LA
Tel: 01246 345727
Fax: 01246 345720
Originally Cock and Pynot Alehouse, this 17thC cottage was the meeting place of noblemen planning their part in the 1688 Revolution; exhibitions with 17thC furniture and video.

SIR RICHARD ARKWRIGHT'S CROMFORD MILL
Mill Lane, Cromford, Derbyshire DE4 3GL
Tel: 01629 824297
Fax: 01629 823256
A guided tour explains the world's first water powered cotton spinning mill. Shops and restaurants also on site.
For further details see page 50

DEVON

ALLHALLOWS MUSEUM
High Street, Honiton, Devon EX14 8HP
Tel: 01404 44966
Fax: 01404 42996
Comprehensive display of Honiton lace and other types of lace.

ASHBURTON MUSEUM
1 West Street, Ashburton,
Newton Abbot, Devon
TQ13 7AB
Tel: 01364 652648
Local items of historical, industrial and geological interest.

AXMINSTER MUSEUM
The Old Courthouse, Church
Street, Axminster, Devon
EX13 5AQ
Tel: 01297 34386
Located in the court room of the old Axminster police station, built c1860.

BAROMETER WORLD MUSEUM
Quicksilver Barn, Merton,
Okehampton, Devon
EX20 3DS
Tel: 01805 603443
Fax: 01805 603344
Unique collection of English barometers through the ages, from 1680 to the present day.

BIDEFORD RAILWAY MUSEUM
Bideford Station,
East-the-Water, Bideford,
Devon EX39 2BB
Tel: 01237 423585
Restored railway station: museum in rebuilt signal box, vintage rolling stock, refreshments in railway carriage.

BRAUNTON & DISTRICT MUSEUM
The Bakehouse Centre, Caen
Street, Braunton, Devon
EX33 1AA
Tel: 01271 816688
Fax: 01271 816400
Former church house with collections of photographs, local shipping, old craft tools and church records.

BRIXHAM MUSEUM
Bolton Cross, Brixham, Devon
TQ5 8LZ
Tel: 01803 856267
Local, social and maritime history of the fishing port of Brixham, through Napoleonic and Victorian periods to present day.

BURTON ART GALLERY & MUSEUM
Kingsley Road, Bideford,
Devon EX39 2QQ
Tel: 01237 471455
Fax: 01237 471455
Examples of North Devon pottery, history of the Long Bridge and galleries with various exhibitions of art and craft, plus gift shop and restaurant.

BYGONES MUSEUM
Fore Street, St Marychurch,
Torquay, Devon TQ1 4PR
Tel: 01803 326108
Life-sized Victorian exhibition street with period rooms, walk through trench; experience large model railways, fantasyland, plus much more.

COBBATON COMBAT COLLECTION
Chittlehampton, Umberleigh,
Devon EX37 9RZ
Tel: 01769 540740
Fax: 01769 540740
Private collection of World War II British, Canadian and Warsaw Pact tanks, trucks, armoured cars and allied equipment.

COLDHARBOUR MILL WORKING WOOL MUSEUM
Coldharbour Mill, Uffculme,
Cullompton, Devon EX15 3EE
Tel: 01884 840960
Fax: 01884 840858
Museum of the Devon wool textiles industry in an 18thC woollen mill.

THE COMBE MARTIN MOTORCYCLE COLLECTION
Cross Street, Combe Martin,
Ilfracombe, Devon EX34 0DH
Tel: 01271 882346
Fax: 01271 882346
Collection of British motorcycles displayed against a background of old petrol pumps, signs and garage equipment. Motoring nostalgia in an old world atmosphere.

COOKWORTHY MUSEUM
Old Grammar School, 108 Fore
Street, Kingsbridge, Devon
TQ7 1AW
Tel: 01548 853235
A 17thC panelled school containing a wide variety of local history displays, old photographs, costume and a farm gallery.

THE CRAWSHAW GALLERY
3 Priory Road, Dawlish, Devon
EX7 9JF
Tel: 01626 862032
Paintings, sketches and ceramics by Alwyn and June Crawshaw and other members of the Crawshaw family.

CROYDE GEM ROCK & SHELL MUSEUM
10 Hobbs Hill, Croyde,
Braunton, Devon EX33 1LZ
Tel: 01271 890407
Colourful display of the world's semi-precious stones, both cut and polished and in their natural state, also worldwide shells.

DARTMOUTH MUSEUM
The Butterwalk, Dartmouth,
Devon TQ6 9PZ
Tel: 01803 832923
Local history and maritime museum in former merchant's house (c1640).

DAWLISH MUSEUM
The Knowle, Barton Terrace,
Dawlish, Devon EX7 9QH
Tel: 01626 865974
Thirteen rooms containing exhibits about Dawlish and the West Country. Large collection of Victoriana, some geology.

THE DEVON GUILD OF CRAFTSMEN
Riverside Mill, Bovey Tracey,
Newton Abbot, Devon
TQ13 9AF
Tel: 01626 832223
Fax: 01626 834220
Grade II listed old mill with exhibition, shop and Egon Ronay listed café. Regularly changing programme of exhibitions and shop featuring contemporary craftwork.

DEVON RAILWAY CENTRE
Buckleigh, Tiverton, Devon
EX16 8RG
Tel: 01736 794440
Railway museum incorporating passenger-carrying narrow gauge railway, model railway exhibition. Preserved Great Western stations and historic railway equipment.

DINGLE'S STEAM VILLAGE
Milford, Lifton, Devon
PL16 0AT
Tel: 01566 783425
Fax: 01566 783584
20,000 sq ft of covered exhibits of steam and vintage road-making and other equipment with playground set in 200-acre sheep farm, river and countryside walks, café and shop.

ELIZABETHAN HOUSE
32 New Street, The Barbican,
Plymouth, Devon PL1 2NA
Tel: 01752 253871
For further details see page 51

ELLIOTT GALLERY
Hillsview, Braunton, Devon
EX33 2LA
Tel: 01271 812100
Art and craft gallery, video, painting courses daily. Four main gallery halls. Paintings in all media, sculpture, crafts. Restaurant.

EXMOUTH MUSEUM
Sheppard's Row, Exeter Road,
Exmouth, Devon EX8 1PP
Tel: 01395 263785
Building housing varied local exhibits on two floors plus adjacent cottage with local artefacts.

FAIRLYNCH ARTS CENTRE & MUSEUM
27 Fore Street, Budleigh
Salterton, Devon EX9 6NP
Tel: 01395 442666
Emphasis on local material: history, nature, archaeology and geology.

FINCH FOUNDRY
Sticklepath, Okehampton,
Devon EX20 2NW
Tel: 01837 840046
Fax: 01837 840046
19thC water-powered edge tool factory with three working water-wheels, driving trip, hammers, grindstone and other machinery.

HANCOCK'S DEVON CIDER
Mill House, Clapworthy Mill,
South Molton, Devon
EX36 4HU
Tel: 01769 572678
Film and self-guided tours of cider press house.

HARTLAND QUAY MUSEUM
Hartland, Bideford, Devon
EX39 6DU
Tel: 01288 331353
Coastal museum with exhibitions on shipwrecks, natural history, coastal trades, geology and history of Hartland Quay.

HENLEY MUSEUM
Anzac Street, Dartmouth,
Devon TQ6 9RY
Collection of relics of Dartmouth with pictorial records of more recent historic events.

THE HERITAGE CENTRE
Queen Anne's Walk, The
Strand, Barnstaple, Devon
EX31 1EU
Tel: 01271 373311
New interactive experience of Barnstaple from Saxon times to 18thC – due to open spring 1998.

HOLSWORTHY MUSEUM
Manor Offices, Holsworthy,
Devon EX22 6DJ
Small rural museum featuring local crafts and objects of interest.

ILFRACOMBE MUSEUM
Runnymede Gardens, Wilder
Road, Ilfracombe, Devon
EX34 8AF
Tel: 01271 863541
Over 20,000 exhibits including natural history, Victoriana, old railways, cobbler's workshop, paintings and photographs of Ilfracombe, and brass rubbings.

JOHN MULVEY SCULPTURE STUDIO
The Garden House, Bickleigh,
Tiverton, Devon EX16 8RN
Tel: 01884 855682
Studio exhibition of bronze sculptures by international sculptor John Mulvey. Visitors welcome by appointment.

LYN & EXMOOR MUSEUM
St Vincent Cottage, Market
Street, Lynton, Devon
EX35 6AF
Tel: 01598 752317
Early 17thC cottage housing art, craft, tool exhibitions representing comprehensive history of Exmoor's past, featuring Victorian kitchen.

MERCHANT'S HOUSE MUSEUM
33 St Andrew's Street,
Plymouth, Devon PL1 2AX
Tel: 01752 304774
Fax: 01752 304775
A 16thC town house – the largest and finest example of its period left in the city.
For further details see page 51

MORWELLHAM QUAY
Morwellham Quay, New
Tavistock, Devon PL19 8JL
Tel: 01822 832766
Fax: 01822 833808
Visitor centre/open-air museum at historic Tamar valley river port. Train ride into old mine workings. Horse-drawn carriage ride. Costumed staff. Costumes to try. Cottages. Workshop trails. Special activities for children.

MUSEUM OF DARTMOOR LIFE
3 West Street, Okehampton,
Devon EX20 1HQ
Tel: 01837 52295
Museum of Dartmoor life tells how people have lived, worked and played on the moor through the centuries.
For further details see page 50

MUSEUM OF NORTH DEVON
The Square, Barnstaple, Devon
EX32 8LN
Tel: 01271 46747
Major regional museum displaying and interpreting the natural and human history of northern Devon.

NATIONAL AMBULANCE HERITAGE CENTRE
Half Bridge, Tavistock, Devon
PL19 9LR
Tel: 01822 840057
Fax: 01822 610066
A complete heritage of the civil and military ambulance services, hospital ships and ambulance trains.

NEWTON ABBOT TOWN & GWR MUSEUM
2a St Paul's Road, Newton
Abbot, Devon TQ12 2HP
Tel: 01626 334675
Fax: 01626 52777
Social history of Newton Abbot from 1BC.

NORTH DEVON MARITIME MUSEUM
Odun House, Odun Road,
Appledore, Bideford, Devon
EX39 1PT
Tel: 01237 422064
All aspects of North Devon's maritime history illustrated by models, photographs and paintings.

PLYMOUTH CITY MUSEUM & ART GALLERY
Drake Circus, Plymouth,
Devon PL4 8AJ
Tel: 01752 304774
Fax: 01752 304775
The Museum's collections cover areas such as entomology, geology, natural history and social history, while the Gallery is home to fine and decorative art collections featuring paintings, prints, silver and Plymouth china.
For further details see page 51

PREHISTORIC HILL SETTLEMENT MUSEUM
Capton, Dartmouth, Devon
TQ6 0JE
Tel: 01803 712452
Museum of prehistoric artefacts and historic trails plus reconstructed Neolithic farmhouse.

ROYAL ALBERT MEMORIAL MUSEUM
Queen Street, Exeter, Devon
EX4 3RX
Tel: 01392 265858
Fax: 01392 421252
Largest museum in the south west.

SALCOMBE MARITIME & LOCAL HISTORY MUSEUM
Town Hall Basement, Market
Street, Salcombe, Devon
TQ8 8DE
Local museum featuring exhibits of local maritime interest, shipbuilding, wreck and rescue, fishing, maritime collection of oil and gouache paintings.

SIDMOUTH MUSEUM
Hope Cottage, Church Street,
Sidmouth, Devon EX10 8LY
Tel: 01395 516139
A 19thC heritage centre conserving and displaying local artefacts of all kinds.

SIMON DREW GALLERY
13 Foss Street, Dartmouth,
Devon TQ6 9DR
Tel: 01803 832832
Exhibitions of ceramics and art.

SOUTH MOLTON MUSEUM
Town Hall, The Square, Broad
Street, South Molton, Devon
EX36 3AB
Tel: 01769 572951
Old fire engines, weights and measures, original charters, giant cider press and large pewter collection.

SPACEX GALLERY
45 Preston Street, Exeter,
Devon EX1 1DF
Tel: 01392 431786
Fax: 01392 431786
Contemporary art gallery.

TEIGNMOUTH MUSEUM
29 French Street, Teignmouth, Devon TQ14 8ST
Tel: 01626 777041
Exhibits include 16thC cannon, artefacts from Armada wreck and local history.

TIVERTON MUSEUM
St Andrew Street, Tiverton, Devon EX16 6PH
Tel: 01884 256295
Comprehensive regional museum.

TOPSHAM MUSEUM
25 The Strand, Topsham, Exeter, Devon EX3 0AX
Tel: 01392 873244
Local riverside museum featuring the history of the port of Topsham, including the shipbuilding era and the wildlife of the Exe estuary.

TORQUAY MUSEUM
529 Babbacombe Road, Torquay, Devon TQ1 1HG
Tel: 01803 293975
Fax: 01803 294186
Devon's oldest museum, displays cover, Agatha Christie, local history, natural history, finds from Kents Cavern, world adornments, Devon regiments and Victorianna, plus temporary exhibitions.

TORRINGTON MUSEUM & ARCHIVE
The Town Hall, Torrington, Devon EX38 8HW
Tel: 01805 624324
Historical items of local interest housed in the old court room and picture room in the town hall.

TOTNES COSTUME MUSEUM – DEVONSHIRE COLLECTION OF PERIOD COSTUME
Bogan House, 43 High Street, Totnes, Devon TQ9 5NP
Tel: 01803 862827
New exhibition of costumes and accessories displayed each season in Bogan House, one of the historic merchant's houses of Totnes recently restored by Mitchell Trust.

TOTNES MUSEUM
70 Fore Street, Totnes, Devon TQ9 5RU
Tel: 01803 863821
A 16thC Tudor merchant's house.

WATERMOUTH CASTLE
Berrynarbor, Ilfracombe, Devon EX34 9SL
Tel: 01271 863879
Fax: 01271 865864
Mechanical music demonstrations, model railway, domestic, dairy and cider-making exhibits, cycle museum, smugglers' dungeon and gardens.

YELVERTON PAPERWEIGHT CENTRE
Leg-o'Mutton Corner, Yelverton, Devon PL20 6AD
Tel: 01822 854250
Fax: 01822 854250
The Broughton Collection: hundreds of glass paperweights both antique and modern.

DORSET

ABBOTSBURY TITHE BARN COUNTRY MUSEUM
New Barn Road, Abbotsbury, Weymouth, Dorset DT3 4JF
Tel: 01305 871817
Extensive collection of rural and agricultural tools and implements from 1700 to the turn of the century.

BLANDFORD FORUM MUSEUM
Beres Yard, Market Place, Blandford Forum, Dorset DT11 7HU
Tel: 01258 450388
The history of Blandford and district with particular emphasis on the period since c1700.

BOURNEMOUTH BEARS
Expo Centre, Old Christchurch Lane, Bournemouth, Dorset BH1 1NE
Tel: 01202 293544
Fax: 01305 268885
Hundreds of bears including old, not so old, traditional, and collectors bears, are exhibited at Dorset's unique Teddy Bear Museum.

BOURNEMOUTH HERITAGE TRANSPORT CENTRE
Bournemouth International Airport, Hurn, Bournemouth, Dorset BH8 9PL
Tel: 01202 485837
Collection of tramcars, trolley buses and diesel buses.

BREDY FARM OLD FARMING COLLECTION
Bredy Farm, Burton Bradstock, Bridport, Dorset DT6 4ND
Tel: 01308 897229
Extensive collection of farm and estate implements, wagons and tools of yesteryear from dairy cultivation, cider making and harvesting.

BRIDPORT MUSEUM
South Street, Bridport, Dorset DT6 3NR
Tel: 01308 422116
Fax: 01308 420659
Interesting stone Tudor building with a variety of exhibits on display.

COACH HOUSE MUSEUM & MUSEUM OF PURBECK STONE INDUSTRY
St George's Close, Langton Matravers, Swanage, Dorset BH19 3HZ
Tel: 01929 423168
Restored coach house of old rectory Langton Matravers.

CORFE CASTLE MUSEUM
The Town Hall, West Street, Corfe Castle, Wareham, Dorset BH20 5HE
Museum containing exhibits of local history and dinosaur footprints.

DINOSAUR DISCOVERY
Expocentre, Old Christchurch Lane, Bournemouth, Dorset BH1 1NE
Tel: 01202 293544
Fax: 01305 268885
Hands-on and computer displays let you discover all there is to know about dinosaurs. It's fascinating fun.

THE DINOSAUR MUSEUM
Icen Way, Dorchester, Dorset DT1 1EW
Tel: 01305 269880
Fax: 01305 268885
This award-winning hands-on museum combines fossils, skeletons, life size dinosaur reconstructions, with audio-visual, interactive and computer displays. Great fun.

DINOSAURLAND
Coombe Street, Lyme Regis, Dorset DT7 3PY
Tel: 01297 443541
Collection of local fossils, skeletons, accompanying video and fossil-hunting walks.

DORSET COUNTY MUSEUM
High West Street, Dorchester, Dorset DT1 1XA
Tel: 01305 262735
Thomas Hardy, history, archaeology, natural history and geology of Dorset in magnificent Victorian building.

GILLINGHAM MUSEUM
Chantry Fields, Gillingham, Dorset SP8 4UA
Tel: 01747 822173
Fax: 01747 823176
Exhibition containing 11–19thC town documents, 1790 fire engine and local railway history.

HARBOUR MUSEUM
West Bay, Bridport, Dorset DT6 4SA
Tel: 01308 420997
Fax: 01308 420659
Converted salt house on one level overlooking the harbour which is now a maritime and local history museum.

KEEP MILITARY MUSEUM
The Keep, Bridport Road, Dorchester, Dorset DT1 1RN
Tel: 01305 264066
Fax: 01305 250373
Exhibits of the Devon Regiment, the Dorset Regiment, the Queen's Own Dorset Yeomanry Militia and Volunteers, and the Devon and Dorset Regiment.

LYME REGIS PHILPOT MUSEUM
Bridge Street, Lyme Regis, Dorset DT7 3QA
Tel: 01297 443370
Fossils, geology, local history and lace exhibitions.

MERLEY HOUSE EXHIBITION CENTRE
Merley, Wimborne Minster, Dorset BH21 3AA
Tel: 01202 886533
Fax: 01202 881415
Grade I Georgian mansion with seven plaster ceilings housing private collection of over 5,000 model cars.

MILL HOUSE CIDER MUSEUM & DORSET COLLECTION OF CLOCKS
Owermoigne, Dorchester, Dorset DT2 8HZ
Tel: 01305 852220
Fax: 01305 854760
Cider equipment of 18th–19thC and collection of long-case and turret clocks.

PORTLAND MUSEUM
217 Wakeham, Portland, Dorset DT5 1HS
Tel: 01305 821804
Local history, folk history, Portland stone and prison.

PRIEST'S HOUSE MUSEUM
23–27 High Street, Wimborne Minster, Dorset BH21 1HR
Tel: 01202 882533
Fax: 01202 882533
Award-winning museum in an historic town house, special exhibitions, childhood gallery, working Victorian kitchen, ironmongers' and stationers' shops.

PURBECK TOY & MUSICAL BOXES MUSEUM
Arne, Wareham, Dorset BH20 5BJ
Tel: 01929 552018
A collection of antique musical boxes, antique and collectors' toys, antique and automata dolls.

THE RED HOUSE MUSEUM & GARDENS
Quay Road, Christchurch, Dorset BH23 1BU
Tel: 01202 482860
Fax: 01202 481924
A charming Georgian building filled with a rich variety of displays and objects all with a local theme. Temporary exhibitions, herb garden, old fashioned roses and herbaceous borders, gift shop and coffee shop.

ROYAL NATIONAL LIFEBOAT INSTITUTION MUSEUM
West Quay Road, Poole, Dorset BH15 1HZ
Tel: 01202 663000
History and development of RNLI shown through pictures, models and paintings.

ROYAL SIGNALS MUSEUM
Blandford Camp, Blandford Forum, Dorset DT11 8RH
Tel: 01258 482248
Fax: 01258 482084
History of army communication from Crimean War to Gulf War.

RUSSELL-COTES ART GALLERY & MUSEUM
Russell-Cotes Road, East Cliff, Bournemouth, Dorset BH1 3AA
Tel: 01202 481800
Fax: 01202 451851
Late Victorian historic house with art galleries, displays of 19th–20thC paintings, decorative art, contemporary craft commissions and world cultures.

SCAPLEN'S COURT MUSEUM
High Street, Poole, Dorset BH15 1DA
Tel: 01202 683138
Fax: 01202 660896
15thC restored town house with central courtyard and walled garden.

SHAFTESBURY ABBEY RUINS & MUSEUM
Park Walk, Shaftesbury, Dorset SP7 8JR
Tel: 01747 852910
Excavated foundations of Shaftesbury Abbey Church.

SHAFTESBURY LOCAL HISTORY MUSEUM
Gold Hill, Shaftesbury, Dorset SP7 8JW
Tel: 01747 852157
Museum containing exhibits of local history and domestic and agricultural implements.

SHELLEY ROOMS
Boscombe Manor, Shelley Park, Bournemouth, Dorset BH5 1NE
Tel: 01202 303571
The Shelley Rooms are part of Boscombe Manor, once the home of Sir Percy Byshe Shelley.

SHERBORNE MUSEUM
Abbey Gate House, Sherborne, Dorset DT9 3BP
Tel: 01935 812252
Displays of local history including prehistory, Roman times, Sherbourne abbey, castles, almhouse, schools, local industry, 18th C silk manufacture.

SOUTHERN ELECTRIC MUSEUM THE OLD POWER STATION
Bargates, Christchurch, Dorset BH23 1QE
Tel: 01202 480467
Fax: 01202 480468
One of the most extensive collections of historic electrical equipment in Great Britain.

THE TANK MUSEUM
Bovington, Wareham, Dorset BH20 6JG
Tel: 01929 405096
Fax: 01929 405360
Largest and most comprehensive museum collection of armoured fighting vehicles in the world.

TITHE BARN MUSEUM & ART CENTRE
Church Hill, Swanage, Dorset BH19 1JU
Tel: 01929 423174
Small museum in old tithe barn.

TOLPUDDLE MARTYRS MUSEUM
4 TUC Memorial Cottages, Tolpuddle, Dorchester, Dorset DT2 7EH
Tel: 01305 848237
Pictures of and literature about the six Martyrs of Tolpuddle who were transported to Australia in 1834.

WAREHAM TOWN MUSEUM
East Street, Wareham, Dorset BH20 4NS
Tel: 01929 553448
Archaeology, geology and social history of area plus collection of T E Lawrence ephemera and photographs.

WATERFRONT MUSEUM
4 High Street, Poole, Dorset (East & North) BH15 1BW
Tel: 01202 683138
Displays in the late 15thC town cellars and Oakleys Mill building tell Poole's maritime history.
For further details see page 51

WEYMOUTH'S WORKING WATER MUSEUM
Sutton Poyntz, Weymouth, Dorset
Tel: 01305 832634
Rural pumping station which has supplied water to Weymouth for 150 years.

EAST RIDING OF YORKSHIRE

BEVERLEY ART GALLERY & MUSEUM
Champney Road, Beverley,
East Riding of Yorkshire
Tel: 01482 887700
Fax: 01482 871857
Permanent collection of works by Beverley-born artist Fred Elwell RA, Victorian and Edwardian works and good topographical collection. Gallery shows with a series of exhibitions from a permanent collection and contemporary art and craft.
For further details see page 51

BRIDLINGTON HARBOUR AQUARIUM & HISTORY MUSEUM
Harbour Road, Bridlington, East
Riding of Yorkshire YO15 3AN
Tel: 01262 670148
Fax: 01262 602041
Photographs, harbour history, models, diarama of fishing techniques, video presentation and North Sea aquarium.

GOOLE MUSEUM & ART GALLERY
c/o ERYC Offices, Church
Street, Goole, East Riding of
Yorkshire DN14 5BG
Tel: 01405 722251
Fax: 01405 722256
Gallery of maritime paintings, many by local artist Reuben Chappell. Changing displays of local and social history. Temporary exhibition programme.

HORNSEA MUSEUM
11 Newbegin, Hornsea, East
Riding of Yorkshire HU18 1AB
Tel: 01964 533443
Folk museum of village life, period rooms including Victorian kitchen, parlour, bedroom, dairy, outbuildings, large garden, shop.

MAJOR BRIDGE PARK
Selby Road, Holme upon
Spalding Moor, York YO4 4HB
Tel: 01430 760992
Nature trail, vintage fairground rides, antique farm and horticultural machinery, vintage wood-working machinery, horses, picnic areas and much more.

MUSEUM OF ARMY TRANSPORT
Flemingate, Beverley, East
Riding of Yorkshire
HU17 0NG
Tel: 01482 860445
Fax: 01482 872767
Army, road, rail, sea and air exhibits excitingly displayed in two huge indoor exhibition halls, plus the last remaining Blackburn Beverley aircraft.

SEWERBY HALL MUSEUM & ART GALLERY
East Riding of Yorkshire
Council Museums Service,
Church Lane, Sewerby,
Bridlington, East Riding of
Yorkshire YO15 1EA
Tel: 01262 677874

WATERWAYS MUSEUM
Dutch Riverside, Goole, East
Riding of Yorkshire
DN14 5TB
Tel: 01405 768730
Fax: 01405 769868
Documents/memorabilia relating to waterways of the North.
For further details see page 51

WITHERNSEA LIGHTHOUSE MUSEUM
Hull Road, Withernsea, East
Riding of Yorkshire HU19 2DY
Tel: 01964 614834
Magnificent view of Withernsea from top of 127ft lighthouse. RNLI and coastguard exhibitions, local history and local girl Kay Kendall 1950s film star memorabilia.

EAST SUSSEX

ANNE OF CLEVES HOUSE MUSEUM
52 Southover High Street,
Lewes, East Sussex BN7 1JA
Tel: 01273 474610
Fax: 01273 486990
Old timber-framed house and workshops housing folk museum.

THE BARLOW COLLECTION
Library Building, University of
Sussex, Falmer, Brighton
BN1 9QE
Tel: 01273 606755
A collection depicting 3,000 years of Chinese civilisation with ceramics, bronzes and jades.

BATTLE MUSEUM OF LOCAL HISTORY
Battle Memorial Hall, High
Street, Battle, East Sussex
TN33 0AQ
Tel: 01424 775955
Museum telling history of Battle of Hastings with diorama and reproduction of Bayeux Tapestry.

BEXHILL MUSEUM
Egerton Road, Bexhill-on-Sea,
East Sussex TN39 3HL
Tel: 01424 787950
Friendly local museum with collections illustrating the geology, natural and local history, and archaeology of the area.

BEXHILL MUSEUM OF COSTUME & SOCIAL HISTORY
Manor Gardens, Upper Sea
Road, Bexhill-on-Sea, East
Sussex TN40 1RL
Tel: 01424 210045
Wide range of period costume from mid-18thC, plus dolls, toys, lace and other items in use during the period.

BOOTH MUSEUM OF NATURAL HISTORY
194 Dyke Road, Brighton,
East Sussex BN1 5AA
Tel: 01273 292777
Fax: 01273 292778
Comprehensive collection of British birds in re-creations of their natural environment, with butterflies, skeletons, fossils and a museum shop.
For further details see page 4

BRIGHTON FISHING MUSEUM
201 Kings Road Arches,
Brighton BN1 1NB
Tel: 01273 723064
Brighton's fishing industry and associated beach leisure are vividly presented in sea front arches used by the local community since the 1860s.

BRIGHTON MUSEUM & ART GALLERY
Church Street, Brighton, East
Sussex BN1 1UE
Tel: 01273 603005
Fax: 01273 608202
Late 19thC Moorish-design historic building with collection of ceramics, art deco, art nouveau, archaeology, local history, non-western art, fine art and costume.
For further details see page 4

THE BRITISH ENGINEERIUM
Nevill Road, Hove, Brighton,
East Sussex BN3 7QA
Tel: 01273 559583
Fax: 01273 566403
A restored working Victorian pumping station with hundreds of model and full-size steam engines, hot air engines, domestic tools and hands-on exhibition for children.
For further details see page 52

BUCKLEYS YESTERDAYS WORLD
89–90 High Street, Battle,
East Sussex TN33 0AQ
Tel: 01424 775378
Fax: 01424 775174
Over 100,000 exhibits in a Wealden Hall house recall shopping and domestic life from 1850 to 1950 accompanied by smells and commentaries. Railway station, play village garden.
For further details see page 52

COUNTRY BYGONES
Heron House, Laughton Road,
Ringmer, Lewes, East Sussex
BN8 5UT
Tel: 01273 813233
Personal collection of household and agricultural bygones.

COURT HALL MUSEUM
Court Hall, High Street,
Winchelsea, East Sussex
TN36 4EU
Tel: 01797 224395
Small local museum with exhibits on Winchelsea and the Cinque Ports and their history plus maps and seals.

CRYPT GALLERY
Off Church Street, Seaford, East
Sussex BN25 2DE
Tel: 01323 891461
Fax: 01273 484166
A modern gallery built around a medieval crypt specialising in top quality contemporary exhibitions.

DITCHLING MUSEUM
Church Lane, Ditchling,
Hassocks, West Sussex
BN6 8TB
Tel: 01273 844744
Mid-Victorian former village school with dioramas, historical displays, costume, farm and domestic equipment. Special exhibitions gallery of the work of 20thC Ditchling craftsmen, Eric Gill, Edward Johnson etc.

FILCHING MANOR & MOTOR MUSEUM
Filching Manor, Filching,
Nr Polegate, East Sussex
BN26 5QA
Tel: 01323 487838
Fax: 01323 486331
15thC Wealden Hall house on site of 600AD priory with collection of over 100 veteran vintage sports and racing cars, Jupiter aircraft and racing motor boats.

FISHERMEN'S MUSEUM
Rock-a-Nore Road, Hastings,
East Sussex TN34 3DW
Tel: 01424 461446
Former fishermen's church by old net sheds now displays local fishing ship models, nets, old photos and the lugger 'Enterprise' built 1912.

FOREDOWN TOWER
Foredown Road, Portslade,
Brighton, East Sussex
BN41 2EW
Tel: 01273 292092
A disused Edwardian water tower home to the Sussex Downs countryside centre and camera obscura, which also has a weather station, exhibition galleries and displays, countryside research and data.
For further details see page 4

GRANGE MUSEUM
The Grange, The Green,
Rottingdean, East Sussex
BNZ 7HA
Tel: 01273 301004
Museum includes: Kipling Room, history of dolls, working model railway, Bob Copper Room (local farming).

HASTINGS EMBROIDERY
Sussex Hall, White Hall Theatre,
Hastings, East Sussex
TN34 1QR
Tel: 01424 781010
A 74m embroidery made in 1966 for the 900th anniversary of Battle of Hastings, showing great historical events since 1066.

HASTINGS MUSEUM & ART GALLERY
Cambridge Road, Hastings, East
Sussex TN34 1ET
Tel: 01424 781155
Fax: 01424 781165
Sussex pottery, Wealden ironwork, European ceramics Pacific ethnography, Native American and grey owl, dinosaurs, natural history. Durbar hall Indian palace.

HASTINGS MUSEUM OF LOCAL HISTORY
High Street, Hastings, East
Sussex TN34 3EW
Tel: 01424 781166
Housed in former town hall, subjects include Norman Conquest, Cinque Ports, fishing, smuggling, archaeology and invention of TV by Logie Baird in 1924.

HEAVEN FARM COUNTRY TOURS MUSEUM & STABLE TEA ROOMS
Heaven Farm, Furners Green,
Uckfield, East Sussex
TN22 3RG
Tel: 01825 790226
Fax: 01825 790881
Ancient farm buildings containing agricultural tools and equipment.

HOVE MUSEUM & ART GALLERY
19 New Church Road, Hove,
Brighton, East Sussex
BN3 4AB
Tel: 01273 779410
Fax: 01273 202275
Museum of art and history with fine collection of English paintings, contemporary crafts and special temporary exhibitions.
For further details see page 4

'HOW WE LIVED THEN' MUSEUM OF SHOPS & SOCIAL HISTORY
20 Cornfield Terrace,
Eastbourne, Sussex BN21 4NS
Tel: 01323 737143
One hundred years of social history (1850–1950) depicted by over 100,000 exhibits displayed in street scenes of authentic old shops and room settings housed in late Regency building.

LEWES CASTLE
Barbican House, 169 High
Street, Lewes, East Sussex
BN7 1YE
Tel: 01273 486290
Fax: 01273 486990
Historic interpretive display of Lewes – 25-minute indoor audio-visual programme, 1:150 scale-model of town c120 years ago.

THE LIFEBOAT MUSEUM
King Edward Parade,
Eastbourne, East Sussex
BN21 4BY
Tel: 01323 730717
Comprehensive collection of lifeboats housed in former boathouse, plus ships in bottles, display of lifesaving equipment and photographs.

MUSEUM OF CHILDHOOD
41 Meeting House Lane,
Brighton BN1 1HB
Tel: 01273 208940
Fax: 01273 202736
World-famous Steiff toys, teddy bears' picnics, china, celluloid and cloth dolls. Children's workhouse tableau – complete with ghost. Snow White scene. Animiated displays.

NEWHAVEN LOCAL & MARITIME MUSEUM
Paradise Leisure Park, Avis
Road, Newhaven, East Sussex
BN9 0DH
Tel: 01273 612530
Exhibits of historical interest local to Newhaven, and of its maritime heritage.

PRESTON MANOR
Preston Drove, Brighton, East
Sussex
Tel: 01273 292843/2
Fax: 01273 608202
An Edwardian gentry home with more than twenty rooms displaying collections of silver, furniture, portraits and Edwardian memorabilia.
For further details see page 4

THE REDOUBT FORTRESS
Royal Parade, Eastbourne, East
Sussex BN21 7AQ
Tel: 01323 410300
Fax: 01323 732240
Fully restored Napoleonic fortress, gun emplacements, battlements, containing, South East England's finest military museum. Displaying medals, uniforms, weapons, badges and equipment.

RIPLEYS MUSEUM OF RURAL LIFE
Bridge Bungalow, Northbridge
Street, Robertsbridge, East
Sussex TN32 5NY
Tel: 01580 880324
Blacksmith's and wheelwright's shop displays, working forge, farm tools and utensils.

THE ROYAL PAVILION
Brighton, East Sussex
BN1 1EE
Tel: 01273 290900
One of the premier royal palaces in Europe, restored to its full Regency glory, showing Indian Mogul architecture, Oriental interiors and collections of furniture, soft furnishings, decorative art, silver gilt and chinoiserie.
For further details see page 4

RYE ART GALLERY STORMONT STUDIO/EASTON ROOMS
Stormont Studio, East Street,
Rye, East Sussex TN31 7JY
Tel: 01797 223218
Main gallery has several exhibitions of fine art of national and regional interest.

SEAFORD MUSEUM OF LOCAL HISTORY
Martello Tower, Esplanade,
Seaford, East Sussex BN25 1JH
Tel: 01323 898222
Converted martello tower.

SUSSEX FARM MUSEUM
Horam Manor Farm, Horam,
Heathfield, East Sussex
TN21 0JB
Tel: 01435 813688
Fax: 01435 813716
Museum with nature trails through woods, streams and open fields. Children's farm, craft workshops, riding, fishing.

SUSSEX TOY & MODEL MUSEUM
52–55 Trafalgar Street,
Brighton, East Sussex
BN1 4EB
Tel: 01273 749494
Museum housed in the arches under Brighton's railway station, with collection of toys and models including cars, trains, planes, dolls, soldiers, buses and forts.
For further details see page 52

TOWNER ART GALLERY & LOCAL MUSEUM
High Street, Old Town,
Eastbourne, East Sussex
BN20 8BB
Tel: 01323 411688
Fax: 01323 648182
18thC house now an art gallery and museum, in beautiful gardens. Lively contemporary and historic exhibitions programme.

WEST BLATCHINGTON WINDMILL
Holmes Avenue, Hove,
Brighton, East Sussex BN3 7L
Tel: 01273 775400
Fax: 01273 207277
Dating from the 1820s, this Grade II listed building still has all the original mill workings in place over five floors.
For further details see page 4

ESSEX

ASHDON VILLAGE MUSEUM
Hill Farm, Ashdon, Saffron
Walden, Essex CB10 2NB
Tel: 01799 584452
Museum of village life.

BARDFIELD CAGE
Bridge Street, Great Bardfield,
Braintree, Essex CM7 4RH
Tel: 01371 810555
Great Bardfield Cage is a 19thC village lock-up.

BARLEYLANDS FARM MUSEUM & VISITOR CENTRE
Barleylands Road, Billericay,
Essex CM11 2UD
Tel: 01268 282090
Fax: 01268 532032
Unique visitors' centre comprising rural museum, animal centre, working craft studios, glass blowing studio with viewing gallery, miniature steam railway and restaurant.

BEECROFT ART GALLERY
Station Road,
Westcliff-on-Sea,
Southend-on-Sea, Essex
SS0 7RA
Tel: 01702 347418
Edwardian building with panoramic estuary views.
For further details see page 53

BRAINTREE DISTRICT MUSEUM
Manor Street, Braintree, Essex
CM7 6HW
Tel: 01376 325266
Fax: 01376 344345
'Threads of Time' is a permanent exhibition housed in a converted Victorian School, telling the story of Braintree District and its important place in our history.

BRENTWOOD MUSEUM
Cemetery Lodge, Lorne Road,
Brentwood, Essex CM14 5HH
Tel: 01277 224012
Small cottage museum covering social and domestic history with special reference to Brentwood.

BRIGHTLINGSEA MUSEUM
1 Duke Street, Brightlingsea,
Colchester, Essex CO7 0EA
Tel: 01206 303185
Maritime social history museum of Brightlingsea (limb of the Cinque Port of Sandwich), showing collection relating to the town's Cinque Port connections.

BURNHAM-ON-CROUCH & DISTRICT MUSEUM
Coronation Road,
Burnham-on-Crouch, Essex
CM0 8AS
Tel: 01621 782562
Small museum devoted to local history with maritime and agricultural features.

CASTLE POINT TRANSPORT MUSEUM SOCIETY
105 Point Road, Canvey Island,
Essex SS8 7TD
Tel: 01268 684272
Museum housing collection of buses, coaches and commercial vehicles in restored condition.

CATER MUSEUM
74 High Street, Billericay, Essex
CM12 9BS
Tel: 01277 622023
Victorian sitting room and bedroom.

CENTRAL MUSEUM & PLANETARIUM
Victoria Avenue,
Southend-on-Sea, Essex
SS2 6EW
Tel: 01702 215131
Fax: 01702 215631
Edwardian building housing displays of archaeology, natural history, social and local history.
For further details see page 53

CHELMSFORD & ESSEX MUSEUM
Oaklands Park, Moulsham
Street, Chelmsford, Essex
CM2 9AQ
Tel: 01245 353066
Fax: 01245 280642
Local/social history, prehistory to present day; Essex Regiment museum, ceramics, coins, costume, glass, rocks and fossils, animals, exhibitions, events, talks.

COLCHESTER CASTLE
Colchester Castle, Colchester,
Essex CO1 1TJ
Tel: 01206 282931
Fax: 01206 282939
Norman keep on foundations of Roman temple with archaeological material including much on Roman Colchester (Camulodunum). Guided tours daily.

COTTAGE MUSEUM
Dunmow Road, Great
Bardfield, Braintree, Essex
Tel: 01371 810555
16thC charity cottage.

CROWN PICTURES/LINDSELL ART GALLERY
Old Crown House, Lindsell,
Dunmow, Essex CM6 3QN
Tel: 01371 870777
Fax: 01371 870369
Art gallery specialising in work by local artists.

DEDHAM ART & CRAFT CENTRE
High Street, Dedham,
Colchester, Essex CO7 6AD
Tel: 01206 322666
Fax: 01206 322231
Constable Country converted red-brick church in famous Dedham village.

DOROTHY L SAYERS CENTRE
Witham Library, 18 Newland
Street, Witham, Essex
CM8 2AQ
Tel: 01376 519625
Fax: 01376 501913
Reference collection of books by and about Dorothy L Sayers.

DUTCH COTTAGE MUSEUM
Canvey Road, Canvey Island,
Essex
Tel: 01268 794005
Early 17thC cottage of one of Vermuyden's Dutch workmen (responsible for drainage schemes in East Anglia).

EAST ANGLIAN RAILWAY MUSEUM
Chappel & Wakes Colne
Station, Colchester, Essex
CO6 2DS
Tel: 01206 242524
Based in a busy Victorian country station, includes steam train rides and minature railway.

EAST ESSEX AVIATION SOCIETY & MUSEUM
Martello Tower, Point Clear, St
Osyth, Clacton-on-Sea, Essex
Tel: 01255 428028
An exhibition of aircraft parts from local recoveries.

EPPING FOREST DISTRICT MUSEUM
39–41 Sun Street, Waltham
Abbey, Essex EN9 1EL
Tel: 01992 716882
Fax: 01992 700427
Tudor and Georgian timber-framed buildings, herb garden, Tudor panelled room.

ESSEX SECRET BUNKER
Crown Building, Shrublands
Road, Mistley, Manningtree,
Essex CO11 1HS
Tel: 01206 392271
Fax: 01206 393847
Essex secret bunker the former Essex County Council nuclear war headquarters.

FEERING & KELVEDON LOCAL HISTORY MUSEUM
Maldon Road, Kelvedon,
Colchester, Essex
Tel: 01376 570307
Artefacts from Roman settlement of Camonium.

FINCHINGFIELD GUILDHALL
Church Hill, Finchingfield,
Braintree, Essex CM7
Tel: 01371 810456
15thC Guildhall.

FIRSTSITE AT THE MINORIES
74 High Street, Colchester,
Essex CO1 1UE
Tel: 01206 577067
Fax: 01206 577161
Exhibitions of 20thC and contemporary art.

FOCAL POINT GALLERY
Southend Central Library,
Victoria Avenue,
Southend-on-Sea SS2 6EX
Tel: 01702 612621 ext 207
Fax: 01702 469241
Photographic gallery showing a programme of temporary exhibitions of contemporary photography.

FRINTON RAILWAY CROSSING COTTAGE & GARDEN
Frinton Gates, Frinton-on-Sea,
Essex CO13 9PN
Records of local history, especially the development of Frinton as a holiday resort.

FRY PUBLIC ART GALLERY
Bridge End Gardens, Castle
Street, Saffron Walden, Essex
CB10 1BD
Tel: 01799 513779
Permanent exhibition of 20thC British artists who have lived and worked in North West Essex.

GORDON'S GIN DISTILLERY
Fenton Way, Laindon, Basildon,
Essex SS15 6SH
Tel: 01268 564082
Fax: 01268 415592
The complete process of gin making and bottling.

HARLOW MUSEUM
Passmores House, Third
Avenue, Harlow, Essex
CM18 6YL
Tel: 01279 454959
Fax: 01279 626094
Five galleries covering the history of the area.

HARWICH LIFEBOAT MUSEUM
Timberfields, off Wellington
Road, Harwich, Essex
CO12 3EJ
Tel: 01255 503429
Lifeboat Museum includes last Clacton off-shore 34ft lifeboat and history of lifeboat service in Harwich.

HARWICH MARITIME MUSEUM
Low Lighthouse, The Green,
Harwich, Essex
Tel: 01255 503429
Special displays related to Royal Navy and commercial shipping. Redoubt, maritime museum, lifeboat museum, treadwheel crane.

HEDINGHAM CASTLE
Castle Hedingham, Halstead,
Essex C09 3DJ
Tel: 01787 460261
Fax: 01787 461473
For further details see page 55

HERITAGE CENTRE
Canvey Village, Canvey Road,
Canvey Island, Essex SS8
Tel: 01268 512220
Housed in the now redundant parish church of St Katherine, built in 1876.

HOLLYTREES MUSEUM
High Street, Colchester, Essex
CO1 1UG
Tel: 01206 282931
Fax: 01206 282925
Georgian house containing displays of costume and social history.

HOUSE ON THE HILL TOY MUSEUM
Stansted Mountfitchet, Stansted,
Essex CM24 8SP
Tel: 01279 813237
Fax: 01279 816391
Exciting animated toy museum covering 7,000sqft featuring a huge collection of toys from Victorian times to the 1970s and offering a nostalgic trip back to childhood.

KELVEDON HATCH NUCLEAR BUNKER
Kelvedon Hall Lane, Kelvedon
Hatch, Brentwood, Essex
CM15 0LB
Tel: 01277 364883
Fax: 01277 372562
Large three-storey ex-government regional HQ buried some 100ft below ground.

LANGDON CONSERVATION CENTRE & PLOTLAND MUSEUM
Third Avenue, Dunton, Basildon, Essex SS16 6EB
Tel: 01268 419095
Fax: 01268 546137
Langdon conservation and visitor centre and Plotland bungalow, built 1934.

LEIGH HERITAGE CENTRE
13a High Street, Leigh-on-Sea, Southend-on-Sea, Essex SS9 2EN
Tel: 01702 470834
Photographic exhibition, historical interpretive displays, Granny's kitchen.

MALDON & DISTRICT AGRICULTURAL & DOMESTIC MUSEUM
47 Church Street, Goldhanger, Maldon, Essex CM9 8AR
Tel: 01621 788647
Museum has extensive collection of farm machinery, domestic items of every kind, products of Maldon Ironworks, printing machines from 1910.

MALDON DISTRICT MUSEUM ASSOCIATION
The Promenade Lodge, 47 Mill Road, Maldon, Essex CM9 5HX
Tel: 01621 842688
Small museum devoted to Maldon Town, with many articles of general and domestic nature, in a charming small listed building.

MALDON MILLENNIUM EMBROIDERY
The Moot Hall, High Street, Maldon, Essex CM9 5PN
Tel: 01621 851553
Forty-two feet of embroidery in seven panels depicts 1,000 years of Maldon's history.

MANGAPPS FARM RAILWAY MUSEUM
Mangapps Farm, Southminster Road, Burnham-on-Crouch, Essex CM0 8QQ
Tel: 01621 784898
Fax: 01621 784898
Large collection of railway relics, restored station, locomotives, coaches and wagons.

MANNINGTREE & DISTRICT LOCAL HISTORY MUSEUM
Manningtree Library, High Street, Manningtree, Essex CO11 1AD
Tel: 01206 392747
Local history museum with displays of old photographs, artefacts, books, local maps and plans.

MARK HALL CYCLE MUSEUM
Off First Avenue, Muskham Road, Harlow, Essex CM20 2LF
Tel: 01279 439680
Fax: 01279 442786
A unique collection of over 80 cycles and accessories illustrating the history of the bicycle from 1818 to the 1980s.

MERSEA ISLAND MUSEUM
High Street, West Mersea, Colchester CO5 8QD
Tel: 01206 385191
Local history and natural history plus display of methods and equipment used in fishing and wildfowling.

THE MINORIES GALLERY
74 High Street, Colchester, Essex CO1 1OE
Tel: 01206 577067
Fax: 01206 577161
Grade A gallery showing a programme of temporary exhibitions of contemporary art, and housed in a converted Georgian house.

NATIONAL MOTORBOAT MUSEUM
Pitsea Hall Country Park, Pitsea, Basildon, Essex SS16 4UW
Tel: 01268 550088
Museum devoted to the history and evolution of the motorboat; racing hydroplanes, power boats and leisure boats.

THE NATIONAL VINTAGE WIRELESS & TELEVISION MUSEUM
The High Lighthouse, Harwich, Essex
Tel: 01206 322606
The museum is set out in 'room sets' of each era tracing the history of broadcasting from Marconi's and Baird's early experiments to present-day developments such as satellite.

NATURAL HISTORY MUSEUM
All Saints Church, High Street, Colchester, Essex CO1 1DN
Tel: 01206 282932
An interesting perspective on the local, natural environment from the Ice Age to the present day.

NORTH WEALD AIRFIELD
North Weald, Epping, Essex CM16 6AA
Tel: 01992 572705
Ground-floor fine old house at former main gate of North Weald Airfield.

PRITTLEWELL PRIORY
Priory Park, Victoria Avenue, Southend-on-Sea, Essex
Tel: 01702 342878
Fax: 01702 355110
Remains of 12thC priory with later additions.
For further details see page 53

SAFFRON WALDEN MUSEUM
Museum Street, Saffron Walden, Essex CB10 1JL
Tel: 01799 510333
Fax: 01799 510550
Friendly family-size museum of local history, decorative arts and ethnography with Great Hall gallery of archaeology and early history. The newly opened natural history gallery has interactive diplays suitable for all ages.

SOUTHCHURCH HALL
Southchurch Hall Close, Southend-on-Sea, Essex
Tel: 01702 476671
Fax: 01702 355110
Moated timber-framed 14thC manor house with Elizabetham extensions set in attractive gardens. Wide range of educational activities.
For further details see page 53

SOUTHEND PIER MUSEUM
Southend Pier, Marine Parade, Southend-on-Sea, Essex SS1 2EL
Tel: 01702 611214/614553
Situated in redundant pier workshops underneath the pier station at the shore end, exhibits include pier trains c1890.

THAXTED GUILDHALL
Town Street, Thaxted, Dunmow, Essex CM6 2LD
Tel: 01371 831339
Fax: 01371 830418
15thC building, permanent display of old photographs and relics, mainly relating to history of Thaxted. Open Sundays Easter to September. Bank holiday weekends.

THURROCK MUSEUM
Thameside Complex, Orsett Road, Grays, Essex RM17 5DX
Tel: 01375 382555
Fax: 01375 392666
An interesting display of artefacts, maps and models showing Thurrock's history from prehistoric to modern times.

TIPTREE TEA ROOM MUSEUM & SHOP WILKIN & SONS LTD
Tiptree, Colchester CO5 0RF
Tel: 01621 815407
Fax: 01621 819468
Tea room and shop with museum displaying how life was, and how the art of jam-making has advanced over the years at Tiptree.

TOY MUSEUM
Dedham Centre, High Street, Dedham, Colchester, Essex CO7 6AD
Tel: 01206 322666
Fax: 01206 322231
Collection of dolls, teddies, toys, games, play houses and pictures displayed in section of beautifully converted church.

TYMPERLEYS CLOCK MUSEUM
Trinity Street, Colchester, Essex CO1 1JN
Tel: 01206 282931
Fax: 01206 282937
Selection of Colchester-made clocks from the Mason collection displayed in 15thC house which Bernard Mason restored and presented to the town.

UNIVERSITY GALLERY
University of Essex, Wivenhoe Park, Colchester CO4 3SQ
Tel: 01206 872074
Fax: 01206 873702
Programme of exhibitions throughout term times.

WALTON HALL FARM MUSEUM
Walton Hall Road, Linford, Stanford-le-Hope, Essex SS17 0RN
Tel: 01375 671874
Main collection housed in 17thC English barn and other farm buildings.

WALTON MARITIME MUSEUM
East Terrace, Walton-on-the-Naze, Essex CO14 8PY
One hundred year-old carefully restored former lifeboat house.

THE WORKING SILK MUSEUM
New Mills, South Street, Braintree, Essex CM7 3GB
Tel: 01376 553393
Fax: 01376 330642
The country's last remaining heirloom silk weavers. See how silk fabric is produced from raw material to finished cloth.

GLOUCESTERSHIRE

BOURTON MODEL RAILWAY EXHIBITION
Box Bush, High Street, Bourton-on-the-Water, Cheltenham, Gloucestershire GL54 2AN
Tel: 01451 820686
Approximately 500 sq ft of some of the finest operating scenic model railway layouts in the country.

BREWERY ARTS
Brewery Court, Cirencester, Gloucestershire GL7 1JH
Tel: 01285 657181
Fax: 01285 644060
Originally a brewery, the building now houses 17 independent craft businesses with a central craft shop, gallery, coffee house, educational facilities, theatre, sculpture studio.

CHELTENHAM ART GALLERY & MUSEUM
Clarence Street, Cheltenham, Gloucestershire GL50 3JT
Tel: 01242 237431
Fax: 01242 262334
17thC Dutch and British paintings, English and Oriental pottery, furniture and notable Arts and Crafts Movement collection inspired by William Morris and Edward Wilson Story.
For further details see page 53

CIRENCESTER LOCK UP
Trinity Road, Cirencester, Gloucestershire GL7 1BR
Tel: 01285 655611
Fax: 01285 643286
Restored two-cell lock up dated 1804 including displays of social history and architectural conservation.

CORINIUM MUSEUM
Park Street, Cirencester, Gloucestershire GL7 2BX
Tel: 01285 655611
Fax: 01285 643286
Collection of antiquities from Roman Britain with full-scale reconstruction of Roman kitchen, dining room and mosaic craftsman's workshop.
For further details see page 54

COTSWOLD COUNTRYSIDE COLLECTION
Fosseway, Northleach, Cheltenham, Gloucestershire GL54 3JH
Tel: 01451 860715
Fax: 01451 860091
Lloyd Baker collection of agricultural history in former house of correction at Northleach.
For further details see page 54

COTSWOLD MOTOR MUSEUM & TOY COLLECTION
Bourton-on-the-Water, Cheltenham, Gloucestershire GL54 2BY
Tel: 01451 821255
Thirty cars and motorcycles on display with a selection of prams, toys and pedal cars.

COWDY GALLERY
31 Culver Street, Newent, Gloucestershire GL18 1DB
Tel: 01531 821173
A gallery showing contemporary glass from studios nationwide.

THE CRAFT COLLECTION
Dundry Nurseries, Bamfurlong, Cheltenham, Gloucestershire GL51 6SL
Tel: 01452 713124
Fax: 01452 857748
A display of old tools and bygones.

DEAN HERITAGE CENTRE
Camp Mill, Soudley, Cinderford, Gloucestershire GL14 2UB
Tel: 01594 822170
Museum displays housed in old corn mill in woodland setting, telling the unique story of the Forest of Dean.

FILKINS GALLERY
Cross Tree, Filkins, Nr Lechlade, Gloucestershire GL7 3JL
Tel: 01367 850385 (evenings)
Gallery in 18thC Cotswold stone barn devoted to the work of local contemporary artists and craftsmen.

THE FOLK MUSEUM
99–103 Westgate Street, Gloucester GL1 2PG
Tel: 01452 526467
Historic timber-framed buildings with new extensions displaying social history, crafts, trades and industries of Gloucestershire.

GLOUCESTER FOLK MUSEUM
99–103 Westgate Street, Gloucester, Gloucestershire GL1 2PG
Tel: 01452 526467
Fax: 01452 330495
15th–17thC timber-framed museum.

GLOUCESTER PRISON MUSEUM
H M Prison Remand Centre, Barrack Square, Gloucester, Gloucestershire GL1 2JN
Tel: 01452 529551
Fax: 01452 310302
Museum covering the history of Gloucester Prison.

GREAT WESTERN RAILWAY MUSEUM
The Old Railway Station, Off Old Station Way, Coleford, Gloucestershire GR16 7LD
Tel: 01594 833569
1883 GWR goods station, 1906 GWR signal box and 1884 small signal box.

HOLST BIRTHPLACE MUSEUM
4 Clarence Road, Pittville, Cheltenham, Gloucestershire GL52 2AY
Tel: 01242 524846
Regency house containing displays on the life and music of Gustav Holst, shows the upstairs–downstairs way of life, including working Victorian kitchen.

THE HOUSE OF THE TAILOR OF GLOUCESTER
9 College Court, Gloucester, Gloucestershire GL1 2NJ
Tel: 01452 422856
House chosen by Beatrix Potter as scene for The Tailor of Gloucester.

JENNER MUSEUM
Church Lane, High Street, Berkeley, Gloucestershire GL13 9BH
Tel: 01453 810631
Fax: 01453 811690
Museum commemorates the life and work of Edward Jenner, the discoverer of the smallpox vaccine.

JET AGE MUSEUM
Hanger 7, Staverton Airport, Staverton, Cheltenham, Gloucestershire GL2 9QY
Tel: 01452 330761
Fax: 01452 549725
A collection of aircraft engines including the superbly restored 1920s Jupiter for the Gloster Gamecock fighter replica.
For further details see page 54

THE JOHN MOORE COUNTRYSIDE MUSEUM
41 Church Street, Tewkesbury, Gloucestershire GL20 5SN
Tel: 01684 297174
Countryside collections past and present.

KEITH HARDING'S WORLD OF MECHANICAL MUSIC
Oak House, High Street, Northleach, Nr Cheltenham, Gloucestershire GL54 3ET
Tel: 01451 860181
Fax: 01451 861133
17thC wool merchant's house with antique clocks, musical boxes, automata and mechanical musical instruments presented as a live entertainment.
For further details see page 54

THE LITTLE MUSEUM (THE MERCHANT'S HOUSE)
45 Church Street, Tewkesbury, Gloucestershire GL20 5SN
Tel: 01684 297174
One of the Abbey cottages built 1450, restored 1970.

NATIONAL WATERWAYS MUSEUM
Llanthony Warehouse, Gloucester Docks, Gloucester, Gloucestershire GL1 2EH
Tel: 01452 318054
Fax: 01452 318066
Three floors of dockside warehouse with lively displays telling the story of Britain's canals.

NATURE IN ART
Wallsworth Hall, Twigworth, Gloucester, Gloucestershire GL2 9PA
Tel: 01452 731422
Fax: 01452 730937
Georgian Mansion dating from 1740 housing a unique collection of the world's finest wildlife art.
For further details see page 39

NORTON HALL ARCHITECTURAL SALVAGE & HERITAGE CENTRE
Norton Barn, Wainlodes Lane, Norton, Gloucester, Gloucestershire GL2 9LN
Tel: 01452 730630
Fax: 01452 731888
Architectural salvage and heritage centre incorporating educational and cultural displays, activities and meeting facilities.

PITTVILLE PUMP ROOM MUSEUM
Pittville Pump Room, Pittville Park, Cheltenham, Gloucestershire GL52 3JE
Tel: 01242 237431
Fax: 01242 526563/262334
Displays of original costume from 1760 to present day.

ROBERT OPIE COLLECTION AT THE MUSEUM OF ADVERTISING & PACKAGING
Albert Warehouse, Gloucester Docks, Gloucester, Gloucestershire GL1 2EH
Tel: 01452 302309
Steeped in nostalgia, the Robert Opie Collection of packaging and advertising brings over 100 years of shopping basket history vividly to life.

SHAMBLES
16–24 Church Street, Newent, Gloucestershire GL18 1PP
Tel: 01531 822144
Fax: 01531 821120
Reconstructed Victorian town set in over an acre comprising cottages, cobbled streets, alleys, square, shops and trade exhibits. Gift shop.

SOLDIERS OF GLOUCESTERSHIRE
Custom House, The Docks, Gloucester, Gloucestershire GL1 2HE
Tel: 01452 522682
Fax: 01452 311116
Listed Victorian building in historic docks, housing collections of Glosters and Royal Gloucestershire Hussars, award winning displays.

TETBURY POLICE MUSEUM
The Old Court House, 63 Long Street, Tetbury, Gloucestershire GL8 8AA
Tel: 01666 504670
Fax: 01666 504670
A collection of items used by the police in the Gloucestershire Constabulary.

TEWKESBURY MUSEUM
64 Barton Street, Tewkesbury, Gloucestershire GL20 5PX
Tel: 01684 295027
Housed in a half-timbered building.

VILLAGE LIFE EXHIBITION
The Old Mill, Bourton-on-the-Water, Cheltenham, Gloucestershire GL54 2BY
Tel: 01451 821255
Reconstruction of an Edwardian village shop complete with bedroom, above bathroom and kitchen.

WELLINGTON AVIATION ART
Bourton/Broadway Road, Moreton-in-Marsh, Gloucestershire GL56 0BG
Tel: 01608 650323
Aviation museum with permanent exhibition of 1939–45 war memorabilia and parts of the Wellington Aircraft.

WINCHCOMBE FOLK & POLICE MUSEUM
Town Hall, High Street, Winchcombe, Cheltenham, Gloucestershire GL54 5HZ
Tel: 01242 602925
The history of Winchcombe from Neolithic times to present day.

WINCHCOMBE RAILWAY MUSEUM & GARDEN
23 Gloucester Street, Winchcombe, Cheltenham, Gloucestershire GL54 5LX
Tel: 01242 620641
A hands-on museum of railway life.

GREATER LONDON

AGE EXCHANGE REMINISCENCE CENTRE
11 Blackheath Village, London SE3 9LA
Tel: 0181 318 9105
Fax: 0181 318 0060
Small museum of everyday life in the 1920s–40s.
For further details see page 60

ALEXANDER FLEMING LABORATORY MUSEUM
St Mary's Hospital, Praed Street, London W2 1NY
Tel: 0171 886 6528
Fax: 0171 886 6739
A visit to the laboratory in which Alexander Fleming discovered penicillin.

ARCHITECTURE CENTRE – ROYAL INSTITUTE OF BRITISH ARCHITECTS
66 Portland Place, London W1N 4AD
Tel: 0171 580 5533
Fax: 0171 255 1541
Continuous series of exhibitions, talks and workshops on architecture, design and the built environment.

ASSOCIATION GALLERY
9–10 Domingo Street, London EC1Y 0TA
Tel: 0171 608 1445
Fax: 0171 253 3007
Photographic exhibitions.

BADEN-POWELL HOUSE
Queen's Gate, London SW7 5JS
Tel: 0171 584 7031
Fax: 0171 590 6902
Exhibition tracing life history of Baden-Powell, founder of the Scout Association.

BANK OF ENGLAND MUSEUM
Bartholomew Lane, London EC2R 8AH
Tel: 0171 601 5545
Fax: 0171 601 5808
An engrossing mix of money, gold, people, forgery, architecture and fun.

BANKSIDE GALLERY
48 Hopton Street, London SE1 9JH
Tel: 0171 928 7521
Fax: 0171 928 2820
The gallery is the home of The Royal Watercolour Society and The Royal Society of Painter-Printmakers.
For further details see page 60

BARBICAN ART GALLERY
Level 3 Barbican Centre, Silk Street, London EC2Y 8DS
Tel: 0171 382 7105 ext 7632
Fax: 0171 628 0364
Part of the Barbican Centre for arts and conferences.

BARNET MUSEUM
31 Wood Street, Barnet, Hertfordshire EN5 4BE
Tel: 0181 440 8066
Samplers, military equipment, costume, photographs and framed photos of the area, local artefacts, archives and World War II display.

BETHLEM ROYAL HOSPITAL ARCHIVES & MUSEUM
The Bethlem Royal Hospital, Monks Orchard Road, Beckenham, Kent BR3 3BX
Tel: 0181 776 4537
Fax: 0181 777 4045
Museum relating to psychiatry.

BETHNAL GREEN MUSEUM OF CHILDHOOD
Cambridge Heath Road, London E2 9PA
Tel: 0181 983 5200
Fax: 0181 983 5225
One of the world's largest toy and nursery displays including dolls, dolls' houses, teddies, trains, children's costume and nursery antiques.

BEXLEY MUSEUM
Hall Place, Bourne Road, Bexley DA115 1PQ
Tel: 01322 526574
The local history museum of the Bexley area, housed in part of a Tudor mansion set in gardens open to the public. Permanent archaeology and natural history displays, temporary exhibitions mainly social history.
For further details see page 61

BISHOPSGATE INSTITUTE
230 Bishopsgate, London EC2M 4QH
Tel: 0171 247 6844
Fax: 0171 375 1794
Local history material and exhibitions of local art groups' work.

BOUNDARY GALLERY
98 Boundary Road, London NW8 0RH
Tel: 0171 624 1126
Exhibitions on monthly basis.

BRAMAH TEA & COFFEE MUSEUM
The Clove Building, Maguire Street, London SE1 2NQ
Tel: 0171 378 0222
Fax: 0171 378 0219
Britain's first tea and coffee museum features hundreds of different coffee grinders and machines, teapots and more.

BRITISH DENTAL ASSOCIATION MUSEUM
64 Wimpole Street, London W1M 8AL
Tel: 0171 935 0875
Fax: 0171 487 5232
Museum concentrates on the development of dentistry in the United Kingdom and on certain technical aspects of the profession.

BRITISH LIBRARY EXHIBITION GALLERIES
96 Euston Road, London NW1 2DB
Tel: 0171 412 7332
Innovative new exhibition galleries with on-site education programmes for Key Stage 2–A Level and the general public. School groups very welcome.
For further details see pages IBC & 61

BRITISH LIBRARY NATIONAL SOUND ARCHIVE
96 Euston Road, London NW1 2DB
Tel: 0171 412 7440
Fax: 0171 412 7441
Holds 1-million discs of all kinds and more than 80,000 hours of recorded tape.
For further details see pages IBC & 61

BRITISH MUSEUM
Great Russell Street, London WC1B 3DG
Tel: 0171 636 1555
Fax: 0171 323 8118
One of the great museums of the world showing the works of humans from all over the world from prehistoric times to the present day.

BROMLEY MUSEUM
The Priory, Church Hill, Orpington BR6 0HH
Tel: 01689 873826
Housed in a medieval/post medieval building standing in formal and informal gardens.
For further details see page 56

BRUCE CASTLE
Lordship Lane, London N17 8NU
Tel: 0181 808 8772
Fax: 0181 808 4118
Exhibitions on local and postal history.

BRUNEI GALLERY
Thornhaugh Street, Russell Square, London WC1H 0XG
Tel: 0171 323 6230
Fax: 0171 323 6010
A venue for special, temporary exhibitions of Asian and African art.

BRUNEL ENGINE HOUSE ROTHERHITHE
Tunnel Road, London SE16 4LF
Tel: 0181 748 3545
Within the original engine house in Tunnel Road SE16, this permanent exhibition commemorates the world's first subaqueous tunnel built by Sir Marc Isambard Brunel and son.

BUILDING CENTRE
26 Store Street, London WC1E 7BT
Tel: 0171 637 1022
Fax: 0171 580 9641
Largest display and source of information on building products/components in Europe. Access to the AXIS database of visual artists.

CABARET MECHANICAL THEATRE
33–34 The Market, Covent Garden, London WC2E 8RE
Tel: 0171 379 7961
Fax: 0171 497 5445
The most important collection of contemporary automata in England today including over 70 hand-made automata which spring into life at the touch of a button.

CABINET WAR ROOMS
Clive Steps, King Charles Street, London SW1A 2AQ
Tel: 0171 930 6961
Fax: 0171 839 5897
The underground headquarters used by Winston Churchill and the British Government during World War II: includes Cabinet Room, Transatlantic telephone room and Map Room.
For further details see page 55

CHURCH FARMHOUSE MUSEUM
Greyhound Hill, Hendon, London NW4 4JR
Tel: 0181 203 0130
Fax: 0181 359 3157
One of the oldest surviving dwelling houses in the London Borough of Barnet. Built about 1660, it was the centre of a busy dairy and hay making farm until the 1930s. The house was opened as a museum in 1955.
For further details see page 61

CLINK PRISON MUSEUM
1 Clink Street, Bankside, London SE1 9DG
Tel: 0171 403 6515
Fax: 0171 403 5813
The history of the Original Clink Prison and bankside brothels in the Bishop of Winchester's Liberty of the Clink.

CLOCK MUSEUM
The Clock Room, Guildhall Library, Aldermanbury, London EC2P 2EJ
Tel: 0171 606 3030 ext 1865
An exceptional collection of historic clocks, watches and marine timekeepers.

CLOWNS INTERNATIONAL CLOWNS' GALLERY & ARCHIVE
1 Hillman Street, London E8 1DY
Tel: 0171 608 0312
Housed in a renovated 1920s building this clown centre provides a national showcase about international clowns and clowning.

COLLEGE OF ARMS
Queen Victoria Street, London EC4V 4BT
Tel: 0171 248 2762
Fax: 0171 248 6448
Mansion built in the 1670s to house the English Officers of Arms and their records and the panelled Earl Marshal's Court.

COMBINED HARVEST
128 Talbot Road, London W11 1JA
Tel: 0171 221 4870
British design and crafts.

CONNAUGHT BROWN GALLERY
2 Albemarle Street, London W1X 3HF
Tel: 0171 408 0362
Fax: 0171 495 3137
Commercial art gallery dealing in 20thC paintings, drawings, watercolours and sculpture.

CONTEMPORARY APPLIED ARTS
2 Percy Street, London W1P 9FA
Tel: 0171 436 2344
Gallery and shop in Fitzrovia showing crafts, including ceramics, glass, textiles, wood, jewellery, pottery and metal.

CRAFTS COUNCIL GALLERY
44a Pentonville Road, London N1 9BY
Tel: 0171 278 7700
Series of exhibitions of high quality contemporary and historical craft.

CROFTON ROMAN VILLA
Crofton Road, Orpington
Tel: 01689 873826
The only Roman Villa in Greater London which is open to the public, showing ten rooms of a villa-house protected inside a public viewing building.
For further details see page 56

CRYSTAL PALACE MUSEUM
Anerley Hill, London SE19 2BA
Tel: 0181 676 0700
The museum tells the story of the Crystal Palace in photographs, by audio and video means, and the display of rare objects from the building.

CUMING MUSEUM
155–157 Walworth Road, London SE17 1RS
Tel: 0171 701 1342
Fax: 0171 903 7415
Worldwide collections of the Cuming family, joined with the history of Southwark, from Roman times to the 19thC.

DE MORGAN FOUNDATION
30 Vicarage Crescent, London SW11 3LD
Tel: 0181 785 6450
Major collection of paintings and drawings by Evelyn de Morgan and ceramics by William de Morgan.
For further details see page 61

DESIGN MUSEUM
28 Shad Thames, London SE1 2YD
Tel: 0171 403 6933
Fax: 0171 378 6540
Visitors of all ages can rediscover 100 years of design history, view state-of-the-art innovations from around the globe and enjoy an extensive programme of critically acclaimed exhibitions on design and architecture.
For further details see page 56

DICKENS HOUSE
48 Doughty Street, London WC1N 2LF
Tel: 0171 405 2127
Fax: 0171 831 5175
Four-floor house housing one of the greatest collections of Dickens' memorabilia.

DIORAMA GALLERY
34 Osnaburgh Street, London NW1 3ND
Tel: 0171 916 5467
Art gallery with work by disabled artists, European exchange exhibitions and mixed media contemporary art.

DULWICH PICTURE GALLERY
College Road, Dulwich Village, London SE21 7AD
Tel: 0181 693 5254
Fax: 0181 693 0923
Thirteen rooms and over 300 pictures on view.
For further details see page 67

EAST HAM NATURE RESERVE
Norman Road, London E6 4HN
Tel: 0181 470 4525
The churchyard of St Mary Magdalene Parish Church, which is managed to protect and support local wildlife.

ERITH MUSEUM
Erith Library, Walnut Tree Road, Erith, Kent DA8 1RS
Tel: 01322 336582
Fax: 01322 522921
Museum situated on the first floor of a library, shows archaeology and history of Erith, especially industrial and maritime.

FAN MUSEUM
12 Crooms Hill, London SE10 8ER
Tel: 0181 305 1441
Fax: 0181 293 1889
This museum is the only venue in the world devoted entirely to the art and craft of the fan.
For further details see page 57

FARADAY'S LABORATORY & MUSEUM
The Royal Institution of Great Britain, 21 Albemarle Street, London W1X 4BS
Tel: 0171 409 2992
Fax: 0171 629 3569
Restored 19thC magnetic laboratory of Michael Faraday with an adjacent display of apparatus.

FLORENCE NIGHTINGALE MUSEUM
Gassiot House, 2 Lambeth Palace Road, London SE1 7EW
Tel: 0171 620 0374
Fax: 0171 922 8079
History of Florence Nightingale told through original objects, audio-visual period settings etc.

FORTY HALL MUSEUM
Forty Hill, Enfield EN2 9HA
Tel: 0181 363 8196
Fax: 0181 367 9098
17th and 18thC furniture and pictures, ceramics, glass, maps, local history and temporary loan exhibitions.
For further details see page 62

FREUD MUSEUM
20 Maresfield Gardens, London NW3 5SX
Tel: 0171 435 2002
Fax: 0171 431 5452
Sigmund Freud's London home containing his library and study.
For further details see page 62

GEFFRYE MUSEUM
Kingsland Road, London E2 8EA
Tel: 0171 739 9893
Fax: 0171 729 5647
English domestic interiors from 1600 to 1950s set in delightful 18thC almshouses with pleasant gardens including walled herb garden.
For further details see page 62

GOLDEN HINDE EDUCATIONAL MUSEUM
St Mary Overie Dock, Cathedral Street, London SE1 9DG
Tel: 0171 403 0123
Full-scale reconstruction of Sir Francis Drake's world famous sailing galleon. Experience life aboard a Tudor warship.

GRANGE MUSEUM OF COMMUNITY HISTORY
Neasden Lane, London NW10 1QB
Tel: 0181 452 8311
Fax: 0181 208 4233
Situated in a converted 18thC cottage, the permanent exhibitions cover the development of the area known today as Brent from the late 18th to 20thC.

GREENWICH BOROUGH MUSEUM
232 Plumstead High Street, London SE18 1JT
Tel: 0181 855 3240
Fax: 0181 316 5754
Local history museum including archaeology, natural history and geology.

GUARDS MUSEUM
Wellington Barracks, Birdcage Walk, London SW1E 6HQ
Tel: 0171 414 3428
Collection of uniforms, colours and artefacts spanning over 300 years of history of the Foot Guards.

GUNNERSBURY PARK MUSEUM
Gunnersby Park, Popes Lane W3 8QL
Tel: 0181 992 1612
Fax: 0181 752 0686
This 18thC house, the former country home of William Hogarth, has been fully restored and now houses an exhibition of Hogarth's life and work.
For further details see page 63

HAMILTONS GALLERY
13 Carlos Place, London W1Y 5AG
Tel: 0171 499 9493
Fax: 0171 629 9919
Monthly photographic exhibitions, permanent print room.

HARROW MUSEUM & HERITAGE CENTRE
Headstone Manor, Pinner View, Harrow, Middlesex HA2 6PX
Tel: 0181 861 2626
Fax: 0181 863 6407
16thC Tithe Barn and moated manor house dating back to the 14thC.

HARROW SCHOOL OLD SPEECH ROOM GALLERY
5 High Street, Harrow, Middlesex HA1 3HP
Tel: 0181 869 1205
Museum contains varied but distinguished collection: Egyptian, Greek and Roman antiquities; English watercolours; Modern British paintings; Horroviana and Natural History.

HAYWARD GALLERY
South Bank Centre, Belvedere Road, London SE1 8XZ
Tel: 0171 928 3144
Fax: 0171 928 0063
The Hayward Gallery has been the originator or host of many of the world's most influential exhibitions since 1968.
For further details see page 63

HEATHROW ROOF GARDEN
Terminal 2, Heathrow Airport, Hounslow, Middlesex UB3 5AP
Tel: 0181 745 5259
Fax: 0181 745 5230
Visitors may watch both the airport and airline activity from the roof of Terminal 2.

HMS BELFAST
Morgan's Lane, Tooley Street, London SE1 2JH
Tel: 0171 407 6434
Fax: 0171 403 0719
Naval vessel which fought in World War II.
For further details see page 55

HOGARTH'S HOUSE
Hogarth Lane, Great West Road, Chiswick, London W4 2QN
Tel: 0181 944 6757
This 18thC house, the former country home of William Hogarth, has been fully restored and now houses an exhibition of Hogarth's life and work.
For further details see page 57

HONOURABLE ARTILLERY COMPANY MUSEUM
Armoury House, City Road, London EC1Y 2BQ
Tel: 0171 382 1530
Fax: 0171 382 1538
History of the company from the 19thC including uniforms, weapons, equipment, applied art, silver and medals.

HORNIMAN MUSEUM & GARDENS
100 London Road, Forest HIll, London SE23 3PQ
Tel: 0181 699 1872
Fax: 0181 291 5506
Museum about the world we live in – our cultures, beliefs, crafts, products and the natural environment.

HOUSE OF DETENTION
Clerkenwell Close, Clerkenwell Green, London EC1R 0AS
Tel: 0171 253 9494
Fax: 0171 251 1897
London's underground prison at Clerkenwell built upon one of London's earliest prison sites originally dating back to 1616.

HUNTERIAN & OTHER MUSEUMS OF THE ROYAL COLLEGE OF SURGEONS

Royal College of Surgeons, 35–43 Lincolns Inn Fields, London WC2A 3PN
Tel: 0171 405 3474 ext 3011
Fax: 0171 405 4438
Museums of anatomy, pathology and odontology; also displays of historical surgical instruments.

IMPERIAL WAR MUSEUM

Lambeth Road, London SE1 6HZ
Tel: 0171 416 5000
Fax: 0171 416 5374
Museum tells the story of 20thC war from Flanders to Bosnia.
For further details see page 55

JAPANESE GALLERY

66d Kensington Church Street, London W8 4BY
Tel: 0171 229 2934
Different Japanese woodcut exhibitions held regularly.

JEWISH MUSEUM – CAMDEN

Raymond Burton House, 129–131 Albert Street, London NW1 7NB
Tel: 0171 284 1997
Fax: 0171 267 9008
Attractive galleries on Jewish history and religious life in Britain and beyond. One of the world's finest collections of Jewish ceremonial art.
For further details see page 58

JEWISH MUSEUM – FINCHLEY

80 East End Road N3 2SY
Tel: 0181 349 1143
Fax: 0181 343 2162
Displays on Jewish immigration and history in London Tailoring and furniture workshops. Moving exhibitions on British-born Holocaust survivor, Leon Greenman.
For further details see page 58

JILL GEORGE GALLERY

38 Lexington Street, London W1R 3HR
Tel: 0171 439 7319
Fax: 0171 287 0478
London's West End contemporary art gallery showing the best in contemporary British and European originals and prints. Monthly exhibition programme.

KEW BRIDGE STEAM MUSEUM

Green Dragon Lane, Brentford, Middlesex TW8 0EN
Tel: 0181 568 4757
Fax: 0181 569 9978
Victorian waterworks housing massive steam-powered pumping engines plus steam railway, water history and waterwheel.

KINGSTON UPON THAMES MUSEUM & HERITAGE SERVICE

Wheatfield Way, Kingston upon Thames, Surrey KT1 2PS
Tel: 0181 546 5386
Fax: 0181 547 6426
Local archaeological finds, the art gallery, the Zoopraxiscope of Eadweard Muybridge and Martinware Pottery.

KIRKALDY TESTING MUSEUM

99 Southwark Street, London SE1 0JF
Tel: 01322 332195
Working equipment and exhibition about the machinery David Kirkaldy designed – to experiment and test the strength of materials to uniform standards.

LEIGHTON HOUSE MUSEUM & ART GALLERY

12 Holland Park Road, London W14 8LZ
Tel: 0171 602 3316
The paintings, drawings and sculpture include works by Leighton, Burne-Jones, Millais, Poynter, Stevens, Alma-Tadema, Cecil and a French bequest.
For further details see page 63

LIVESEY MUSEUM

682 Old Kent Road, London SE15 1JF
Tel: 0171 639 5604
Fax: 0171 277 5384
The Livesey Museum runs a changing programme of lively and unusual interactive exhibitions for children up to the age of 12, their parents, carers and schools.

LLEWELLYN ALEXANDER GALLERY

124–126 The Cut, London SE1 8LN
Tel: 0171 620 1322
Fax: 0171 928 9469
Art exhibitions of living British artists with a new exhibition each month. Also large collection of miniatures.

LONDON CANAL MUSEUM

12–13 New Wharf Road, London N1 9RT
Tel: 0171 713 0836
Museum devoted to the commercial and social history of the canals and the long forgotten trade in natural ice.

LONDON FIRE BRIGADE MUSEUM

Winchester House, 94a Southwark Bridge Road, London SE1 0EX
Tel: 0171 587 2894
Fax: 0171 587 2878
Fire service appliances, equipment and other memorabilia dating back to the 17thC.

LONDON GAS MUSEUM

British Gas Plc, Twelvetrees Crescent, London E3 3JH
Tel: 0171 538 4982
Fax: 0171 538 0781
Small museum illustrates the history of the gas industry with particular emphasis on London.

LONDON SILVER VAULTS

Chancery House, 53–64 Chancery Lane, London WC2A 1QT
Tel: 0171 242 3844
Fax: 0171 405 5648
Forty shops containing the largest display of silver under one roof in the world.

LONDON TOY & MODEL MUSEUM

21–23 Craven Hill, Bayswater, London W2 3EN
Tel: 0171 706 8000
Fax: 0171 706 8823
After extensive refurbishment there are now over 20 themed galleries housing toys, from trains to dolls, and working models; also a ride-on carousel and steam train in garden.

LONDON TRANSPORT MUSEUM

39 Wellington Street, Covent Garden, London WC2E 7BB
Tel: 0171 379 6344
Fax: 0171 836 4118
Spectacular displays of buses, trams and trains reveal the fascinating story of travel, people and London.

LORDS TOURS

Lords Grounds, London NW8 8QN
Tel: 0171 432 1033
Expert guided tours of Lords including the Long Room, the MCC Museum, Real Tennis Court, the Mound Stand, Indoor School and the Lords Shop. Open throughout the year (except major matches and preparation days). Admission charge – group rates available.

MALL GALLERIES

The Mall, London SW1Y 5BD
Tel: 0171 930 6844
Fax: 0171 839 7830
Exhibitions, by a number of art societies throughout the year, of contemporary art mainly by British artists in traditional media.

MANOR PARK LIBRARY & MUSEUM

Romford Road, London E12 5SY
Tel: 0181 514 0274
Tells the story of Newham and its people.

MARKFIELD BEAM ENGINE & MUSEUM

Markfield Road, South Tottenham, London N15 4RB
Tel: 0181 800 7061
A restored 1886 Beam pumping engine housed in its original building.
For further details see page 40

MARX MEMORIAL LIBRARY

37A Clerkenwell Green, London EC1R 0DU
Tel: 0171 253 1485
Fax: 0171 253 1485
Specialist subscription library. Marxism and social sciences, Spanish Civil War, US Labour movement, peace, early radicals and Chartists. Historic building.

MARYLEBONE CRICKET CLUB (MCC)

Lord's Cricket Ground, London NW8 8QN
Tel: 0171 423 1033
Fax: 0171 286 9545
Expert guided tours of Lord's that take in the Long Room, the MCC Museum, the Mound Stand, the Indoor Cricket School and the Real Tennis Court; telephone for tour schedule.

MEDICI GALLERIES

7 Grafton Street, Bond Street, London W1X 3LA
Tel: 0171 629 5675
Features a changing display of contemporary work including paintings, sculpture, ceramics and limited-edition prints.

MERTON HERITAGE CENTRE

The Canons, Madeira Road, Mitcham CR4 4HD
Tel: 0181 640 9387
Based at The Canons, a beautiful historic house in Mitcham, the Heritage Centre tells the story of Merton and its people, through a changing programme of exhibitions and special events.
For further details see page 63

MICHAEL PARKIN GALLERY

11 Motcomb Street, London SW1X 8LB
Tel: 0171 235 8144
Fax: 0171 245 9846
Art gallery dealing in modern British art from 1860 to present day.

MUSEUM OF ARTILLERY IN THE ROTUNDA

Repository Road, London SE18 4DN
Tel: 0181 316 5402
Museum traces the design and manufacture of cannon-type weapons with sections on small arms and automatic weapons, fuses and detonators, and the larger weapons.
For further details see page 64

MUSEUM OF GARDEN HISTORY

St Mary-at-Lambeth, Lambeth Palace Road, London SE1 7LB
Tel: 0171 261 1891
Fax: 0171 401 8869
Memorial to the work of the Tradescants, royal gardeners to Charles I and Henrietta Maria. Replica 17thC garden, Charles II.
For further details see page 64

MUSEUM OF INSTRUMENTS

Royal College of Music, Prince Consort Road, London SW7 2BS
Tel: 0171 589 3643 ext 4346
Fax: 0171 589 7740
Six hundred exhibits including the Donaldson, Tagore, Hipkins, Ridley and Hartley collections; keyboard, stringed and wind instruments from the 16th–19thC.

MUSEUM OF LONDON

150 London Wall, London EC2Y 5HN
Tel: 0171 600 3699 ext 290
Fax: 0171 600 1058
The galleries illustrate over 2,000 years of the capital's social history from prehistoric times to the present day

MUSEUM OF RICHMOND

Old Town Hall, Whittaker Avenue, Richmond, Surrey TW9 1TP
Tel: 0181 332 1141
Housed in old town hall (1893).

THE MUSEUM OF RUGBY AT TWICKENHAM

Rugby Football Union, Rugby Road, Twickenham TW1 1DZ
Tel: 0181 892 2000/8877
Fax: 0181 892 2817
Audio-visual and interactive displays on the history of rugby with scrum machine and mock-ups of dressing room, medical room and commentary box.
For further details see page 58

MUSEUM OF THE MOVING IMAGE

South Bank, Waterloo, London SE1 8XT
Tel: 0171 928 3535
The museum is a celebration of cinema and television.

MUSEUM OF THE ORDER OF SAINT JOHN

St John's Gate, St John's Lane, London EC1M 4DA
Tel: 0171 253 6644
A 16thC gateway housing artefacts relating to the knights of St John and St John Ambulance.
For further details see page 65

MUSICAL MUSEUM

368 High Street, Brentford TW8 0BD
Tel: 0181 560 8108
Exciting trip into the history of recorded sound with demonstrations of an amazing collection of automatic musical instruments.
For further details see page 64

N R OMELL GALLERY

6 Duke Street, St James, London SW1Y 6BN
Tel: 0171 839 6223
Fax: 0171 930 1625
Private art gallery specialising in 18th and 19thC marine oil paintings.

NATIONAL ARMY MUSEUM

Royal Hospital Road, Chelsea, London SW3 4HT
Tel: 0171 730 0717
Fax: 0171 823 6573
The story of the British soldier in peace and war through five centuries.

NATIONAL GALLERY

Trafalgar Square, London WC2N 5DN
Tel: 0171 747 2424
Fax: 0171 747 2431
Superb collection of Western European painting from 1260–1900. Most of Europe's greatest artists represented.

NATIONAL MARITIME MUSEUM

Romney Road, Greenwich, London SE10 9NF
Tel: 0181 858 4422
Fax: 0181 312 6632
Britain's maritime heritage illustrated through artefacts, models, paintings, navigation instruments, archives, photographs, regular exhibitions and a children's gallery.
For further details see page 38

NATIONAL PORTRAIT GALLERY
St Martin's Place, London WC2H 0HE
Tel: 0171 306 0055
Fax: 0171 306 0056
Permanent collection of portraits of famous British men and women from the Middle Ages to the present day.
For further details see page 64

NATIONAL POSTAL MUSEUM
King Edward Building, King Edward Street, London EC1A 1LP
Tel: 0171 776 3636
One of the most important and extensive collections of postage stamps in the world, including the Phillips and Berne Collections.
For further details see page 65

NATURAL HISTORY MUSEUM
Cromwell Road, London SW7 5BD
Tel: 0171 938 9123
Fax: 0171 938 9290
Home of the wonders of the natural world, one of the most popular museums in the world and one of London's finest landmarks.
For further details see page 65

NEW ACADEMY GALLERY AND BUSINESS ART GALLERIES
34 Windmill Street, Fitzrovia, London W1P 1HH
Tel: 0171 323 4700
Fax: 0171 436 3059
The New Academy Gallery exhibits a wide range of paintings, sculpture and original prints by leading and emerging British artists.
For further details see page 65

NORTH WOOLWICH OLD STATION MUSEUM
Pier Road, London E16 2JJ
Tel: 0171 474 7244
History of the Great Eastern Railway.

OLD OPERATING THEATRE MUSEUM & HERB GARRET
9a St Thomas' Street, London SE1 9RY
Tel: 0171 955 4791
Restored 1822 women's operating theatre is the only 19thC operating theatre in England.

ORLEANS HOUSE GALLERY
Riverside, Twickenham TW1 3DJ
Tel: 0181 892 0221
Fax: 0181 744 0501
Art gallery sited in picturesque woodland garden by the Thames.
For further details see page 66

PERCIVAL DAVID FOUNDATION OF CHINESE ART
53 Gordon Square, London WC1H 0PD
Tel: 0171 387 3909
Fax: 0171 383 5163
The Percival David foundation houses the finest collection of 10th–18thC ceramics outside China.
For further details see page 66

PETRIE MUSEUM OF EGYPTIAN ARCHAEOLOGY
University College London, London WC1E 6BT
Tel: 0171 387 7050 ext 2884
A university teaching collection open to the public.

PHOTOGRAPHERS' GALLERY
5 & 8 Great Newport Street, London WC2H 7HY
Tel: 0171 831 1772
Fax: 0171 836 9704
Photographic exhibitions, original photographic print sales room and photographic bookshop with magazines and postcards.

PITSHANGER MANOR MUSEUM
Mattock Lane, London W5 5EQ
Tel: 0181 567 1227
Fax: 0181 567 0595
Country home of architect Sir John Soane and rebuilt by him 1800–1804. New contemporary art gallery showing international exhibitions opened in 1996.

POLISH INSTITUTE & SIKORSKI MUSEUM
20 Princes Gate, London SW7 1PT
Tel: 0171 589 9249
Polish militaria.

POLLOCK'S TOY MUSEUM
1 Scala Street, London W1P 1LT
Tel: 0171 636 3452
Toys of all kinds – dolls, dolls' houses, Victorian nursery, toy theatres, teddy bears, tin toys, folk toys worldwide.

PUMPHOUSE EDUCATIONAL MUSEUM
Lavender Pond and Nature Park, Lavender Road off Rotherhithe Street, London SE16 1DZ
Tel: 0171 231 2976
Private collection of artefacts from the Thames foreshore in Rotherhithe. A 3-hectare nature park and pond. Hands-on exhibition for schools 'now and then'.

PUPPET CENTRE TRUST
BAC, Lavender Hill, London SW11 5TN
Tel: 0171 228 5335
Puppet Centre has a small permanent exhibition of figures, a reference library and information and specialist book and materials sales facilities.

QUEEN'S GALLERY BUCKINGHAM PALACE
Buckingham Palace Road, London SW1A 1AA
Tel: 0171 839 1377
Once the Palace chapel, the gallery has constantly changing exhibitions allowing the general public glimpses of rarely seen works of art from the Royal Collection.

RAGGED SCHOOL MUSEUM
46–50 Copperfield Road, London E3 4RR
Tel: 0181 980 6405
Fax: 0181 983 3481
Museum about the East End, in canalside warehouses which once housed Barnardo's largest ragged school.

ROYAL ACADEMY OF ARTS
Burlington House, Piccadilly, London W1V 0DS
Tel: 0171 439 7438
Fax: 0171 434 0837
Oldest society in Great Britain devoted solely to the fine arts.

ROYAL AIR FORCE MUSEUM
Grahame Park Way, London NW9 5LL
Tel: 0181 200 1763
Fax: 0181 205 8044
Britain's National Museum of aviation features over 70 full size aircraft, Flight Simulator, Jet Provost Trainer & Eurofighter 2000 Theatre. 'Fun n Flight' interactive gallery opening in March 1998.

ROYAL COLLEGE OF ART
Kensington Gore, London SW7 2EU
Tel: 0171 590 4444
Fax: 0171 590 4500
Regular student work-in-progress exhibitions and visiting exhibitions such as the 20thC British Art Fair.

ROYAL FUSILIERS MUSEUM
HM Tower of London, London EC3N 4AB
Tel: 0171 488 5611
Exhibits illustrate the history of the Royal Fusiliers.

ROYAL LONDON HOSPITAL ARCHIVES CENTRE & MUSEUM
Royal London Hospital, Whitechapel, London E1 1BB
Tel: 0171 377 7000 ext 3364
Fax: 0171 377 7077
Archives and museum housed in the crypt of a fine 19thC Gothic church where the story of the Royal London Hospital (founded 1740) is told.

ROYAL MILITARY SCHOOL OF MUSIC (KNELLER HALL)
Kneller Road, Whitton, Middlesex TW2 7DU
Tel: 0181 898 5533
Fax: 0181 898 7906
Listed building rebuilt 1848.

ROYAL MINT SOVEREIGN GALLERY
7 Grosvenor Gardens, London SW1W 0BH
Tel: 0171 931 7977
Fax: 0171 630 6592
The new Royal Mint Sovereign Gallery relates the 500 year-old history of the famous gold coin.

SAATCHI COLLECTION
98a Boundary Road, London NW8 0RH
Tel: 0171 624 8299
Fax: 0171 624 3798
Exhibits of contemporary art – paintings, photographs, sculpture and installations.

SALVATION ARMY HERITAGE CENTRE
3rd Floor Salvationist Publishing & Supplies Ltd, 117–121 Judd Street, London WC1H 9NN
Tel: 0171 387 1656
Fax: 0171 387 3768
Exhibits concentrate on history of early Salvation Army.

SCIENCE MUSEUM
Exhibition Road, London SW7 2DD
Tel: 0171 938 8000
Fax: 0171 938 8118
Over 200,000 different exhibits covering almost every imaginable sector of science, technology, industry and medicine.

SERPENTINE GALLERY
Kensington Gardens, London W2 3XA
Tel: 0171 402 6075
Fax: 0171 402 4103
The gallery provides a platform for contemporary artists both British and international.

SHAKESPEARE'S GLOBE EXHIBITION
New Globe Walk, Bankside, London SE1 9DT
Tel: 0171 902 1500
Fax: 0171 902 1515
The Exhibition uses dioramas, graphics, videos and models to tell the story of William Shakespeare's 'workplace': Elizabethan Bankside.

SHERLOCK HOLMES MUSEUM
221b Baker Street, London NW1 6XE
Tel: 0171 935 8866
Grade II listed lodging house.

SIR JOHN SOANE'S MUSEUM
13 Lincoln's Inn Fields, London WC2A 3BP
Tel: 0171 405 2107
Fax: 0171 831 3957
Former residence of Sir John Soane, architect of the Bank of England.

SOSEKI MUSEUM IN LONDON
80b The Chase, London SW4 0NG
Tel: 0171 720 8718
Fax: 0181 684 9925
Private terraced house, now converted into a museum which is devoted to Soseki Natsume, one of the distinguished Japanese novelists who lived there from 1900 to 1902.

SOUTH LONDON GALLERY
65 Peckham Road, London SE5 8UH
Tel: 0171 703 6120
Fax: 0171 252 4730
The South London Gallery is over 100 years' old but it has become a focus for the exhibition of contemporary art in south east London.

SPENCER HOUSE
27 St James's Place, London SW1 1NR
Tel: 0171 499 8620
Fax: 0171 493 5765
Built for the first Earl Spencer, this 18thC town house has a fine collection of paintings and furniture on display.
For further details see page 59

TATE GALLERY
Millbank, London SW1P 4RG
Tel: 0171 887 8000
Fax: 0171 887 8007
The Tate Gallery holds the national collection of British painting from 1500 to the present day, the Turner Collection and the national collection of 20thC painting and sculpture.
For further details see page 66

THEATRE MUSEUM
Russell Street, London WC2E 7PA
Tel: 0171 836 7891
Fax: 0171 836 5148
Five galleries include permanent display of history of performance in the United Kingdom.

THOMAS CORAM FOUNDATION FOR CHILDREN
40 Brunswick Square, London WC1N 1AZ
Tel: 0171 278 2424
Fax: 0171 837 8084
Coram Museum housing the Foundling Hospital Collection works of art by Hogarth, Gainsborough and Reynolds, Handel memorabilia, furniture and clocks.

THE TOWER BRIDGE EXPERIENCE
Tower Bridge, London SE1 2UP
Tel: 0891 600 210
Fax: 0171 357 7935
Transports visitors back in time to the 1890s to discover how and why the bridge came to be built and gives them a chance to visit the original Victorian engine rooms and to see the London skyline from the top of the Thames.
For further details see page 66

TWININGS
216 The Strand, London WC2R 1AP
Tel: 0171 353 3511
It was at these premises in 1706 that the famous company of R Twining was founded.

UPMINSTER TITHE BARN & AGRICULTURAL FOLK MUSEUM
Hall Lane, Upminster, Essex RM14 1AU
Tel: 01708 447535
15thC thatched barn with domestic and agricultural items on show.

VALENCE HOUSE MUSEUM
Becontree Avenue, Dagenham, Essex RM8 3HT
Tel: 0181 592 4500 ext 4293
Fax: 0181 595 8307
Local history museum and gallery – in mainly 17thC timber-framed and plastered manor house on partly moated site.

VESTRY HOUSE MUSEUM
Vestry Road, Walthamstow, London E17 9NH
Tel: 0181 509 1917 ext 4391
Reconstructed Victorian parlour and police cell, domestic display, the Bremer car and exhibits on local crafts and industry housed in an 18thC workhouse.

VICTORIA & ALBERT MUSEUM
Cromwell Road, South Kensington, London SW7 2RL
Tel: 0171 938 8500
Fax: 0171 938 8379
The world's finest museum of the decorative arts.
For further details see page 67

WALLACE COLLECTION
Hertford House, Manchester Square, London W1M 6BN
Tel: 0171 935 0687
Fax: 0171 224 2155
Permanent collection of European paintings, furniture, porcelain miniatures and sculpture plus arms and armour.
For further details see page 59

WANDLE INDUSTRIAL MUSEUM
The Vestry Hall Annexe, London Road, Mitcham, Surrey CR4 3UD
Tel: 0181 648 0127
Fax: 0181 685 0249
Established in 1983 by local people with the main aim of creating a riverside museum that reflects the rich heritage of the Wandle Valley.

WANDSWORTH MUSEUM
The Courthouse, 11 Garratt Lane, London SW18 4AQ
Tel: 0181 871 7074
Fax: 0181 871 4602
Museum tells the story of the area that is now the London Borough of Wandsworth from prehistoric times to the present day.
For further details see page 60

WELLCOME TRUST
The Wellcome Building, 183 Euston Road, London NW1 2BE
Tel: 0171 611 8351
Fax: 0171 611 8416
Headquarters of medical research charity, is home to several exhibitions including 'Science for Life': a permanent exhibition on medical science and 'History of Medicine' gallery.
For further details see page 39

WELLINGTON MUSEUM (APSLEY HOUSE)
149 Piccadilly, Hyde Park Corner, London W1V 9FA
Tel: 0171 499 5676
Fax: 0171 493 6576
The Iron Duke's London palace housing his famous collection of paintings, porcelain, silver, sculpture, orders and decorations.

WESTMINSTER ABBEY MUSEUM
The East Cloister, Westminster Abbey, London SW1P 3PA
Tel: 0171 222 5152/233 0019
Fax: 0171 233 2072
The Abbey's famous collection of Royal and other effigies forms the centrepiece of the exhibition, with other attractions including replicas of Coronation regalia and surviving panels of medieval glass.

WHITECHAPEL ART GALLERY
Whitechapel High Street, London E1 7QX
Tel: 0171 522 7888
Fax: 0171 377 1685
Housed behind a striking Art Nouveau front, a wide range of temporary exhibitions, generally of modern art, are displayed throughout the year.

WILLIAM MORRIS GALLERY
Lloyd Park, Forest Road, London E17 4PP
Tel: 0181 527 3782
Fax: 0181 527 7070
Mid 18thC house, boyhood home of William Morris with permanent exhibition on his life and work.

WIMBLEDON LAWN TENNIS MUSEUM
All England Lawn Tennis and Croquet Club, Church Road, Wimbledon, London SW19 5AE
Tel: 0181 946 6131
Fax: 0181 944 6497
View the world famous Centre Court and Championship trophies plus video highlights of great players through the ages in action.

WIMBLEDON MUSEUM OF LOCAL HISTORY
26 Lingfield Road, London SW19 4QD
Tel: 0181 296 9914
Victorian building (1858).

WIMBLEDON WINDMILL MUSEUM
Windmill Road, Wimbledon Common, London SW19 5NR
Tel: 0181 947 2825
This hollow-post windmill (1817) houses a museum depicting the history of windmills and windmilling in Britain.

WINSTON CHURCHILL'S BRITAIN AT WAR EXPERIENCE
64–66 Tooley Street, London Bridge, London SE1 2TF
Tel: 0171 403 3171
Fax: 0171 403 5104
Theme museum about the Second World War and how the British coped with the day-to-day life, rationing, blackouts and air raids.

WOODLANDS ART GALLERY
90 Mycenae Road, London SE3 7SE
Tel: 0181 858 5847
Fax: 0181 858 5847
Contemporary art gallery housed on ground floor of a Georgian mansion situated in attractive gardens.

WORLD OF SILK
David Evans and Company, Bourne Road, Crayford, Kent DA1 4BP
Tel: 01322 559401
Fax: 01322 550476
Demonstrations of hand silk printing.

GREATER MANCHESTER

ASTLEY CHEETHAM ART GALLERY
Trinity Street, Stalybridge, SK15 2BN
Tel: 0161 338 2708
Fax: 0161 303 8200
Exhibitions change monthly and cover all aspects of fine art and craft.

BOLTON MUSEUM & ART GALLERY
Le Mans Crescent, Bolton BL1 1SE
Tel: 01204 22311 ext 2191
Galleries including archaeology, zoology, geology, natural history, Egyptology, aquarium and art gallery.

BURY ART GALLERY & MUSEUM
Moss Street, Bury, Greater Manchester BL9 0DG
Tel: 0161 253 5879
Fax: 0161 705 5915
Wrigley collection of Victorian paintings by Turner, Constable, Landseer, Cox etc.
For further details see page 67

CITY ART GALLERIES
Mosley Street, Princess Street, Manchester, M2 3JL
Tel: 0161 236 5244
Fax: 0161 236 7369
Paintings, sculpture, ceramics, silver, glass and furniture including works by Constable, Stubbs, Gainsborough and a famous collection of Pre-Raphaelites.

CORGI HERITAGE CENTRE
53 York Street, Heywood, Rochdale, Lancashire OL10 4NR
Tel: 01706 365812
Fax: 01706 627811
Opened in June 1995 the Corgi Heritage Centre is located on two levels fronted by a retail area.

THE FUSILIERS' MUSEUM, LANCASHIRE
Wellington Barracks, Bolton Road, Bury, Lancashire BL8 2PL
Tel: 0161 764 2208
The history of the Lancashire Fusiliers 1688–1968. The Royal Regiment of Fusilers 1968 to date.

GALLERY OF ENGLISH COSTUME
Platt Hall, Rusholme, Manchester M14 5LL
Tel: 0161 224 5217
One of the finest collections of English costume outside London.

GREATER MANCHESTER POLICE
Newton Street, Manchester M1 1ES
Tel: 0161 856 3287
Fax: 0161 856 3286
Museum displays depicting the history of policing in Greater Manchester housed in an original Victorian police station.

HERITAGE INTERPRETATION SECTION
Wigan Pier, Wallgate, Wigan, Greater Manchester WN3 4EU
Tel: 01942 323666
Fax: 01942 828540
Life in Wigan in the 1900s with 'The Way we Were', professional theatre company. World's largest steam mill engine, Victorian schoolroom and day visitor facilities.

LANCASHIRE MINING MUSEUM
Buile Hill Park, Eccles Old Road, Salford, Lancashire M6 8GL
Tel: 0161 736 1832
Two reproduction coal mines; history of Coalmining Gallery situated in a Georgian House.

MANCHESTER JEWISH MUSEUM
190 Cheetham Hill Road, Manchester M8 8LW
Tel: 0161 834 9879
Fax: 0161 832 7353
Former Spanish and Portuguese synagogue (1874), now restored to its former glory. Grade II listed building. Displays relate the history of the Manchester Jewish community. Heritage trails and special events are conducted throughout the year, and a busy education programme operates.
For further details see page 68

MANCHESTER MUSEUM
The University, Oxford Road, Manchester M13 9PL
Tel: 0161 275 2634
Fax: 0161 275 2676
Collections of archaeology, archery, egyptology, botany, entomology, ethnology, geology, numismatics, zoology, live snakes, lizards and fish.
For further details see page 67

MANCHESTER UNITED FOOTBALL CLUB MUSEUM & TOUR CENTRE
Manchester United Football Club, Old Trafford, Manchester M16 0RA
Tel: 0161 872 1661
Fax: 0161 930 2904
Tour of Manchester United football ground.

MEMORIAL ART GALLERY
Wellington Road South, Stockport, Cheshire SK3 8AB
Tel: 0161 474 4453
Fax: 0161 480 4960
Temporary exhibitions change every month. Workshops available with most exhibitions.

MUSEUM OF THE MANCHESTERS
Ashton Town Hall, Market Place, Ashton-under-Lyne, Lancashire OL6 7JU
Tel: 0161 344 3078
History of the Manchester regiment set in the context of the local society in which it was based.

MUSEUM OF SCIENCE & INDUSTRY IN MANCHESTER
Liverpool Road, Castlefield, Manchester M3 4FP
Tel: 0161 832 2244/1830
Fax: 0161 833 2184
The Museum of Science and Industry in Manchester based in the world's oldest passenger railway station with galleries to educate and entertain.
For further details see page 68

MUSEUM OF TRANSPORT MANCHESTER
Boyle Street, Cheetham, Manchester M8 8UW
Tel: 0161 205 2122
One of the largest transport collections in the country including 70 buses.

OLDHAM ART GALLERY
Union Street, Oldham, Greater Manchester OL1 1DN
Tel: 0161 911 4653
Fax: 0161 627 1025
Lively programme of temporary exhibitions with an emphasis on contemporary British art.

OLDHAM MUSEUM
Greaves Street, Oldham, Greater Manchester OL1 1DN
Tel: 0161 911 4657
Exhibitions interpreting Oldham including a re-creation of an Edwardian street.
For further details see page 68

ORDSALL HALL MUSEUM
Taylorson Street, Salford, Manchester M5 3EX
Tel: 0161 872 0251
Tudor half-timbered great hall dating from early 16thC (some parts earlier) with period rooms including Victorian kitchen; social and local history display upstairs.

PUMP HOUSE PEOPLE'S HISTORY MUSEUM
Left Bank, Bridge Street, Manchester M3 3ER
Tel: 0161 839 6061
The Museum displays and reconstructs over 200 years of social and labour history.

ROCHDALE PIONEERS MUSEUM
31 Toad Lane, Rochdale, Lancashire OL12 0NU
Tel: 0161 832 4300
Original Co-op shop opened by Pioneers in 1844, with period equipment and furnishings.

SADDLEWORTH MUSEUM & ART GALLERY
High Street, Uppermill, Nr Oldham OL3 6HS
Tel: 01457 874093
The museum of a unique Yorkshire parish and its people on the Lancashire side of the Pennines.

SALFORD MUSEUM & ART GALLERY
Peel Park, The Crescent, Salford, Lancashire M5 4WU
Tel: 0161 736 2649
Fax: 0161 745 9490
Building (1850) with later additions, L S Lowry collections, Lark Hill Place Victorian Gallery, temporary exhibitions.

SMITHILLS HALL MUSEUM
Smithills Deane Road, Bolton BL1 7NP
Tel: 01204 41265
14thC Lancashire manor-house with appropriate furnishings.

STOCKPORT ART GALLERY
War Memorial Building, Wellington Road South, Stockport, Cheshire SK3 8AB
Tel: 0161 474 4451
Fax: 0161 480 4960
Stockport Art Gallery provides a changing exhibitions programme of regional, national and international significance.

STOCKPORT MUSEUM
Vernon Park, Turncroft Lane, Offerton, Stockport, Cheshire SK1 4AR
Tel: 0161 474 4460
History of Stockport from pre-history to present day including architecture and environmental gallery.

VIEWPOINT PHOTOGRAPHY GALLERY
Old Fire Station, The Crescent, Salford, Greater Manchester M5 4NZ
Tel: 0161 737 1040
Fax: 0161 745 7806
Viewpoint is a modern exhibition space based in the old fire-station on Salford Crescent which provides a continually changing programme of photography exhibitions of the region.

WHITWORTH ART GALLERY
The University of Manchester, Oxford Road, Manchester M15 6ER
Tel: 0161 275 7450
Fax: 0161 275 7451
The Whitworth is home to internationally famous collection of British watercolours, textiles and wallpapers as well as an impressive range of modern and historic prints.

HAMPSHIRE

AIRBORNE FORCES MUSEUM
RHQ The Parachute Regiment, Browning Barracks, Aldershot, Hampshire GU11 2BU
Tel: 01252 349619
Briefing models of World War II (Bruneval, Normandy, Arnhem and Rhine crossing) and post war operations including Suez and the Falklands campaign.

ALDERSHOT MILITARY MUSEUM
Queens Avenue, Aldershot, Hampshire GU11 2LG
Tel: 01252 314598
Fax: 01252 342942
Exhibition telling the story of the army camp at Aldershot, Home of the British Army.
For further details see page 69

ALLEN GALLERY
Church Street, Alton, Hampshire GU34 2BW
Tel: 01420 82802
Houses an important collection of ceramics from 13thC to the present day with requent temporary exhibitions.
For further details see page 69

ANDOVER MUSEUM
6 Church Close, Andover, Hampshire SP10 1DP
Tel: 01264 366283
Fax: 01264 339152
New permanent and temporary displays in an old grammar school depicting stories of the town and its countryside.
For further details see page 69

ARMY PHYSICAL TRAINING CORPS MUSEUM
Fox Lines, Queens Avenue, Aldershot, Hampshire GU11 2LB
Tel: 01252 347168
Fax: 01252 340785
General history of Army Physical Training Corps including historical documents and pamphlets tracing the development of physical training in the army from 1860 to present day.

BALFOUR MUSEUM OF HAMPSHIRE RED CROSS HISTORY
Red Cross House, Weeke, Winchester, Hampshire SO22 5JD
Tel: 01962 869721
Fax: 01962 869721
A small purpose-built museum opened in 1994 to preserve and display a collection of uniforms, photographs and documents of the history on the Red Cross.

THE BEAR MUSEUM
38 Dragon Street, Petersfield, Hampshire GU31 4JJ
Tel: 01730 265108
World-renowned collection of antique teddy bears displayed in Edwardian toy-shop setting.

BEATRICE ROYAL ART GALLERY
Nightingale Avenue, Eastleigh, Hampshire SO50 3JJ
Tel: 01703 610592
Fax: 01703 610596
The largest commercial gallery in Southern England.

BISHOP'S WALTHAM MUSEUM
Brook Street, Bishop's Waltham, Southampton SO3 1GH
Tel: 01489 894970
Displays illustrating the many ages of the parish history and pre-history and includes many items from the prosperous Victorian era.

BREAMORE COUNTRYSIDE MUSEUM
Breamore, Fordingbridge, Hampshire SP6 2DF
Tel: 01725 512468
Farm buildings in a walled garden provide a fascinating insight into the days when a village was self sufficient.

BURSLEDON WINDMILL
Windmill Lane, Bursledon, Southampton, Hampshire SO31 8BG
Tel: 01703 404999
Hampshire's only working windmill on a magnificent hilltop setting. Traditional, timber-framed barn and granary, farm pond and nature trail. School visits by arrangement.
For further details see page 69

BUTSER ANCIENT FARM
Bascomb Copse, Nr Chalton, Horndean, Waterlooville, Hampshire PO8 0QE
Tel: 01705 598838
Reconstruction of Iron Age buildings.

CALLEVA MUSEUM
Rectory Gardens, Bramley Road, Silchester, Reading RG7 2LU
Tel: 0118 970 0825
The museum houses a pictorial record of the Roman Town of Calleva Atrebatum.

CHAPEL HOUSE GALLERY
Dummer, Basingstoke, Hampshire RG25 2AD
Tel: 01256 397 295
Small gallery showing regular exhibitions of art (approx 6 per year).

CHARLES DICKENS BIRTHPLACE MUSEUM
393 Old Commercial Road, Portsmouth PO1 4QL
Tel: 01705 827261
Fax: 01705 875276
Birthplace of the famous novelist in 1812. This small terrace has been restored, decorated and furnished in the Regency style appropriate to his parents.

THE CITY MUSEUM
The Square, Winchester, Hampshire SO23 9ES
Tel: 01962 863064
Museum housing exhibits on archaeology and history of Winchester with reconstruction of 19thC shops.
For further details see page 69

CUMBERLAND HOUSE NATURAL HISTORY MUSEUM
Eastern Parade, Southsea, Portsmouth PO4 9RF
Tel: 01705 827261
Fax: 01705 875276
Geology and natural history of the Portsmouth area, dinosaurs and other fossil remains. Fresh water aquarium and butterfly house.

CURTIS MUSEUM
High Street, Alton, Hampshire GU34 1BA
Tel: 01420 82802
Fax: 01420 84227
Geology and archaeological finds. Collection of children's toys and display on hops and brewing.
For further details see page 69

EASTLEIGH MUSEUM
25 High Street, Eastleigh, Hampshire SO50 5LF
Tel: 01703 643026
Contains a re-creation of an 1930s engine driver's home and steam engine footplate. Frequent temporary exhibitions gallery.
For further details see page 69

EMSWORTH MUSEUM
10b North Street (above the Fire Station), Emsworth, Hampshire PO10 7DD
Tel: 01243 378091
Building c1900, formerly offices of Old Warblington District Council.

FLAGSHIP PORTSMOUTH
Porter's Lodge, 1–7 College Road, HM Naval Base, Portsmouth PO1 3LJ
Tel: 01705 839766
The world's greatest historic ships – Mary Rose, HMS Victory, HMS Warrior plus 'Warships by Water' Tours and Dockyard Apprentice Exhibition.

FLORA TWORT GALLERY & RESTAURANT
Church Path Studio, 21 The Square, Petersfield, Hampshire GU32 1HS
Tel: 01730 260756
Charming gallery showing the paintings of a pre-war Petersfield artist. Includes a popular restaurant.
For further details see page 69

FORT BROCKHURST
Gunners Way, Elson, Gosport, Hampshire PO12 4OS
Tel: 01705 581059

FORT NELSON – THE ROYAL ARMOURIES MUSEUM OF ARTILLERY
Down End Road, Fareham, Hampshire PO17 6AN
Tel: 01329 233734
Fax: 01329 822092
1860s Victorian fort depicting the life of volunteer soldiers. Fort Nelson houses the nation's collection of artillery through the ages.

GOSPORT MUSEUM
Walpole Road, Gosport, Hampshire PO12 1NS
Tel: 01705 588035
Fax: 01705 501951
Recently refurbished museum on history of the town with an imaginative geology gallery, new art gallery featuring temporary exhibitions. New coffee shop.
For further details see page 69

GOSS & CRESTED CHINA CENTRE & MUSEUM
62 Murray Road, Horndean, Waterlooville, Hampshire PO8 9JL
Tel: 01705 597440
Fax: 01705 591975
Museum of Victorian/Edwardian heraldic china souvenier ware and the world's largest showroom of Goss and crested china for sale.

THE GUILDHALL GALLERY
The Guildhall, The Broadway, Winchester, Hampshire SO23 9LJ
Tel: 01962 848269
Victorian Guildhall, situated in the Broadway, housing a gallery with changing programme of exhibitions often by local artists and groups.
For further details see page 69

THE GURKHA MUSEUM
Peninisula Barracks, Romsey Road, Winchester, Hampshire SO23 8TS
Tel: 01962 842832
Fax: 01962 877597
History of Gurkhas' service to the Crown 1815–1993; militaria, badges, medals, figures and uniforms.

HAVANT MUSEUM & ART GALLERY
56 East Street, Havant, Hampshire PO9 1BS
Tel: 01705 451155
Fax: 01705 498707
New displays on local themes, including railways, local industries, and wildfowling. Nationally important collection of firearms, which included Buffalo Bill's rifle. Programme of temporary exhibitions.
For further details see page 69

HISTORIC RESOURCES CENTRE
75 Hyde Street, Winchester, Hampshire SO23 7DW
Tel: 01962 848269
Houses collections of old photographs and the site and monuments record for the area.
For further details see page 69

HOLLYCOMBE STEAM COLLECTION IRON HILL
Midhurst Road, Liphook, Hampshire GU30 7LP
Tel: 01428 724900
Three steam railways, one ascending to spectacular views. Traction engine rides. Steam farm. Unique bioscope with engine fairground organ and films. Steam fairground.

JOHN HANSARD GALLERY
The University Southampton, Highfield, Southampton SO17 1BJ
Tel: 01703 592158
Fax: 01703 593939
Exhibitions of contemporary art, craft and photography.

THE KINGS ROYAL HUSSARS REGIMENTAL MUSEUM
Peninsula Barracks, Romsey Road, Winchester, Hampshire SO23 8TS
Tel: 01962 828539
Fax: 01962 828538
Victorian uniforms, paintings, medals, 1914 dug-out, photographs, armoured vehicles.

LIGHT INFANTRY MUSEUM
Peninsula Barracks, Romsey Road, Winchester, Hampshire SO23 8TS
Tel: 01962 828550
Fax: 01962 828500
Museum depicting the modern light infantry soldier, the origins of the regiment and the life of the battalions around the world.

MANOR FARM COUNTRY PARK
Pylands Lane, Bursledon, Southampton
Tel: 01489 787055
Fax: 01489 790357
Traditional Hampshire farmstead – range of buildings, farm animals, machinery and equipment pre-1950s farmhouse and 13thC church.

MUSEUM OF ARCHAEOLOGY
Gods House Tower, Winkle Street, Southampton SO14 2NY
Tel: 01703 635904
Fax: 01703 339601
The building is a 15thC tower used as part of the medieval defences.

MUSEUM OF ARMY FLYING
Middle Wallop, Stockbridge, Hampshire SO20 8DY
Tel: 01980 674421
Fax: 01264 781694
Award-winning and unique collection of flying machines and displays depicting the role of army flying since late 19thC.
For further details see page 68

MUSEUM OF THE IRON AGE
6 Church Close, Andover, Hampshire SP10 1DP
Tel: 01264 366283
Fax: 01264 339152
Dramatically tells the story of Danebury Iron Age Hillfort, with finds from many years of excavation. Displays recently updated.
For further details see page 69

NATIONAL MOTOR MUSEUM
John Montagu Building,
Beaulieu, Brockenhurst,
Hampshire SO42 7ZN
Tel: 01590 612345
Fax: 01590 612624
*The National Motor museum at
Beaulieu has over 250 exhibits
showing history of motoring from
1895, plus motoring memorabilia.*

NEW FOREST MUSEUM
High Street, Lyndhurst,
Hampshire SO43 7NY
Tel: 01703 283914
*Exhibition telling the story of the
New Forest – history, traditions,
characters and wildlife.*

**OATES MUSEUM & GILBERT
WHITE'S HOUSE**
The Wakes, High Street,
Selborne, Alton, Hampshire
GU34 3JH
Tel: 01420 511275
*Historic house and garden home of
Gilbert White, author of 'The
Natural History of Selborne'.*

**PORTSMOUTH CITY MUSEUM
& RECORD OFFICE**
Museum Road, Portsmouth
PO1 2LJ
Tel: 01705 827261
Fax: 01705 875276
*Local history displays, paintings,
room settings from 17thC to 1950s.
Fine and decorative art gallery and
regularly changing exhibitions.*

**QUEEN ALEXANDRA'S ROYAL
ARMY NURSING CORPS
MUSEUM**
Keogh Barracks, Ash Vale,
Aldershot, Hampshire
GU12 5RQ
Tel: 01252 340320
Fax: 01252 340224
*The history of military nursing from
1854 to present day.*

**ROCKBOURNE ROMAN
VILLA**
Rockbourne, Fordingbridge,
Hampshire SP6 3PG
Tel: 01725 518541
*Remains of largest known Roman
villa in Hampshire. Superb
mosaics, part of unusual
underfloor heating system and
outline of the villa's 40 rooms.
Recently refurbished displays of
fascinating objects found at site.
Collections of artefacts available
for handling by school groups.*
For further details see page 69

**ROYAL ARMY DENTAL CORPS
HISTORICAL MUSEUM**
DDA & HQ RADC, Evelyn
Woods Road, Aldershot,
Hampshire GU11 2LS
Tel: 01252 347976
Fax: 01252 340224
*Items of Corps historical interest and
a collection of early dental
instruments.*

**ROYAL GREEN JACKETS
MUSEUM**
Peninsula Barracks, Romsey
Road, Winchester, Hampshire
SO23 8TS
Tel: 01962 863846
Fax: 01962 828500
*Collection illustrating the history of
the Royal Green Jackets and the
three famous regiments from which
they were formed.*

**THE ROYAL HAMPSHIRE
REGIMENT MUSEUM &
MEMORIAL GARDEN**
Serles House, Southgate Street,
Winchester, Hampshire
SO23 9EG
Tel: 01962 863658
Fax: 01962 888302
*History of the regiment
(1702–1992).*

ROYAL MARINES MUSEUM
Southsea, Hampshire PO4 9PX
Tel: 01705 819385
Fax: 01705 838420
*History of Royal Marines – 1664
to present day, including many
topics covered by Key Stages 1–4
(both military and social).*

ROYAL NAVAL MUSEUM
Buildings 1–7 College Road,
HM Naval Base, Portsmouth
PO1 3LJ
Tel: 01705 839766
*The only museum in Britain
devoted to the overall history of the
Royal Navy.*

ST BARBE MUSEUM
New Street, Lymington,
Hampshire SO41 9BH
Tel: 01590 676969
Fax: 01590 679997
*New town centre museum
presently being developed. Art
gallery now reopened showing
programme of temporary
exhibitions. Main gallery reopens
Autumn 1998.*
For further details see page 69

**SAMMY MILLER MUSEUM
(TRANSPORT)**
Bashley Cross Road, New
Milton, Hampshire BH25 5SJ
Tel: 01425 620777
Fax: 01425 619696
*One of the world's largest collections
of racing trials and historic
motorcycles.*

SEARCH
50 Clarence Road, Gosport,
Hampshire PO12 1BU
*Hampshire museum's
award-winning, hands-on centre
for history and natural history
providing superb facilities for
primary schools. Informal tours,
open days and staff meetings
catered for. Free information pack
for teachers.*
For further details see page 69

**SOUTHAMPTON CITY ART
GALLERY**
Civic Centre, Commercial
Road, Southampton SO14 7LP
Tel: 01703 832758
Fax: 01703 832153
*Major collection of British and
European paintings and sculpture
from the 14th–20thC with
emphasis on 20thC British Art.*

**SOUTHAMPTON HALL OF
AVIATION**
Albert Road South,
Southampton SO15 1GB
Tel: 01703 635830
*Seventeen aircraft including the
Spitfire MK24, world record
breaking Schneider Trophy 56B,
massive Sandringham Flying Boat,
replica AVRO 504J, aero engines,
artefacts etc.*

**SOUTHAMPTON MARITIME
MUSEUM**
Wool House, Town Quay,
Southampton SO14 2AR
Tel: 01703 223941
Fax: 01703 339601
*Medieval stone warehouse with
timber roof.*

**SUBMARINE WORLD/ROYAL
NAVY SUBMARINE MUSEUM &
HMS ALLIANCE**
Haslar Jetty Road, Gosport,
Hampshire PO12 2AS
Tel: 01705 529217
Fax: 01705 511349
*National memorial museum of
submarine service including guided
tour of HMS Alliance,
audio-visuals and Royal Navy's
first submarine.*

TREADGOLDS OF PORTSEA
Bishop Street, Portsmouth,
Hampshire PO1 3DA
Tel: 01705 824745
Fax: 01705 837310
*Ironmongers and iron and steel
merchants established in 1809
and trading until 1988, the
business remained untouched by
the 20thC. The museum brings
to life a unique piece of social and
industrial history. Educational
facilities for schools and resource
pack for use with a new resource
room now available.*
For further details see page 69

TUDOR HOUSE MUSEUM
St Michael's Square, Bugle
Street, Southampton SO14 2AD
Tel: 01703 332513
Fax: 01703 339601
*Large half-timbered Tudor house
with exhibitions on Tudor,
Georgian and Victorian domestic
and local history.*

**WESTBURY MANOR
MUSEUM**
84 West Street, Fareham,
Hampshire PO16 0JJ
Tel: 01329 824895
Fax: 01329 825917
*Situated in the town centre, the
museum boasts high quality
displays on many local themes,
including the local strawberry
industry and industrial history.
Educational facilities for schools
and resource pack for use with a
new resource room now available.*
For further details see page 69

THE WESTGATE
High Street, Winchester,
Hampshire
Tel: 01962 848269
*Museum housing the city's
collection of standard weights and
measures and the Tudor painted
ceiling.*
For further details see page 69

WILLIS MUSEUM
Old Town Hall, Market Place,
Basingstoke, Hampshire
RG21 7QD
Tel: 01256 465902
Fax: 01256 471455
*One of Hampshire's liveliest local
museums with vibrant new
displays depicting Basingstoke in
the last 200 years. Coffee lounge
and children's play corner.
Handling collections and gallery
workshops for schools.*
For further details see page 69

HARTLEPOOL

HARTLEPOOL ART GALLERY
Church Square, Hartlepool
TS24 7EQ
Tel: 01429 869706
Fax: 01429 523477
*The art gallery has a varied
programme of art and craft
exhibitions.*
For further details see page 69

HARTLEPOOL HISTORIC QUAY
Maritime Avenue, Hartlepool
TS24 0XZ
Tel: 01429 860006
Fax: 01429 867332
*Teesside Development
Corporation's Hartlepool Historic
Quay is an exciting reconstruction of
a seaport of the 1800s with
buildings and lively quayside
authentically reconstructed.*

MUSEUM OF HARTLEPOOL
Jackson's Dock, Marina,
Hartlepool TS24 0XZ
Tel: 01429 222255
Fax: 01429 523477
*The award-winning museum
includes archaeological and local
historical and maritime exhibits
featuring the original lighthouse
light, and the paddle steamer
Wingfield Castle.*
For further details see page 69

HEREFORD & WORCESTER

THE ALMONRY
Abbey Gate, Evesham,
Worcestershire WR11 4BG
Tel: 01386 446944
Fax: 01386 442348
*Heritage centre with displays of
Evesham Abbey, Battle of
Evesham, and general exhibits of
local historic interest.*

**AVONCROFT MUSEUM OF
HISTORIC BUILDINGS**
Stoke Heath, Bromsgrove,
Hereford & Worcester B60 4JR
Tel: 01527 831886
Fax: 01527 876934
*Re-erected buildings saved from
destruction including a working
windmill, a timber prefab and
industrial buildings. Also now
includes the national telephone kiosk
collection.*

BEWDLEY MUSEUM
Load Street, Bewdley,
Hereford & Worcester
DY12 2AJ
Tel: 01299 403573
*Local history, craft and industries
of the Wyre Forest.*
For further details see page 70

**BIRMINGHAM & MIDLAND
MUSEUM OF TRANSPORT**
Chapel Lane, Wythall,
Birmingham, West Midlands
B47 6JX
Tel: 01564 826471
*Operating transport museum with
over 100 vehicles, specialising in
buses, coaches and battery electric
vehicles.*

BORDESLEY ABBEY
Abbey Meadows, Needle Mill
Lane, Redditch, Worcestershire
B97 6RR
Tel: 01527 62509
Cistercian Abbey founded c1140.

**BROADWAY TEDDY BEAR
MUSEUM**
76 High Street, Broadway,
Worcestershire WR12 7AJ
Tel: 01386 858323
*Collection of old bears and dolls and
demonstration of how they are made.*

BROMSGROVE MUSEUM
26 Birmingham Road,
Bromsgrove, Worcestershire
B61 0DD
Tel: 01527 831809
*Past industries and craft gallery
including local and social history.*

**BUTTON MUSEUM & BUTTON
SHOP**
Kyrle Street, Ross-on-Wye,
Herefordshire HR9 7DB
Tel: 01989 566089
*A museum devoted entirely to
buttons, covering 200 years of
fashion, working clothes, uniforms
and leisure pursuits.*

**CHURCHILL HOUSE
MUSEUM**
Venns Lane, Hereford,
Hereford & Worcester
HR1 1DE
Tel: 01432 267409
*Costumes, furniture and paintings
of 18th and 19thC.*
For further details see page 70

CIDER MUSEUM
21 Ryelands Street, Hereford,
Hereford & Worcester
HR4 0LW
Tel: 01432 354207
*Explores the fascinating history of
cider making through different
sources of information, including
machinery, small objects, documents,
photos and memorabilia.*

THE COMMANDERY
Sidbury, Worcester,
Worcestershire WR1 2HU
Tel: 01905 355071
*A 15thC timber-framed building
containing period rooms and civil
war exhibits. Special events staged
throughout the year.*

ELGAR'S BIRTHPLACE
Crown East Lane, Lower
Broadheath, Hereford &
Worcester
Tel: 01905 333224
*The cottage in which Edward Elgar
was born, now houses a museum of
photographs, musical scores, letters
and records associated with the
composer.*

**FORGE MILL NEEDLE
MUSEUM & BORDESLEY
ABBEY VISITOR CENTRE**
Needle Mill Lane, Riverside,
Redditch, Worcestershire
B98 8HY
Tel: 01527 62509
Fax: 01527 584619
*Archaeology visitors centre, showing
finds from medieval Abbey
excavation on a changing site.*

FRAMED
46 Friar Street, Worcester,
Worcestershire WR1 2NA
Tel: 01905 28836
*Contemporary fine art gallery selling
original paintings, sculpture and
prints in old timber-framed building.*

HEREFORD & WORCESTER COUNTY MUSEUM
Hartlebury Castle, Hartlebury, Kidderminster, Worcestershire DY11 7XZ
Tel: 01299 250416
Housed in north wing of Bishop's Palace; exhibits restored cider mill, costume and horse-drawn vehicles, including gypsy caravans, crafts and industry of county.

HEREFORD CITY MUSEUM AND ART GALLERY
Broad Street, Hereford, Hereford & Worcester HR4 9AU
Tel: 01432 364691
Regional natural history, local geology and bee-keeping display with observation hive.
For further details see page 70

HEREFORDSHIRE REGIMENTAL MUSEUM
Harold Street (TA Centre), Hereford, Herefordshire HR1 2QX
Tel: 01432 359917
Relics of the Regiment including uniforms, weapons, badges, maps, pictures and photographs.

LEDBURY HERITAGE CENTRE & GALLERY
Church Lane, Ledbury, Herefordshire
Tel: 01531 635680
Restored timber-framed building in picturesque cobbled Church Lane.

LEOMINSTER FOLK MUSEUM
Etnam Street, Leominster, Herefordshire HR6 8AQ
Tel: 01568 615186
Local-history museum including items of agricultural interest from Iron Age and Saxon maps to costumes.

THE LION GALLERY
Lion House, 15 Broad Street, Leominster, Herefordshire HR6 8BT
Tel: 01568 611898
Lively gallery run for and by local artists and craftworkers selling a wide selection of the highest quality work.

THE LOST STREET MUSEUM
Palma Court, 27 Brookend Street, Ross-on-Wye, Herefordshire HR9 7EE
Tel: 01989 562752
Complete Edwardian street of shops including tobacconist, glasswear, grocers, chemist, clothes store, pub and many others.

MALVERN MUSEUM
Abbey Gateway, Abbey Road, Malvern, Worcestershire WR14 3ES
Tel: 01684 567811
Abbey Gateway, the medieval gatehouse to Malvern Monastery. Illustrates Malvern's history from early times to present day.

THE MUSEUM OF WORCESTER PORCELAIN
Severn Street, Worcester, Worcestershire WR1 2NE
Tel: 01905 23221
Fax: 01905 617807
The largest and most comprehensive collection of Worcester porcelain in the world, covering the period from start of manufacture in 1751 to present day.

OLD CHAPEL GALLERY
East Street, Pembridge, Leominster, Herefordshire HR6 9HB
Tel: 01544 388842
Fax: 01544 388842
Crafts Council selected gallery.

THE OLD HOUSE
High Town, Hereford, Hereford & Worcester HR1 2AA
Tel: 01432 364598
One of Hereford's finest buildings showing furnished rooms and interpretive displays.
For further details see page 70

OMBERSLEY GALLERY
Church Terrace, Ombersley, Worcestershire WR9 0EP
Tel: 01905 620655
Fax: 01905 620655
The Gallery is one of the listed buildings of Ombersley, displaying paintings and pottery, and a small amount of woodwork and glass.

SAINT JOHN MEDIEVAL MUSEUM
Coningsby Hospital, Widemarsh Street, Hereford, Herefordshire HR4 9HN
Tel: 01432 272837
Small museum and chapel dating back to 13thC.

TENBURY MUSEUM
Goffs School, Cross Street, Tenbury Wells, Worcestershire
Tel: 01584 811669
Containing relics of Tenbury and old local history items including hop picking and items relating to Dr Henry Hickman, pioneer of anaesthesia.

TUDOR HOUSE MUSEUM OF LOCAL LIFE
Friar Street, Worcester, Worcestershire WR1 2NA
Tel: 01905 722349
Social and domestic history of Worcester.

UPTON HERITAGE CENTRE
Pepperpot, Church Street, Upton-upon-Severn, Worcester, Worcestershire WR8 0HT
Tel: 01684 592679
Restored Bell Tower, oldest surviving building in the town and local landmark.

WATERWORKS MUSEUM
Broomy Hill, Hereford, Herefordshire
Tel: 01432 361147
A vertical triple expansion condensing pump engine, inverted vertical 2-cylinder pumping engine, coal-fired Lancashire boiler, Tangee single-cylinder diesel triple throw pump.

WORCESTER CITY MUSEUM & ART GALLERY
Foregate Street, Worcester, Worcestershire WR1 1DT
Tel: 01905 25371
Busy programme of art exhibitions and events; River Severn display; collections of Worcestershire Regiment and Yeomanry Calvary; 19thC chemist's shop.

WYE VALLEY HERITAGE CENTRE
Chestnuts, Doward, Symonds Yat West, Ross-on-Wye, Herefordshire HR9 6DZ
Tel: 01600 890474
Fax: 01600 890327
Set in woodland location, museum houses one of the country's largest collections of historic farm machinery, vintage tractors and rural bygones.

WYEBRIDGE INTERIORS
Wyebridge House, Bridge Street, Hereford, Herefordshire HR4 9DG
Tel: 01432 350722
Fax: 01432 344076
Restored 16thC building overlooking river Wye adjoining 14thC Grade I listed Old Wye Bridge. Display of birds and beasts by international sculptor Walnety Pytel.

HERTFORDSHIRE

ASHWELL VILLAGE MUSEUM
Swan Street, Ashwell, Baldock, Hertfordshire SG7 5QH
Tel: 01462 742155
Collection of village bygones and agricultural implements set in a small but interesting timber building.

FIRST GARDEN CITY HERITAGE MUSEUM
296 Norton Way South, Letchworth, Hertfordshire SG6 1SU
Tel: 01462 482710
Fax: 01462 486056
Displays relating to the Garden City movement and the social history of Letchworth including a collection of Parker and Unwin architectural drawings.

THE HENRY MOORE FOUNDATION
Dane Tree House, Perry Green, Much Hadham, Hertfordshire SG10 6AF
Tel: 01279 843333
Fax: 01279 843647
Sculpture garden and studios. Visits by appointment.

HERTFORD MUSEUM
18 Bull Plain, Hertford, Hertfordshire SG14 1DT
Tel: 01992 582686
A 17thC building with main exhibits on archaeology and natural and local history of Hertfordshire.

HITCHIN MUSEUM & ART GALLERY
Paynes Park, Hitchin, Hertfordshire SG5 1EQ
Tel: 01462 422946
Fax: 01462 434883
Converted 19thC house on two floors with displays of costume, local history, reconstructed 19th century pharmacy, Hertfordshire Yeomanry and temporary exhibitions.

LETCHWORTH MUSEUM
Broadway, Letchworth, Hertfordshire SG6 3PF
Tel: 01462 685647
Fax: 01462 481879
Museum features local natural history, archaeological displays and a programme of temporary exhibitions.

LOWEWOOD MUSEUM
High Street, Hoddesdon, Hertfordshire EN11 8BH
Tel: 01992 445596
Located in a Georgian House the museum contains displays relating to the history of the borough of Broxbourne.

MILL GREEN MUSEUM & MILL
Mill Green, Hatfield, Hertfordshire AL9 5PD
Tel: 01707 271362
Fax: 01707 272511
An 18thC watermill restored to working order; museum in an adjoining miller's house shows local and social history, archaeology, craft tools and Victorian kitchen.
For further details see page 71

MOSQUITO AIRCRAFT MUSEUM
PO Box 107, Salisbury Hall, London Colney, St Albans, Hertfordshire AL2 1BU
Tel: 01727 822051
Restoration and preservation of a range of De Havilland aircraft including the first Mosquito.

MUSEUM OF ST ALBANS
Hatfield Road, St Albans, Hertfordshire AL1 3RR
Tel: 01727 819340
Fax: 01727 837472
Purpose-built as a museum in 1898, displays include craft tools and local and natural history, telling the St Albans story from Roman times to the present day.
For further details see page 70

RHODES MEMORIAL MUSEUM & COMMONWEALTH CENTRE
South Road, Bishop's Stortford, Hertfordshire CM23 3JG
Tel: 01279 651746
Birthplace of Cecil John Rhodes, two Victorian villas made to look as one. Exhibition of his life and times.

ST ALBANS ORGAN MUSEUM
320 Camp Road, St Albans, Hertfordshire AL1 5PE
Tel: 01727 851557
Fax: 01727 851557
Collection of organs by Mortier, DeCap and Bursens, Steinway and Weber duo-art reproducing pianos, Mills Violano Virtuoso, music boxes and Wurlitzer & Rutt theatre pipe organs.

STEVENAGE MUSEUM
St George's Way, Stevenage, Hertfordshire SG1 1XX
Tel: 01438 354292
A lively museum which tells the story of Stevenage from the Stone Age to the present.

VERULAMIUM MUSEUM
St Michaels, St Albans, Hertfordshire AL3 4SW
Tel: 01727 819339
Fax: 01727 859919
The museum of everyday life in Roman Britain.
For further details see page 70

WALTER ROTHSCHILD ZOOLOGICAL MUSEUM
Akeman Street, Tring, Hertfordshire HP23 6AP
Tel: 01442 824181
Fax: 01442 890693
Once the private collection of Lionel Walter, 2nd Baron Rothschild, more than 4,000 animal and bird specimens on display in a unique Victorian setting.
For further details see page 71

WARE MUSEUM
The Priory Lodge, 89 High Street, Ware, Hertfordshire SG12 9AL
Tel: 01920 487848
An independent museum featuring the 'Story of Ware' from the Roman town, through the malting industry of the 18th–20thC, to modern times.

WATFORD MUSEUM
194 High Street, Watford WD1 2HG
Tel: 01923 232297
Fax: 01923 232297
Museum building built in 1775 with displays of local history, brewing, printing and archaeology.

WELWYN ROMAN BATHS
Welwyn By-Pass, Welwyn Village, Hertfordshire AL6 9HT
Tel: 01707 271362
Baths are a small part of a villa which was built at the beginning of 300AD and occupied for over 150 years; villa had at least four buildings.
For further details see page 71

ISLE OF WIGHT

BEMBRIDGE LIFEBOAT STATION
Lane End, Bembridge, Isle of Wight PO35 5ST
Tel: 01983 872044
Off-shore lifeboat on slipway at end of 250-yard pier.

BEMBRIDGE MARITIME MUSEUM & SHIPWRECK CENTRE
Sherbourne Street, Bembridge, Isle of Wight PO35 55B
Tel: 01983 872223
Fax: 01983 873125
A museum devoted to displaying nautical heritage.

BLACKGANG SAWMILL – WORLD OF TIMBER
Blackgang Chale, Nr Ventnor, Isle of Wight PO38 2HN
Tel: 01983 730330
Fax: 01983 731267
Exhibition of woodworking and woodland trades with engines and mill gardens.

THE CLASSIC BOAT CENTRE
Seaclose Wharf, Town Quay, Newport, Isle of Wight PO30 2EF
Tel: 01983 533493
Collection of sailing and motor boats dating from 1870.

COWES MARITIME MUSEUM
Beckford Road, Cowes, Isle of
Wight PO31 7SG
Tel: 01983 293341
*Museum containing boats, paintings
and models depicting the maritime
history of Cowes and the Isle of
Wight.*

GUILDHALL MUSEUM
High Street, Newport, Isle of
Wight
Tel: 01983 823366

**THE ISLAND AEROPLANE
COMPANY LTD**
Embassy Way, Sandown
Airport, Sandown, Isle of Wight
PO36 9PJ
Tel: 01983 404448
Fax: 01983 404448
*Collection of 20 aircraft
(1909–1950s), engines,
instruments and components.*

**JULIA MARGARET CAMERON
TRUST LTD**
Dimbola Lodge Terrace Lane,
Freshwater Bay, Isle of Wight
PO40 9QE
Tel: 01983 756814
Fax: 01983 755578
*The house is the former home of
Julia Margaret Cameron.*

**LILLIPUT ANTIQUE DOLL &
TOY MUSEUM**
High Street, Brading, Isle of
Wight PO36 0DJ
Tel: 01983 407231
*Over 2,000 antique dolls and toys
dating from c2000BC to c1945.
Many unusual and rare items on
display.*

LONGSHOREMAN'S MUSEUM
The Esplanade, Ventnor, Isle of
Wight PO38 1JT
Tel: 01983 853176
*Local historical and nautical
exhibition: models, artefacts, antique
engravings and photographs
depicting Victorian and Edwardian
Ventnor.*

**MUSEUM OF SMUGGLING
HISTORY**
Botanic Garden, Ventnor, Isle of
Wight PO38 1UL
Tel: 01983 853677
*Unique underground museum with
hundreds of exhibits and exciting
tableaux showing the history of
smuggling over 700 years.*

NOSTALGIA TOY MUSEUM
High Street, Godshill, Ventnor,
Isle of Wight PO38 3HZ
Tel: 01983 840181
*Models 1945–1970 including toys
by Dinky, Corgi, Matchbox,
Triang, Hornbey, etc.*

OLD TOWN HALL MUSEUM
High Street, Brading, Sandown,
Isle of Wight PO36 0DJ
Tel: 01983 407560
*Well-preserved ancient relics and
history of Brading.*

QUAY ARTS CENTRE
Sea Street, Newport, Isle of
Wight PO30 5BD
Tel: 01983 528825
Fax: 01983 526606
*The Quay Arts Centre is housed in
an 18thC warehouse in the old
docks area of Newport known as
'Little London'.*

RAINBOWS END
39 Cross Street, Cowes, Isle of
Wight PO31 7TA
Tel: 01983 291672
*Art and craft gallery featuring dolls'
houses and accessories, rocks and
minerals, local pictures and
engravings, collectables old and new.*

**SANDOWN GEOLOGY
MUSEUM**
Sandown Library, High Street,
Sandown, Isle of Wight
PO36 8AF
Tel: 01983 404344
*Display of fossils and rocks from the
Island – particularly dinosaurs.*

SIR MAX AITKEN MUSEUM
The Prospect, 83 High Street,
Cowes, Isle of Wight PO31 7AJ
Tel: 01983 295144
*A museum featuring many maritime
artefacts of sailing vessels from
Nelson to modern times.*

**WIRELESS MUSEUM
PUCKPOOL PARK**
Seaview, Ryde, Isle of Wight
PO34 5AR
Tel: 01983 567665
Fax: 01983 64708
*Display of radios and television
receivers tells the story of
broadcasting from its inception in the
early 1920s; exhibition shortwave
transmitting station.*

KENT

ASHFORD BOROUGH MUSEUM
The Church Yard, Ashford,
Kent TN23 1QG
Tel: 01233 620771
*Former grammar school built in
1635 now housing local history
exhibits.*

THE BAY MUSEUM
Beach Road, St Margaret's Bay,
Dover, Kent CT15 6DZ
Tel: 01304 852764
*Museum with items of local and
marine interest covering the First
and Second World War periods.*

BRATTLE FARM MUSEUM
Five Oak Lane, Staplehurst,
Tonbridge, Kent TN12 0HE
Tel: 01580 891222
*Agricultural tractors, machinery,
horse-drawn and hand implements,
tools and domestic bygones.*

**BRENZETT AERONAUTICAL
MUSEUM**
Ivychurch Road, Brenzett,
Romney Marsh, Kent
Tel: 01797 344747
*Wide display of aircraft engines
relating to World War II.*

**C M BOOTH COLLECTION OF
HISTORIC VEHICLES**
Falstaff Antiques, 63–67 High
Street, Rolvenden, Cranbrook,
Kent TN17 4LP
Tel: 01580 241234
*Display includes unique collection of
Morgan cars, 1913–1935.*

**CANTERBURY HERITAGE
MUSEUM**
Stour Street, Canterbury,
Kent
Tel: 01227 452747
Fax: 01227 455047
*Treasures from 2,000 years of
Canterbury history housed in a
medieval building on River Stour
including Stephenson's Invicta
steam locomotive and Saxon gold.*
For further details see page 71

**CANTERBURY ROMAN
MUSEUM**
Butchery Lane, Canterbury,
Kent
Tel: 01227 785575
Fax: 01227 455047
*New museum around the
preserved remains of a Roman
town house with fine mosaics,
hands-on area and computer
generated reconstructed images of
archaeological excavations on site.*
For further details see page 71

**CHUFFA TRAINS RAILMANIA
MUSEUM**
82 High Street, Whitstable, Kent
CT5 1AZ
Tel: 01227 277339
*Museum tells the history of Britain's
railways, especially the Canterbury
and Whitstable line. Children's
activity area and some interactive
displays.*

COURT HALL MUSEUM
High Street, Milton Regis,
Sittingbourne, Kent
*Unique Kentish 15thC
timber-framed court building set
among attractive buildings of Old
Milton with pictorial display on
Milton's royal heritage.*

CRAMPTON TOWER MUSEUM
High Street, Broadstairs, Kent
Tel: 01843 862078
*Museum dedicated to the works of
T R Compton (1816–1888) civil
engineer. Also local transport and
Canterbury stagecoach*

CRANBROOK MUSEUM
Carriers Road, Cranbrook, Kent
TN17 3JX
Tel: 01580 712368
A 15thC timber building.

**DARTFORD BOROUGH
MUSEUM**
Market Street, Dartford
DA1 1EU
Tel: 01322 343555
*Programme of temporary exhibitions
covering the history of the Dartford
area from prehistoric to Victorian
times.*

**DEAL MARITIME & LOCAL
HISTORY MUSEUM**
22 St Georges Road, Deal, Kent
CT14 6BA
Tel: 01304 375816
*Exhibits relating to history of Deal,
especially maritime.*

DEAL TOWN HALL EXHIBITION
Town Hall, High Street, Deal,
Kent CT14 6BB
Tel: 01304 380546
*Collections of Victoriana,
17th–20thC pictures, costumes and
antique dolls.*

DICKENS HOUSE MUSEUM
2 Victoria Parade, Broadstairs,
Kent CT10 1QS
Tel: 01843 862853
*Museum of Dickens' letters and
possessions.*
For further details see page 72

**DOLPHIN YARD SAILING
BARGE MUSEUM**
Crown Quay Lane,
Sittingbourne, Kent ME10 3SN
Tel: 01795 424132
*Original sailing barge yard restored
as museum, and site for restoration
of old barges with models, plans,
photographs, tools and navigational
instruments.*

DOVER MUSEUM
Market Square, Dover, Kent
CT16 1PB
Tel: 01304 201066
Fax: 01304 241186
*Museum tells the story of the town's
history since prehistoric times using
original artefacts, fine arts and
models.*

DOVER TRANSPORT MUSEUM
Old Park Barracks, Honeywood
Road, Whitfield, Dover, Kent
CT16 2HQ
Tel: 01304 822409
*Vehicles, photographs and models,
model tramway and local history
displays covering land sea and air.*

FINCHCOCKS
Goudhurst, Cranbrook, Kent
TN17 1HH
Tel: 01580 211702
Fax: 01580 211007
*Fine early Georgian house with
gardens set in parkland and
housing a remarkable collection of
historical keyboard instruments in
full playing order.*
For further details see page 72

**FOLKESTONE MUSEUM & ART
GALLERY**
2 Grace Hill, Folkestone, Kent
CT20 1HD
Tel: 01303 850123
Fax: 01303 242907
*Museum of local, natural and social
history and archaeology.*

FORT LUTON MUSEUM
Magpie Hall Road, Chatham,
Kent ME4 5XJ
Tel: 01634 813969
*Restored Victorian fort containing
museum, model museum and model
railway.*

GRAND SHAFT
Snargate Street, Dover, Kent
Tel: 01304 201200
*A 140ft triple Napoleonic staircase
built in 1809, used by troops as a
short-cut between forts and barracks,
on the Western Heights to Dover
town and harbour.*

GRAVESHAM MUSEUM
High Street, Gravesend, Kent
DA11 0BQ
Tel: 01474 323159
*Exhibition on history and
development of Gravesend district
over last 200 years.*

GUILDHALL & MUSEUM
Cattle Market, Sandwich, Kent
CT13 9AE
Tel: 01304 617197
Fax: 01304 614780
*Displaying Cinque Ports robes,
Mayor's chair, weights and
measures, seals and other local items
in historical building.*

GUILDHALL MUSEUM
High Street, Rochester, Kent
ME1 1QU
Tel: 01634 848717
Fax: 01634 827980
*Late 17thC Guildhall wing on
theme of life in Medway towns in
19th and 20thC.*

THE HEADCORN GALLERY
17 High Street, Headcorn,
Ashford, Kent TN27 9NH
Tel: 01622 890108
*Gallery featuring established British
contemporary artists. Galley
featuring established British
contemporary artists, large selection
of artist produced prints, also
ceramics and sculpture. Frequent solo
exhibitions.*

HERBFARM PERFUMERY
Broad Oak Road, Canterbury,
Kent CT2 0PP
Tel: 01227 458755
Fax: 01227 455629
*Working perfume museum where
visitors can see plants, herbs,
essential oils and flowers collected
from all over the world.*

THE HISTORIC DOCKYARD
Chatham, Kent ME4 4TE
Tel: 01634 812551
Fax: 01634 826918
Historic 80-acre 18thC dockyard.

**HYTHE LOCAL HISTORY
ROOM**
Oaklands, 1 Stade Street, Hythe,
Kent CT21 6BG
Tel: 01303 266152/3
Fax: 01303 262912
*Historical displays on local history,
the Cinque Ports Confederation and
the Small Arms School.*

**KENT BATTLE OF BRITAIN
MUSEUM**
Hawkinge Airfield, Hawkinge,
Folkestone, Kent CT18 7AG
Tel: 01303 893140
*Largest collection of related items
from the Battle of Britain together
with uniforms, vehicles, photos,
letters and charts in old airfield
buildings.*

**LASHENDEN AIR WARFARE
MUSEUM**
Headcorn Aerodrome,
Headcorn, Ashford, Kent
TN27 9HX
Tel: 01622 890226
Fax: 01622 890876
*Piloted VI flying bomb and other
items of British and German
wartime equipment, radios, engines
etc.*

LYDD TOWN MUSEUM
Old Fire Station, Queens Road,
Lydd, Romney Marsh, Kent
TN29 9AN
Tel: 01797 366566
*Exhibits of local interest and an
original 'Merryweather' 1890 fire
manual, Horse Bus c1890, a
19thC Landau Dungeness beach
cart and agricultural implements.*

MAIDSTONE MUSEUM & ART GALLERY
St Faith's Street, Maidstone, Kent ME14 1LH
Tel: 01622 754497
Fax: 01622 602193
Historic building housing outstanding collections of Kentish archaeology and history, natural history, and fine and applied art and costume.
For further details see page 73

MAISON DIEU
Town Hall, Biggin Street, Dover, Kent CT16 1DL
Tel: 01304 201200
Once pilgrims' hostel, dating from 1203.

MAISON DIEU
Ospringe Street, Ospringe, Faversham, Kent ME13 8TW
Tel: 01795 534542
Early 16thC timber-framed building incorporating fragments of 13thC hospital and shelter for pilgrims with displays on local history and archaeology.

MARITIME MUSEUM RAMSGATE
The Clock House, Pier Yard, Royal Harbour, Ramsgate, Kent CT11 8LS
Tel: 01843 587765
Fax: 01843 587765
Four galleries devoted to local and national maritime heritage, history of navigation, relics from Goodwin Sands wrecks, RNLI, historic ship collection and restored dry dock.

MINSTER GATEHOUSE
Union Road, Minster-in-Sheppey, Sheerness, Kent ME12 2HW
Tel: 01795 872303
Stone-built medieval gatehouse of former Benedictine nunnery containing three floors of local maps, photographs, artefacts, costumes and fossils.

MUSEUM OF KENT LEISURE
Lock Lane, Sandling, Maidstone, Kent ME14 3LD
Tel: 01622 763936
Fax: 01622 662024
Historic buildings with displays on Kent's history plus orchards, hops, vegetable and herb gardens, and farmyard.

NEW HALL MUSEUM
New Hall Close, Dymchurch, Romney Marsh, Kent TN29 0LF
Tel: 01303 872142
Fax: 01303 874788
Old court room (1575) containing small museum of Romney Marsh exhibits, maps and charts.

OLD BROOK PUMPING STATION
The Brook, Chatham, Kent
Pumping station featuring large diesel-operated pumps used for sewage and rain water pumping until 1956.

OLD TOWN GAOL
Town Hall, High Street, Dover, Kent CT16 1DQ
Tel: 01304 202723
Situated beneath Dover's medieval town hall; full re-creation of Victorian prison life, sights and sounds using latest audio visual techniques.

OLD TOWN HALL LOCAL HISTORY MUSEUM
Market Place, Margate, Kent CT9 1ER
Tel: 01843 231213
Fax: 01843 887765
Various aspects of local and maritime history housed in original 1690 town commissioners' building with 1820 police station and court.

PEMBROKE LODGE MUSEUM
2/4/6 Station Approach, Birchington-on-Sea, Kent CT7 9RD
Tel: 01843 841649
Building dating from 1891 with paintings and family portraits and family history centre.

POWELL COTTON MUSEUM QUEX HOUSE & GARDENS
Quex Park, Birchington, Kent CT7 0BH
Tel: 01843 842168
Fax: 01843 846661
Regency house with period furniture etc.
For further details see page 72

THE PRECINCT TOY COLLECTION
38 Harnet Street, Sandwich, Kent CT13 9ES
Tel: 01304 621114
Interesting collection of dolls, dolls' houses, mechanical toys, miniatures and other displays dating from about 1860.

RAF MANSTON SPITFIRE & HURRICANE MEMORIAL BUILDING
Royal Air Force Manston, Manston, Ramsgate, Kent CT12 5BS
Tel: 01843 823351 ext 6219
Purpose-built pavilion houses World War II static Spitfire, Hurricane and many other exhibits associated with the aircraft, World War II and RAF Manston.

RAMSGATE MOTOR MUSEUM
West Cliff Hall, West Cliff, Ramsgate, Kent CT11 9JK
Tel: 01843 581948
Over 130 cars and motorcycles dating from the Victorian era to the present day.

ROMAN PAINTED HOUSE
New Street, Dover, Kent CT17 9AJ
Tel: 01304 203279
Remains of well-preserved Roman mansion (hotel) with unique early 300AD frescos.

ROYAL ENGINEERS MUSEUM
Prince Arthur Road, Gillingham, Kent ME4 4UG
Tel: 01634 406397
Fax: 01634 822371
The characters, lives and work of Britain's soldier-engineers 1066 to present day.

ROYAL MUSEUM & ART GALLERY WITH BUFFS REGIMENTAL MUSEUM
18 High Street, Canterbury, Kent CT1 2RA
Tel: 01227 452747
Fax: 01227 455047
Canterbury's art museum including fine arts, rare porcelain and antiques. Special exhibitions gallery. Buffs museum with extensive displays of Gallantry Awards and silver.

THE SALTER COLLECTION
18 Gladstone Road, Deal, Kent CT14 7ET
Tel: 01304 361471
Museum in a Victorian house containing costumes dating from 1785 to the 1950s displayed against a domestic background.

SEVENOAKS MUSEUM
Sevenoaks Library, Buckhurst Lane, Sevenoaks, Kent TN13 1LQ
Tel: 01732 452384/453118
Fax: 01732 742682
The story of Sevenoaks and district is shown using fossils, archaeological artefacts, photographs, domestic, trade and commercial items, tools and a small boat.

SHOREHAM AIRCRAFT MUSEUM
High Street, Shoreham, Sevenoaks, Kent TN14 7TB
Tel: 01959 524416
Fax: 01959 524416
Collection of memorabilia relating to the aerial combats fought over south east England between the Luftwaffe and RAF during the 1939–45 war.

TENTERDEN & DISTRICT MUSEUM
Station Road, Tenterden, Kent TN30 6HN
Tel: 01580 764310
Well-displayed maps, pictures and exhibits on Tenterden's history, Cinque Ports, hops, The Weald and Victorian domestic life.

TIME-BALL TOWER
Victoria Parade, Deal, Kent CT14 7BP
Tel: 01304 360897
Originally a 19thC semaphore tower adapted for use as time-ball in 1853.

TUNBRIDGE WELLS MUSEUM & ART GALLERY
Civic Centre, Mount Pleasant, Royal Tunbridge Wells, Kent TN1 1JN
Tel: 01892 547221
Frequent art and craft exhibitions and displays of local history, Tunbridge ware, dolls and toys, archaeology and natural history.

THE TYRWHITT-DRAKE MUSEUM OF CARRIAGES
Mill Street, Maidstone, Kent ME15 6YE
Tel: 01622 754497
Finest collection of horse-drawn vehicles in country.

WATERLOO MUSEUM
Crow Hill, Broadstairs, Kent CT10 1HN
Tel: 01843 865044
Museum on three floors with treasures and memorabilia including weaponry, costumes, battle plans, detailed models and diorama of British squares withstanding French assaults.

WEST GATE MUSEUM
St Peter's Street, Canterbury, Kent
Tel: 01227 452747
Fax: 01227 455047
Explore one of England's finest medieval fortified gatehouses with defensive features including 'murder holes'. Panoramic views from the battlements. Arms and armour displays.

WHITSTABLE MUSEUM & GALLERY
Oxford Street, Whitstable, Kent CT5 1DB
Tel: 01227 276998
Fax: 01227 772379
A coastal museum exploring the sea-faring traditions of the town with special features on divers, shipbuilders and oyster-fishers.

KINGSTON-UPON-HULL

FERENS ART GALLERY
Queen Victoria Square, Hull HU1 3RA
Tel: 01482 613902
Fax: 01482 613710
Old Masters, marine paintings, 20thC and contemporary works.

HANDS ON HISTORY
South Church Side, Hull
Fax: 01482 613710
Hull's oldest secular building.

HULL & EAST RIDING MUSEUM
33 High Street, Hull HU1 1PS
Tel: 01482 613902
Fax: 01482 613710
The museum explores the story of Hull and the East Riding area, covering geology and archaeology.

STREETLIFE – HULL MUSEUM OF TRANSPORT
High Street, Hull HU1 1PS
Tel: 01482 613902
Fax: 01482 613710
Horse-drawn vehicles, motor vehicles 1890 to 1910 with the very rare Ryde Pier and Kitson trams.

TOWN DOCKS MUSEUM
Queen Victoria Square, Hull HU1 3DX
Tel: 01482 613902
Fax: 01482 613710
Whaling, fishing and trawling exhibits.

UNIVERSITY OF HULL ART COLLECTION
University of Hull, Cottingham Road, Hull HU6 7RX
Tel: 01482 465035
Fax: 01482 465192
Collection of British art paintings, drawings and sculpture (1890–1940) including works by Sickert Steer, Lucien Pissarro, Augustus John, Stanley Spencer, Epstein and Moore.

YORKSHIRE WATER'S MUSEUM
Springhead Pumping Station, Springhead Avenue, Hull HU5 5HZ
Tel: 01482 652283
The museum is set in an operational pumping station of the Victorian era and is centred around a Bell's Lightfoot Cornish Beam Engine.

LANCASHIRE

BACUP NATURAL HISTORY SOCIETY
24 Yorkshire Street, Bacup, Lancashire OL13 9AE
Tel: 01706 875687
Industrial and domestic bygones, fossils, flints, butterflies.

BANCROFT MILL ENGINE MUSEUM
Gillians Lane (off Colne Road), Barnoldswick, Colne, Lancashire BB8 6QF
Tel: 01282 865626
Mill engine running in steam with ancillary equipment including Cornish and Lancashire boilers, looms etc.

BLACKBURN MUSEUM & ART GALLERY
Museum Street, Blackburn, Lancashire BB1 7AJ
Tel: 01254 667130
Oil and watercolour paintings, icons, manuscripts, textiles from India and Pakistan.
For further details see page 73

BRITISH COMMERCIAL VEHICLE MUSEUM
King Street, Leyland, Preston PR5 1LE
Tel: 01772 451011
Fax: 01772 623404
The museum contains the finest collection of historic commercial vehicles in Europe including the world famous Popemobile, horse-drawn and steam vehicles and fire engines.

BRITISH IN INDIA MUSEUM
Newtown Street, Colne, Lancashire BB8 0JJ
Tel: 01282 870215/613129
Fax: 01282 870215
The museum occupies a building very close to the centre of Colne, showing the history of the British in India.

BYGONE TIMES
Times House, The Green, Eccleston, Chorley, Lancashire PR7 5PD
Tel: 01257 453780
Fax: 01257 450197
Themed American displays of antiques and bric-a-brac for both browsers and buyers.

EANAM WHARF VISITOR CENTRE
Eanam Wharf, Blackburn, Lancashire BB1 5BL
Tel: 01254 56557
Fax: 01254 662590
Permanent exhibition interpreting impact of Leeds–Liverpool canal on Blackburn.

FLEETWOOD MUSEUM
Queens Terrace, Fleetwood, Lancashire FY7 6BT
Tel: 01253 876621
Fax: 01253 878088
Deep-sea fishing, inshore fishing and maritime displays on the history of Fleetwood, its maritime connections and local environment.

GRUNDY ART GALLERY
Queen Street, Blackpool, Lancashire FY1 1PX
Tel: 01253 751701
Art gallery with permanent collection and temporary exhibitions.

HARRIS MUSEUM & ART GALLERY
Market Square, Preston, Lancashire PR1 2PP
Tel: 01772 258248
Fax: 01772 886764
Magnificent Greek revival building showing collections of fine and decorative art, costume and social history as well as an acclaimed programme of temporary exhibits.

HAWORTH ART GALLERY (TIFFANY GLASS)
Haworth Park, Manchester Road, Accrington, Lancashire BB5 2JS
Tel: 01254 233782
Local authority art gallery.

HELMSHORE TEXTILE MUSEUMS
Higher Mill Holcombe Road, Helmshore, Rossendale, Lancashire BB4 4NP
Tel: 01706 226459
Fax: 01706 218554
Textile machinery, waterwheel and many working exhibits especially carding engines and cotton spinning mules.

JUDGES LODGINGS MUSEUM
Church Street, Lancaster, Lancashire LA1 1YS
Tel: 01524 32808
Town House: furnished rooms with Gillow furniture.

LANCASHIRE MUSEUM
Stanley Street, Preston PR1 4YP
Tel: 01772 264075
Fax: 01772 264079
Courthouse built in 1826.

LANCASTER CITY MUSEUM
Market Square, Lancaster, Lancashire LA1 1HT
Tel: 01524 64637
Fax: 01524 841692
A social history museum. Roman, Victorian and 1930s. Activities for schools.

LANCASTER MARITIME MUSEUM
Custom House, St George's Quay, Lancaster, Lancashire LA1 1RB
Tel: 01524 64637
Fax: 01524 841692
Custom house (1764) and 18thC warehouse telling the story of the historic port of Lancaster, the fishing industry of Morecombe Bay and much more.

MID PENNINE ARTS
Mid Pennine Gallery, Yorke Street, Burnley, Lancashire BB11 1HD
Tel: 01282 421986
Fax: 01282 429513
Non-permanent exhibitions of contemporary art.

MUSEUM OF YORKSHIRE DALES LEAD MINING
Old Grammar School, School Lane, Earby, Colne, Lancashire BB8 6QF
Tel: 01282 814686
Yorkshire Dales lead-mining relics, mine tubs, miners' personal effects tools, and mine plans etc.

PETER SCOTT GALLERY
Lancaster University, Lancaster, Lancashire LA1 4YW
Tel: 01524 593057
Fax: 01524 592603
Two galleries showing a programme of temporary exhibitions of the visual arts, including craft and photographs, and often showing contemporary work. Painting and sculpture.

THE QUEEN'S LANCASHIRE REGIMENT REGIMENTAL MUSEUM
Fulwood Barracks, Fulwood, Preston, Lancashire PR2 8AA
Tel: 01772 260362
Fax: 01772 260583
Housed in one of Preston's finest 19thC listed buildings, situated in a Regular Army barracks, is the Museum and Chapel of the Queen's Lancashire Regiment.

RIBCHESTER ROMAN MUSEUM
Riverside, Ribchester, Preston PR3 3XS
Tel: 01254 878261
Original displays containing coins, pottery, inscriptions, and complementary models bring Roman Ribchester to life. Includes remains of the Roman fort.

ROSSENDALE FOOTWEAR HERITAGE MUSEUM
Gaghills Mill, off Burnley Road East, Waterfoot, Rossendale, Lancashire BB4 9AS
Tel: 01706 215417
Footwear museum located in mill built 1900; using footwear, machinery and photographs from the Lambert Howarth collection.

ROSSENDALE MUSEUM
Whitaker Park, Haslingden Road, Rawtenstall, Rossendale, Lancashire BB4 6RE
Tel: 01706 217777 ext 335
Fax: 01706 250037
The Museum is housed in the former home of a 19thC woollen manufacturer and set in pleasant parkland in the heart of the industrial north east of Lancashire.

STEAMTOWN RAILWAY MUSEUM LTD
Warton Road, Carnforth, Lancashire LA5 9HX
Tel: 01524 732100
Fax: 01524 735518
Ex BR Engine Shed housing over 30 main line and industrial locomotives.

TOWNELEY HALL ART GALLERY & MUSEUM
Todmorden Road, Burnley, Lancashire BB11 3RQ
Tel: 01282 424213
Fax: 01282 436138
Country house with art galleries, museum of local history, environmental study centre and permanent collections with changing exhibitions.

TOY & TEDDY BEAR MUSEUM
373 Clifton Drive North, Lytham St Annes, Lancashire FY8 2PA
Tel: 01253 713705
A museum of childhood displayed in a fine period building with a well-balanced collection of old toys, teddy bears and children's fashions; fun quiz for everybody.

WEAVERS TRIANGLE VISITOR CENTRE
85 Manchester Road, Burnley, Lancashire BB11 1JZ
Tel: 01282 452403
Visitor centre is an information centre for Weavers Triangle, a well-preserved Victorian industrial area with displays of history of area, buildings and cotton industry.

LEICESTERSHIRE

ABBEY PUMPING STATION
Corporation Road, Abbey Lane, Leicester LE4 5PX
Tel: 0116 266 1330
Housed in Abbey Pumping Station which is a Victorian sewerage works of 1891 and home to beautifully conserved fully working beam engines.

ASHBY-DE-LA-ZOUCH MUSEUM
North Street, Ashby-de-la-Zouch, Leicestershire LE65 1HU
Tel: 01530 560090
Permanent display of Ashby and district's history with annual temporary exhibitions of local interest.

BELGRAVE HALL
Church Road, Belgrave, Leicester LE4 5PE
Tel: 0116 266 6590
Fax: 0116 261 3063
A small Queen Anne country house 1709–13 with 17th–19thC period room setting.

THE BELL FOUNDRY MUSEUM & TAYLORS BELLFOUNDRY
Freehold Street, Loughborough, Leicestershire LE11 1AR
Tel: 01509 233414
Fax: 01509 263305
Scheduled building.

BOSWORTH BATTLE TOURIST INFORMATION CENTRE AND COUNTRY PARK
Sutton Cheney, Market Bosworth, Leicestershire CV13 0AD
Tel: 01455 290429
For further details see page 73

DONINGTON GRAND PRIX COLLECTION
Donington Park, Castle Donington, Derby DE74 2RP
Tel: 01332 811027
Fax: 01332 812829
World's largest public display of Grand Prix racing cars.

FOXTON CANAL MUSEUM
Middle Lock, Gumley Road, Foxton, Market Harborough, Leicestershire LE16 7RA
Tel: 0116 279 2657
Ten working locks, canal museum and education workshop.

THE FRANK HAYNES GALLERY
50 Station Road, Great Bowden, Market Harborough, Leicestershire LE16 7HN
Tel: 01858 464862
Two galleries, one for exhibitions of paintings etc, the other offering studio pottery.

THE GUILDHALL
Guildhall Lane, Leicester LE1 5FQ
Tel: 0116 253 2569
14thC Medieval hall of Corpus Christi Guild.

HALLATON MUSEUM
Hog Lane, Hallaton, Market Harborough, Leicestershire LE16 8UE
Tel: 01858 555216
Small museum with exhibits of local interest, agricultural and domestic.

THE HARBOROUGH MUSEUM
Council Offices, Adam and Eve Street, Market Harborough, Leicestershire LE16 7AG
Tel: 01858 432468
Fax: 01858 462766
Museum illustrating local history of Harborough area particularly the town's role as a market and social focus.

JEWRY WALL MUSEUM & SITE
St Nicholas Circle, Leicester LE1 4LB
Tel: 0116 247 3021
Fax: 0116 251 2257
Archaeology/history of Leicestershire to 1485. Public baths of Roman Leicester.

JOHN DORAN GAS MUSEUM
Aylestone Road, Leicester LE2 7QH
Tel: 0116 253 5506
All aspects of gas industry in Britain and East Midlands in particular.

KEGWORTH MUSEUM
52 High Street, Kegworth, Derby DE74 2DA
Tel: 01509 673801
Museum of village exhibits, Royal British Legion and other visiting exhibitions.

LEICESTER ROYAL INFIRMARY HISTORY MUSEUM
Leicester Royal Infirmary, Knighton Street, Leicester
Tel: 0116 254 1414
History of Royal Infirmary.

LEICESTERSHIRE MUSEUM & ART GALLERY
96 New Walk, Leicester LE1 7EA
Tel: 0116 255 4100
Fax: 0116 247 3005
Collections of 18th–20thC English paintings and drawings.

LUTTERWORTH MUSEUM
Churchgate, Lutterworth, Leicestershire LE17 4AN
Tel: 01455 284733
Displays of Victorian agriculture, roman relics from 60AD, fieldwalker display of palaeolithic, neolithic and bronze age.

THE MAGAZINE GATEWAY
Oxford Street, Leicester LE2 7BY
Tel: 0116 255 5889
Late 14thC gatehouse containing Museum of the Royal Leicestershire Regiment (17th Foot).

THE MANOR HOUSE
Manor Road, Donington le Heath, Coalville, Leicester, Leicestershire LE67 2FW
Tel: 01530 831259
Superbly restored Medieval Manor House with fine oak furnishings, herb gardens and tempting Barn Tea-room.

MELTON CARNEGIE MUSEUM
Thorpe End, Melton Mowbray, Leicestershire LE13 1RB
Tel: 01664 569946
Fax: 01664 569946
Museum illustrating the natural and local history of the Borough of Melton.

NEWARKE HOUSES MUSEUM
The Newarke, Leicester LE2 7BY
Tel: 0116 247 3222
Fax: 0116 247 0403
Local history and crafts from 1485.

THE OLD RECTORY MUSEUM
Rectory Place, Loughborough, Leicestershire LE11 1UW
Tel: 01509 232419
Archaeological objects found in and around Loughborough. Charnwood forest canal, Victorianna display, Garendon Abbey display.

RUTLAND COUNTY MUSEUM
Catmos Street, Oakham, Rutland LE15 6HW
Tel: 01572 723654
Fax: 01572 757576
Museum of Rutland life. Farm equipment, vehicles, rural tradesmen's tools, domestic collections, archaeology. 1794 indoor riding school. Volunteer soldier gallery. Café.

RUTLAND RAILWAY MUSEUM
Ashwell Road, Cottesmore, Oakham, Leicestershire LE15 7BX
Tel: 01572 813203
Museum of industrial railways with particular emphasis on local ironstone quarry railways.

SNIBSTON DISCOVERY PARK
Ashby Road, Coalville, Leicester, Leicestershire LE67 3LN
Tel: 01530 510851
Fax: 01530 813301
All weather and award-winning science and industrial heritage museum.
For further details see page 94

WILLIAM CAREY EXHIBITION
Central Baptist Church, Charles Street, Leicester LE1 1LA
Tel: 0116 273 8447
Tableaux of life of William Carey, letters, photos and mementoes of missionary work in India.

WYGSTON'S HOUSE
Museum of Costume, 12 Applegate, St Nicholas Circle, Leicester LE1 5LD
Tel: 0116 247 3056
Fax: 0116 262 0964
Late medieval building with later additions.

LINCOLNSHIRE

ALFORD MANOR HOUSE MUSEUM
The Manor House, West Street, Alford, Lincolnshire LN13 9DJ
Tel: 01507 463073
Thatched 17thC manor house in own grounds housing a museum which includes the history of the house and general local history.

ALLIED FORCES MUSEUM
Main Road (Church Road), Stickford, Boston, Lincolnshire PE22 8ES
Tel: 01205 480317
Private collection including a display of military motorcycles, heavy vehicles, weaponry, uniforms and medals.

AYSCOUGHFEE HALL MUSEUM
Churchgate, Spalding, Lincolnshire PE11 2RA
Tel: 01775 725468
Fax: 01775 762715
Displays on land drainage, agriculture, horticulture, wildfowling, local history and Spalding.

THE BARN GALLERY
18 West Street, Osbournby,
Sleaford, Lincolnshire
NG34 0DS
Tel: 01529 455631
Fax: 01529 455631
*Art gallery with seasonal exhibitions
of wildlife and country
pictures/prints featuring local and
international artists.*

BATTLE OF BRITAIN
MEMORIAL FLIGHT
RAF Coningsby, Coningsby,
Lincoln LN4 4SY
Tel: 01526 344041
Fax: 01526 344041
*Working collection with the only
flying Lancaster bomber in Europe,
five Spitfires, two Hurricanes,
Dakota and other World War II
memorabilia.*

BOSTON GUILDHALL
MUSEUM
South Street, Boston,
Lincolnshire PE21 6HT
Tel: 01205 365954
Fax: 01205 359401
*A 15thC building, 16thC
kitchens.*
For further details see page 74

CHURCH FARM MUSEUM
Church Road South, Skegness,
Lincolnshire PE25 2HF
Tel: 01754 766658
Fax: 01754 766658
*Bernard Best Collection of
agricultural objects in 19thC
farmhouse and buildings.*

GEESON BROS MOTORCYCLE
MUSEUM & WORKSHOP
2, 4 & 6 Water Lane, South
Witham, Grantham,
Lincolnshire NG33 5PH
Tel: 01572 767280/768195
*Eight British motorcycles dating back
to 1913, most restored to new
condition in our workshop.*

THE GORDON BOSWELL
ROMANY MUSEUM
Clay Lake, Spalding,
Lincolnshire PE12 6BL
Tel: 01775 710599
*Collection of Romany Vardo's
horse-drawn caravans, and carts and
harness.*

GRANTHAM MUSEUM
St Peter's Hill, Grantham,
Lincolnshire NG31 6PY
Tel: 01476 568783
Fax: 01476 592457
*Collection relating to history,
natural history and archaeology of
Grantham and district. Features,
Isaac Newton, Romans, WW
II–the Dambusters.*

THE INCREDIBLY FANTASTIC
OLD TOY SHOW
26 Westgate, Lincoln LN1 3BD
Tel: 01522 520534
*Exciting collection covering two
centuries of toys, old pier machines,
videos, push-buttons, music, photos,
distorting mirros. Nostalgia and fun.*

LEGBOURNE RAILWAY
MUSEUM
The Old Station, Legbourne,
Louth, Lincolnshire LN11 8LH
Tel: 01507 603116
*Restored Great Northern country
station frontage.*

THE LIFEBOAT STATION
Boathouse, Tower Esplanade,
Skegness, Lincolnshire
PE25 3HJ
Tel: 01754 763011
*Visitors may see the offshore and
inshore lifeboats.*

LINCOLNSHIRE AVIATION
HERITAGE CENTRE
The Airfield, East Kirkby,
Spilsby, Lincolnshire PE23 4DE
Tel: 01790 763207
*Part of wartime bomber airfield
including restored control tower.*

LINCOLNSHIRE ROAD
TRANSPORT MUSEUM
Whisby Road, Doddington
Road, Lincoln LN6 3QT
Tel: 01522 500566
*A display of over 40 historic and
classic vehicles dating from the
1920s to the late 1960s.*

LOUTH MUSEUM
4 Broadbank, Louth,
Lincolnshire LN11 0EQ
Tel: 01507 601211
*Butterflies and moths, stuffed birds,
craft and industry, fossil and
geological specimens, printing press
and typeface.*

MAGDALEN MUSEUM
St John's Street, Wainfleet,
Skegness, Lincolnshire
PE24 4DL
Tel: 01754 880307
*Exhibits of local history all donated
or lent by people living locally.*

MAWTHORPE MUSEUM
Woodlands, Mawthorpe, Alford,
Lincolnshire LN13 9LU
Tel: 01507 462336
A museum of life in Lincolnshire.

MUSEUM OF
ENTERTAINMENT
Millgate, Whaplode St
Catherine, Spalding,
Lincolnshire PE12 6SD
Tel: 01406 540379
*The home of entertainment. Take a
guided tour of mechanical music,
organs, marionettes, fairground.
circus, radio, TV and much more.*

MUSEUM OF LINCOLNSHIRE
LIFE
Burton Road, Lincoln LN1 3LY
Tel: 01522 528448
Fax: 01522 521264
*The region's largest social history
museum, everything from a teapot to
a tank.*

PINCHBECK PUMPING ENGINE
& LAND DRAINAGE MUSEUM
Off West Marsh Road, Spalding,
Lincolnshire PE11 3UW
*Demonstrations given in restored
steam pumping station; collection of
rare hand tools and displays on land
reclamation, drainage and modern
conservation work.*

SPALDING BULB MUSEUM &
HORTICULTURAL EXHIBITION
Birchgrove Garden Centre,
Surfleet Road, Pinchbeck,
Spalding, Lincolnshire
PE11 3XY
Tel: 01775 680490
Fax: 01775 680656
*A slide presentation theatre with
undercover exhibits and artefacts,
detailing the history of the flower
bulb industry in South Lincolnshire.*

STAMFORD MUSEUM
Broad Street, Stamford,
Lincolnshire PE9 1PJ
Tel: 01780 766317
Fax: 01780 480363
*Displays illustrate the development
of Stamford, an important historic
town, including customs, trades and
people.*

USHER GALLERY
Lindum Road, Lincoln
LN2 1NN
Tel: 01522 527980
Fax: 01522 560165
*Regional art gallery with
outstanding collection of fine and
decorative arts.*

WILLOUGHBY MEMORIAL
TRUST GALLERY
Lenton House, Lenton,
Grantham, Lincolnshire
NG33 4HB
Tel: 01476 550380
*A 17thC grammar school, now
library reading room and gallery.
Exhibitions from Easter to
November changing monthly.*

WOODHALL SPA COTTAGE
MUSEUM
Iddesleigh Road, Woodhall Spa,
Lincolnshire LN10 6SH
Tel: 01526 353775
*The Victorian Boulton and Paul
sectional bungalow houses displays
on Woodhall Spa history plus an
ancillary exhibition on 617
Squadron, The Dambusters.*

YE OLDE CURIOSITY MUSEUM
61 Victoria Road, Mablethorpe,
Lincolnshire LN12 2AF
Tel: 01507 472406
*Collection of 4,500 old glass
lampshades.*

MERSEYSIDE

ANYTHING TO DECLARE
HM CUSTOMS & EXCISE
NATIONAL MUSEUM
Merseyside Maritime
Museum, Albert Dock,
Liverpool, Merseyside
L3 4AQ
Tel: 0151 207 0001
Fax: 0151 478 4777
*Visitors can join the exciting
search for smuggled goods at
Liverpool's newest museum.*
For further details see page 75

ATKINSON ART GALLERY
Lord Street, Southport,
Merseyside PR8 1DH
Tel: 01704 533133 ext 2110
*19th–20thC oil paintings,
watercolours, prints, drawings,
modern sculpture and temporary
exhibitions.*
For further details see page 75

THE BEATLES STORY
Britannia Vaults, Albert Dock,
Liverpool, Merseyside L3 4AA
Tel: 0151 709 1963
Fax: 0151 708 0039
*Liverpool's number 1
award winning visitor attraction.*

BOTANIC GARDENS MUSEUM
Churchtown, Southport,
Merseyside PR9 7ND
Tel: 01704 27547
*Local history, lifeboats, growth of
Southport, Victorian natural history,
dolls, toys, costume and porcelain.*

BRITISH LAWNMOWER
MUSEUM
106–114 Shakespeare Street,
Southport, Lancashire PR8 5AJ
Tel: 01704 501336
Fax: 01704 500564
*Over 200 restored lawnmowers and
memorabilia from 1830s. A tribute
to the garden machine industry over
the last 170 years. Large archive.*

LADY LEVER ART GALLERY
NMGM PO Box 33, 127 Dale
Street, Liverpool, Merseyside
L69 3LA
Tel: 0151 478 4136
Fax: 0151 478 4140
*First Lord Leverhulme's
magnificent collection of British
paintings 1750–1900, British
furniture, Wedgewood and
oriental porcelain.*
For further details see page 75

LIVERPOOL MUSEUM
NMGM PO Box 33, 127 Dale
Street, Liverpool, Merseyside
L69 3LA
Tel: 0151 478 4616
Fax: 0151 478 4777
*Displays on five floors include
vivarium and aquarium, land
transport, natural history,
antiquities, ethnology and space
and time.*
For further details see page 75

LIVERPOOL MUSEUM
NATURAL HISTORY CENTRE
NMGM PO Box 33, 127 Dale
Street, Liverpool, Merseyside
L69 3LA
Tel: 0151 478 4291
*Explore the fascinating world of
natural history. If you've found a
fossil on the beach the Natural
History Centre is the place to look
for the answers.*
For further details see page 75

MERSEYSIDE MARITIME
MUSEUM
Albert Dock, Liverpool,
Merseyside L3 4AQ
Tel: 0151 478 4499
Fax: 0151 478 4590
Restored 19thC docks.
For further details see page 75

MUSEUM OF LIVERPOOL
LIFE
Albert Dock, Liverpool,
Merseyside L3 1PZ
Tel: 0151 478 4080
Fax: 0151 478 4090
*This new museum explores the
history of Liverpool, its people,
and their contribution to national
life.*
For further details see page 75

OPEN EYE GALLERY
28–32 Wood Street, Liverpool
L1 4AQ
Tel: 0151 709 9460
Fax: 0151 709 3059
*Exhibitions of national, regional
and international photographers.
Education programme aimed at
young people and school groups.*

PILKINGTON GLASS MUSEUM
Prescot Road, St Helens,
Merseyside WA10 3TT
Tel: 01744 692499
Fax: 01744 692727
*Fine collection of vessel glass from all
periods.*

PORT SUNLIGHT HERITAGE
CENTRE
95 Greendale Road, Port
Sunlight, Wirral, Merseyside
L62 4XE
Tel: 0151 644 6466
Fax: 0151 645 8973
*A picturesque 19thC garden
village on the Wirral, built by
William Hesketh Lever for his
soap factory workers. It was
named after Lever's famous
Sunlight Soap.*
For further details see page 75

PRESCOT MUSEUM OF CLOCK
& WATCH MAKING
34 Church Street, Prescot,
Merseyside L34 3LA
Tel: 0151 430 7787
Fax: 0151 430 7219
*Display of clock and watchmaking
and local history.*

RAINFORD ART GALLERY
Gamble Building, Victoria
Square, St Helens, Merseyside
WA10 4DY
Tel: 01744 456950
*Art gallery with permanent collection
of Victorian water colours.*

TATE GALLERY LIVERPOOL
Albert Dock, Liverpool,
Merseyside L3 4BB
Tel: 0151 709 3223
Fax: 0151 709 3122
*Tate Gallery Liverpool exhibits
the national collection of modern
art in the north of England.*
For further details see page 75

UNIVERSITY OF LIVERPOOL
ART GALLERY
3 Abercromby Square,
Liverpool, Merseyside L69 3BX
Tel: 0151 794 2347
Fax: 0151 708 2343
*Selection from university collections
housed in early 19thC merchant's
house.*

WALKER ART GALLERY
William Brown Street,
Liverpool, Merseyside L3 8EL
Tel: 0151 478 4178
Fax: 0151 478 4090
*Outstanding general collection of
European paintings from 1330;
specially notable for Italian and
Netherlandish painting
14th–16thC; British art
1840–1910.*
For further details see page 75

WESTERN APPROACHES
1 Rumford Street, Liverpool,
Merseyside L2 3SZ
Tel: 0151 227 2008
*Visit the former top secret
underground HQ for the Battle of
the Atlantic in the heart of
Liverpool.*

MIDDLESBROUGH

CAPTAIN COOK BIRTHPLACE
MUSEUM
Stewart Park, Marton,
Middlesbrough TS7 6AS
Tel: 01642 311211
Fax: 01642 813781
*Early life and voyages of Captain
Cook and the countries he visited.
Shop, tearoom, disabled access,
endeavour room, resource centre.*

DORMAN MUSEUM
Linthorpe Road, Middlesbrough
TS5 6LA
Tel: 01642 813781
Fax: 01642 813781
Displays of local, social and natural history.

MIDDLESBROUGH ART GALLERY
320 Linthorpe Road,
Middlesbrough TS1 4AW
Tel: 01642 247445
Fax: 01642 247445
Late Victorian house, 20thC art collection, temporary exhibitions of contemporary art and related events.

NORFOLK

100TH BOMB GROUP MEMORIAL MUSEUM
Common Road, Dickleburgh,
Diss, Norfolk IP21 4PH
Tel: 01379 740708
Museum housed in original World War II control tower.

ALBY BOTTLE MUSEUM
Alby Craft Centre, Cromer
Road, Erpingham, Norfolk
Tel: 01263 761327
The only bottle museum in East Anglia.

ALBY LACE MUSEUM & STUDY CENTRE/STITCHES & LACE
Cromer Road, Alby Hill,
Norwich, Norfolk NR11 7QE
Tel: 01263 768002
Lace exhibits up to 300 years' old.

ANCIENT HOUSE MUSEUM
White Hart Street, Thetford,
Norfolk IP24 1AA
Tel: 01842 752599
A museum of Thetford and Breckland life in a remarkable early Tudor house.

BISHOP BONNERS COTTAGE MUSEUM
St Withburga Lane, East
Dereham, Norfolk NR19 1ED
Tel: 01362 860096
Built 1502.

BRESSINGHAM STEAM MUSEUM & GARDENS
Bressingham, Diss, Norfolk
IP22 2AB
Tel: 01379 687386
Fax: 01379 688085
Working vintage steam engines and six acres of gardens.

BRIDEWELL MUSEUM
Bridewell Alley, Norwich,
Norfolk NR2 1AQ
Tel: 01603 667228
Fax: 01603 765651
Displays illustrating local industry during the past 200 years.

BURSTON STRIKE SCHOOL
Burston, Diss, Norfolk
IP22 3TP
Tel: 01379 741565
Erected in 1917 after pupils went on strike from county school after the wrongful dismissal of teachers, strike lasted 1914–39.

CHARLES BURRELL MUSEUM
Minstergate, Thetford, Norfolk
Tel: 01842 751166
The Charles Burrell steam museum draws together an impressive collection of exhibits to tell the story of Charles Burrell and Son (1770–1932).

CITY OF NORWICH AVIATION MUSEUM
Old Norwich Road, Horsham
St Faith, Norwich, Norfolk
NR10 3JF
Tel: 01603 861348
Exhibition building containing Norfolk aeronautical history and aero engines. Eight aircraft on show. Entry to cockpit at certain times.

CROMER LIFEBOAT MUSEUM & LIFEBOAT
The Pier and Gangway, Cromer,
Norfolk NR27 0HY
Tel: 01263 512503
Models, pictures, photographs.

CROMER MUSEUM
East Cottages, Tucker Street,
Cromer, Norfolk NR27 9HB
Tel: 01263 513543
Fax: 01263 511651
Late Victorian fisherman's cottage, displays on local history, geology, natural history and archaeology.

DISS MUSEUM
Market Place, Diss, Norfolk
IP22 3AB
Tel: 01379 650618
Changing displays reflecting the history of Diss and its local area. Dip into 10,000 years of local history with a variety of changing displays.

DUNHAM MUSEUM
Little Dunham, King's Lynn,
Norfolk PE32 2DJ
Tel: 01760 723073
Exhibition building showing collection of old working tools, bygones and machinery.

ELIZABETHAN HOUSE MUSEUM
4 South Quay, Great Yarmouth,
Norfolk NR30 2QH
Tel: 01493 855746
Merchant's house with late Georgian front and 16thC panelled rooms.

FAKENHAM MUSEUM OF GAS & LOCAL HISTORY
Hempton Road, Fakenham,
Norfolk
Tel: 01328 863150
Complete small town gasworks with local history section, displays of working gas meters and working exhausters.

FENLAND & WEST NORFOLK AVIATION MUSEUM (BAMBERS GARDEN CENTRE)
Old Lynn Road, West Walton,
Wisbech, Cambridgeshire
PE14 7DA
Tel: 01945 585946
Fax: 01945 474307
Vampire T11 and Lightning aircraft, uniforms, aero engines, aircraft components, artefacts, radio equipment, souvenir shop, memorabilia, models, replica Spitfire cockpit.

FORNCETT INDUSTRIAL STEAM MUSEUM
Low Road, Forncett St Mary,
Norwich, Norfolk NR16 1JJ
Tel: 01508 488277
Unique collection of large industrial steam engines including one that used to open Tower Bridge.

GREAT YARMOUTH MUSEUMS EXHIBITION GALLERIES
Central Library, Tolhouse
Street, Great Yarmouth, Norfolk
NR30 2SH
Tel: 01493 745526
Fax: 01493 745459
Galleries on the first floor of library housing temporary art exhibitions.

GUILDHALL OF ST GEORGE
27 King Street, King's Lynn,
Norfolk PE30 1HA
Tel: 01553 774725
Fax: 01553 770591
Regional Arts Centre.

HOBBIES MUSEUM OF FRETWORK & CRAFT CENTRE
34–36 Swaffham Road,
Dereham, Norfolk NR19 2QZ
Tel: 01362 692985
Fax: 01362 699145
Museum of fretwork machines dating back to 1900, magazines and hobbies weeklies from 1895 and samples of old fretwork designs.

ICENI VILLAGE & MUSEUMS
Cockley Cley, Swaffham,
Norfolk PE37 8AG
Tel: 01760 724588
Fax: 01760 721339
Iceni tribal-village reconstruction believed to be on original site.

INSPIRE HANDS-ON SCIENCE CENTRE
St Michael's Church, Coslany
Street, Norwich, Norfolk
Tel: 01603 612612
Fax: 01603 616721
Inspire is a hands-on science centre housed in a medieval church.

LYNN MUSEUM
Market Street, King's Lynn,
Norfolk PE30 1NL
Tel: 01553 775001
Mid-Victorian church includes natural history, archaeology, local history and temporary exhibitions.

MARITIME MUSEUM
Marine Parade, Great Yarmouth,
Norfolk NR30 2EN
Tel: 01493 842267
Maritime history of Norfolk with herring fishery and Norfolk wherry; large collection of ship models, World War II and home front, World War I and home front.

MUCKLEBURGH COLLECTION
Weybourne Old Military Camp,
Weybourne, Holt, Norfolk
NR25 7EG
Tel: 01263 588210
Fax: 01263 588425
3,000 exhibits of military history including 16 tanks, 150 armoured vehicles, guns and missiles. Tank demonstrations daily during summer.

THE MUSTARD SHOP
3 Bridewell Alley, Norwich,
Norfolk NR2 1AQ
Tel: 01603 627889
Fax: 01603 627889
Decorated 19thC-style shop which houses a museum with a series of displays illustrating the history of Colmans mustard.

NORFOLK MOTORCYCLE MUSEUM
Railway Yard, North Walsham,
Norfolk NR28 0DS
Tel: 01692 406266
Motorcycles dating from 1920 to 1960.

NORFOLK RURAL LIFE MUSEUM
Beech House, Gressenhall,
Dereham, Norfolk NR20 4DR
Tel: 01362 860563
Fax: 01362 860385
Former workhouse illustrating history of Norfolk over the last 200 years, with traditional working farm, rare breeds, demonstrations and events.

NORWICH CASTLE MUSEUM
Norwich Museum Service,
Norwich, Norfolk NR1 3JU
Tel: 01603 223624
Fax: 01603 765651
Large collection of art, including an important collection by Norwich School of Artists.
For further details see page 76

THE NORWICH GALLERY
Norwich School of Art and
Design, St Georges Street,
Norwich, Norfolk NR3 1BB
Tel: 01603 610561
Fax: 01603 615728
Temporary exhibitions of contemporary art, design and crafts.

OLD MERCHANT'S HOUSE
Row 111, South Quay, Great
Yarmouth, Norfolk NR30 2RQ
Tel: 01493 857900
Typical 17thC town houses.

PICTURECRAFT OF HOLT
23 Lees Courtyard, Off Bull
Street, Holt, Norfolk
NR25 6HP
Tel: 01263 711040
Fax: 01263 711151
Main art gallery exhibits 19 artists' work which changes every three weeks.

REEPHAM STATION
Station Road, Reepham,
Norwich, Norfolk NR10 4LJ
Tel: 01603 871187
Traffic-free cycle hire along the 26 mile Marriott's Way (former railway route).

ROYAL NORFOLK REGIMENTAL MUSEUM
Shirehall, Market Avenue,
Norwich, Norfolk NR1 3JQ
Tel: 01603 223649
Displays about the County Regiment from 1685.

SAINSBURY CENTRE FOR VISUAL ARTS
University of East Anglia,
Norwich, Norfolk NR4 7TJ
Tel: 01603 456060
Fax: 01603 259401
The Robert and Lisa Sainsbury Collection of modern and non-modern art is wide-ranging and of international importance.

SAINT PETER HUNGATE CHURCH MUSEUM
Princes Street, Norwich,
Norfolk NR3 1AE
Tel: 01603 667231
A 15thC church with fine hammerbeam roof and Norwich painted glass.

SEETHING AIRFIELD CONTROL TOWER
Station 146, Seething Airfield,
Seething, Norwich, Norfolk
Tel: 01502 561396
Renovated original wartime control tower holding 448th bomb group honour roll and World War II exhibits.

SHELL MUSEUM
Glandford, Holt, Norfolk
NR25 7JR
Tel: 01263 740081
Exhibits of shells, fossils, pottery and objects of local history.

SHERINGHAM MUSEUM
Station Road, Sheringham,
Norfolk NR26 8RE
Tel: 01263 822895
Fax: 01263 822097
Local history museum.

SHIREHALL MUSEUM
Common Place, Little
Walsingham, Norfolk
NR22 6BP
Tel: 01328 820510
A Georgian country courthouse, local museum and Tourist Information Centre.

STRUMPSHAW OLD HALL STEAM MUSEUM & FARM MACHINERY COLLECTION
Low Road, Strumpshaw,
Norwich NR13 4HR
Tel: 01603 714535
Many steam engines, beam engines, mechanical organs, narrow gauge railway, and working toy train for children.

SWAFFHAM MUSEUM
Town Hall, London Street,
Swaffham, Norfolk PE37 7DQ
Tel: 01760 721230
Fax: 01760 720469
An 18thC building, formerly brewer's main house.

TALES OF THE OLD GAOL HOUSE
The Old Gaol House, Saturday
Market Place, King's Lynn,
Norfolk PE30 5DQ
Tel: 01553 763044
A personal stereo tour of the Old Gaol House tells the true stories of Lynn's infamous murderers, highwaymen and even witches.

THURSFORD COLLECTION
Thursford Green, Thursford,
Fakenham, Norfolk NR21 0AS
Tel: 01328 878477
Fax: 01328 878415
Live musical show every opening.

TOAD HOLE COTTAGE MUSEUM
How Hill, Ludham, Great
Yarmouth, Norfolk NR29 5PG
Tel: 01692 678763
An 18thC building with five small rooms plus Broads information area.

TOLHOUSE MUSEUM
Tolhouse Street, Great
Yarmouth, Norfolk
Tel: 01493 858900
One of the oldest municipal buildings in England.

TOWN HOUSE MUSEUM
46 Queen Street, King's Lynn,
Norfolk PE30 5DQ
Tel: 01553 773450
Fax: 01553 775001
The past comes to life in this newly opened museum with historic room displays including costume toys, a working Victorian kitchen and a 1950s living room.

TRUE'S YARD HERITAGE CENTRE

3–5 North Street, King's Lynn, Norfolk PE30 1QW
Tel: 01553 770479
Fax: 01553 765100
Two fully-restored fishermen's cottages, with research facilities for tracing ancestry in King's Lynn; museum gift shop and tea room.

WELLS MARITIME MUSEUM

Old Lifeboat House, The Quay, Wells-next-the-Sea, Norfolk NR23 1AT
Tel: 01328 711646
Fax: 01328 710623
Maritime history of Wells housed in Old Lifeboat House.

WOLFERTON STATION MUSEUM

Wolferton, King's Lynn, Norfolk PE31 6HA
Tel: 01485 540674
Former royal station retiring rooms built for Edward VII and Queen Alexandra.

WYMONDHAM HERITAGE MUSEUM

Bridewell, Norwich Road, Wymondham, Norfolk
Tel: 01362 850154
Award-winning museum, established in 1984, moved to Bridewell in 1996. Housed in an old prison. Exhibits of historic and local origin.

NORTH EAST LINCOLNSHIRE

CLEETHORPES DISCOVERY CENTRE

Lakeside, King's Road, Cleethorpes, North East Lincolnshire DN35 0AG
Tel: 01472 323232
Fax: 01472 323233
One of Europe's top ten estuaries for wildlife. Award-winning exhibitions and environmental education programmes for all ages.

IMMINGHAM MUSEUM

Margaret Street, Immingham, Grimsby, North East Lincolnshire DN40 1LE
Tel: 01469 577066
The Great Central Railway and the creation of a port.

NATIONAL FISHING HERITAGE CENTRE

Alexandra Dock, Grimsby, North East Lincolnshire DN31 1UZ
Tel: 01472 323345
Fax: 01472 344887
Spectacular 1950s' steam trawler experience.

NORTH LINCOLNSHIRE

BAYSGARTH HOUSE MUSEUM

Baysgarth Leisure Park, Caistor Road, Barton-upon-Humber, North Lincolnshire DN18 6AH
Tel: 01652 632318
An 18thC house with period room displays.

NORMANBY HALL COUNTY PARK

Normanby, Scunthorpe, North Lincolnshire DN15 9HU
Tel: 01724 720588
Fax: 01724 721248
A Regency mansion set in 350 acres of parkland with a farming museum, Victorian laundry and walled garden.
For further details see page 76

SCUNTHORPE MUSEUM & ART GALLERY

Oswald Road, Scunthorpe, North Lincolnshire DN15 7BD
Tel: 01724 843533
Regional museum for North Lincolnshire, with local collections of archaeology, social history, natural sciences and history of Scunthorpe's steel industry.

NORTH SOMERSET

THE HELICOPTER MUSEUM

The Airport, Locking Moor Road, Weston-super-Mare BS22 8PP
Tel: 01934 635227
Fax: 01934 822400
Unique collection of helicopters and autogyros with background displays on history, developments, how they work and uses.

THE TIME MACHINE

Burlington Street, Weston-super-Mare BS23 1PR
Tel: 01934 621028
Fax: 01934 612526
Victorian building reflecting the archaeology, natural and social history of the area. Feature Clara's cottage and period house fitted in detail.

NORTH YORKSHIRE

ARCHAEOLOGICAL RESOURCE CENTRE

St Saviourgate, York YO1 2NN
Tel: 01904 654324
Fax: 01904 640029
Visitors can touch the past, handling ancient finds of pottery and bone, stitching Roman sandals and picking a Viking padlock.

BAR CONVENT MUSEUM & GALLERY

17 Blossom Street, York YO2 2AH
Tel: 01904 643238
Fax: 01904 631792
One of the finest Georgian buildings in York, housing a chapel built in 1767 which is still in regular use.

BECK ISLE MUSEUM OF RURAL LIFE

Bridge Street, Pickering, North Yorkshire YO18 8DU
Tel: 01751 473653
Bygones of Victorian age with something of interest to all ages; many rooms including grocer's shop, children's room, printer's workshop, costume room and kitchen.

BEDALE MUSEUM

Bedale Hall, Bedale, North Yorkshire DL8 1AA
Tel: 01677 424604
This fascinating little museum is housed in the Georgian wing of Bedale Hall.

CAPTAIN COOK MEMORIAL MUSEUM

Grape Lane, Whitby, North Yorkshire YO22 4BE
Tel: 01947 601900
18thC merchant's house where Captain Cook lodged when apprenticed to John Walker the owner.

CAPTAIN COOK SCHOOLROOM MUSEUM

101 High Street, Great Ayton, Middlesbrough, Cleveland TS9 6NB
Relics belonging to Cook and his family; maps of the period; model of family cottage transported to Melbourne, Australia in 1934; Cook memorabilia.

THE CRAVEN MUSEUM

Town Hall, High Street, Skipton, North Yorkshire BD23 1AH
Tel: 01756 706407
Fax: 01756 706412
Folk history, archaeology, geology, costume, lead mining – a small museum which is crammed full of curios guaranteed to have something of interest for everybody.

DALES COUNTRYSIDE MUSEUM

Station Yard, Hawes, North Yorkshire DL8 3NT
Tel: 01969 667494
Fax: 01969 667494
Tells the story of the people and landscape of the treasured Yorkshire dales, past and present.

FILEY MUSEUM

8–10 Queen Street, Filey, North Yorkshire YO14 9HB
Tel: 01723 513640
Fishing, lifeboat, rural, domestic, local and photographic items.

GREEN HOWARDS MUSEUM

Trinity Church Square, Richmond, North Yorkshire DL10 4QN
Tel: 01748 822133
Fax: 01748 826561
Three hundred years of regimental history; founded in 1688; its campaigns from 1690 onwards illustrated in three galleries with original uniforms, gallantry awards, medals and silver.

IMPRESSIONS GALLERY OF PHOTOGRAPHY

29 Castlegate, Castle Walk, York YO1 1RN
Tel: 01904 654724
Fax: 01904 651509
Photographic exhibitions, changing every eight weeks, of local, national and international interest; also talks and workshops.

MALTON MUSEUM

Town Hall, Market Place, Malton, North Yorkshire YO17 0LT
Tel: 01653 695136
Archaeological collections from Malton Norton and the surrounding Ryedale area, plus changing temporary exhibitions each year.

MERCER ART GALLERY

Swan Road, Harrogate, North Yorkshire HG1 2SS
Tel: 01423 503340
Fax: 01423 840026
Exhibitions feature the Harrogate permanent collections plus a programme of contemporary shows and the Kent collection of foreign antiquities.

MICKLEGATE BAR MUSEUM

Micklegate Bar, York
Tel: 01904 634436
Fax: 01904 612490
An 800 year-old royal gateway to city on the city-wall walk.

MUSEUM OF BADGES & BATTLEDRESS

Old Methodist Chapel, The Green, Crakehall, Bedale, North Yorkshire DL8 1HP
Tel: 01677 424444
Two floors of uniforms, badges, equipment of the British Army, RAF, Civil Defence, ARP, Observer Corps, Women's Services and Land Army from 1900 to present day.

MUSEUM OF VICTORIAN WHITBY

Sandgate, Whitby, North Yorkshire YO22 4DB
Tel: 01947 601221
First section contains Victorian 'lane' with shops' interiors and yards.

MUSIC IN MINIATURE EXHIBITION

Albion Road, Robin Hood's Bay, Whitby, North Yorkshire YO22 4SW
Tel: 01947 880512
Permanent exhibition of 50 one-twelfth-scale dioramic models set in illuminated recesses – depicting man's love of music from stone age to space age.

NATIONAL RAILWAY MUSEUM

Leeman Road, York YO2 4XJ
Tel: 01904 621261
Fax: 01904 686247
Experience nearly 200 years of technical and social history on the railways and see the way they shaped the world.

NIDDERDALE MUSEUM

Council Offices, Pateley Bridge, Harrogate, North Yorkshire HG3 5LE
Tel: 01423 711225
Wide variety of exhibits relating to Nidderdale life; complete cobblers shop, Victorian living room, chemist shop and haberdashers display.

OLD COURTHOUSE MUSEUM

Castle Grounds, Knaresborough, North Yorkshire
Tel: 01423 869274
Local history of ancient market town and Civil War exhibition.

THE REAL AEROPLANE MUSEUM

The Aerodrome, Breighton, Selby, North Yorkshire YO8 7DH
Tel: 01757 289065
Fax: 01757 289065
Four hangars, 50 vintage aircraft plus club room.

THE REGIMENTAL MUSEUM

3 Tower Street, York YO1 1SB
Tel: 01904 662790
Regimental museum of the Royal Dragoon Guards and the Prince of Wales's Own Regiment of Yorkshire – uniforms, weapons, pictures, silver and medals.

RICHARD III MUSEUM

Monk Bar, Monkgate, York
Tel: 01904 634191
The museum allows the visitor to decide whether King Richard III of England was an evil monster or loyal ruler in this reconstructed modern-day 'trial'.

RICHMONDSHIRE MUSEUM

Ryder's Wynd, Richmond, North Yorkshire DL10 4JA
Tel: 01748 825611
History of Richmond and Richmondshire from prehistoric times to the present.

RIPON PRISON & POLICE MUSEUM

St Marygate, Ripon, North Yorkshire HG4
Tel: 01765 690799
Displays and exhibits trace the development from 17thC to present day of the police and the prison service using Victorian cells of former Liberty Gaol.

RIPON WORKHOUSE MUSEUM

Sharow View, Allhallowgate, Ripon, North Yorkshire HG4
Tel: 01765 690799
Museum established in the Men's Casual Wards (1877) of Ripon's Victorian workhouse buildings.

ROTUNDA MUSEUM

Vernon Road, Scarborough, North Yorkshire
Tel: 01723 374839
Fax: 01723 376941
Local history and archaeology, pottery, prehistoric remains from North York Moors, displays of Mesolithic lakeside settlement at Star Carr and Bronze Age skeleton.

ROYAL PUMP ROOM MUSEUM

Crescent Road, Harrogate, North Yorkshire HG1 2RY
Tel: 01423 503340
Fax: 01423 840026
Site of original sulphur well (the strongest well in Britain) where visitors can sample the spa, waters, also history of the spa, and changing exhibitions.
For further details see page 76

RYEDALE FOLK MUSEUM

Hutton-le-Hole, York YO6 6UA
Tel: 01751 417367
Reconstructed local buildings including cruck-framed long houses, Elizabethan manor house, furnished cottages, craftsmen's tools and household/agricultural implements.

SCARBOROUGH MILLENNIUM

Harbourside, Scarborough, North Yorkshire YO11 1PG
Tel: 01723 501000
Fax: 01723 365272
An epic adventure through 1000 years. The future and past will never look the same again.

SCARBOROUGH MUSEUMS AND GALLERY
Lundesborough Lodge, Scarborough, North Yorkshire YO11 2PW
Tel: 01723 367326
Fax: 01723 376941
Scarborough museums and galleries together offer a range of educational opportunities to suit all ages.

SION HILL HALL
Kirby Wiske, Thirsk, North Yorkshire YO7 4EU
Tel: 01845 587206
Fax: 01845 587206
Large collection of antique furniture, porcelain and pictures of all periods displayed in Edwardian country house c1913.

SUTCLIFFE GALLERY
1 Flowergate, Whitby, North Yorkshire YO21 3BA
Tel: 01947 602239
A display devoted to Frank Meadow Sutcliffe's maritime and rural 19thC photographs.

SWALEDALE FOLK MUSEUM
Reeth Green, Reeth, Richmond, North Yorkshire DL11 6QT
Tel: 01748 884373
Museum reflects history traditions and social history of the dale including lead mining, hand knitting, agriculture, brass bands, domestic pastimes and religion.

THIRSK MUSEUM
16 Kirkgate, Thirsk, North Yorkshire YO7 1PQ
Tel: 01845 524510
Exhibits of local life and industry and cricket memorabilia – the building was the home of Thomas Lord, founder of Lords cricket ground in London.

UPPER WHARFEDALE MUSEUM
6 The Square, Grassington, Skipton, North Yorkshire BD23 5AQ
Tel: 01756 752800
An 18thC Dales cottage, farming, geology, archaeology, lead mining and items of local interest.

WHITBY ARCHIVES HERITAGE CENTRE
1st/2nd Floors, 17–18 Grape Lane, Whitby, North Yorkshire YO22 4BA
Tel: 01947 600170
Permanently changing display of pictures of old Whitby, ephemera and other items.

WHITBY LIFEBOAT MUSEUM (RNLI)
Pier Road, Whitby, North Yorkshire YO21 3PU
Tel: 01947 602001
Last pulling lifeboat of the RNLI now preserved, models of lifeboats and other types of vessel, diorama of 'Rohilla' wreck and local history of the Whitby R.NLI.

WHITBY MUSEUM
Pannett Park, Whitby, North Yorkshire YO21 1RE
Tel: 01947 602908
Captain James Cook material, fossils, ship models, Whitby jet ornaments, whaling, the Scoresbys, local history, geology, archaeology, bygones and costumes.

WORDSWORTH GALLERY
Gallows Hill, Ruston, Scarborough, North Yorkshire YO13 9QF
Tel: 01723 863298
Fax: 01723 862287
Exhibition devoted to William Wordsworth, Mary Hutchinson, Samuel Taylor Coleridge and their connections with the property; art gallery, tea and coffee rooms.

YORK CASTLE MUSEUM
The Eye of York, York YO1 1RY
Tel: 01904 653611
Fax: 01904 671078
England's most popular museum of everyday life including reconstructed streets and period rooms, Edwardian park costume and jewellery, arms and armour craft workshops.

YORK CITY ART GALLERY
Exhibition Square, York YO1 2EW
Tel: 01904 551861
Fax: 01904 551866
Seven centuries of European painting from early Italian gold-ground panels to the art of the 20thC.

YORK MINSTER
Deangate, York YO1 2JA
Tel: 01904 624426
The largest Gothic cathedral in England.

YORK MINSTER VISITOR & CONFERENCE CENTRE
St William's College, 5 College Street, York YO1 2JF
Tel: 01904 637134
Fax: 01904 654604
15thC home of Minster chantry priests.

YORK STORY
St Mary's Church, Castlegate, York, North Yorkshire
Tel: 01904 628632
The York Story brings the history of the city to life through models, reconstructions and videos.

YORKSHIRE AIR MUSEUM & ALLIED AIR FORCES MEMORIAL
Elvington Airfield, Halifax Way, Elvington, York YO4 5AU
Tel: 01904 608595
Fax: 01904 608246
Central part of original World War II airfield authentically restored, including control tower.

YORKSHIRE CARRIAGE MUSEUM
Yore Mill, Aysgarth Falls, Leyburn, North Yorkshire DL8 3SR
Tel: 01969 663399
Fax: 01969 663699
Ex-water-powered cotton mill three storeys high, now houses some 50 horse-drawn vehicles including coaches, fire engines, hansom cab, haunted coach and coaching impediments.

YORKSHIRE MUSEUM
Museum Gardens, York YO1 2DR
Tel: 01904 629745
Fax: 01904 651221
Permanent collection includes archaeology, geology, decorative art and numismatics; also temporary exhibitions.

YORKSHIRE MUSEUM OF FARMING
Murton Park, Murton, York YO1 3UF
Tel: 01904 489966
Fax: 01904 489159
This 8-acre site incorporates farming museum, Derwent Valley light railway and replica dark age village used by schools.

NORTHAMPTONSHIRE

ABINGTON MUSEUM
Abington Park, Park Avenue South, Northampton, Northamptonshire NN1 5LW
Tel: 01604 31454
Grade I listed building set in attractive public park.
For further details see page 77

ALFRED EAST ART GALLERY
Sheep Street, Kettering, Northamptonshire
Tel: 01536 534381
Fax: 01536 534370
Collection of work by Sir Alfred East RA, Thomas Cooper Gotch and contemporary artists.

THE CANAL MUSEUM
Stoke Bruerne, Towcester, Northamptonshire NN12 7SE
Tel: 01604 862229
Fax: 0115 935 0988
Traditional decorated items, model boat replica, horse, replica cabin, boat engines, photos illustrating history of Britain's canals and waterways.

CARPET BAGGER AVIATION MUSEUM
Sunnyvale Farm & Nursery, off Lamport Road, Harrington, Northampton NN6 9PF
Tel: 01604 686608
Exhibits and history of carpet bagger operations.

CENTRAL MUSEUM & ART GALLERY
Guildhall Road, Northampton, Northamptonshire NN1 1DP
Tel: 01604 639415
Fax: 01604 238720
Collection of footwear through the ages.
For further details see page 77

COUGHTON GALLERIES LTD
The Old Manor, Arthingworth, Market Harborough, Leicestershire LE16 8JT
Tel: 01858 525436
Fax: 01858 525535
Picture gallery within The Old Manor House and Gardens; expert discussion available on paintings from Lady Isabel.

DAVENTRY MUSEUM MOOT HALL
Market Square, Daventry, Northamptonshire NN11 4BH
Tel: 01327 302463
Permanent exhibition depicting social and local history of Daventry district.

HUNSBURY HILL INDUSTRIAL MUSEUM
Hunsbury Hill Road, West Hunsbury, Hunsbury Hill, Northampton
On site of former ironstone workings with railway engines and wagons from local iron works.

MANOR HOUSE MUSEUM
Sheep Street, Kettering, Northamptonshire
Tel: 01536 534219
Kettering's past.

MUSEUM OF THE NORTHAMPTONSHIRE REGIMENT
Abington Park, Northampton
Tel: 01604 631454
History of the Northamptonshire Regiment from 1741 to 1960.

NASEBY BATTLE & FARM MUSEUM
Purlieu Farm, Naseby, Northampton NN6 7DD
Tel: 01604 740241
Miniature layout of Battle of Naseby with commentary (10 mins).

NATIONAL DRAGONFLY MUSEUM
Ashton Mill, Ashton, Northampton PE8 5LB
Tel: 01832 272427
Discover the wonder and plight of dragonflies. TV microscope link, working Victorian power house, craft room and bygones.

RUSHDEN HISTORICAL TRANSPORT SOCIETY MUSEUM
Rushden Railway Station, Station Approach, Rushden, Northamptonshire NN10 0AW
Tel: 01933 318988
Midland Railway branch station building c1893.

TURNER'S MUSICAL MERRY-GO-ROUND
Queen Eleanor Vale, Newport Pagnell Road, Wootton, Northampton NN4 6HU
Tel: 01604 763314
Fax: 01604 705695
Wurlitzer theatre organ, fairground organs collection and merry-go-round.

WOLLASTON MUSEUM
104 High Street, Wollaston, Wellingborough, Northamptonshire NN29 7RJ
Tel: 01933 664468
Local boot and shoe making.

NORTHUMBERLAND

BERWICK BARRACKS
The Parade, Berwick-upon-Tweed TD15 1DF
Tel: 01289 304493
Barracks designed 1717–21 and garrisoned until 1964.

BERWICK-UPON-TWEED MAIN GUARD
Palace Street, Berwick-upon-Tweed, Northumberland TD15 1HN
Eighteenth century neo-classical military guardhouse rehabilitated by Berwick Civic Society and developed as an interpretative centre for Berwick walls and fortifications.

BERWICK-UPON-TWEED MUSEUM & ART GALLERY
Ravensdowne Barracks, Berwick-upon-Tweed TD15 1DQ
Tel: 01289 330933
Fax: 01289 330540
The museum is housed in the historic Berwick Barracks and contains collections of fine and decorative art and local history displayed in innovative ways.

BONDGATE GALLERY
22 Narrowgate, Alnwick, Northumberland NE66 1JG
Contemporary exhibitions by regional artists.

BORDER HISTORY MUSEUM
The Old Gaol, Hallgate, Hexham, Northumberland NE46 3NH
Tel: 01434 652349
Set in the old gaol (1330) the museum illustrates, through displays and audio-visual effects, the border warfare of 15thC and 16thC and the Jacobite rebellion of 1715.

CHATTON GALLERY
Church House, Chatton, Alnwick, Northumberland NE66 5PU
Tel: 01668 215494
A wide range of contemporary art and sculpture.

CHERRYBURN: THOMAS BEWICK BIRTHPLACE MUSEUM
Cherryburn Station Bank, Mickley, Stocksfield, Northumberland NE43 7DB
Tel: 01661 843276
Birthplace cottage (1700) and farmyard.

EARLE HILL HOUSEHOLD & FARMING MUSEUM
Langleford Road, Wooler, Northumberland NE71 6RH
Tel: 01668 281243
Household and farm antiques including farm kitchen range.

FENWICK GALLERY
21 Castle Street, Warkworth, Morpeth, Northumberland NE65 0UW
Tel: 01665 711136
Art gallery displaying and selling some of its finest work locally and nationally.

GRACE DARLING MUSEUM
Radcliffe Road, Bamburgh, Northumberland NE69 7AE
Tel: 01668 214465
Museum commemorates the rescue, by Grace and her father, of the nine survivors from the wreck of the Forfarshire.

HEATHERSLAW CORNMILL
Cornhill-on-Tweed, Northumberland TD12 4TJ
Tel: 01890 820338
Fax: 01890 820384
Restored working 19thC cornmill producing flour and pearl barley.

HEXHAM MOOTHALL LIBRARY
Market Place, Hexham, Northumberland NE46 3NH
Tel: 01434 652351
Fax: 01434 652425
A 15thC building. Gallery space for solo artists and groups to hire. Victorians, 2nd WW, in library.

HOUSE OF HARDY MUSEUM & COUNTRY STORE
Willowburn, Alnwick, Northumberland NE66 2PF
Tel: 01665 602771
Fax: 01665 602389
Manufacturer of finest fishing tackle in the world.

LADY WATERFORD HALL
Ford Village, Ford, Berwick-upon-Tweed TD15 2TQ
Tel: 01890 820224
Fax: 01890 820384
Water-colour murals by Louisa, Marchioness of Waterford.

MARINE LIFE CENTRE & FISHING MUSEUM
8–10 Main Street, Seahouses, Northumberland NE68 5RG
Tel: 01665 721257
Ground floor seawater aquarium, first-floor fisherman's museum and cottage and second-floor exhibition area and museum.

MORPETH CHANTRY BAGPIPE MUSEUM
The Chantry, Bridge Street, Morpeth, Northumberland NE61 1PJ
Tel: 01670 519466
Fax: 01670 511326
Set in a 13thC church building this unusual museum specialises in the history and development of Northumbrian small pipes and their music.

NORHAM STATION MUSEUM
Station House, Norham, Berwick-upon-Tweed TD15 2LW
Tel: 01289 382217
Station site, signal box, loading docks, coal cells, lime cells, porters' room and model railway.

OLD SCHOOL GALLERY
The School House, Carrshield, Hexham, Northumberland NE47 8AA
Tel: 01434 345396
School converted into picture gallery with workshop and demonstrations.

REGIMENTAL MUSEUM
King's Own Scottish Borderers, The Barracks, Berwick-upon-Tweed TD15 1DG
Tel: 01289 307426
Fax: 01289 331928
The regimental museum of the King's Own Scottish Borderers. Situated with their regimental headquarters in the oldest purpose-built barracks in Britain.

ROMAN ARMY MUSEUM – CARVORAN
Greenhead, Northumberland, via Carlisle, Northumberland CA6 7JB
Tel: 01697 747485
Fax: 01697 747487
Audio-visual effects, video, films, general display and educational facilities.

VINDOLANDA & THE ROMAN MUSEUM
Chesterholm Museum, Bardon Mill, Hadrian's Wall, Hexham, Northumberland NE47 7JN
Tel: 01434 344277
Fax: 01434 344060
Visitors may inspect the remains of the Roman fort and settlement and see the extraordinary finds in the superb museum.

WINE & SPIRIT MUSEUM & VICTORIAN CHEMIST SHOP
Palace Green, Berwick-upon-Tweed TD15 1HN
Tel: 01289 305153
Fax: 01289 302501
Artefacts from the wine and spirit industry and also a reconstructed chemist shop and free sample of Lindisfarne Mead.

WOODHORN CHURCH EXHIBITION CENTRE
Woodhorn Village, Ashington, Northumberland NE63 9YA
Tel: 01670 817371
Redundant 11thC church converted into an exhibition centre. Open April to October only.

WYLAM RAILWAY MUSEUM
Falcon Centre, Falcon Terrace, Wylam, Northumberland NE41 8EE
Tel: 01661 852174
Displays show importance of Wylam in the history of railway development and the work of famous local railway pioneers – George Stephenson, Timothy Hackworth and William Hedley.

NOTTINGHAMSHIRE

BASSETLAW MUSEUM
Amcott House, Grove Street, Retford, Nottinghamshire DN22 6JU
Tel: 01777 706741
Local history and archaeology of Bassetlaw with displays of bygones and decorative arts.

BREWHOUSE YARD MUSEUM OF SOCIAL HISTORY
Castle Boulevard, Nottingham NG7 1FB
Tel: 0115 948 3504 ext 3684
Fax: 0115 935 0653
Five 17thC cottages at foot of Castle Rock showing daily life in Nottingham, includes use of rock-cut cellars.

BRITISH HOROLOGICAL INSTITUTE
Upton Hall, Upton, Newark, Nottinghamshire NG23 5TE
Tel: 01636 813795
Fax: 01626 812258
Georgian/Victorian manor house featuring watches, clocks, horological tool collection and library.

CALVERTON FOLK MUSEUM
Main Street, Calverton, Nottingham
Tel: 0115 965 2836
Period furniture and clothing.

THE CANAL MUSEUM
Canal Street, Nottingham
Tel: 0115 959 8835
Fax: 0115 935 0988
Former canal warehouse with landing areas and wharves.

D H LAWRENCE BIRTHPLACE MUSEUM
8a Victoria Street, Eastwood, Nottingham NG16 3AW
Tel: 01773 763312
House furnished as at time of Lawrence family occupation and D H Lawrence's birth in 1885.

THE D H LAWRENCE 'SONS & LOVERS' COTTAGE
28 Garden Road, Eastwood, Nottingham NG16 3FW
Tel: 01773 763312
Home of Lawrence family 1887–91 with same garden layout and ground floor furnished as in 'Sons and Lovers'.

THE GALLERIES OF JUSTICE
Shire Hall, High Pavement Lace Market, Nottingham NG1 1HN
Tel: 0115 952 0555
Fax: 0115 952 0557
A museum of law incorporating the major crime and punishment experience: Condemned! Located in and around a 19thC courthouse and county gaol.

THE HARLEY GALLERY
Welbeck, Worksop, Nottinghamshire S80 3LW
Tel: 01909 501700
Fax: 01909 488747
Housed in a unique stone building in the heart of the Dukeries, the gallery shows varied arts and crafts exhibitions.
For further details see pages 40 & 77

IBTE TELECOMMUNICATIONS MUSEUM
Queen Street, Worksop, Nottinghamshire S8 7DR
Tel: 01909 483680
The museum offers an insight into the history and development of the telecommunications industry.

THE LACE CENTRE
Severn's Building, Castle Road, Nottingham NG1 6AA
Tel: 0115 941 3539
Housed in a medieval building a lace exhibition and retail of genuine locally made Nottingham lace.

THE LACE HALL
3–5 High Pavement, Nottingham NG1 1HF
Tel: 0115 948 4221
The Lace Hall is set in a converted chapel containing magnificent stained glass windows.

LAXTON HERITAGE MUSEUM
Lilac Farm, Laxton, Newark, Nottinghamshire NG22 0NX
Tel: 01777 870376
Farm buildings (1760).

MANSFIELD MUSEUM & ART GALLERY
Leeming Street, Mansfield, Nottinghamshire NG18 1NG
Tel: 01623 663088
Geography, geology, natural history and images of Mansfield past and present.

MILLGATE MUSEUM OF SOCIAL & FOLK LIFE
48 Millgate, Newark, Nottinghamshire NG24 4TS
Tel: 01636 679403
Fax: 01636 613279
Museum portraying local social and folk life.

MINIATURE WORLD MUSEUM
Beechfield House, West Stockwith, Doncaster, South Yorkshire DN10 4EY
Tel: 01427 890982
Three-storey Georgian house built about 1710.

MUSEUM OF COSTUME & TEXTILES
51 Castlegate, Nottingham NG1 6AF
Tel: 0115 915 5555
Fax: 0115 915 3599
Georgian houses containing Lord Middleton collection of 17thC costume and embroideries, plus extensive collection relating to Nottingham's lace industry.

NEWARK AIR MUSEUM
The Airfield, Winthorpe, Newark, Nottinghamshire NG24 2NY
Tel: 01636 707170
Aircraft parts and memorabilia.

NEWARK MUSEUM
Appletongate, Newark, Nottinghamshire NG24 1JY
Tel: 01636 702358
Collections of local archaeology and history, some natural history and Militaria.

NOTTINGHAM CASTLE MUSEUM & ART GALLERY
Nottingham NG1 6EL
Tel: 0115 915 3691
Fax: 0115 915 3653
A 17thC residence on site of medieval royal castle, fine and decorative arts, multi-cultural displays, temporary exhibitions, education programme.

NOTTINGHAM INDUSTRIAL MUSEUM
Courtyard Buildings, Wollaton Park, Nottingham NG8 2AE
Tel: 0115 915 3910
18thC stables presenting history of Nottingham's industries: printing, pharmacy, hosiery and lace.

PIERREPONT GALLERY
Thoresby Park, Ollerton, Newark, Nottinghamshire NG22 9EP
Tel: 01623 822365
Fax: 01623 822315
The Pierrepont Gallery is in the old stables at Thoresby Park.

RUDDINGTON FRAMEWORK KNITTERS MUSEUM
Chapel Street, Ruddington, Nottingham NG11 6HE
Tel: 0115 984 6914
Unique complex of early 19thC framework-knitters cottages and workshops restored to original use.

THE UNIVERSITY OF NOTTINGHAM ARTS CENTRE
University Park, Nottingham, Nottinghamshire NG7 2RD
Tel: 0115 951 5791
Fax: 0115 951 3194
The Djanogly art gallery shows temporary exhibitions of historical and contemporary art.

VICTORIAN CARRIAGES
Pasture Farm, Main Street, Kirton, Newark, Nottinghamshire NG22 9LP
Tel: 01623 836291
Working carriage driving centre and museum.

THE VINA COOKE MUSEUM OF DOLLS & BYGONE CHILDHOOD
The Old Rectory, Cromwell, Newark, Nottinghamshire NG23 6JE
Tel: 01636 821364
Large collection of dolls, prams, cots, toys, dolls' houses, costumes. Also handmade dolls depicting royalty, film stars etc. Unique location.

WILLIAM BOOTH MEMORIAL COMPLEX
14 Notintone Place, Sneinton Road, Nottingham NG2 4QG
Tel: 0115 950 3927
The Salvation Army Museum is the birthplace of the founder, William Booth.

WOLLATON HALL & NATURAL HISTORY MUSEUM
Wollaton Park, Nottingham NG8 2AE
Tel: 0115 928 1333
Elizabethan house built 1580–88 by Sir Francis Willoughby, now housing Natural History Museum (botany, zoology, geology).

WORKSOP MUSEUM
Public Library and Museum, Memorial Avenue, Worksop, Nottinghamshire S80 2BP
Tel: 01909 472408
Local history and archaeology of Worksop and the Dukeries.

OXFORDSHIRE

ABINGDON MUSEUM
County Hall, Market Place, Abingdon, Oxfordshire OX14 3HG
Tel: 01235 523703
Fax: 01235 536814
Formerly the County Hall for Berkshire dating from 1678. A spectacular setting for exhibitions of local history, arts and crafts.

ASHMOLEAN MUSEUM
Beaumont Street, Oxford, Oxfordshire OX1 2PH
Tel: 01865 278000
Fax: 01865 278018
Oxford University's Museum of Fine and Applied Art and Archaeology, housing paintings, ceramics and glass from Europe and Asia, and antiquities from ancient Egypt and Rome.
For further details see page 78

B. T. MUSEUM
35 Speedwell Street, Oxford, Oxfordshire OX1 1RH
Tel: 01865 246601

BANBURY MUSEUM
8 Horsefair, Banbury, Oxfordshire OX16 0AA
Tel: 01295 259855
Fax: 01295 270556
Museum of local history with temporary exhibition gallery, shop and tourist information centre.

BATE COLLECTION OF MUSICAL INSTRUMENTS
Faculty of Music, St Aldates, Oxford, Oxfordshire OX1 1DB
Tel: 01865 276139

BENSON VETERAN CYCLE MUSEUM
61 Brook Street, Benson, Wallingford, Oxfordshire OX10 6LH
Tel: 01491 838414
Veteran and vintage cycles dating from 1818–1925 (by appointment only).

BISHOP'S PALACE
Mount House, Church Green, Witney, Oxfordshire
The excavated ruin of the palace of the Bishops of Winchester.
For further details see page 77

BLOXHAM VILLAGE MUSEUM
Church Street, Bloxham, Banbury, Oxfordshire OX15 4ET
Tel: 01295 720283
Museum housed in one room in an ancient building. Changing exhibitions reflecting past life in the village displayed in one room and in an ancient court house.

BODLEIAN LIBRARY
Broad Street, Oxford OX1 3BG
Tel: 01865 277165
Fax: 01865 277187/2
Early books and manuscript works on view in Exhibition Room.

BOHUN GALLERY
15 Reading Road, Henley-on-Thames, Oxfordshire RG9 1AB
Tel: 01491 576228
Fax: 01491 576228
Artists shown by the gallery include: John Piper, June Redfern, Elizabeth Frink and the estate of Julian Trevelyan etchings.

CHARLBURY MUSEUM
Corner House, Market Street, Charlbury, Oxford
Tel: 01608 810060
Collection of local tools and other items from the town's past, an Oxfordshire wagon and old photographs.

CHIPPING NORTON LOCAL HISTORY SOCIETY MUSEUM
High Street, Chipping Norton, Oxfordshire
Local history exhibits of local industry, eg Bliss Tweed Mill, Hitchmans Brewery, old photographs, etc.

CHRIST CHURCH PICTURE GALLERY
Canterbury Quadrangle, Christ Church, Oxford OX1 1DP
Tel: 01865 276172
Fax: 01865 202429
Christ Church Picture Gallery designed in 1968 by Powell and Moya holds 300 paintings and 2,000 drawings by famous artists Van Dyck, Leonardo, Michelangelo and Rubens.

COGGES FARM MUSEUM
Church Lane, Witney, Oxfordshire OX8 6LA
Tel: 01993 772602
Fax: 01993 703056
Manor House with furnished rooms, Victorian working farm, walled garden, history and nature trails, demonstrations and special events.
For further details see page 77

DORCHESTER ABBEY MUSEUM
Abbey Guest House, Dorchester on Thames, Wallingford, Oxfordshire OX10 7HH
Tel: 01865 340703
Besides the Abbey itself the small museum (formerly the Abbey guest house) houses a display of artefacts which illustrate Dorchester's history.

GRANARY MUSEUM OF BYGONES
Butlin Farm, Claydon, Banbury, Oxfordshire OX17 1EP
Tel: 01295 690258
Private farming museum including tractors and stationary engines from the time of Victoria to the 1950s.

THE GUILDHALL
Abbey Close, Abingdon, Oxfordshire OX14 3JE
Tel: 01235 524085
Guildhall complex is a working building with Magistrates' courts, Vale and Town committee meetings and social/community functions.

THE MG CAR CLUB LIMITED
Kimber House, 12 Cemetery Road, Abingdon, Oxfordshire OX14 1FF
Tel: 01235 555552
For MG enthusiasts; home of the MG Marque.

MUSEUM OF MODERN ART OXFORD
30 Pembroke Street, Oxford, Oxfordshire OX1 1BP
Tel: 01865 722733
Fax: 01865 722573
Centre for 20thC arts with a constantly changing exhibition programme, combining new historical perspectives with a range of work from across the world.
For further details see page 78

MUSEUM OF OXFORD
St Aldates, Oxford, Oxfordshire OX1 1DD
Tel: 01865 815559
History of Oxford with graphics, models, reconstructed period rooms, Elizabethan inn parlour, 18thC students' room and 19thC Jericho kitchen.
For further details see page 77

MUSEUM OF THE HISTORY OF SCIENCE
Broad Street, Oxford OX1 3AZ
Tel: 01865 277280
Fax: 01865 277288
Displays include scientific instruments, fine Islamic and European astrolabes, early chemical apparatus, clocks, medical instruments and original penicillin apparatus.

THE OXFORD STORY
6 Broad Street, Oxford OX1 3AJ
Tel: 01865 790055
Fax: 01865 791716
A blend of scholarship, technology and audio-visual techniques bringing the University's past to life.

OXFORD UNIVERSITY MUSEUM OF NATURAL HISTORY
Parks Road, Oxford, Oxfordshire OX1 3PW
Tel: 01865 272950/270949
Fax: 01865 272970
Fascinating Victorian-Gothic building with displays of animals, insects, birds, fossils, dinosaurs, gemstones and Alice's Dodo.
For further details see page 78

OXFORDSHIRE COUNTY MUSEUM
Fletcher's House, Park Street, Woodstock, Oxfordshire OX20 1SN
Tel: 01993 811456
Chronological history of the culture of Oxfordshire and its people.
For further details see page 77

PENDON MUSEUM
Long Wittenham, Abingdon, Oxfordshire OX14 4QD
Tel: 01865 407365
Finely detailed miniature landscape, village and railways depicting the 1930s era in the Vale of White Horse and Dartmoor.

PITT RIVERS MUSEUM
Parks Road, Oxford, Oxfordshire OX1 3PW
Tel: 01865 270949
Fax: 01865 270943
Impressive collections from all periods and places including Ancient Egypt, Americas, Africa, Australia, grouped by technology or function. Ideal for cross-curricular studies.
For further details see page 78

REGIMENTAL MUSEUM OXFORDSHIRE & BUCKINGHAMSHIRE LIGHT INFANTRY
TA Centre, Slade Park, Headington, Oxford OX3 7JJ
Tel: 01865 780128
Exhibitions of medals, uniforms and other militaria of the Oxfordshire and Buckinghamshire Light Infantry

RIVER AND ROWING MUSEUM
Mill Meadows, Henley-on-Thames, Oxfordshire RG9 1BF
Tel: 01491 415600
Fax: 01491 415601
New museum covering three interwoven themes: the Thames, the sport of rowing and the town of Henley-on-Thames – due to open summer 1998.

SWALCLIFFE BARN
Shipston Road, Swalcliffe, Nr Banbury, Oxfordshire OX15
Tel: 01295 788278
A half-cruck barn built by New College Oxford between 1401 and 1407. Exhibitions of agricultural vehicles and Swalcliffe village history.
For further details see page 77

SWINFORD MUSEUM
Filkins, Lechlade, Gloucestershire GL7 3JQ
Tel: 01367 860209
Tools and artefacts relating to domestic life and rural trades and crafts in past centuries collected in this Cotswold village of Filkins

THE TOLSEY MUSEUM
126 High Street, Burford, Oxfordshire OX18 4QU
Tel: 01993 823236
Small museum housed in early Tudor courthouse.

TOM BROWN'S SCHOOL MUSEUM
The Old School, Broad Street, Uffington, Faringdon, Oxfordshire SN7 7RA
Tel: 01367 820259
Exibition of the life and works of Thomas Hughes.

VALE & DOWNLAND MUSEUM & VISITOR CENTRE
The Old Surgery, Church Street, Wantage, Oxfordshire OX12 8BL
Tel: 01235 771447
Fax: 01235 774316
Converted town-house, once a doctor's surgery, with permanent displays on local history and archaeology, and exhibitions of local art and crafts. Refurbishment is in progress in main gallery, due to re-open in June 1998.

WALLINGFORD MUSEUM
Flint House, High Street, Wallingford, Oxfordshire OX10 0DB
Tel: 01491 835065
Small attractive 15thC house, first floor converted for museum ground floor entrance.

REDCAR AND CLEVELAND

GUISBOROUGH MUSEUM
West Gate, Sunnyfield House, Guisborough, Cleveland TS14 6AY
Tel: 01287 634595/632016
Museum of social history.

KIRKLEATHAM OLD HALL MUSEUM
Kirkleatham, Redcar, Cleveland TS10 5NW
Tel: 01642 479500
Fax: 01642 474199 .
Displays depicting local life, industry, commerce, local history, sea rescue, artists, social and natural history.

MARGROVE HERITAGE CENTRE
Margrove Park, Boosbeck, Saltburn TS12 3BZ
Tel: 01287 610368
A permanent gallery reflecting the archaeology, geology and natural history of the area, temporary exhibition programme, activites and events.

RNLI ZETLAND LIFEBOAT MUSEUM
5 King Street, Redcar, North Yorkshire TS10 3PF
Tel: 01642 494311
Listed building housing the Zetland, oldest surviving lifeboat in the world built 1802 by H Greathead.

SIR WILLIAM TURNER HOSPITAL
Kirkleatham, Redcar, Cleveland TS10 4QT
Tel: 01642 477035
Founded in 1676 as Almshouses for the poor.

TOM LEONARD MINING MUSEUM
Deepdale, Skinningrove, Saltburn-by-the-Sea, Cleveland TS13 4AA
Tel: 01287 642877
Ironstone mining museum with underground working experience.

SHROPSHIRE

THE AEROSPACE MUSEUM
Cosford, Shifnal, Shropshire TF11 8UP
Tel: 01902 374872/374112
Fax: 01902 374813
Extensive aircraft collection, rockets and missiles, aero engines.
For further details see page 78

BLISTS HILL OPEN AIR MUSEUM
Ironbridge Gorge Museum, Ironbridge, Telford, Shropshire TF7 5DU
Tel: 01952 433522
Fax: 01952 588016
This working Victorian town of 50 acres includes the only wrought-iron works in the western world.
For further details see page 79

THE CHILDHOOD & COSTUME MUSEUM
Newmarket Building, Postern Gate, Bridgnorth, Shropshire WV16 4AA
Tel: 01746 764636
Building built in 1857 in the Italian style from local bricks.

CLIVE HOUSE MUSEUM
College Hill, Shrewsbury, Shropshire SY1 1LT
Tel: 01743 354811
Fax: 01743 358411
Shrewsbury town-house associated with Clive of India, contains fine collections of Shropshire porcelains, paintings, natural and social history.

CLUN LOCAL HISTORY MUSEUM
Clun Town Hall, Clun, Craven Arms, Shropshire SY7 8JT
Tel: 01588 640681
Small 1-room museum.

COALBROOKDALE FURNACE & MUSEUM OF IRON
Ironbridge Gorge Museum, Ironbridge, Telford, Shropshire
Tel: 01952 433522
Fax: 01952 432204
Blast furnace where iron was first smelted in 1709 using coke.
For further details see page 79

COALPORT CHINA MUSEUM
Ironbridge Gorge Museum, Ironbridge, Telford, Shropshire TF8 7AW
Tel: 01952 580650
Displays of Coalport china, china making and the people who once worked at the factory canal.
For further details see page 79

COLEHAM PUMPING STATION
Longden Coleham, Longden, Shrewsbury, Shropshire SY3 7DN
Tel: 01743 362947
Two double expanding Victorian beam pumping engines in brick pumping house; built in 1901.

IRONBRIDGE GORGE MUSEUM
Ironbridge, Telford, Shropshire TF8 7AW
Tel: 01952 433522
Fax: 01952 432204
World's first cast-iron bridge, Museum of the River Visitor Centre, Tar Tunnel, Jackfield Tile Museum, Coalport China Museum, Rosehill House, Blists Hill Museum and Museum of Iron.
For further details see page 79

IRONBRIDGE TOLLHOUSE
The Iron Bridge, Ironbridge, Telford, Shropshire TF8 7AW
Tel: 01952 884391
The original tollhouse opened 1781 to collect tolls from all passengers crossing the iron bridge.
For further details see page 79

JACKFIELD TILE MUSEUM
Ironbridge Gorge Museum, Jackfield, Telford, Shropshire TF8 7AN
Tel: 01952 882030
Museum of decorative tiles located on a site of former Craven Dunnills' Victorian factory.
For further details see page 79

LUDLOW MUSEUM
11–13 Castle Street, Ludlow, Shropshire SY8 1AS
Tel: 01584 873857
The history of Ludlow from Norman times to the 20thC.

MIDLAND MOTOR MUSEUM
Stanmore Hall, Stourbridge Road, Bridgnorth, Shropshire WV15 6DT
Tel: 01746 762992
Fax: 01746 768104
Over 100 sports racing cars and motorcycles from 1920s–1980s.

MUCH WENLOCK MUSEUM
High Street, Much Wenlock, Shropshire TF13 6HR
Tel: 01952 727773
Displays of archaeology, natural history and social history, including Wenlock Olympics. Hands-on session in geology and the Victorians. Fieldwork available.

MUSEUM OF THE RIVER VISITOR CENTRE
Ironbridge Gorge Museum, Ironbridge, Telford, Shropshire TF8 7NH
Tel: 01952 432405
Fax: 01952 432204
Exhibition centre introducing the various museum sites and the use and abuse of water.
For further details see page 79

OSWESTRY TRANSPORT MUSEUM
Oswald Road, Oswestry, Shropshire SY11 1RE
Tel: 01691 671749
Railway and bicycle museum, includes over 11 engines and over 100 bicycles which display their history and development.

ROWLEY'S HOUSE MUSEUM
Barker Street, Shrewsbury, Shropshire SY1 1QH
Tel: 01743 361196
Major regional museum in a timber-framed 16thC building and adjoining 17thC brick mansion.

SHREWSBURY CASTLE & SHROPSHIRE REGIMENTAL MUSEUM
Castle Gates, Shrewsbury, Shropshire SY1 2AT
Tel: 01743 358516
Museum depicting history of The King's Shropshire Light Infantry, The Shropshire Yeomanry and The Shropshire Royal Horse Artillery, housed in historic castle buildings.

THE SHREWSBURY QUEST
193 Abbey Foregate, Shrewsbury, Shropshire SY2 6AH
Tel: 01743 243324
Fax: 01743 244342
Re-created on part of Shrewsbury Abbey's original grounds, the Shrewsbury Quest re-creates Shrewsbury's medieval monastic life within the 12thC.

SOMERSET

ADMIRAL BLAKE MUSEUM
Blake House, Blake Street, Bridgwater, Somerset TA6 3NB
Tel: 01278 456127
Fax: 01278 444076
Museum of local history and archaeology, with Robert Blake and the Civil War, Monmouth Rebellion, maritime and local art collections.

BLUE ANCHOR RAILWAY MUSEUM
Blue Anchor Station, Blue Anchor, Minehead, Somerset TA24 6LB
Tel: 01643 821092
Museum of small exhibits dedicated to the Great Western Railway, particularly in the West Country, at a working period station on Britain's longest preserved railway.

CASTLE CARY & DISTRICT MUSEUM & PRESERVATORY SOCIETY
The Market House, Castle Cary, Somerset BA7 7BG
Tel: 01963 350680
General display of items of local interest.

CHARD & DISTRICT MUSEUM
Godworthy House, High Street, Chard, Somerset TA20 1QL
Tel: 01460 65091
16thC buildings housing displays showing history of local area, farming, rural industries, social life, early aviation and much more.

CREWKERNE & DISTRICT MUSEUM
Heritage Centre, Market Square, Crewkerne, Somerset TA18 7JU
Tel: 01460 73441
New local history museum in renovated 16thC building – due to open late 1998/early 1999.

DUNSTER DOLLS' MUSEUM
Memorial Hall, High Street, Dunster, Minehead, Somerset TA24 6SF
Tel: 01643 821220
Varied collection of over 700 dolls from many periods, costume and foreign and ethnic, Christening robes, and dolls' houses.

FLEET AIR ARM AVIATION EXPERIENCE
RNAS Yeovilton, Ilchester, Somerset BA22 8HT
Tel: 01935 840077
Fax: 01935 840181
Forty historic naval aircraft, displays, models, uniforms and other artefacts.

FORGOTTEN WORLD – FORMERLY WHEELWRIGHTS & GYPSY MUSEUM
Webbington, Loxton, Axbridge, Somerset BS26 2HX
Tel: 01934 750841
Exhibition of wheelwright's old tools, collection of gypsy caravans, gypsy artefacts and photographs.

FROME MUSEUM
1 North Parade, Frome, Somerset BA11 1AT
Tel: 01373 464487
Artefacts of local interest.

HAYNES MOTOR MUSEUM
Sparkford, Yeovil, Somerset BA22 7LH
Tel: 01963 440804
Fax: 01963 441004
Motor vehicles and memorabilia covering the years from the turn of the century to the present day.

ILCHESTER MUSEUM
Town Hall and Community Centre, High Street, Ilchester, Yeovil, Somerset BA22 8NQ
Tel: 01935 841247
A display showing the history of Ilchester from pre-history to 20thC in finds found locally: text, pictures and photographs.

KING JOHN'S HUNTING LODGE
The Square, Axbridge, Somerset BS26 2AP
Tel: 01934 732012
Early Tudor merchant's house extensively restored in 1971, now houses museum of local history and archaeology.

MUSEUM OF SOUTH SOMERSET
Hendford, Yeovil, Somerset BA20 1UN
Tel: 01935 24774
Fax: 01935 752281
Collections of glassware and costumes. Roman artifacts, old newspaper works. Gloving industry. Social history.

PERRY'S CIDER MILL
Dowlish Wake, Ilminster, Somerset
Tel: 01460 52681
Working cider farm with museum of cider presses, wagons, farm tools and photographic displays.

RURAL LIFE MUSEUM
The Abbey Barn, Chilkwell Street, Glastonbury, Somerset BA6 8BD
Tel: 01485 831197
Museum of Somerset countryside, with permanent displays, temporary exhibitions, events, demonstrations. Magnificent 14thC abbey barn.

SHOE MUSEUM
C & J Clark Limited, High Street, Street, Somerset BA16 0YA
Tel: 01458 43131 ext 2320
Fax: 01458 841894
Shoes from Roman times to the present day, documents, photographs, advertising material, machinery and hand tools.

SOMERSET & DORSET RAILWAY MUSEUM
Washford Station, Washford, Watchet, Somerset TA23 0PP
Tel: 01984 640869
Museum of Somerset and Dorset; railway relics, working replica signal box, collection of locomotives and rolling stock.

SOMERSET COUNTY MUSEUM
Taunton Castle, Castle Green, Taunton, Somerset TA1 4AA
Tel: 01823 320201
Housed in Taunton Castle and displays feature: archaeology, ceramics, costume, silver, the Somerset Military Museum and a 16thC almshouse.
For further details see page 79

SOMERSET CRICKET MUSEUM
7 Priory Avenue, Taunton, Somerset TA1 1XX
Tel: 01823 275893
Display of Somerset County Cricket Club memorabilia housed in a renovated 16thC priory barn.

SOMERSET RURAL LIFE MUSEUM
Abbey Farm, Chilkwell Street, Glastonbury, Somerset BA6 8DB
Tel: 01458 831197
Fax: 01458 831197
Magnificent 14thC abbey barn, also Victorian farmhouse and yard.
For further details see page 79

WATCHET MARKET HOUSE MUSEUM
Market Street, Watchet, Somerset TA23 0AN
Tel: 01984 631345
History of Watchet and area. Fossils, Roman British artifacts, Saxon mint, industrial and maritime exhibits, models, painting, photographs and video.

WELLINGTON MUSEUM
28 Fore Street, Wellington, Somerset TA21 8AQ
Tel: 01823 664747
Listed building housing permanent displays relating to the local woollen industry and the Duke of Wellington as well as changing displays relating to the town's past.

WELLS MUSEUM
8 Cathedral Green, Wells, Somerset BA5 2UE
Tel: 01749 673477
Local archaeology and cave finds. Samplers, medieval statuary, social history.

WEST SOMERSET RURAL LIFE MUSEUM
The Old School, Allerford, Minehead, Somerset TA24 8HN
Tel: 01643 862529
Victorian museum housed in the old school building with a large hall, smaller schoolroom, thatched roof and garden by the river.

SOUTH YORKSHIRE

ABBEYDALE INDUSTRIAL HAMLET
Abbeydale Road South, Sheffield S7 2QW
Tel: 0114 236 7731
Working museum.

BISHOPS HOUSE
Meersbrook Park, Norton Lees Lane, Sheffield, South Yorkshire S8 9BE
Tel: 0114 255 7701
A 16thC timber-framed farmhouse.
For further details see page 80

CANNON HALL MUSEUM
Cawthorne, Barnsley, South Yorkshire S75 4AT
Tel: 01226 790270
Fax: 01226 792117
Remodelled in the 18th century this elegant country house is now a museum with fine collections of pottery, pewter, glass, furniture and paintings.
For further details see page 39

CLIFTON PARK MUSEUM
Clifton Lane, Rotherham, South Yorkshire S65 2AA
Tel: 01709 823633
Local pottery, antiquities, natural and social history, fine art.
For further details see page 79

COOPER GALLERY
Church Street, Barnsley, South Yorkshire S70 2AH
Tel: 01226 242905
Fax: 01226 773599
Frequently changing exhibitions of contemporary fine art, craft and mixed media.

CUSWORTH HALL MUSEUM OF SOUTH YORKSHIRE LIFE
Cusworth Hall, Cusworth Lane, Doncaster, South Yorkshire DN5 7TU
Tel: 01302 782342
Fax: 01302 782342
Georgian mansion in landscaped park containing Museum of South Yorkshire Life.

DONCASTER MUSEUM & ART GALLERY
Chequer Road, Doncaster, South Yorkshire DN1 2AE
Tel: 01302 734293
Fax: 01302 735409
Regional collections of human and natural history, art, glass and ceramics, militaria.

FIRE POLICE MUSEUM SHEFFIELD
101–109 West Bar, Sheffield S3 8PT
Tel: 0114 249 1999
Fax: 0114 249 1999
Massive fire police station, full of exhibits from fire engines to famous murders. One of Britain's best family museums.

GRAVES ART GALLERY
Surrey Street, Sheffield, South
Yorkshire S1 1XZ
Tel: 0114 273 5158
Fax: 0114 273 5994
*Collection of British and
European painting, drawing and
sculpture; Islamic pottery; Indian
and Japanese art; frequent
temporary exhibitions.*
For further details see page 80

KELHAM ISLAND MUSEUM
Alma Street (off Corporation
Street), Sheffield, South
Yorkshire S3 8RY
Tel: 0114 272 2106
Fax: 0114 275 7847
*Major museum of Sheffield industry
with 12,000hp working steam
engine; working Little Mesters –
cutler, grinder, forger; Bessemer steel
converter.*

ROTHERHAM ART GALLERY
The Arts Centre, Rotherham,
South Yorkshire S65 1JH
Tel: 01709 382121
Fax: 01709 823653
*Modern gallery with changing
temporary exhibitions, many local
in origin but some from outside
the area.*
For further details see page 79

RUSKIN GALLERY & RUSKIN CRAFT GALLERY
101 Norfolk Street, Sheffield,
South Yorkshire S1 2JE
Tel: 0114 273 5299
Fax: 0114 273 5994
*Houses John Ruskin's
(1819–1900) collection of Guild
of St George originally formed
1875.*
For further details see page 80

SANDTOFT TRANSPORT CENTRE
Belton Road, Sandtoft,
Doncaster, South Yorkshire
DN8 5SX
Tel: 01724 711391
Fax: 01724 711391
*Working trolleybus system at home
of Britain's largest single collection of
trolleybuses and motorbuses.
Museum includes period shops and
exhibitions.*

SHEFFIELD BUS MUSEUM
Tinsley Tram Sheds, Sheffield
Road, Tinsley, Sheffield S9 2FY
Tel: 0114 255 3010
Fax: 0114 268 3679
*Collection ranges from the period
1926–1976 and comprises over 20
assorted buses and coaches.*

SHEFFIELD CITY MUSEUM & MAPPIN ART GALLERY
Weston Park, Sheffield, South
Yorkshire S10 2TP
Tel: 0114 276 5619
Fax: 0114 275 0957
*World-famous cutlery: Old
Sheffield Plate; also ceramics,
paintings, glass and clocks,
archaeology, wildlife, geology,
weather and on-going programme
of temporary exhibitions.*
For further details see page 80

SITE GALLERY (MEDIA ART PHOTOGRAPHY)
1 Brown Street, Sheffield
S1 2BS
Tel: 0114 281 2077
*Newly redeveloped gallery showing
contemporary artwork, offering a
darkroom and digital imaging
facilities and courses, bookshop and
reading room.*

SOUTH YORKSHIRE AIRCRAFT MUSEUM
Home Farm, Firbeck, Worksop,
Nottinghamshire S81 8JR
Tel: 01909 812168
*Collection of Rolls-Royce
aero-engines, Hawker Hunter, De
Havilland Vampire, English Electric
Lightning, Jet Provost and
Westland Scout.*

SOUTH YORKSHIRE RAILWAY CO LTD
Barrow Road, Meadowhall,
Sheffield S9 1HN
Tel: 0114 242 4405
*Over 70 locomotives including steam
engines plus other exhibits including
guard's vans, rail cranes, wagons,
etc.*

TRADITIONAL HERITAGE MUSEUM
605 Ecclesall Road, Sheffield
S11 8PR
Tel: 0114 282 6296
Fax: 0114 276 8251
*The museum houses a collection of
social and industrial history artefacts
which illustrate life and work in
Sheffield during the period
1850–1950.*

VICTORIA JUBILEE MUSEUM
Taylor Hill, Cawthorne,
Barnsley, South Yorkshire
S75 4HH
Tel: 01226 790545
*Part cruck-frame, part post-and-truss
construction.*

WORTLEY TOP FORGE
Cote Lane, Thurgoland,
Sheffield
Tel: 0114 288 7576
*A 17thC iron forge, three water
wheels, ancient monument.*

YORK & LANCASTER REGIMENTAL MUSEUM
The Arts Centre, Walker
Place, Rotherham, South
Yorkshire S65 1JH
Tel: 01709 382121
*The displays cover the story of the
regiment and of the men who
served during its 200 year
history. The extensive regimental
archive is housed at the museum
and can be visited by
appointment.*
For further details see page 79

STAFFORDSHIRE

THE ANCIENT HIGH HOUSE
Greengate Street, Stafford,
Staffordshire ST16 2HS
Tel: 01785 240204
Fax: 01785 240204
*England's largest timber-framed
town house, with rooms set out to
show its 400-year history.*
For further details see page 81

THE BASS MUSEUM
PO Box 220, Horninglow
Street, Burton-upon-Trent,
Staffordshire DE14 1YQ
Tel: 01283 511000
ext 3604/3505
Fax: 01283 513509
*The brewing story, interactive
exhibits, award-winning
education service, guided brewery
tours, vintage vehicles and the
famous Bass shire horses.*
For further details see page 81

BOROUGH MUSEUM & ART GALLERY
The Brampton,
Newcastle-under-Lyme,
Staffordshire ST5 0QP
Tel: 01782 619705
*Local history, ceramics, militaria,
gallery of childhood, clocks,
Victorian street scene and an aviary,
temporary exhibition programme.*

CHURNET VALLEY RAILWAY
Cheddleton Station, Station
Road, Cheddleton, Moorland,
Staffordshire ST13 7EE
Tel: 01538 360522
Fax: 01538 360522
*Station building, Grade II listed
house, shop and museum set in
Churnet Valley. Steam locomotives
diesel locos and coaches and other
rolling stock. Steam days through
year.*

ETRURIA INDUSTRIAL MUSEUM
Lower Bedford Street, Etruria,
Stoke-on-Trent, Staffordshire
ST4 7AF
Tel: 01782 287557
Fax: 01782 260192
*Etruscan bone mill with coal fired
boiler, 1820s beam engine and
grinding machinery, also
balcksmith's forge and canal
warehouse activities.*
For further details see page 80

FORD GREEN HALL
Ford Green Road,
Smallthorne, Stoke-on-Trent,
Staffordshire ST6 1NG
Tel: 01782 233195
Fax: 01782 233194
*A fully-furnished timber-framed
farmhouse of 1624 with 18thC
brick additions and small period
garden.*
For further details see page 80

GLADSTONE POTTERY MUSEUM
Uttoxeter Road, Longton,
Stoke-on-Trent, Staffordshire
ST3 1PQ
Tel: 01782 319232/311378
Fax: 01782 598640
*A 19thC pottery where potters
demonstrate traditional skills
daily.*
For further details see page 80

HOOD & BROOMFIELD FINE ART
29 Albert Street,
Newcastle-under-Lyme,
Staffordshire ST5 1JP
Tel: 01782 626859
Fax: 01782 639257
*19thC inn gallery with fascinating
pictures of the potteries and
moorlands.*

IZAAK WALTON'S COTTAGE
Worston Lane, Shallowford,
Stafford, Staffordshire
ST15 0PA
Tel: 01785 760278
*A registered museum of fishing
with rooms set out in the style of
the 17thC.*
For further details see page 81

LICHFIELD HERITAGE CENTRE
Market Square, Lichfield,
Staffordshire WS13 6LG
Tel: 01543 256611
Fax: 01543 414749
*Heritage exhibition and treasury.
A V theatre key stage 2 activity
based school visits. Coffee shop, gift
shop, spire viewing platform.*

MINTON MUSEUM
Royal Doulton Minton House,
London Road, Stoke-on-Trent,
Staffordshire ST4 7QD
Tel: 01782 292292
Fax: 01782 292099
*Display spanning two centuries of
porcelain. Exhibits include pate sur
pate bone china tableware majolica
and vases.*

MUSEUM OF THE STAFFORDSHIRE REGIMENT
Whittington Barracks, Lichfield,
Staffordshire WS14 9PY
Tel: 0121 311 3229
Fax: 0121 311 3205
*Uniforms, badges, medals, weapons
and war trophies of the Regiment
from 1705; including militia and
volunteers.*

THE POTTERIES MUSEUM
Bethesda Street, Hanley,
Stoke-on-Trent, Staffordshire
ST1 3DW
Tel: 01782 232323
Fax: 01782 232500
*Internationally famous collections
of pottery and porcelain;
pre-eminent in Staffordshire
ceramics.*
**For further details see pages 80
& 38**

THE ROUND HOUSE GALLERY
38 High Street, Tutbury,
Burton-upon-Trent,
Staffordshire DE13 9LS
Tel: 01283 814964
*Situated in the heart of the historic
village.*

ROYAL DOULTON VISITOR CENTRE
Nile Street, Burslem,
Stoke-on-Trent, Staffordshire
ST6 2AJ
Tel: 01782 292434
*Fully guided factory tours,
museums, demonstration areas,
cinema, restaurant and extensive
shop. Open seven days a week.
Factory tours Monday to Friday
only.*

SAMUEL JOHNSON BIRTHPLACE MUSEUM
Breadmarket Street, Lichfield,
Staffordshire WS13 6LG
Tel: 01543 264972
Fax: 01543 258441
*In the house in which he was born is
a museum to Dr Johnson; his life,
work, friends and contemporaries.*

SHIRE HALL GALLERY
Market Square, Stafford,
Staffordshire ST16 2LD
Tel: 01785 278345
Fax: 01785 278327
*Annual programme of
contemporary art, craft and
photography exhibitions.
Historical courtrooms open to the
public.*
For further details see page 81

STAFFORD CASTLE & VISITOR CENTRE
Newport Road, Stafford,
Staffordshire ST16 1DJ
Tel: 01785 257698
*The site of a Norman fortress
with a Visitor Centre that houses
an exhibition of archaeological
artefacts discovered during
extensive excavations, a hands-on
display and a video presentation.*
For further details see page 81

TAMWORTH CASTLE
The Holloway, Tamworth,
Staffordshire B79 7LR
Tel: 01827 63563
Fax: 01827 52567
*This 12thC castle has 15
furnished rooms and features The
Tamworth Story, a hands-on
exhibition tracing the history of
the town.*
For further details see page 82

UTTOXETER HERITAGE CENTRE
34–36 Carter Street, Uttoxeter,
Staffordshire ST14 8EU
Tel: 01889 567176
*17thC timber-framed building with
displays of aspects of Uttoxeter's
history.*

WEDGWOOD VISITOR CENTRE
Barlaston, Stoke-on-Trent,
Staffordshire ST12 9ES
Tel: 01782 204141
Fax: 01782 204402
*Visitor Centre is located in the
Wedgwood factory which lies within
500-acre country estate.*

WILLIAM SALT LIBRARY
Eastgate Street, Stafford,
Staffordshire ST16 2LZ
Tel: 01785 255276
*18thC town house containing
books, documents and illustrative
material relating to history of
Staffordshire.*

STOCKTON-ON-TEES

BILLINGHAM ART GALLERY
Queensway, Billingham,
Cleveland TS23 2LN
Tel: 01642 555443
*A purpose-built gallery with a lively
programme of local, national and
international art, and arts and crafts
workshops.*

GREEN DRAGON MUSEUM
Theatre Yard,
Stockton-on-Tees, Cleveland
TS18 1AT
Tel: 01642 674308
*A local history museum set in a
Georgian warehouse, with displays
exploring Stockton's past, present
and future.*

PRESTON HALL MUSEUM

Yarm Road, Stockton-on-Tees, Cleveland TS18 3RH
Tel: 01642 781184
A Georgian country house, set in a park.

390TH BOMB GROUP MEMORIAL AIR MUSEUM

Parham Airfield, Parham, Woodbridge, Suffolk
Tel: 01728 621373
Museum housed in original control tower, refreshment sale hut and archive building. Including museum of British resistance organisation.

ABBEY VISITOR CENTRE

Samons Tower, Abbey Precinct, Bury St Edmunds, Suffolk IP33 1RS
Tel: 01284 763100
Fax: 01284 757079
The Abbey Visitor centre is housed in Samson's Tower, part of the west front of the now ruined Abbey of St Edmund.
For further details see page 82

BECCLES & DISTRICT MUSEUM

Former Sir John Leman School Building, Ballygate, Beccles, Suffolk NR34 9ND
Tel: 01502 715722
Printing artefacts, cultural and domestic items, model of town in 1841, natural history, discovery boxes and Grade I listed building.

BRANDON HERITAGE CENTRE

George Street, Brandon, Suffolk IP27 0BX
Tel: 01842 813707
Details of the flint, fur and forestry industries in the Brandon area together with a local interest section housed in former Fire Station premises.

BUNGAY MUSEUM

Waveney District Council Office, Broad Street, Bungay, Suffolk NR35 1EE
Tel: 01986 892176
History of Bungay and its printing works.

BURY ST EDMUNDS ART GALLERY

Cornhill, Bury St Edmunds, Suffolk IP33 1BT
Tel: 01284 762081
Fax: 01284 750774
Housed in a fine Robert Adam's building, the gallery organises a changing programme of fine art and crafts exhibitions.

CHRISTCHURCH MANSION

Christchurch Park, Ipswich, Suffolk IP4 2BE
Tel: 01473 253246
Fax: 01473 210328
Tudor mansion built in 1548, houses fine and applied art displays. One of the best collections of Gainsborough and Constables outside London. Temporary exhibition programme.
For further details see page 82

DUNWICH MUSEUM

St James's Street, Dunwich, Saxmundham, Suffolk IP17 3EA
Tel: 01728 648796
History of Dunwich from Roman times chronicling its disappearance into the sea.

DUNWICH UNDERWATER EXPLORATION EXHIBITION

The Orford Craft Shop, Orford, Woodbridge, Suffolk IP12 2LN
Tel: 01394 450678
Fax: 01394 450678
Exhibits showing progress in the underwater exploration of the former city and underwater studies off the Suffolk coast.

EAST ANGLIA TRANSPORT MUSEUM

Chapel Road, Carlton Colville, Lowestoft, Suffolk NR33 8BL
Tel: 01502 518459
A working museum with one of the widest ranges of street transport vehicles on display and in action.

GAINSBOROUGH'S HOUSE

46 Gainsborough Street, Sudbury, Suffolk CO10 6EU
Tel: 01787 372958
Fax: 01787 376991
Birthplace of Thomas Gainsborough (1727–88) displaying more of the artist's work than any other gallery; also a varied programme of contemporary art exhibitions.
For further details see page 83

GRANARY MUSEUM

The Granary, Flatford, East Bergholt, Colchester, Suffolk CO7 6UL
Tel: 01206 298111
Fax: 01206 298111
Building and exhibits.

HALESWORTH & DISTRICT MUSEUM

The Almshouses, Steeple End, Halesworth, Suffolk IP19 8LL
Tel: 01986 873030
Two rooms in Almshouses plus former fire engine shed adjacent to library and under art gallery.

HAVERHILL & DISTRICT LOCAL HISTORY CENTRE

Town Hall, High Street, Haverhill, Suffolk
Tel: 01440 714962
A collection of over 2,000 items relating to Haverhill and district.

HMS GANGES ASSOCIATION MUSEUM

Unit 4 & 5, Shotley Marina, Shotley Gate, Ipswich IP9 1JQ
Tel: 01473 684749
History of HMS Ganges contained in two-roomed museum with photographs, artefacts and documentation.

IPSWICH MUSEUM

High Street, Ipswich, Suffolk IP1 3QH
Tel: 01473 213761
Fax: 01473 281274
Victorian museum displays Suffolk archaeology, natural history, British birds, Tudor and Stuart, Ipswich and people of the world.
For further details see page 83

IPSWICH TRANSPORT MUSEUM

Old Trolleybus Depot, Cobham Road, Ipswich, Suffolk IP3 9JD
Tel: 01473 832260
Fax: 01473 832260
Museum features over 90 vehicles built or operated in and around Ipswich together with other associated displays and small exhibits.

LANMAN MUSEUM

Framlingham Castle, Framlingham, Woodbridge, Suffolk IP13 9AJ
Tel: 01728 724189
Rural exhibits relating to everyday life in Framlingham and surrounding area, including paintings and photographs.

LAXFIELD & DISTRICT MUSEUM

The Guildhall, High Street, Laxfield, Woodbridge, Suffolk IP13 8DU
Tel: 01986 798421
The museum is housed in the early 16thC Guildhall opposite All Saint's church in the centre of Laxfield.

LONG SHOP MUSEUM

Main Street, Leiston, Suffolk IP16 4ES
Tel: 01728 832189
An award-winning museum with three exhibition halls full of items from our glorious age of steam.

LOWESTOFT & EAST SUFFOLK MARITIME MUSEUM

Sparrows Nest Park, Whapload Road, Lowestoft, Suffolk NR32 1XG
Tel: 01502 561963
Models of fishing and commercial ships, old and new shipwright's tools and fishing gear. Lifeboat display, drifters cabin, picture gallery.

LOWESTOFT MUSEUM

Broad House, Nicholas Everitt Park, Lowestoft, Suffolk NR33 9JR
Tel: 01502 511457
Local history, Lowestoft porcelain, fossils, flint implements and medieval artefacts from local sites.

MANOR HOUSE MUSEUM

Honey Hill, Bury St Edmunds, Suffolk IP33 1HF
Tel: 01284 757072
Fax: 01284 757079
Clocks and watches of all kinds and many other types of time-keeping instruments.
For further details see page 82

MECHANICAL MUSIC MUSEUM TRUST

Blacksmith Road, Cotton, Stowmarket, Suffolk IP14 4QN
Tel: 01449 613876
A selection of fairground organs, pipe organs, street pianos, music boxes, polyphons and many other musical items, all demonstrated.

MID SUFFOLK LIGHT RAILWAY SOCIETY MUSEUM

Brockford Station, Brockford, Suffolk
Tel: 01473 742358
Re-created Mid Suffolk Light Railway station with exhibits relating to Mid Suffolk Light Railway.

MILDENHALL & DISTRICT MUSEUM

6 King Street, Mildenhall, Bury St Edmunds, Suffolk IP28 7EX
Tel: 01638 716970
Local voluntary museum housed in early 19thC building.

MOOT HALL & MUSEUM

Aldeburgh, Suffolk IP15 5DS
Tel: 01728 453295
A 16thC listed ancient building with museum of items of local interest, including paintings and ship burial finds.

MOYSE'S HALL MUSEUM

Cornhill, Bury St Edmunds, Suffolk IP33 1DX
Tel: 01284 757488
Fax: 01284 757079
Norman domestic building containing local history and archaeology of West Suffolk.
For further details see page 82

MUSEUM OF EAST ANGLIAN LIFE

Stowmarket, Suffolk IP14 1DL
Tel: 01449 612229
East Anglia's open-air museum set in 70 acres of Suffolk countryside.

NATIONAL HORSERACING MUSEUM

99 High Street, Newmarket, Suffolk CB8 8JL
Tel: 01638 667333/560222
Fax: 01638 665600
Five galleries telling of the development of horseracing and the individuals involved.
For further details see page 83

NORFOLK & SUFFOLK AVIATION MUSEUM

The Street, Flixton, Bungay, Suffolk NR35 1NZ
Tel: 01986 986644
Twenty-four aircraft on display together with large indoor display of smaller items connected with the history of aviation. Admission free.

ORFORD MUSEUM

Rear of Crown & Castle Hotel, Orford, Woodbridge, Suffolk IP12
Tel: 01394 450421
Local history museum.

ROYAL NAVAL PATROL SERVICE ASSOCIATION MUSEUM

Sparrows Nest, Lowestoft, Suffolk NR32 1XG
Tel: 01502 586250
Fax: 01502 586250
Photographs from World War II of crews, minesweepers and anti-submarine vessels. Models of ship, mine sweepers, and anti submarine vessels. Ratings and officers of the 1939/45 conflict.

SOUTHWOLD LIFEBOAT MUSEUM

Gun Hill, Southwold, Suffolk IP18 6RH
Tel: 01502 723600
RNLI models, photographs of lifeboat and relics from old boats.

SOUTHWOLD MUSEUM

Bartholomew Green, Southwold, Suffolk IP18 6HZ
Tel: 01502 722437
Local history, archaeology and natural history.

SOUTHWOLD SAILORS READING ROOM

East Cliff, Southwold, Suffolk IP18 6EI
Tel: 01502 723782
Building of character where retired seamen have a social club and reading room.

SUE RYDER FOUNDATION MUSEUM

Sue Ryder Foundation Headquarters, Cavendish, Sudbury, Suffolk CO10 8AY
Tel: 01787 280252
Fax: 01787 280548
Displays showing the reason for establishing the Sue Ryder Foundation and its work, past, present and future.
For further details see page 84

SUFFOLK HORSE MUSEUM

The Market Hill, Woodbridge, Suffolk IP12 4LU
Tel: 01394 380643
An indoor exhibition about the Suffolk Punch breed of heavy horse.

TOLLY COBBOLD BREWERY & THE BREWERY TAP

Cliff Road, Ipswich, Suffolk IP3 0AZ
Tel: 01473 231723
Fax: 01473 280045
Fully guided brewery tours – taste the malt, smell the hops and see the UK's largest collection of commemorative bottled beers.

WOODBRIDGE MUSEUM

5a Market Hill, Woodbridge, Suffolk IP12 4LP
Tel: 01394 380502

WOOLPIT & DISTRICT MUSEUM

The Institute, Woolpit, Bury St Edmunds, Suffolk IP30
Tel: 01359 240822
A 17thC timber-framed building with one permanent display of brickmaking and other displays, changing yearly, depicting life of a Suffolk village.

BOURNE HALL MUSEUM

Bourne Hall, Spring Street, Ewell, Surrey KT17 1UF
Tel: 0181 796 7265
Old tools, clothes, household goods and machinery re-create yesterday's Epsom and Ewell.

BRITISH RED CROSS MUSEUM & ARCHIVES

Barnett Hill, Wonersh, Guildford, Surrey GU5 0RF
Tel: 01483 898595
Fax: 01483 898595
Museum shows history of Red Cross movement, particularly the British, from 1870.

BROOKLANDS MUSEUM

Brooklands Road, Weybridge, Surrey KT13 0QN
Tel: 01932 857381
Fax: 01932 855465
The birthplace of British motorsport and aviation with an historic collection of cars and aircraft displayed in original buildings.

CHERTSEY MUSEUM
The Cedars, 33 Windsor Street,
Chertsey, Surrey KT16 8AT
Tel: 01932 565764
Fax: 01932 571118
*Regency house with museum of local
history archaeology and costume.
Varied temporary exhibitions and
events programme.*

COBHAM BUS MUSEUM
Redhill Road, Cobham, Surrey
KT11 1EF
Tel: 01932 864078
*Collection of vintage buses dating
from 1925 to 1958.*

**DORKING & DISTRICT
MUSEUM**
62a West Street, Dorking,
Surrey RH4 1BS
Tel: 01306 743821
*Small museum containing pictures
and relics of local interest. Also
library with large collection of
archives and photographs.*

EAST SURREY MUSEUM
1 Stafford Road, Caterham,
Surrey CR3 6JG
Tel: 01883 340275
*Local history museum with
geological and archaeological
displays, crafts, artefacts and other
changing exhibitions.*

THE EGHAM MUSEUM
Literary Institute, High Street,
Egham, Surrey TW20 9EW
Tel: 01344 843047
*Museum in Literary Institute
containing local historical and
archaeological items, clocks,
paintings, documents and
photographs.*

ELMBRIDGE MUSEUM
Church Street, Weybridge,
Surrey KT13 8DE
Tel: 01932 843573
Fax: 01932 846552
*Collections covering local, natural
and social history, archaeology
and costume.*
For further details see page 39

GODALMING MUSEUM
109a High Street, Godalming,
Surrey GU7 1AQ
Tel: 01483 426510
Fax: 01483 869495
*Museum set in an interesting
timber-framed house.*

**GUILDFORD HOUSE
GALLERY**
155 High Street, Guildford,
Surrey GU1 3AJ
Tel: 01483 444740
Fax: 01483 444742
*Exhibition gallery in recently
restored 17thC house. Varied
exhibitions programme throughout
the year. Tea shop and gift shop.*
For further details see page 84

GUILDFORD MUSEUM
Castle Arch, Quarry Street,
Guildford, Surrey GU1 3SX
Tel: 01483 444750
Fax: 01483 444750
*17thC house with collections of local
history.*

**THE HANNAH PESCHAR
GALLERY**
Black and White Cottage,
Standon Lane, Ockley, Dorking,
Surrey RH5 5QR
Tel: 01306 627269
Fax: 01303 627662
*Controlled wilderness of an intimate
water-garden designed by Anthony
Paul; an exhibition of British
contemporary sculpture and ceramics
among architectural plants, such as
reeds/ferns, and four ponds.*

**HASLEMERE EDUCATIONAL
MUSEUM**
78 High Street, Haslemere,
Surrey GU27 2LA
Tel: 01428 642112
Fax: 01428 645234
*Founded 1888, museum's
collections include natural history,
geology, archaeology and local
history items.*

**LEATHERHEAD MUSEUM OF
LOCAL HISTORY**
Hampton Cottage, 64 Church
Street, Leatherhead, Surrey
KT22 8DP
Tel: 01372 386348
*A 17thC listed timber-framed
cottage housing exhibitions on
Leatherhead and the surrounding
area including Ashtead pottery and
Ashtead Roman Villa.*

MUSEUM OF FARNHAM
Willmer House, 38 West Street,
Farnham, Surrey GU9 7DX
Tel: 01252 715094
Fax: 01252 715094
*Award-winning museum with
imaginative displays interpreting the
history of the Farnham area.*

THE NEW ASHGATE GALLERY
Wagon Yard, Farnham, Surrey
GU9 7PS
Tel: 01252 713208
Fax: 01252 737398
*Monthly exhibitions of the work of
contemporary professional artists and
makers. Also craft gallery and
jewellery workshop.*

**ROYAL EARLSWOOD
HOSPITAL MUSEUM**
Shopping Centre, The Belfry,
Redhill, Surrey RH1 6JL
Tel: 0188 373 4000
Small museum in working hospital.

RURAL LIFE CENTRE
Reeds Road, Tilford, Farnham,
Surrey GU10 2DL
Tel: 01252 795571/792300
Fax: 01252 795571
*Museum with farm machines,
implements, wagons, etc.*

SURREY HEATH MUSEUM
Surrey Heath House, Knoll
Road, Camberley, Surrey
GU15 3HD
Tel: 01276 704284
*Museum concerned with local history
and environment of Surrey Heath.*

THE WATTS GALLERY
Down Lane, Compton,
Guildford, Surrey GU3 1DQ
Tel: 01483 810235
*Memorial gallery containing pictures
and sculptures by G F Watts.*

THE WESTCOTT GALLERY
4 Guildford Road, Westcott,
Dorking, Surrey RH4 3NR
Tel: 01306 876261
*Gallery with main exhibits
including paintings of the 19th and
20thC and contemporary Surrey
artists.*

TYNE AND WEAR

**ARBEIA ROMAN FORT &
MUSEUM**
Baring Street, South Shields,
Tyne and Wear NE33 2BB
Tel: 0191 456 1369
Fax: 0191 427 6862
*Roman fort, remains of gateway,
fort wall and defences.*

BEDE'S WORLD
Church Bank, Jarrow, Tyne
and Wear NE32 3DY
Tel: 0191 489 2106
Fax: 0191 4282361
*Museum, parish church and farm
focuses on life and times of the
Venerable Bede (673–735AD)
and early medieval Northumbria.*
For further details see page 84

HANCOCK MUSEUM
Barras Bridge, Newcastle upon
Tyne NE2 4PT
Tel: 0191 222 6765
Fax: 0191 222 6753
*Magnificent collections of birds,
mammals, insects, fossils and
minerals as well as exciting special
exhibitions including Land of the
Pharaohs and Living Planet.*

HATTON GALLERY
The University of Newcastle
upon Tyne, Newcastle upon
Tyne NE1 7RU
Tel: 0191 222 6057
Fax: 0191 261 1182
*Temporary exhibitions of
contemporary art.*

LAING ART GALLERY
Higham Place, Newcastle upon
Tyne NE1 8AG
Tel: 0191 232 7734
Fax: 0191 222 0952
*Paintings and watercolours including
works by Northumbrian-born artist
John Martin; award-winning
interactive displays 'Art on
Tyneside' and 'Children's Gallery';
café and shop.*

MILITARY VEHICLE MUSEUM
Exhibition Park Pavilion,
Newcastle upon Tyne NE2 4PZ
Tel: 0191 281 7222
*Military history through the 20thC
displayed by vehicles, uniforms and
equipment. WWI trench and
home-front displays.*

**MONKWEARMOUTH STATION
MUSEUM**
North Bridge Street,
Monkwearmouth, Sunderland
SR5 1AP
Tel: 0191 567 7075
*Take a look inside a real Victorian
train station and visit the fascinating
ticket office.*

MUSEUM OF ANTIQUITIES
The University, Newcastle upon
Tyne NE1 7RU
Tel: 0191 222 7849
Fax: 0191 222 8516
*Regional antiquities 6000 BC to
17thC, ideal place to start tour of
Hadrian's wall.*

**NEWBURN HALL MOTOR
MUSEUM**
Townfield Gardens, Newburn,
Newcastle upon Tyne
NE15 8PY
Tel: 0191 264 2977
*Period buildings built for the 4th
Northumberland Fusiliers.*

**NEWCASTLE DISCOVERY
MUSEUM**
Blandford House, Blandford
Square, Newcastle upon Tyne
NE1 4JA
Tel: 0191 232 6789 ext 449
Fax: 0191 230 2614
*Discovery Museum offers a wide
variety of experiences for all the
family to enjoy.*

**NORTH EAST AIRCRAFT
MUSEUM**
Old Washington Road,
Sunderland SR5 3HZ
Tel: 0191 519 0662
*A collection of aircraft and aero
engines. Displays depicting the
wartime activites of the Royal
Observor Corps and other items of
aviation interest.*

**PEOPLE'S MUSEUM OF
MEMORABILIA & NEWCASTLE
ANTIQUE CENTRE**
42–44 Grainger Street,
Newcastle upon Tyne NE1 5JG
Tel: 0191 221 1534
*The People's Museum of
Memorabilia is a streetscape museum
portraying a local history study of
commercial and domestic life from
the 18thC to post-war period.*

RYHOPE ENGINES MUSEUM
Sunderland SR2 0ND
Tel: 0191 516 0212
Victorian waterworks 1868.

**THE SHEFTON MUSEUM OF
GREEK ART & ARCHAEOLOGY**
Department of Classics, The
University, Newcastle upon
Tyne NE1 7RU
Tel: 0191 222 7966
Fax: 0191 222 5432
*Small but important collection of
Greek and Etruscan antiquities from
the Bronze Age to the Hellenistic
period.*

SHIPLEY ART GALLERY
Prince Consort Road,
Gateshead, Tyne and Wear
NE8 4JB
Tel: 0191 477 1495
Fax: 0191 477 1495
*The Shipley is home to one of the
largest collections of contemporary
craft in Northern England.*

SOUTH SHIELDS MUSEUM
Ocean Road, South Shields,
Tyne and Wear NE33 2AU
Tel: 0191 456 8740
Fax: 0191 456 7850
*Visit the fascinating reconstruction of
William Black Street where famous
novelist Catherine Cookson grew
up. Learn about South Tyneside's
history.*

**STEPHENSON RAILWAY
MUSEUM**
Middle Engine Lane, North
Shields, Tyne and Wear
NE29 8SX
Tel: 0191 262 2627
*Railway engines and rolling stock
including Killingworth Billy, one of
George Stephenson's early
locomotives built in 1826.*

**SUNDERLAND MUSEUM &
ART GALLERY**
Borough Road, Sunderland
SR1 1PP
Tel: 0191 565 0723
Fax: 0191 565 0713
*The wildlife and geology of the north
east, the history of Sunderland and
its industries, glass, pottery,
shipbuilding and coal mining.*

TRINITY MARITIME CENTRE
29 Broad Chare, Quayside,
Newcastle upon Tyne
NE1 3DQ
Tel: 0191 261 4691
*Museum contains models of sailing
ships, colliers, tankers, naval vessels,
and a model of the quayside as it
was in 1775.*

**TYNEMOUTH VOLUNTEER
LIFE BRIGADE**
Spanish Battery, Tynemouth,
North Shields, Tyne and Wear
NE30 4DD
Tel: 0191 252 0933
*The brigade was formed in 1864 to
assist HM Coastguard in the rescue
of seamen wrecked on this coast.*

**UNIVERSITY GALLERY
UNIVERSITY OF
NORTHUMBRIA AT
NEWCASTLE**
Library Building, Sandyford
Road, Newcastle upon Tyne
NE1 8ST
Tel: 0191 227 4424
*First-floor main library; entrance on
Sandyford Road.*

**WASHINGTON 'F' PIT
MUSEUM**
Albany Way, District 2,
Washington, Tyne and Wear
Tel: 0191 4167640
Fax: 0191 5650713
Colliery engine house and headgear.

WINLATON COTTAGE FORGE
Church Street, Winlaton,
Blaydon-on-Tyne, Tyne and
Wear NE21 6AR
Tel: 0191 414 3223
Building dating from 1691.

WARWICKSHIRE

ABBEY BARN
Abbey Fields, Kenilworth,
Warwickshire
Tel: 01926 853574
*Small museum housed in medieval
building formerly part of the Abbey
of St Mary the Virgin.*

**ANNE HATHAWAY'S
COTTAGE**
Cottage Lane, Shottery,
Stratford-upon-Avon,
Warwickshire CV37 9HH
Tel: 01789 292100
Fax: 01789 414372
For further details see page 85

**ANTIQUE DOLL & TEDDIES
COLLECTION**
Golden Cross Inn, Wixford
Road, Arden's Grafton, Nr
Bidford-on-Avon,
Warwickshire B50 4LG
Tel: 01789 772420
*Three hundred year-old public house
with large restaurant added in the
1930s which holds main exhibition.*

ASHORNE HALL NICKELODEON
Ashorne Hill, Leamington Spa, Warwickshire CV33 9QN
Tel: 01926 651444
Fax: 01203 367213
A presentation of automatically played musical instruments and vintage cinema with Compton organ accompanying silent films.

HALL'S CROFT
Old Town, Stratford-upon-Avon, Warwickshire CV37 6BG
Tel: 01789 292107
Fax: 01789 414372
For further details see page 85

HARVARD HOUSE AND THE NEISH PEWTER COLLECTION
High Street, Startford-upon-Avon, Warwickshire CV37 6HB
Tel: 01789 204016
Fax: 01789 296083
This Elizabethan town house is an appropriate setting for the nationally important Neish Collection of pewter, which ranges from Roman times to the 19thC.

HERITAGE MOTOR CENTRE
Banbury Road, Gaydon, Warwick, Warwickshire CV35 0BJ
Tel: 01926 641188
Fax: 01926 641555
Purpose-built transport museum containing collection of historic British cars.

JAMES GILBERT RUGBY FOOTBALL MUSEUM
5 St Matthews Street, Rugby, Warwickshire CV21 3BY
Tel: 01788 542426
Fax: 01788 540795
Original 19thC building of the Gilbert family who made the first rugby balls for the game and for the Rugby school.

LORD LEYCESTER HOSPITAL
High Street, Warwick, Warwickshire CV34 4BH
Tel: 01926 491422
A group of 14thC buildings converted into a home for old soldiers in 1571 and still serving that purpose.

MARY ARDEN'S HOUSE & SHAKESPEARE COUNTRYSIDE MUSEUM
Station Road, Wilmcote, Warwickshire CV37 9UN
Tel: 01789 293455
Fax: 01789 414327
For further details see page 85

MONTPELIER GALLERY
8 Chapel Street, Stratford-upon-Avon, Warwickshire CV37 3EP
Tel: 01789 261161
Gallery selling paintings and original etchings, glass, jewellery and ceramics.

MUSEUM OF COUNTRY BYGONES TRUST
Louisa Ward Close, Marton, Rugby, Warwickshire CV23 9SA
Tel: 01926 633361
A small museum displaying a collection of rural and domestic paraphernalia including tools of the wheelwright, saddler, thatcher and shepherd plus farm tools and dairy equipment.

NEW PLACE/NASH'S HOUSE
Chapel Street, Stratford-upon-Avon, Warwickshire CV37 6EP
Tel: 01789 292325
Fax: 01789 414372
For further details see page 85

NUNEATON LIBRARY
Church Street, Nuneaton, Warwickshire CV11 4DR
Tel: 01203 384027
Fax: 01203 350125
Contains local history collection and George Eliot collection of photos, letters, first editions, biography and criticism.

NUNEATON MUSEUM & ART GALLERY
Riversley Park, Nuneaton, Warwickshire CV11 5TU
Tel: 01203 350720
Fax: 01203 376551
Local history, archaeology, art, George Eliot collection plus changing exhibitions from local artists and touring exhibitions.

RUGBY SCHOOL MUSEUM
10 Little Church Street, Rugby, Warwickshire CV21 3AW
Tel: 01788 574117
Fax: 01788 565871
Rugby School Museum tells the story of the school scene of Tom Brown's Schooldays and contains the earlier memorabilia of the game invented on the School Close.

SAINT JOHN'S HOUSE
St John's, Warwick, Warwickshire CV34 4NF
Tel: 01926 412132 ext 2021
A branch of the county museum in 17thC house.

SHAKESPEARE'S BIRTHPLACE TRUST
The Shakespeare Centre, Henley Street, Stratford-upon-Avon, Warwickshire CV37 6QW
Tel: 01789 204016
Fax: 01789 296083
For further details see page 85

TEDDY BEAR MUSEUM
19 Greenhill Street, Stratford-upon-Avon, Warwickshire CV37 6LF
Tel: 01789 293160
The Teddy Bear Museum is housed in an Elizabethan building with a collection of teddy bears from the turn of the century including some of the oldest.

WARWICK DOLL MUSEUM
Oken's House, Castle Street, Warwick, Warwickshire CV34 4BP
Tel: 01926 495546
A branch of the county museum in a half-timbered medieval house containing displays on the history of dolls.

WARWICKSHIRE MUSEUM
Market Place, Warwick, Warwickshire CV34 4SA
Tel: 01926 412501 ext 2500
Fax: 01926 419840
Exhibits include geology (with giant Plesiosaur fossil), wildlife, history of Warwickshire and the great Sheldon tapestry map.

WARWICKSHIRE YEOMANRY MUSEUM
The Court House, Jury Street, Warwick, Warwickshire CV34 4EW
Tel: 01926 492212
Fax: 01926 494837
Uniforms, arms, swords, sabres and selected silver.

WELLESBOURNE AVIATION MUSEUM
Control Tower Entrance, Wellesbourne, Warwick, Warwickshire CV35 9JJ
Tel: 01926 855031
Underground bunker converted to museum and above ground museum containing aviation memorabilia and static aircraft.

WEST MIDLANDS

AVERY HISTORICAL MUSEUM
Foundry Lane, Smethwick, Warley, West Midlands B66 2LP
Tel: 0121 558 1112 ext 1951
Collection of weighing scales, weights and records and instruments relating to the history of weighing.

BANTOCK HOUSE MUSEUM
Bantock Park, Finchfield Road, Wolverhampton, West Midlands WV3 9LQ
Tel: 01902 552195
Fax: 01902 552196
Main collections of 18thC and 19thC Midland Japanned ware, tin, iron, papiermache, wood.

BARBER INSTITUTE OF FINE ARTS
University of Birmingham, Edgbaston, Birmingham, West Midlands B15 2TS
Tel: 0121 414 7333
Fax: 0121 414 3370
One of the finest small picture galleries in the world housing an outstanding permanent collection of Old Masters and modern paintings, drawings and sculpture including masterpieces by Bellini, Rubens, Poussin, Murillo, Gainsborough, Rosetti, Whistler, Monet, Degas and Magritte.
For further details see page 85

BERKSWELL MUSEUM
The Cottage, Lavender Hall Lane, Berswell, West Midlands CV7 7BL
Tel: 01676 534981
Collection of memorabilia; farm implements, Victorian household items, church and parish documents.

BILSTON ART GALLERY & MUSEUM
Mount Pleasant, Bilston, Wolverhampton, West Midlands WV14 7LU
Tel: 01902 409143
Art Gallery housing temporary community exhibitions.
For further details see page 86

BIRCHILLS CANAL MUSEUM
Old Birchills, Walsall, West Midlands
Tel: 01922 645778
Small museum about life on the canals housed in a former Boatman's rest at the top of the eight Walsall locks on the Walsall canal.

BIRMINGHAM MUSEUM & ART GALLERY
Chamberlain Square, Birmingham, West Midlands B3 3DH
Tel: 0121 235 2834
Fine and applied art, archaeology and local history collections all displayed in the same building.
For further details see page 86

BIRMINGHAM MUSEUM OF SCIENCE & INDUSTRY
146 Newhall Street, Birmingham, West Midlands B3 1RZ
Tel: 0121 235 1661
Steam engines, aircraft, veteran cars and motorcycles.

BIRMINGHAM RAILWAY MUSEUM
670 Warwick Road, Tyseley, Birmingham, West Midlands B11 2HL
Tel: 0121 707 4696
Fax: 0121 764 4645
A live steam-museum featuring a fine collection of locomotives, specialist coaches and goods wagons.

BLACK COUNTRY LIVING MUSEUM
Tipton Road, Dudley, West Midlands DY1 4SQ
Tel: 0121 557 9643
Fax: 0121 557 4242
Open-air museum, old fashioned village with shops, houses, workshops, pub, 1920s cinema, electric tramway, underground, coal mine and canal tunnel.
For further details see page 85

BROADFIELD HOUSE GLASS MUSEUM
Compton Drive, Kingswinford, West Midlands DY6 9NS
Tel: 01384 812745
Fax: 01384 812746
Internationally famous collection of British Glass from 17thC to present day focusing on achievements of local Stourbridge glass industry.

CADBURY WORLD
Linden Road, Bournville, Birmingham, West Midlands B30 2LD
Tel: 0121 451 4180
Fax: 0121 451 1366
Story of chocolate from Aztec times to present day includes chocolate making-demonstration and children's fantasy factory.

THE COVENTRY TOY MUSEUM
Whitefriars Gate, Much Park Street, Coventry, West Midlands CV1 2LT
Tel: 01203 227560
Toy museum is housed in building of historic interest, Whitefriars Gate built in 1352.

DUDLEY MUSEUM & ART GALLERY
St James's Road, Dudley, West Midlands DY1 1HU
Tel: 01384 453575
Fax: 01384 453576
Award-winning geological gallery, The Time Trail. Changing programme of popular exhibitions. New for 1998 'Watch With Mother', 'Art Attack'.

THE GAS HALL
Birmingham Museum and Art Gallery, Chamberlain Square, Birmingham, West Midlands B3 3DH
Tel: 0121 303 1966
Fax: 0121 303 1394
Exhibition hall housing temporary touring collections.

HERBERT ART GALLERY & MUSEUM
Jordan Well, Coventry, West Midlands CV1 5QP
Tel: 01203 832381
Fax: 01203 832410
Local exhibits including social history, natural history, visual arts and archaeology.

IKON GALLERY
Oozells Street, Brindleyplace, Birmingham
Tel: 0121 643 0708
Fax: 0121 643 2254
Re-opening January 1998, this gallery hosts a varied programme of contemporary art exhibitions.

JEROME K JEROME BIRTHPLACE MUSEUM
Belsize House, Bradford Street, Walsall, West Midlands WS1 1PN
Tel: 01922 653116
Classical stuccoed terraced building in 1850s parlour setting housing Jerome K Jerome exhibition including photographs and personal items.

JEWELLERY QUARTER DISCOVERY CENTRE
75–79 Vyse Street, Hockley, Birmingham, West Midlands B18 6HA
Tel: 0121 554 3598
Fax: 0121 554 9700
The story of jewellery making in Birmingham with a visit around a 'time capsule' jewellery factory.
For further details see page 86

LAPWORTH MUSEUM
School of Earth Sciences, Birmingham University, Edgbaston, Birmingham, West Midlands B15 2TT
Tel: 0121 414 4173
Minerals, rocks, fossils and stone implements from the UK and around the world.

LOCK MUSEUM
54 New Road, Willenhall, West Midlands WV13 2DA
Tel: 01902 634542
Lock museum in Victorian locksmith's house and workshop.

LUNT ROMAN FORT
c/o Coventry Museum Service, Jordan Well, Warwickshire CV1 5QP
Tel: 01203 832381
Fax: 01203 832410
A 1stC Roman turf and timber fort, with reconstructed features. Guided tours available. Shop, toilets, museum and parking on site.

MAYPOLE GALLERY
Maypole House, Maypole
Street, Wombourne,
Wolverhampton, West Midlands
WV5 9JB
Tel: 01902 897452
*Gallery specialising in ceramics,
dolls and paintings.*

MIDLAND AIR MUSEUM
Coventry Airport, Baginton,
Coventry, West Midlands
CV8 3AZ
Tel: 01203 301033
*Collection of over 28 historic
aeroplanes.*

MUSEUM OF BRITISH ROAD TRANSPORT
St Agnes Lane, Hales Street,
Coventry, West Midlands
CV1 1NN
Tel: 01203 832425
*160 cars and commercial vehicles
from 1896 to present day.*
For further details see page 86

NATIONAL MOTORCYCLE MUSEUM
Coventry Road, Bickenhill,
Solihull, West Midlands B92 0EJ
Tel: 01675 443311
Fax: 0121 711 3153
*Museum with a collection of 700
British machines from 1898 to the
present day housed in a new
building of a high architectural
standard.*

OLDWYCH GALLERY
Oldwych House Farm, Oldwych
Lane, Fen End, Kenilworth,
Warwickshire CV8 1NR
Tel: 01676 533552
*Art gallery and painter's studio in
converted barn on working farm.*

SOHO HOUSE
Soho Avenue (off Soho
Road), Handsworth,
Birmingham, West Midlands
B18 5LB
Tel: 0121 554 9122
*This restored 18thC museum was
home to industrialist Matthew
Boulton, manufacturer of silver,
steam engines and coins.*
For further details see page 86

STUART CRYSTAL EXPERIENCE & FACTORY TOUR
Wordsley, Stourbridge, West
Midlands DY8 4AA
Tel: 01384 828282
*Famous Redhouse Cone museum,
factory shop, glass repair service and
factory tours.*

WALSALL LEATHER MUSEUM
Wisemore, Walsall, West
Midlands WS2 8EQ
Tel: 01922 721153
Fax: 01922 725827
*Housed in a restored Victorian
factory this working museum tells
the story of Walsall's traditional
trade.*

WALSALL MUSEUM & ART GALLERY
Central Library, Lichfield
Street, Walsall, West Midlands
WS1 1TR
Tel: 01922 653116
*Walsall Inside Out is a
permanent exhibition of the
histories of Walsall and its people.*
For further details see page 86

WEDNESBURY ART GALLERY & MUSEUM
Holyhead Road, Wednesbury,
West Midlands WS10 7DF
Tel: 0121 556 0683
Fax: 0121 505 1625
*Edwin Richard's collection of 19thC
paintings. A permanent display of
Ruskin pottery and an ethnographic
collection of a 19thC lady.*

WEST MIDLANDS POLICE MUSEUM
639 Stratford Road, Sparkhill
Police Station, Birmingham,
West Midlands B11 4EA
Tel: 0121 626 7181
Fax: 0121 626 7066
*Police exhibits through the ages
housed in Victorian court house
complete with a mock cell.*

WILLENHALL MUSEUM
Willenhall Library, Walsall
Street, Willenhall, West
Midlands WV13 2EX
Tel: 01902 366513
*A museum about the people of
Willenhall and their town, the
capital of the British Lock Industry.*

WOLVERHAMPTON ART GALLERY & MUSEUM
Lichfield Street,
Wolverhampton, West
Midlands WV1 1DU
Tel: 01902 552055
*Collections of 18th and 19thC
fine art, 20thC pop and
contemporary art and local history
room.*
For further details see page 87

WEST SUSSEX

AMBERLEY MUSEUM
Houghton Bridge, Amberley,
Arundel, West Sussex
BN18 9LT
Tel: 01798 831370
*Open-air working museum on
36-acre site with craftsmen,
narrow gauge railway, motor
buses and electricity hall.*
For further details see page 87

ARUNDEL MUSEUM & HERITAGE CENTRE
61 High Street, Arundel, West
Sussex BN18 9AJ
Tel: 01903 882344
*Story of Arundel and its people,
including photographs, models,
tools, weapons and clothes, relating
to local trades and shipping.*

CHICHESTER DISTRICT MUSEUM
29 Little London, Chichester,
West Sussex PO19 1PB
Tel: 01243 784683
Fax: 01243 776766
*Museum displays history of
Chichester district including geology,
archaeology and social history. Also
hands-on activities and small gift
shop.*

COULTERSHAW WATER PUMP
Coultershaw Mill, Station Road,
Petworth, West Sussex
GU28 0JE
Tel: 01903 505626
*A waterwheel-driven beam pump
(1782) to supply Petworth house
and town. Also warehouse and lock
(1785) of Rother navigation.*

CRAWLEY MUSEUM CENTRE
Goffs Park House, Old Horsham
Road, Southgate, Crawley,
West Sussex RH11 8PE
Tel: 01293 539088
*Local history museum established in
1992.*

DOLL HOUSE MUSEUM
Station Road, Petworth, West
Sussex GU28 0BF
Tel: 01798 344044
Fax: 01798 343858
*Over 100 modern, inhabited and
furnished dolls' houses.*

EAST GRINSTEAD TOWN MUSEUM
East Court, College Lane, East
Grinstead, West Sussex
RH19 3LT
Tel: 01342 712087
*Upstairs wing of listed 1769
building in public park.*

FORGE NORTH AMERICAN INDIAN MUSEUM
Forge Cottage, The Green,
Horsted Keynes, Haywards
Heath, West Sussex RH17 7AT
Tel: 01825 790314
*Native American artefacts from the
period 1850–1990.*

THE GUILDHALL MUSEUM
Priory Park, Priory Road,
Chichester, West Sussex
Tel: 01243 784683
A 13thC church of the Greyfriars.

HENFIELD MUSEUM
(Henfield Parish Council)
Village Hall, High Street,
Henfield, West Sussex
BN5 9DB
Tel: 01273 492546
Fax: 01273 494898
*Small local-history museum
reflecting village life from
Victorian era to 1950s.*
For further details see page 87

HORSHAM MUSEUM
9 The Causeway, Horsham,
West Sussex RH12 1HE
Tel: 01403 254959
*Folk museum showing domestic and
rural life, local crafts, toys,
pre-history, geology and exotica.*

IFIELD WATERMILL
Hyde Drive, Ifield West,
Crawley, West Sussex
RH11 0PL
Tel: 01293 539088
*Partly restored corn mill in a
picturesque setting. Local history
and milling displays.*

LANNARDS GALLERY
Okehurst Road, Billingshurst,
West Sussex RH14 9HR
Tel: 01403 782692
Fax: 01403 786157
Octagonal cedarwood/pine gallery.

LITTLEHAMPTON MUSEUM
Manor House, Church Street,
Littlehampton, West Sussex
BN17 5EP
Tel: 01903 715149
Fax: 01903 731690
*Interesting local history/archaeology
museum with active display and
education programmes.*

MARLIPINS MUSEUM
High Street, Shoreham-by-Sea,
West Sussex BN43 5DA
Tel: 01273 462994
*A 12thC secular building with fine
architectural features housing
museum of the history of Shoreham
as a port with maritime paintings
and models.*

MECHANICAL MUSIC & DOLL COLLECTION
Church Road, Portfield,
Chichester, West Sussex
PO19 4HN
Tel: 01243 785421/372646
Fax: 01243 370299
*Extensive collection of fully restored
and working mechanical musical
items – street pianos, barrel organs,
music boxes, phonographs plus fine
Victorian dolls housed in Victorian
church.*

MUSEUM OF D-DAY AVIATION
Shoreham Airport,
Shoreham-by-Sea, West Sussex
PO20 7EF
Tel: 0374 971971
*Typhoon and Tempest Gallery,
Spitfire, uniforms, medals, special
D-Day section, Horsa Glider,
further aircraft, original air sea rescue
boat and RAF fire engines.*

PETWORTH COTTAGE MUSEUM
346 High Street, Petworth,
West Sussex GU28 0AU
Tel: 01798 342100
Fax: 01798 343467
*A Leconfield estate-worker's cottage
restored and furnished as it might
have been in about 1910 when the
estate was at the height of its power
and prosperity.*

THE ROYAL MILITARY POLICE MUSEUM
Rousillon Barracks, Broyle
Road, Chichester, West Sussex
PO19 4BN
Tel: 01243 534225
*Museum, in keep built 1803, now
home of Royal Military Police.*

SCULPTURE AT GOODWOOD
Hat Hill Copse, Goodwood,
Chichester, West Sussex
PO18 0QP
Tel: 01243 538449
Fax: 01243 531853
*A changing collection of
contemporary British sculpture set in
20 acres of beautiful grounds on the
South Downs overlooking
Chichester.*

STEYNING MUSEUM
The Museum, Church Street,
Steyning, West Sussex
BN44 3YB
Tel: 01903 813333
*The story of Steyning through the
ages, plus regular temporary
exhibitions.*

TANGMERE MILITARY AVIATION MUSEUM
Tangmere, Chichester, West
Sussex PO20 6ES
Tel: 01243 775223
Fax: 01243 789490
*Famous WW II fighter airfield now
museum containing relics, maps,
photos, displays, working models
and Spitfire simulator.*

WEALD & DOWNLAND OPEN AIR MUSEUM
Singleton, Chichester, West
Sussex PO18 0EU
Tel: 01243 811348
Fax: 01243 811475
*Open-air museum of rescued historic
buildings from south east England
reconstructed on Downland Country
Park site.*

WORTHING MUSEUM & ART GALLERY
Chapel Road, Worthing,
West Sussex BN11 1HP
Tel: 01903 239999 ext 2528
Fax: 01903 236277
*Local history, archaeology,
costume, toys and geology
exhibits.*
For further details see page 87

WEST YORKSHIRE

1853 GALLERY
Salts Mill, Victoria Road,
Saltaire, Shipley, West Yorkshire
BD18 3LB
Tel: 01274 531163
Fax: 01274 531184
*Comprehensive art galleries,
featuring David Hockney, situated
within this historic mill building.*

ARMLEY MILLS
Canal Road, Armley, Leeds,
West Yorkshire
Tel: 0113 263 7861
Fax: 0113 263 7861
*Once the world's largest woollen
mills, this museum is housed in a
unique fire-proof building of
1806, on an impressive island
site in the River Aire.*
For further details see page 88

AUTOMOBILIA TRANSPORT MUSEUM
Billy Lane, Old Town, Hebden
Bridge, West Yorkshire
HX7 8RX
Tel: 01422 844775
Fax: 01422 842884
*Unique collection of Austin 7s, a
range of pre-war Morris cars and
MG British motor cycles, bicycles,
fashion, war-time display and model
cars.*

BAGSHAW MUSEUM
Wilton Park, Batley, West
Yorkshire WF17 0AS
Tel: 01924 326155
Fax: 01924 326164
*Victorian mansion with objects from
around the world including ancient
Egypt, the Orient, Amazon
rainforest. Local and natural history.*

BANKFIELD MUSEUM
Boothtown Road, Halifax, West
Yorkshire HX3 6HG
Tel: 01422 354823
Fax: 01422 349020
*Mansion house of a 19thC
mill-owner now housing a large
costume/textile museum, military
museum and fine art displays.*

BATLEY ART GALLERY
Market Place, Batley, West
Yorkshire WF17 5DA
Tel: 01924 326090
Fax: 01924 326308
*Special exhibitions throughout the
year featuring contemporary art, craft
and photography.*

BRADFORD INDUSTRIAL & HORSES AT WORK MUSEUM
Moorside Mills, Moorside Road, Bradford, West Yorkshire BD2 3HP
Tel: 01274 631756
Fax: 01274 636362
Original 19thC spinning mill complex complete with mill owner's house, back-to-back cottages and job master's stables with working shire horses.

BRONTE PARSONAGE MUSEUM
Church Street, Haworth, Keighley, West Yorkshire BD22 8DR
Tel: 01535 642323
Fax: 01535 647131
Manuscripts, personal effects, furniture and drawings belonging to the Bronte family housed in this small Georgian parsonage which is furnished as in the Brontes' day.

CALDERDALE INDUSTRIAL MUSEUM
Central Works, Square Road, Halifax, West Yorkshire HX1 0QG
Tel: 01422 358087
Fax: 01422 349310
Discover how lives were changed by industrialisation.

CANAL MUSEUM
Savile Town Wharf, Mill Street East, Dewsbury, West Yorkshire WF12 9BD
Tel: 01924 467976
Waterways museum in stable buildings.

CARTWRIGHT HALL ART GALLERY
Lister Park, Bradford, West Yorkshire BD9 4NS
Tel: 01274 493313
Fax: 01274 481045
Built 1904, in Baroque style, as an art gallery.

CASTLEFORD MUSEUM ROOM
Castleford Library, Carlton Street, Castleford, West Yorkshire WF10 1BB
Tel: 01977 722085
Victorian Castleford – small hands-on display.

CLIFFE CASTLE MUSEUM
Spring Gardens Lane, Keighley, West Yorkshire BD20 6LH
Tel: 01535 618230
Fax: 01535 610536
Natural and social history of local area, local geology gallery, mineral gallery, local pottery, toys, dolls, games and temporary exhibitions.

COLNE VALLEY MUSEUM
Cliffe Ash, Golcar, Huddersfield HD7 4PY
Tel: 01484 659762
Three weaver's cottages of the 1840s with restored weaver's workshop, living room and reconstructed clog maker's workshop.

COLOUR MUSEUM
Perkin House, PO Box 244, Providence Street, Bradford, West Yorkshire BD1 2PW
Tel: 01274 390955
Fax: 01274 392888
Britain's only museum of colour uses visitor-operated exhibits to look at light-colour dyeing and textile printing.
For further details see page 88

DEAN CLOUGH
Dean Clough, Halifax, West Yorkshire HX3 5AX
Tel: 01422 344555
Fax: 01422 341148
A network of six stunning galleries showing contemporary art and design; Dean Clough is also home to the Henry Moore Studio, highly acclaimed Design House Restaurant and the Viaduce Theatre.

DEWSBURY ART GALLERY
Dewsbury Museum, Crow Nest Park, Heckmondwike Road, Dewsbury, West Yorkshire WF13 2SA
Tel: 01924 468171
Fax: 01924 464952
Permanent exhibition of children in art.

DEWSBURY MUSEUM
Crow Nest Park, Heckmondwike Road, Dewsbury, West Yorkshire WF13 2SA
Tel: 01924 325100
Fax: 01924 325109
Set in parkland and housed in the historic Crow Nest Mansion, Dewsbury Museum is devoted to the magical theme of childhood.

EUREKA! THE CHILDREN'S MUSEUM
Discovery Road, Halifax, West Yorkshire HX1 2NE
Tel: 01422 330069
Fax: 01422 300275
Eureka! is the first museum of its kind designed especially for children up to the age of 12 with over 400 hands-on exhibits.

FULNECK MORAVIAN MUSEUM
55–57 Fulneck, Pudsey, West Yorkshire LS28 8NT
Tel: 0113 256 4862
Two 17thC cottages, Victorian parlour and kitchen, weaving chamber, Moravian embroidery, folk exhibits and 1822 hand-pulled fire engine.

THE GISSING CENTRE
2–4 Thompson's Yard, Westgate, Wakefield, West Yorkshire WF1 2TP
Small suite of rooms in Georgian town house where novelist George Gissing lived from birth to age 13.

THE HENRY MOORE INSTITUTE
74 The Headrow, Leeds LS1 3AA
Tel: 0113 234 3158
Fax: 0113 246 1481
The Institute has four gallery spaces for temporary exhibitions.

HEPTONSTALL MUSEUM
Heptonstall, Hebden Bridge, West Yorkshire HX7
Tel: 01422 843738
Fax: 01422 843738
A 17thC stone school-building with old school-furniture and items of local domestic, historic and agricultural interest; includes coiners exhibition.

HORSFORTH MUSEUM
5 The Green, Horsforth, Leeds LS18 5JB
Tel: 0113 258 9411
Housed in former council chambers a small friendly local-history museum covering a wide range of aspects of Horsforth's past.

HUDDERSFIELD ART GALLERY
Princess Alexandra Walk, Huddersfield HD1 2SU
Tel: 01484 221964
Permanent collection of British paintings, drawings, sculpture and graphics from mid 19thC to date. Touring exhibitions programme.

KIRKSTALL ABBEY
Abbey Road, Kirkstall, Leeds, West Yorkshire LS5 3EH
Tel: 0113 275 5821
Fax: 0113 274 9439
Formerly great gatehouse to Abbey, three streets of full-size reconstructed shops and houses.
For further details see page 88

LAST OF THE SUMMER WINE EXHIBITION
Scarfold, off Hollowgate, Holmfirth, Huddersfield, West Yorkshire
Tel: 01484 681408
Collection of photographs and memorabilia connected with the television series 'Last of the Summer Wine'.

LEEDS CITY ART GALLERY
The Headrow, Leeds, West Yorkshire LS1 3AA
Tel: 0113 247 8248
Fax: 0113 244 9689
Art gallery containing paintings, sculptures, prints and drawings of the 19thC and 20thC.
For further details see page 88

LEEDS CITY MUSEUM
Municipal Buildings, The Headrow, Leeds, West Yorkshire LS1 3AA
Tel: 0113 247 8275
Collections are shown in natural history, multicultural and archaeological galleries with a particular emphasis on the Yorkshire region. Free admission.
For further details see page 88

LEEDS INDUSTRIAL MUSEUM
Armley Mills, Canal Road, Leeds LS12 2QF
Tel: 0113 263 7861
Built in 1806 and once the world's largest woollen mill, Armley now houses the city's varied collections of industrial history.

LOTHERTON HALL
Aberford, Leeds LS25 3EB
Tel: 0113 281 3259
Edwardian house with fine and decorative arts and furniture on display.

MANOR HOUSE
Castle Yard, Ilkley, West Yorkshire LS29 9DT
Tel: 01943 600066
A 17thC town school-building with old school-furniture and items of local domestic, historic and ... A picturesque Elizabethan building on the site of a Roman fort. Museum and art gallery.

MUSEUM OF THE HISTORY OF EDUCATION
Parkinson Court, University of Leeds, Leeds LS2 9JT
Tel: 0113 233 4665
Diverse collection of educational artefacts and documents housed in a small museum.

NATIONAL COAL MINING MUSEUM FOR ENGLAND
Caphouse Colliery, New Road, Overton, Wakefield, West Yorkshire WF4 4RH
Tel: 01924 848806
Fax: 01924 840694
Exciting award-winning museum of the English coalfields including guided underground tour in authentic old workings, surface displays and working steam winder.

NATIONAL MUSEUM OF PHOTOGRAPHY FILM & TELEVISION
Pictureville, Bradford, West Yorkshire BD1 1NQ
Tel: 01274 727488
Fax: 01274 394540
Free exhibitions, workshops and tours, on photography, film and television. Media education events, films and INSET also available.

OTLEY MUSEUM
Civic Centre, Cross Green, Otley, West Yorkshire LS21 1HD
Tel: 01943 461052
Museum holds a comprehensive collection of objects, artefacts and documentary material related to development of Otley and district since pre-historic period.

PIECE HALL ART GALLERY & CALDERDALE KALEIDOSCOPE
Halifax, West Yorkshire HX1 1PR
Tel: 01422 358087
Fax: 01422 349310
Regular changing programme of challenging contemporary exhibitions also the new Calderdale kaleidoscope display.

PONTEFRACT MUSEUM
Salter Row, Pontefract, West Yorkshire WF8 1BA
Tel: 01977 722741
Art Nouveau building of considerable interest; the museum has displays on archaeology and history of ancient borough of Pontefract from pre-historic times to recent past.

ROYAL ARMOURIES
Armories Drive, Leeds, West Yorkshire LS10 1LT
Tel: 0113 220 1990
Fax: 0113 220 1997
History in action at Britain's newest museum.

SANDAL CASTLE
Manygates Lane, Wakefield, West Yorkshire
Tel: 01924 305796
Ruins of the 13thC stone castle of the Warenne family. Excavation finds displayed in Wakefield Museum. Open dawn to dusk all year. Access for wheelchair users.
For further details see page 89

SHIBDEN HALL
Lister's Road, Halifax, West Yorkshire HX3 6XG
Tel: 01422 352246
Fax: 01422 348440
Early 15thC half-timber-framed house with period room settings from 17thC; barn with collection of horse-drawn vehicles, outhouses and workshops.

SMITH ART GALLERY
Halifax Road, Brighouse, West Yorkshire HD6 2AF
Tel: 01484 719222
Fax: 01484 719222
Two fine-art galleries purpose-built at the turn of the century, now housing a wide range of temporary exhibitions of art and craft.

TEMPLE NEWSAM HOUSE
Leeds, West Yorkshire LS15 0AE
Tel: 0113 264 7321
Fax: 0113 260 2285
A furnished Jacobean/Tudor house with a collection of fine and decorative arts.

TETLEY'S BREWERY WHARF
The Waterfront, Leeds LS1 1QG
Tel: 0113 242 0666
Fax: 0113 245 1925
Brings to life the story through the ages of probably the greatest of British traditions – the pub, tour, museum and shire horses.

THACKRAY MEDICAL MUSEUM
Beckett Street, Leeds, West Yorkshire LS9 7LN
Tel: 0113 244 4343
Fax: 0113 247 0219
Explore the sights, sounds and smells of Victorian slum life. Find out how people really lived 150 years ago. Look into keyhole surgery and walk through a giant gut.
For further details see page 88

THWAITE MILLS
Thwaite Lane, Stourton, Leeds, West Yorkshire LS10 1RP
Tel: 0113 249 6453
Fax: 0113 277 6737
Two 18ft working waterwheels, extensive water-powered grinding machinery, three-storey Victorian mill building and engineering workshops with blacksmith's forge.
For further details see page 88

UNIVERSITY GALLERY LEEDS
Parkinson Building, Woodhouse Lane, Leeds LS2 9JT
Tel: 0113 233 2777
Changing displays from the University's collection of 19thC and 20thC British art and busy temporary exhibition schedule.

VICTORIAN REED ORGAN MUSEUM
Victoria Hall, Victoria Road, Saltaire, Shipley, West Yorkshire BD18
Tel: 01274 585601
A display of approximately 75 reed organs in this private collection – from tiny Book harmonium to large three manual and pedal, there is also advertising material from the period.

VINTAGE RAILWAY CARRIAGE MUSEUM
Ingrow Railway Station, Ingrow, Keighley, West Yorkshire BD21 1AH
Tel: 01535 680425
Fax: 01535 646472
Collection of historic railway coaches plus elderly steam locomotives, used in over 30 television productions.

WAKEFIELD ART GALLERY
Wentworth Terrace,
Wakefield, West Yorkshire
WF1 3QW
Tel: 01924 305796
Fax: 01924 305770
Significant early sculptures by Henry Moore and Barbara Hepworth. Important work by other major British artists, European schools and other periods.
For further details see page 89

WAKEFIELD MUSEUM
Wood Street, Wakefield, West
Yorkshire WF1 2EW
Tel: 01924 305351
The story of Wakefield and its complex history. Also the exotic and eccentric natural history collections of Victorian explorer, Charles Waterton.
For further details see page 89

YORKSHIRE SCULPTURE PARK
Bretton Hall, West Bretton,
Wakefield, West Yorkshire
WF4 4LG
Tel: 01924 830642
Fax: 01924 830614
A leading international open-air gallery with changing exhibitions of contemporary sculpture is set within 260 acres of beautiful 18thC landscaped grounds.

WILTSHIRE

ALEXANDER KEILLER MUSEUM
Avebury, Marlborough,
Wiltshire SN8 1RF
Tel: 01672 539250
Founded by Alexander Keiller in 1930s the museum contains one of the most important pre-historic archaeology collections in Britain.

ATHELSTAN MUSEUM
Cross Hayes, Malmesbury,
Wiltshire SN16 9BZ
Tel: 01666 822143
Exhibits of local history including coins minted in Malmesbury, lace-making displays, early fire engine and tricycle.

ATWELL-WILSON MOTOR MUSEUM
Downside, Stockley Lane,
Calne, Wiltshire SN11 0NF
Tel: 01249 813119
Motor museum with vintage, post-vintage and classic cars, including American models.

ATWORTH MUSEUM
Poplar Farm Barn, Bradford
Road, Atworth, Melksham,
Wiltshire SN12 8HY
Tel: 01225 852160
Local history of the village.

BEDWYN STONE MUSEUM
Great Bedwyn, Marlborough,
Wiltshire SN8 3NX
Tel: 01672 870234
Fax: 01672 871211
The exhibits consist of a large number of carved stone features, mostly humorous.

BRADFORD-ON-AVON MUSEUM
Bridge Street,
Bradford-on-Avon, Wiltshire
BA15 1BY
Tel: 01225 863280
Fax: 01225 868647
The main feature of the museum is the re-creation of the Christopher Pharmacy which was opened in 1863 and closed in 1986.

CRICKLADE MUSEUM
16 Calcutt Street, Cricklade,
Swindon, Wiltshire SN6 6BB
Tel: 01793 750756
Local archaeology, Roman site and Saxon town details, pictures, bygones and local history.

DEVIZES MUSEUM
41 Long Street, Devizes,
Wiltshire SN10 1NS
Tel: 01380 727369
Fax: 01380 722150
Archaeological displays and exhibitions including finds from important Bronze Age, Iron Age and Roman sites in Wiltshire.
For further details see page 89

FOX TALBOT MUSEUM OF PHOTOGRAPHY
Lacock, Chippenham, Wiltshire
SN15 2LG
Tel: 01249 730459
Museum dedicated to the life and work of William Henry Fox Talbot inventor of the positive/negative photographic process.

GREAT WESTERN RAILWAY MUSEUM
Faringdon Road, Swindon,
Wiltshire SN1 5BJ
Tel: 01793 466555
Fax: 01793 484073
Historic Great Western Railway locomotives, wide range of nameplates, models, illustrations, posters and tickets.

JOHN CREASEY MUSEUM
The Library, Market Place,
Salisbury, Wiltshire SP1 1BL
Tel: 01722 324145
Gallery devoted to contemporary art.

THE KENNET & AVON CANAL MUSEUM
The Canal Centre Couch Lane,
Devizes, Wiltshire SN10 1EB
Tel: 01380 721279
Fax: 01380 727870
Exhibition tells of the creation of the waterways link connecting London and Bristol which emerged as a direct result of the Industrial Revolution.

MARKET LAVINGTON MUSEUM
Church Street, Market
Lavington, Devizes, Wiltshire
SN10 4DT
Tel: 01380 818736
All aspects of life in the village of Market Lavington up to the present day.

MERE LIBRARY & MUSEUM
Barton Lane, Church Street,
Mere, Warminster, Wiltshire
BA12 6SA
Tel: 01747 860546
Displays of local history and items of general interest which change at approximately two-monthly intervals.

RAILWAY VILLAGE MUSEUM
34 Faringdon Road, Swindon,
Wiltshire SN1 5BJ
Tel: 01793 466555
Fax: 01793 484073
Foreman's house in original Great Western Railway village.

RICHARD JEFFERIES MUSEUM
Marlborough Road, Coate,
Swindon, Wiltshire SN3 6AA
Tel: 01793 463000 ext 6561
Farmhouse in which Jefferies was born.

THE ROYAL GLOUCESTERSHIRE BERKSHIRE & WILTSHIRE REG MUSEUM
The Wardrobe, Cathedral Close,
Salisbury, Wiltshire SP1 2EX
Tel: 01722 414536
Collections include uniforms, silver, medals, paintings, photographs, textiles, historic house and gardens.

ST PETER'S CHURCH
High Street, Marlborough,
Wiltshire SN8 1HQ
Tel: 01672 511453
Permanent art and crafts display, coffee and snacks, and book shop in an historic redundant church.

SALISBURY & SOUTH WILTSHIRE MUSEUM
The King's House, 65 The
Close, Salisbury, Wiltshire
SP1 2EN
Tel: 01722 332151
Fax: 01722 325611
Outstanding archaeology, (Stonehenge, early man, Pitt Rivers collection), Salisbury history, ceramics, costume, arts, exhibitions, six awards, Grade I listed.

SWINDON MUSEUM & ART GALLERY
Bath Road, Swindon, Wiltshire
SN1 4BA
Tel: 01793 493188
Fax: 01793 541685
Archaeology, geology and social history of Swindon and North Wiltshire.

THE TROWBRIDGE MUSEUM
The Shires, Court Street,
Trowbridge, Wiltshire
BA14 8AT
Tel: 01225 751339
Fax: 01225 777147
Living history, Trowbridge history and archaeology, working with wool, Victorian times and schooldays, the home front, and the Tudors.

WARMINSTER DEWEY MUSEUM
Warminster Library, Three
Horseshoes Mall, Warminster,
Wiltshire BA12 9BT
Tel: 01985 216022
Exhibition of the local history of Warminster and the surrounding district including the Manley collection of fossils.

THE WILTON CARPET FACTORY LTD
King Street, Wilton, Salisbury,
Wiltshire SP2 0AY
Tel: 01722 744919
Fax: 01722 744445
Manufacture of carpet.

WILTSHIRE FIRE DEFENCE & BRIGADES MUSEUM
Fire Brigade Headquarters, The
Manor House, Potterne,
Devizes, Wiltshire SN10 5PP
Tel: 01380 723601
Fax: 01380 727000
Fire defence collection of Wiltshire with examples of early hand pumps, uniforms, helmets, fire fighting equipment, breathing apparatus, photographs and documents.

YELDE HALL MUSEUM
Market Place, Chippenham,
Wiltshire
Tel: 01249 651488
Local collections of photographs and artefacts.

NORTHERN IRELAND

BELFAST

ARCHES GALLERY
2 Holywood Road, Belfast
BT4 1NT
Tel: 01232 459031
A wide variety of paintings mainly by Irish artists.

BELFAST CITY HALL
Donegall Square, Belfast
Tel: 01232 320202 ext 2346
Magnificent building of Portland stone, completed 1906.

BELL GALLERY
13 Adelaide Park, Belfast
BT9 6FX
Tel: 01232 662998
Changing programme of contemporary Irish art.

CAVEHILL GALLERY
18 Old Cavehill Road, Belfast
Tel: 01232 776784
Various exhibitions. Two large group shows annually. Painting and sculpture with some Batik/stitch.

EAKIN GALLERY
237 Lisburn Road, Belfast
Tel: 01232 668522
Mixed exhibitions of contemporary Irish artists.

FENDERESKY GALLERY
2 University Road, Belfast
BT7 1NH
Tel: 01232 235245
Fax: 01232 246748
Temporary exhibitions of paintings and sculpture, video and installation works by contemporary Irish artists.

FERNHILL HOUSE: THE PEOPLE'S MUSEUM
Glencairn Road, Glencairn, Belfast BT13 3PT
Tel: 01232 715599
Fax: 01232 715582
The history of Greater Shankill and the story of the people from the early 19thC to the present.

LAGAN LOOKOUT CENTRE
1 Donegall Quay, Belfast
BT1 3EA
Tel: 01232 315444
Fax: 01232 311955
Background to the River Lagan's weir explained, with industrial and folk history of the harbour. Bus tour of Laganside development sites.

THE MAGEE GALLERY
455–457 Ormeau Road, Belfast
BT57 3GQ
Tel: 01232 693830
Permanent display of paintings by Irish and European artists, with temporary shows.

NORTHERN IRELAND WAR MEMORIAL BUILDING
9–13 Waring Street, Belfast
BT1 2DW
Tel: 01232 320392
Exhibition depicting Northern Ireland during the Second World War, with a section on air raids.

OLD MUSEUM ARTS CENTRE
7 College Square North, Belfast
BT1 6AR
Tel: 01232 235053
Monthly exhibitions, mainly from emerging artists, with a focus on lens-based work and installations.

ORMEAU BATHS GALLERY
18a Ormeau Avenue, Belfast
BT2 8HS
Tel: 01232 321402
Continuous programme of monthly shows featuring a wide range of contemporary work by Irish artists.

QUEEN'S VISITOR CENTRE
Queen's University, University Road, Belfast
Tel: 01232 335252
Historical exhibitions and memorabilia on Queen's University.

ROYAL ULSTER CONSTABULARY MUSEUM
Brooklyn, Knock Road, Belfast
BT5 6LE
Tel: 01232 650222
Uniforms, photographs and equipment of the Irish Constabulary since its formation in 1822.

ROYAL ULSTER RIFLES MUSEUM
War Memorial Building, Waring Street, Belfast BT1 2EW
Tel: 01232 232086
Preserved relics of the Royal Ulster Rifles and its predecessor foot regiments raised in 1793 plus the World War II exhibition.

TANK GALLERY
75a Fitzwilliam Street, Belfast
Tel: 01232 230500
Irish contemporary art.

TOM CALDWELL GALLERY
40–42 Bradbury Place, Belfast
BT7 1RT
Tel: 01232 323226
Contemporary Irish and British painting, sculpture and ceramics.

ULSTER MUSEUM
Botanic Gardens, Stranmillis Road, Belfast BT9 5AB
Tel: 01232 383000
Fax: 01232 383003
Noted for its Irish antiquities, art collections and natural sciences. New early Ireland gallery, handling sessions and tours of art galleries.

YELLOW BLUE GALLERY
Boucher Crescent, Belfast
Tel: 01232 660791
Irish art.

COUNTY ANTRIM

ANDREW JACKSON CENTRE
Boneybefore, Larne Road, Carrickfergus, County Antrim
BT38 7DG
Tel: 01960 366455
Site of ancestral home of Andrew Jackson, 7th US President (1829–1837), with exhibition on his life and career.

ARTHUR ANCESTRAL HOME
Dreen, Cullybackey, Ballymena, County Antrim BT42 2DE
Tel: 01266 880781
Ancestral home of Chester Alan Arthur, 21st US President (1881–1885).

BALLANCE HOUSE
118a Lisburn Road, Glenavy, County Antrim
Tel: 01846 648492
Birthplace of John Ballance, New Zealand prime minister 1891–1893.

BALLYCASTLE MUSEUM
59 Castle Street, Ballycastle, County Antrim BT54 6AS
Tel: 012657 62942
Folk social history of the Glens in the town's 18thC courthouse.

BALLYMONEY MUSEUM & HERITAGE CENTRE
33 Charlotte Street, Ballymoney, County Antrim
Tel: 012656 62280
Exhibits on Ballymoney and north Antrim.

BROOKHALL HISTORICAL FARM
2 Horse Park, Magheragall, Lisburn, Co. Antrim BT28 2QU
Tel: 01846 621712
Farming museum with duck pond, animals, gardens and display of farming tools.

CARRICKFERGUS GASWORKS
Irish Quarter West, Carrickfergus, County Antrim
BT38 8AS
Tel: 01960 351438
Exhibition of gas making machinery and gas equipment.

CASTLECAT STUDIO GALLERY
76 Castlecat Road, Bushmills, County Antrim BT57 8TW
Tel: 01265 741682
Studio gallery showing contemporary paintings by James McNulty.

CAUSEWAY SCHOOL MUSEUM
Causeway Road, Bushmills, County Antrim BT57 8SU
Tel: 012657 31777
Fax: 012657 32142
Take your desk in a 1920s classroom with inkwells and splodgy pens.

CLOTWORTHY ARTS CENTRE
Antrim Castle Gardens, Randalstown Road, Antrim, County Antrim BT41 4LH
Tel: 01849 428000
Exhibits a variety of work from a worldwide selection of artists with up to three temporary displays running concurrently.

DUNLUCE CENTRE
10 Sandhill Drive, Portrush, County Antrim BT56 8BF
Tel: 01265 824444
Fax: 01265 825125
Special effects show of local history and folklore, hi-tech interactive nature trail and an action/adventure motion simulation thrill ride.

DUNSEVERICK MUSEUM
Dunseverick Harbour, Bushmills, County Antrim
Nautical exhibits include Spanish Armada artefacts, a steamboat gauge and recovered coat from 'Titanic'.

FORD FARM PARK & MUSEUM
8 Low Road, Islandmagee, County Antrim BT40 3RD
Tel: 01960 353264
Small country museum in former farm outhouse with fishing nets, lobster pots and farming implements.

GIANT'S CAUSEWAY CENTRE
44 Causeway Road, Bushmills, County Antrim BT57 8SU
Tel: 012657 31855
Fax: 012657 32537
Geology, flora and fauna of the region.

HARMONY HILL ARTS CENTRE
54 Harmony Hill, Lisburn, County Antrim BT27 4ES
Tel: 01846 678219
Temporary shows, mainly displaying work from local and touring visual arts exhibitors. Arts and crafts classes and workshops.

IRISH LINEN CENTRE & LISBURN MUSEUM
Market Square, Lisburn, County Antrim BT28 1AG
Tel: 01846 663377
Fax: 01846 672624
Ulster's greatest industry re-created with weaving workshop, hand looms and audio visuals.

KNIGHT RIDE
Antrim Street, Carrickfergus, County Antrim BT38 7DG
Tel: 01960 366455
Fax: 01960 350350
Monorail ride through the history of Carrickfergus from 581AD.

LARNE & DISTRICT HISTORICAL CENTRE
Old Carnegie Library, 2 Victoria Road, Larne, County Antrim BT40 1RN
Tel: 01574 279482
Exhibits include a country kitchen from the turn of the century, a smithy and family history material.

LARNE INTERPRETIVE CENTRE
Tourist Information Centre, Narrow Gauge Road, Larne, County Antrim BT40 1XB
Tel: 01574 260088
Story of the building of the Antrim Coast Road.

LESLIE HILL FARM PARK
Ballymoney, County Antrim
Tel: 01265 666803
Horse-trap and pony rides through an 18thC estate; includes museum, adventure playground and walled garden.

MILLTOWN HOUSE GALLERY
35 Derriaghy Road, Lisburn, County Antrim BT28 3SQ
Tel: 01232 301328
Private house with a programme that concentrates mainly on fine art exhibitions. See Arts Link Ireland for dates, or by appointment.

MORROW'S SHOP MUSEUM
13 Bridge Street, Ballymena, County Antrim
Tel: 01266 653663
Local history exhibits.

OLD BUSHMILLS DISTILLERY
2 Distillery Road, Bushmills, County Antrim BT57 8XH
Tel: 01265 731521
Fax: 01265 731339
Oldest whiskey distillery in the world, established in 1608. Guided tour of whiskey making process and whiskey tasting

RATHLIN ISLAND BOATHOUSE CENTRE
The Harbour, Rathlin Island, County Antrim
Tel: 01265 763591
History and photographs on Rathlin Island – six miles from Ballycastle on the north Antrim coast.

ROYAL IRISH REGIMENT MUSEUM
St Patrick's Barracks, Ballymena, County Antrim
Tel: 01266 661383

VILLAGE GALLERY
4 Bendooragh Road, Bendooragh, Ballymoney, County Antrim BT53 7ND
Tel: 01265 665528
Traditional and contemporary Irish art.

WATERTOP OPEN FARM
188 Cushendall Road, Ballyvoy, Ballycastle, County Antrim BT54 6RL
Tel: 012657 62576
Farm tours, sheep shearing (July–August), ornamental game birds, museum.

COUNTY ARMAGH

ARMAGH COUNTY MUSEUM
The Mall East, Armagh
BT61 9BE
Tel: 01861 523070
Fax: 01861 522631
Prehistory of the city and county with costumes, natural history room, library and art gallery.

ARMAGH PLANETARIUM
College Hill, Armagh
BT61 9DB
Tel: 01861 523689
Fax: 01861 526187
Explore the universe with hands-on computers in the Hall of Astronomy.

CARDINAL O'FIAICH HERITAGE CENTRE
Slatequarry Road, Cullyhanna, County Armagh BT35 0JH
Tel: 01693 868757
Fax: 01693 868757
Exhibition on Cardinal Tomas O'Fiaich (1923–90) who was born near Cullyhanna.

DAN WINTER'S ANCESTRAL HOME
9 The Diamond, Derryloughran Road, Loughgall, County Armagh BT61 8PH
Tel: 01762 851344
Maps and relics of the Battle of the Diamond (1795).

LOUGH NEAGH DISCOVERY CENTRE
Oxford Island, Craigavon, County Armagh BT66 6NJ
Tel: 01762 322205
Fax: 01762 347438
The wildlife, history and management of Lough Neagh and Oxford Island are interpreted here.

MULLAGHBAWN FOLK MUSEUM
Tullymacrieve, Mullaghbawn, County Armagh
Tel: 01693 888278
Thatched roadside museum furnished as a traditional farmhouse.

NAVAN (EMAIN MACHA) CENTRE
81 Killylea Road, Armagh, County Armagh BT60 4LD
Tel: 01861 525550
The hillfort, capital of the Kings of Ulster from 600BC, is interpreted at the nearby Navan Centre.

PALACE STABLES HERITAGE CENTRE
Friary Road, Armagh BT60 4EL
Tel: 01861 529629
Guided tour of 'A Day in the life of the Palace' (1776), plus living history characters bringing the experience to life.

ROYAL IRISH FUSILIERS MUSEUM
Sovereign's House, The Mall,
Armagh BT61 9DL
Tel: 01861 522911
Story of the regiment (1793–1968).

SAINT PATRICK'S TRIAN
40 English Street, Armagh
BT61 7BA
Tel: 01861 521801
Fax: 01861 528329
The Armagh Story and The Land of Lilliput (an adaptation of Swift's Gulliver's Travels).

COUNTY DOWN

ARDS ART CENTRE
Town Hall, Conway Square,
Newtownards, County Down
BT23 4DB
Tel: 01247 810803
Programme of exhibitions featuring contemporary artists from Northern Ireland, examining a wide range of media, accompanied by art-lab workshop series.

THE ART GALLERY HILLSBOROUGH
12 Main Street, Hillsborough,
County Down BT26 6AE
Tel: 01846 689896
Ongoing programme of temporary exhibitions, often displaying paintings by contemporary young artists.

THE BAY TREE GALLERY
118 High Street, Holywood,
County Down BT18 9HW
Tel: 01232 426414
Frequently updated selection of exhibitions, the majority of which feature work by local artists.

BRONTE HOMELAND INTERPRETIVE CENTRE
Churchill Road,
Drumballyroney, Rathfriland,
County Down BT34 5PH
Tel: 018206 31152
Drumballyroney school and church, where Patrick Bronte, father of the novelist sisters, taught and preached, both built in 1780.

BURREN HERITAGE CENTRE
15 Bridge Road, Burren,
Warrenpoint, County Down
BT34 3QT
Tel: 016937 73378
Interpretation of the Burren district of South Down from prehistory to the 16thC.

DOWN COUNTY MUSEUM
The Mall, English Street,
Downpatrick, County Down
BT30 6AH
Tel: 01396 615218
Fax: 01396 615590
Restored county gaol with cells plus history of County Down. Special events and schools programme.

MUSEUM OF CHILDHOOD
92 Main Street, Saintfield,
County Down
Tel: 01238 519270
Thousands of toys, books, prams and clothes from the Victorian era to the 1960s.

NEWRY MUSEUM & ARTS CENTRE (CARROLL GALLERY)
Bank Parade, Newry, County
Down BT35 6HP
Tel: 01693 66232
History of the Gap of the North, robes of the Order of St Patrick and Nelson's table from HMS Victory.

NORTH DOWN HERITAGE CENTRE
Town Hall, Bangor Castle,
Bangor, County Down
BT20 4BT
Tel: 01247 271200
Fax: 01247 271370
The Ballycroghan Swords, dating from 500BC, and a 900AD handbell found near Bangor.

ROUTE 66
94 Dundrum Road, Newcastle,
County Down BT33 0LN
Tel: 01396 725223
American automobiles from the 1930s including a 1959 Cadillac.

SCARVA VISITOR CENTRE
Main Street, Scarva, County
Down BT63
Tel: 01762 832163
History of canals in Ireland, the building of the Newry canal and the history of Scarva.

SOMME HERITAGE CENTRE
233 Bangor Road,
Newtownards, County Down
BT23 7PH
Tel: 01247 823202
Fax: 01247 823202
Reconstruction of elements of the Battle of the Somme in 1916.

ULSTER FOLK & TRANSPORT MUSEUM
153 Bangor Road, Cultra,
Holywood, County Down
BT18 0EU
Tel: 01232 428428
Fax: 01232 427925
Some 30 buildings showing urban and rural Ulster social history c1900. Extensive transport galleries. All forms of transport.

COUNTY FERMANAGH

CARROTHERS FAMILY HERITAGE MUSEUM
Carrybridge Road, Tamlaght,
Lisbellaw, County Fermanagh
BT74 4NN
Tel: 01365 387278
Small private museum preserves a thousand items collected by the Carrothers family.

CASTLE ARCHDALE COUNTRY PARK: VISITOR CENTRE
Three miles south of Kesh,
County Fermanagh
Tel: 01365 621588
Exhibition on the Battle of the Atlantic.

DEVENISH ISLAND
Lough Erne, County Fermanagh
Famous for its perfect 12thC round tower and ruined Augustinian abbey, the island also has a small museum.

ENNISKILLEN CASTLE
Castle Barracks, Enniskillen,
County Fermanagh BT74 7HL
Tel: 01365 325000
Fax: 01365 327342
Famous castle, once the stronghold of Gaelic Chieftains, with exhibitions on the Maguires and the landscape and people of Fermanagh.

EXPLORE ERNE EXHIBITION
Gateway Centre, Corry,
Belleek, County Fermanagh
Tel: 01365 658866
The story of the formation of Lough Erne and its effect on the people who live around its shores.

FOLKLIFE DISPLAY
Lisnaskea Library, Drumhaw,
Lisnaskea, County Fermanagh
BT92 0JB
Tel: 01365 721222
Exhibition of rural life in Fermanagh.

ROSLEA HERITAGE CENTRE
Monaghan Road, Roslea,
County Fermanagh BT92 7QY
Tel: 01365 751750
An 1874 schoolhouse with old school desks.

VINTAGE CYCLE MUSEUM
64 Main Street, Brookeborough,
County Fermanagh
Tel: 01365 531206
Over 60 bicycles on show including an 1870s bike with levers.

COUNTY LONDONDERRY

BELLAGHY BAWN
Castle Street, Bellaghy, County
Londonderry
Tel: 01648 386812
Exhibits include local history and the writings of Bellaghy-born Seamus Heaney and other living Northern poets.

EARHART CENTRE & WILDLIFE SANCTUARY
Ballyarnet Racecourse Society,
Racecourse Road, Ballyarnet,
Londonderry BT48 7UF
Tel: 01504 354040
Cottage exhibition on Amelia Earhart, the first woman to fly the Atlantic solo, who landed in the field here in 1932.

THE FIFTH PROVINCE
Calgach Centre, Butcher Street,
Londonderry
Tel: 01504 373177
The history of the Celts in Ireland

FOYLE VALLEY RAILWAY CENTRE
Foyle Road, Londonderry BT48
Tel: 01504 265234
Features working models and narrow gauge networks.

GARVAGH MUSEUM & HERITAGE CENTRE
Garvagh High School, Main
Street, Garvagh, County
Londonderry
Tel: 01266 557924
Farming implements, eel fishing boat, Stone Age artefacts, jaunting car and Victorian clothes. Victorian kitchen and bedroom, rock fossil collection.

HARBOUR MUSEUM
Harbour Square, Londonderry
Tel: 01504 377331
The maritime history of Derry City.

MCGILLOWAY GALLERY
Shipquay Street, Londonderry
BT48 6ND
Tel: 01504 366011
Modern Irish paintings.

ORCHARD GALLERY
14 Bishop Street, Londonderry
BT48 6PW
Tel: 01504 269675
Displays of photographs, paintings and recordings relating to local history, with an ongoing programme of temporary exhibitions.

PLANTATION OF ULSTER VISITOR CENTRE
50 High Street, Draperstown,
County Londonderry
Tel: 01648 28113
The story of the Ulster Plantation in the 1600s.

RIVERSIDE THEATRE GALLERY
Riverside Theatre, University of
Ulster, Coleraine, County
Londonderry BT52 1SA
Tel: 01265 324449
Holds monthly exhibitions featuring a wide range of work.

ST COLUMB'S CATHEDRAL
Londonderry
Tel: 01504 267313
Built in 1633, the Cathedral includes audio-visuals on the seige of 1688/9 and the history of the cathedral.

SPRINGHILL
Moneymore, Magherafelt,
Co. Londonderry BT45 7NQ
Tel: 01648 748210
Fax: 01648 748210
Costume museum in the grounds of a 17thC manor house.

TOWER MUSEUM
Union Hall Place,
Londonderry, County
Londonderry BT48 6LU
Tel: 01504 372411
History of the city from prehistoric times.
For further details see page 89

COUNTY TYRONE

AN CREAGAN VISITOR CENTRE
Mid Ulster Enterprises –
Creggan Ltd, Creggan, Omagh,
County Tyrone BT79 9AF
Tel: 01662 761112
Fax: 01662 761116
Archaeology, history, natural environment and culture of Creggan and the Sperrins.

BENBURB VALLEY HERITAGE CENTRE
89 Tullymore Road, Benburb,
County Tyrone BT71 7LZ
Tel: 01861 549752
Fax: 01861 549713
This 19thC weaving factory preserves an impressive array of machinery used in linen making.

CASTLEDERG VISITOR CENTRE
26 Lower Strabane Road,
Castlederg, County Tyrone
Tel: 01662 670795
Stories from the area on hi-tech video wall, plus model of the Alamo Fort.

COACH & CARRIAGE MUSEUM
Blessingbourne, Fivemiletown,
County Tyrone BT75 0QS
Tel: 01365 521221
Among the numerous coaches on display is an 1825 London to Oxford stagecoach. Also non-flying helicopter.

CORNMILL HERITAGE CENTRE
Limeside, Coalisland, County
Tyrone BT71 4LP
Tel: 01868 748532
Story of Coalisland's industrial history.

DONAGHMORE HERITAGE CENTRE
Pomeroy Road, Donaghmore,
County Tyrone BT70 3HG
Tel: 01868 767039
Fax: 01868 767663
Converted national school (1883) preserves photographs, townland maps, documents and artefacts from local industries.

GRAY'S PRINTER MUSEUM
49 Main Street, Strabane,
County Tyrone BT82 8AU
Tel: 01504 884094
Display of 19thC hand printing presses.

KINTURK CULTURAL CENTRE
7 Kinturk Road, Cookstown,
County Tyrone
Tel: 016487 36512
History of the Lough Neagh fishing and eel industry.

NEWTOWNSTEWART GATEWAY CENTRE
Grange Court Complex, 21–27
Moyle Road, Newtownstewart,
County Tyrone BT78 4AP
Tel: 01662 662414
Exhibition of militaria, old toys, Victoriana, and photographic and agricultural equipment.

SPERRIN HERITAGE CENTRE
274 Glenelly Road, Plumbridge,
County Tyrone
Tel: 01662 648142
Natural history and gold-mining exhibits.

TOURIST INFORMATION CENTRE GALLERY
1 Market Street, Omagh,
County Tyrone BT78 1EE
Tel: 01662 245321
Fax: 01662 243888
Displays mixed media exhibitions by local and touring artists.

ULSTER HISTORY PARK
Cullion, Omagh, County
Tyrone BT79 7SU
Tel: 01662 648188
Fax: 01662 648011
Human history of settlement in Ireland from 8000BC to the 17thC.

ULSTER-AMERICAN FOLK PARK
2 Mellon Road, Castletown,
Omagh, County Tyrone
BT78 5QY
Tel: 01662 243292
The story of 200 years of emigration to North America.
For further details see page 89

THE US GRANT HOMESTEAD
45 Dergina Road,
Dungannon, County Tyrone
BT70 1TW
Tel: 01662 557133
House of grandfather of Ulysses Simpson Grant, 18th US President (1869–77). Visitor centre. Agricultural implements display. Pond and wildlife garden.

WILSON ANCESTRAL HOME
Dergalt, Strabane, Co. Tyrone
Tel: 01504 883735
This thatched white-washed house belonged to the grandfather of Woodrow Wilson, 28th US president 1913–21.

SCOTLAND

ABERDEEN

ABERDEEN

ABERDEEN ART GALLERY
Schoolhill, Aberdeen
AB10 1FQ
Tel: 01224 646333
Fax: 01224 632133
Permanent collection of 18th–20thC art with emphasis on contemporary art, oil paintings, watercolours, prints, drawings, sculpture and decorative arts.
For further details see page 90

ABERDEEN MARITIME MUSEUM
Shiprow, Aberdeen AB1 2BY
Tel: 01224 337700
Display themes on local shipbuilding, fishing, North Sea oil, ship models and paintings with a major new complex opened in 1997.
For further details see page 90

CARNEGIE MUSEUM
The Town Hall, Inverurie,
Aberdeen AB51 9SN
Tel: 01771 622906
Local history museum specialising in archaeology.

GALLERY HEINZEL
21 Spa Street, Aberdeen
AB1 1PU
Tel: 01224 625629

GORDON HIGHLANDERS MUSEUM
St Lukes, Viewfield Road,
Aberdeen, Grampian AB1 7XH
Tel: 01224 318174
Exhibitions of paintings, weapons, uniforms, colours and trophies of the famous regiment. Audio-visual theatre.

JONAH'S JOURNEY
Rosemount Place, Aberdeen
AB2 4YW
Tel: 01224 620111/648041
An ancient world, third world educational daytrip.

MARISCHAL MUSEUM
University of Aberdeen,
Marischal College, Aberdeen
AB10 1YS
Tel: 01224 274301
Fax: 01224 645519
Houses objects from all over the world collected by generations of friends and graduates of the university.

PROVOST SKENE'S HOUSE
Guestrow (off Broad Street),
Aberdeen AB10 1AS
Tel: 01224 641086
17thC furnished house with period room settings and displays of local history, domestic life and archaeology.
For further details see page 90

THE TOLBOOTH
Castle Street, Aberdeen
Tel: 01224 621167
Fax: 01224 632133
Originally the city's prison, it brings the history of Aberdeen to life and tells how the witches, debtors, criminals and felons incarcerated there, spent their days.
For further details see page 90

ABERDEENSHIRE

ABERDEENSHIRE FARMING MUSEUM
Aden Country Park, Mintlaw,
by Peterhead, Aberdeenshire
AB42 8QF
Tel: 01771 622906
Fax: 01771 622884
Relive the story of the North East farming life over the last 200 years in the Aden Estate Story. Visit Hareshowe, a working farm set in the 1950s. Award winning displays and audio visual shows.

ARBUTHNOT MUSEUM
St Peter Street, Peterhead,
Aberdeenshire AB42 1QD
Tel: 01779 477778
Fax: 01771 622884
Local history museum including fishing and whaling section, large local photograph collection and temporary exhibitions programme.

BANCHORY MUSEUM
Bridge Street, Banchory,
Kincardineshire AB42 5QF
Tel: 01771 622906
Displays on local history and wildlife. Features the life of Banchory born musician and composer J. Scott Skinner.

BANFF MUSEUM
High Street, Banff, Grampian
Tel: 01771 622906
One of Scotland's oldest museums, founded in 1823. Award winning natural history display, local geography and collection of Banff silver, arms and armour.

BRANDER MUSEUM
The Square, Huntly,
Aberdeenshire
Tel: 01771 62 2906
Extensive collection of communion tokens. A display about Huntly-born author George Macdonald and local history displays.

GARLOGIE MILL POWER HOUSE
Aberdeenshire Heritage H.Q.,
Aden Country Park, Mintlaw,
Aberdeenshire
Tel: 01771 622906

GRAMPIAN TRANSPORT MUSEUM
Alford, Aberdeenshire
AB33 8AE
Tel: 01975 562292
Fax: 01975 562180
Regional road and rail transport history as reflected through extensive collection of vehicles of all types and ages.

LITTLE TREASURES DOLLS HOUSE MUSEUM
Petersfield, Kemnay,
Aberdeenshire AB51 5PR
Tel: 01467 642332

MAUD RAILWAY MUSEUM
Maud Station, Aberdeenshire
Tel: 01771 622906
Relive the great days of stream trains at the former Maud Railway Station. Displays and railway memorabilia.

NORTHFIELD FARM MUSEUM
New Pitsligo, Fraserburgh,
Aberdeenshire AB43 4PX
Tel: 01771 653504
Exhibition with farm machinery, vintage tractors, stationary engines and vintage motorbikes on display. Smithy, engineers, line shafting work shop.

OLD MANSE GALLERY
Western Road, Insch,
Aberdeenshire AB52 6RZ
Tel: 01464 820392
Fax: 01464 820318
Art gallery plus hand made carpets of Oriental and Celtic design.

SCOTLAND'S LIGHTHOUSE MUSEUM
Kinnaird Head, Fraserburgh,
Aberdeenshire AB43 5DU
Tel: 01346 511022
Fax: 01346 511033
Unique collection of lighthouse artefacts from across Scotland, including a guided tour of the original Kinnaird Head lighthouse.

TOLBOOTH MUSEUM
The Harbour, Stonehaven,
Aberdeenshire
Tel: 01771 622906
Local history, fishing and temporary exhibitions.

TOLQUHON GALLERY
Tolquhon, Tarves, Ellon,
Aberdeenshire AB41 7LP
Tel: 01651 842343
Gallery exhibiting original paintings, prints, sculpture and studio crafts.

ANGUS

ANGUS FOLK MUSEUM
Kirkwynd, Glamis, Forfar,
Angus DD8 1RT
Tel: 01307 840288
Collection of early furnishings, clothing, domestic utensils and agricultural implements from the County of Angus.

ARBROATH MUSEUM – SIGNAL TOWER
Ladyloan, Arbroath, Angus
DD11 1PU
Tel: 01241 875598
Displays of Arbroath's rich fishing and maritime history, flax textile and engineering trades housed in Stevenson's 1813 shore station for the Bell Rock lighthouse.

GLENESK FOLK MUSEUM
The Retreat, Glenesk, Angus
DD9 7YT
Tel: 01356 670254
Exhibition depicting ways of life in the Glen during the 19th–20thC.

MONTROSE AIR STATION MUSEUM
Waldron Road, Broomfield,
Montrose, Angus DD10 9BB
Tel: 01674 672035
The original station headquarters, built in 1915, houses a collection of memorabilia depicting the station from 1913 to 1950.

MONTROSE MUSEUM & ART GALLERY
Angus Council Museums,
Panmure Place, Montrose,
Angus DD10 8HE
Tel: 01674 673232
Fax: 01307 462590
Extensive local collections covering the history of Montrose, with exhibitions featuring the maritime history of the port, the natural history of Angus and local art.

ARGYLL AND BUTE

ARCTIC PENGUIN
Maritime Heritage Centre,
Inveraray Pier, Inveraray, Argyll
PA32 8UY
Tel: 01499 302213
Exhibition tracing the history of the Clyde shipbuilding industry.

AUCHINDRAIN TOWNSHIP OPEN-AIR MUSEUM
Inveraray, Argyll PA32 8XN
Tel: 01499 500235
An original Highland township restored and presented to illustrate the life of the Highlander in the past.

BUTE MUSEUM
Bute Museum Trustees, Stuart
Street, Rothesay, Isle of Bute
PA20 0BR
Tel: 01700 502248
Fax: 01700 505067
The Centre of archaeological, natural history, historical, archival and general history relating to the island of Bute.

CAMPBELTOWN MUSEUM
Hall Street, Campbeltown,
Argyll
Tel: 01586 552366
Collections of archaeology and natural history with some local history and maritime material. Displays on the landscape and birdlife of Kintyre.

COMBINED OPERATIONS MUSEUM
Argyll Estates Office, Inveraray,
Argyll PA32 8XE
Tel: 01499 500218
Pictures, models and memorabilia commemorating the stationing of 250,000 troops in Inveraray between 1930–45 where combined operations began.

EASDALE ISLAND FOLK MUSEUM
5 Easdale Island, Oban, Argyll
PA34 4TB
Tel: 01852 300370

INVERARAY JAIL
Church Square, Inveraray,
Argyll PA32 8TX
Tel: 01499 302381
Fax: 01499 302195
The museum consists of a 19thC court house with two prisons and features guides dressed in traditional costume.

KILMARTIN HOUSE
Kilmartin, Argyll PA31 8RQ
Tel: 01546 510278
Museum and archaeological centre tracing 5,000 years of human history in the Kilmartin valley.

THE MUSEUM OF ISLAY LIFE
Port Charlotte, Isle of Islay
PA48 7UA
Tel: 01496 850358
Local island museum with artefacts illustrating everyday Islay life, both past and present.

BORDERS

AIKWOOD TOWER
Ettrick Valley, by Selkirk
TD7 5HJ
Tel: 01750 52253
This restored 16thC border tower contains the James Hogg exhibition, featuring the life and work of the important 19thC Scottish writer.

CASTLE JAIL & JEDBURGH MUSEUM
Castlegate, Jedburgh,
Roxburghshire TD8 6QD
Tel: 01835 863254
A Howard reform jail, built in 1823, on the site of the former Jedburgh Castle and gallows.

COLDSTREAM MUSEUM
Market Square, Coldstream,
Berwickshire TD12 4BD
Tel: 01890 882630
Local history museum featuring a section on the Coldstream Guards.

EYEMOUTH MUSEUM
Market Place, Eyemouth,
Berwickshire TD14 5HE
Tel: 01890 750678

HALLIWELL'S HOUSE MUSEUM & GALLERY
Scottish Borders Council, High
Street, Selkirk TD7 4JX
Tel: 01750 20096
Selkirk's oldest surviving dwelling house now creates for the present day visitor its past role as a home and ironmonger's shop.

HAWICK MUSEUM
Wilton Lodge Park, Hawick,
Roxburghshire TD9 7JL
Tel: 01450 373457
Fax: 01450 378506
Social history, local industries (particularly knitwear), natural history and fine local collections, Scottish paintings, temporary exhibitions in the Scott Gallery, and Jimmy Guthrie display.

THE HIRSEL COUNTRY PARK
The Estate Office, Coldstream,
Berwickshire TD12 4LP
Tel: 01890 882834
Fax: 01890 882834
Tools from the Estate's past – archaeology, agriculture, forestry, blacksmiths, natural and family history, geology, craft house and workshops.

JIM CLARK ROOM
44 Newtown Street, Duns,
Berwickshire TD11 3AU
Tel: 01361 883960
Fax: 01361 884104
Trophies, memorabilia, film and photographs from the career of the motor racing hero who was twice world champion (1963 and 1965).

JOHNNIE ARMSTRONG GALLERY
Henderson's Knowe,
Teviothead, by Hawick,
Roxburghshire TD9 0LF
Tel: 01450 850237
Display of original 16th–17thC arms and armour, associated with the Raiving period.

KELSO MUSEUM & TOURIST INFORMATION CENTRE
Turret House, Abbey Court, Kelso TD5 7JA
Tel: 01573 225470
Once used as a skinner's workshop, the house has displays reconstructing a skinner's business, as well as areas reflecting Kelso's growth as a market town.

KITTIWAKE GALLERY & ARTISTS WORKSHOP
Units 1 & 2 The Steading, Northfield, St Abbs, Berwickshire TD14 5QF
Tel: 01890 771504

PEEBLES GALLERY
6 Newby Court, Peebles, Borders EH45 8AL
Tel: 01721 724747
Specialises in miniatures and carries a large selection of original work.

ROBERT SMAIL'S PRINTING WORKS
7/9 High Street, Innerleithen, Peeblesshire EH44 6HA
Tel: 01896 830206
This 130-year-old printing works, a time-capsule of local history and the printing methods of yesteryear, has a water-wheel and working machinery.

SIR WALTER SCOTT'S COURTROOM
Scottish Borders Council Museum Service, Market Place, Selkirk, Selkirkshire TD7 4BT
Tel: 01750 20096
Fax: 01750 23282
Opened in 1994, the exhibition tells the story of the novelist Sir Walter Scott and his role as sheriff of the county of Selkirk.

THE STATION GALLERY & ARTISTS STUDIO
Palma Place, Melrose, Borders TD6 9PR
Tel: 01896 823631
The studio of Bruce Dobson and a gallery displaying his work.

TEDDY MELROSE: SCOTLAND'S TEDDY BEAR MUSEUM
The Wynd, Melrose, Roxburghshire TD6 9LB
Tel: 01896 822464
Records the heritage of British teddy bear makers, also Winnie, Paddington and Rupert with their creative story. Open May to October.

TWEEDALE MUSEUM
Chambers Institute, High Street, Peebles, Borders EH45 9AJ
Tel: 01721 724820
Fax: 01721 724424
Displays of local history, craftwork, contemporary art.

CLACKMANNAN

GLASGOW VENNEL ART GALLERY
10 Glasgow Vennel, Irvine, Clackmannan KA12 0BD
Tel: 0129 427 5059
Fax: 0129 427 5059
An exciting, changing programme of contemporary arts and crafts exhibitions. The gallery includes the "Heckling Shop" where Robert Burns worked and the Lodging House where he lived in 1781.
For further details see page 93

DUMFRIES AND GALLOWAY

THE CLATTERINGSHAWS FOREST WILDLIFE CENTRE
Clatteringshaws, Nr New Galloway
Tel: 01644 420285
Displays relating to wildlife, ecology and forest management.

CRAIGCLEUCH SCOTT EXPLORERS' MUSEUM
Langholm, Dumfriesshire DG13 0NY
Tel: 01387 380137

CREETOWN GEM & ROCK MUSEUM
Chain Road, Creetown, Dumfries and Galloway DG8 7HJ
Tel: 01671 820357
Fax: 01671 820554
World class collection of minerals, crystals, gemstones from around the world. AV display, interactive computers, shop and tearoom.

DESIGNS GALLERY
179 King Street, Castle Douglas, Kirkcudbrightshire DG7 1DZ
Tel: 01556 504552
Gallery and sculpture garden.

DUMFRIES & GALLOWAY AVIATION MUSEUM
Old Control Tower, Heathhall Industrial Estate, Heathhall, Dumfries and Galloway DG1 3PH
Tel: 01387 256409
Display on aircraft and aviation memorabilia.

DUMFRIES MUSEUM & CAMERA OBSCURA
The Observatory, Dumfries DG2 7SW
Tel: 01387 253374
Fax: 01387 265081
Natural history, archaeology and folk collections.

ELLISLAND FARM
Municipal Buildings, Buccleuch Street, Dumfries DG1 2AD
Tel: 01387 253166

GALLOWAY DEER MUSEUM
Kirroughtree Visitor Centre, Newton Stewart, Wigtownshire, Dumfries and Galloway DG8
Tel: 01644 420285

GLEN TROOL VISITOR CENTRE
Stroan Bridge, Glentroe, Bargrennan, Newton Stewart DG8 6FZ
Tel: 01671 840302
Exhibition tracing the history of the Glen.

GRETNA GREEN
The World Famous Old Blacksmiths Shop Centre, Gretna Green, Dumfriesshire DG16 5EA
Tel: 0146 133 8441/338224
Fax: 0146 133 8442
Situated on the Scottish/English border. It is famous for runaway marriages, it has the anvil and coach museum telling the Gretna Green story, and Blacksmith's cottage. Tartan and tweed shop, restaurants, arts centre.

HARBOUR COTTAGE GALLERY
12 Castle Street, Kirkcudbright, Dumfries and Galloway DG6 4JA
Tel: 01577 330073
Gallery exhibiting the work of local artists.

JOHN PAUL JONES COTTAGE MUSEUM & VISITOR CENTRE
Arbigland, Kirkbean, Kirkcudbrightshire, Dumfries and Galloway DG2 8BQ
Tel: 01387 880613
Based around the cottage in which John Paul Jones, the "Father of the American Navy" spent his first 13 years before becoming an apprentice in the merchant navy.

KIRROUGHTREE VISITOR CENTRE
Stronard, Palnure, Newton Stewart DG8 7BE
Tel: 01671 402420
Exhibition comprises a Forest Enterprise display and an audio-visual presentation on forest management, harvesting and design.

MOFFAT MUSEUM
The Old Bakehouse, The Neuk, Moffat, Dumfriesshire DG10
Tel: 01683 220868

THE NEWTON STEWART MUSEUM
York Road, Newton Stewart, Wigtownshire DG8 6HH
Tel: 01671 402472
Collections of items from the social, domestic and farming history of Mid-Galloway.

OLD BRIDGE HOUSE MUSEUM
Mill Road, Dumfries DG2 7BE
Tel: 01387 256904
17thC house with six period and historical rooms.

SANQUHAR TOLBOOTH MUSEUM
High Street, Sanquhar DG4 6BN
Tel: 01659 50186
Adam-designed town house (1735) with displays covering local history, geology and knitting.

SAVINGS BANKS MUSEUM
Ruthwell, Dumfries DG1 4NN
Tel: 01387 870640

SHAMBELLIE HOUSE MUSEUM OF COSTUME
New Abbey, Dumfries, Dumfries and Galloway DG2 8HQ .
Tel: 01387 850375
Fax: 01387 850461
Victorian country home containing costumes from 1850s to 1920s. Tearoom, gift shop, picnic area, wooded grounds.
For further details see page 90

SOPHIES PUPPEN STUBE AND DOLLS HOUSE MUSEUM
29 Queen Street, Newton Stewart, Wigtownshire, Dumfries and Galloway DG8 6JR
Tel: 01671 403344
Fax: 01671 403344
Collection of 50 dolls' houses and room settings furnished in miniature detail depicting life through the ages.

STEWARTRY MUSEUM
St Mary Street, Kirkcudbright DG6 4AQ
Tel: 01557 331643
Displays the archaeology, history and natural history of the Stewartry District.

STRANRAER MUSEUM
55 George Street, Stranraer, Wigtownshire DG9 7JP
Tel: 01776 705088
Fax: 01776 704420
Permanent exhibition on farming, archaeology and polar explorers, John and James Clark Ross, temporary exhibition programme.

TOLBOOTH ART CENTRE
High Street, Kirkcudbright
Tel: 01557 331556
Housed in the town's historic tolbooth which dates back to 1629, now providing gallery accommodation for the best of the museum services painting collection.

WHITHORN PRIORY AND MUSEUM
Whithorn, Wigtownshire, Dumfries and Galloway
Tel: 01988 500700
A fine collection of early Christian stone, including the Latinus stone, the earliest Christian memorial in Scotland, and the Monreith Cross, the finest of the Whithorn school of crosses.

DUNDEE

BARRACK STREET MUSEUM
Barrack Street, Dundee DD1 1PG
Tel: 01382 432067
Fax: 01382 432070
This natural history museum has an art and nature gallery with temporary exhibitions exploring environmental themes and the influence of nature on the arts.

BROUGHTY CASTLE MUSEUM
Arts & Heritage, Dundee City Council, Broughty Ferry, Dundee DD5 2BE
Tel: 01382 436916
A former estuary fort housing displays on local history, arms and armour, seashore life and Dundee's whaling story, with an observation area offering fine views.

FRIGATE UNICORN
Victoria Dock, Dundee, Angus DD1 3JA
Tel: 01382 200900
Launched in 1824, this is the oldest British-built warship afloat.

MCMANUS GALLERIES
Albert Square, Dundee DD1 1DA
Tel: 01382 432020
Fax: 01382 432052
Museum with displays relating to the history of Dundee and an art gallery showing a programme of temporary exhibitions.

MILLS OBSERVATORY
Arts & Heritage, Dundee City Council, Balgay Park, Dundee DD2 2UB
Tel: 01382 435846
Fax: 01382 435962
Attractions at Britain's only full-time public observatory include a small planetarium, an audio-visual presentation, an exhibition of telescopes and scientific instruments and the chance to view the night sky during the winter months.

ST MARY'S TOWER
c/o McManus Galleries, Albert Square, Dundee DD1 1DA
Tel: 01382 432020
Fax: 01382 432052
A restored 15thC steeple tower that can be viewed by arrangement.

VERDANT WORKS
West Henderson Wynd, Dundee
Tel: 01382 225282
Fax: 01382 221612
A restored 19thC jute works surrounding a cobbled courtyard. Visitors can view the period office and discover why Dundee became the jute capital of the world.

EAST AYRSHIRE

BAIRD HISTORY CENTRE & MUSEUM
Cumnock, Ayrshire KA18 1AD
Tel: 01290 421701
A local history museum and district history centre featuring local pottery and wooden ware in conjunction with a programme of temporary exhibitions.

BOSWELL MUSEUM & MAUSOLEUM
Auchinleck Boswell Society, Peden Place, 88 Main Street, Auchinleck, Ayrshire KA18 2AG
Tel: 01290 420931

BURNS HOUSE MUSEUM
4 Castle Street, Mauchline, Ayrshire KA5 5BZ
Tel: 01290 550045

DICK INSTITUTE MUSEUM & ART GALLERY
Elmbank Avenue, Kilmarnock, Ayrshire KA1 3BU
Tel: 01563 526401
Fax: 01563 529661
The art galleries and two museum galleries showing fine art, local history, natural sciences, archaeology, industry and frequent temporary exhibitions.

EAST DUNBARTONSHIRE

AULD KIRK MUSEUM
The Cross, Kirkintilloch, Glasgow G66 1AB
Tel: 0141 775 1185
Fax: 0141 777 7649
Permanent displays of local life and industry, and temporary exhibitions of art, photography, local history, archaeology and social and industrial history.

BARONY CHAMBERS
The Cross, Kirkintilloch, Glasgow G66 1AB
Tel: 0141 775 1185
Fax: 0141 777 7649
Resource room, temporary exhibitions only.

THOMAS MUIR MUSEUM
Library, 170 Kirkintilloch Road,
Bishopbriggs G64 2LX
Tel: 0141 772 4513

EAST LOTHIAN

DUNBAR TOWN HOUSE MUSEUM
High Street, Dunbar, East
Lothian EH42 1ER
Tel: 01368 863734
*Historic 16thC town house with a
hands-on archaeology display,
photographs of old Dunbar and
temporary exhibitions.*

JANE WELSH CARYLLE MUSEUM
2 Lodge Street, Haddington,
East Lothian EH41 3DX
Tel: 01620 823738
Fax: 01620 823738
*Authentic 18thC home of Jane
Bailey-Welsh, who was born in
Haddington and later married
Thomas Carlyle.*

MUSEUM OF FLIGHT
East Fortune Airfield, East
Lothian EH39 5LF
Tel: 01620 880308
Fax: 01620 880355
*Scotland's national collection of
aviation, based on a Second
World War airfield.*
For further details see page 90

MYRETON MOTOR MUSEUM
Aberlady, East Lothian
EH32 0PZ
Tel: 01875 870288
*Motor cars, motorcycles, bicycles,
commercial vehicles and military
vehicles from the 1880s.*

NORTH BERWICK MUSEUM
School Road, North Berwick,
East Lothian
Tel: 01620 895457
Fax: 01620 828201
*Local history, archaeology, wildlife
and golf.*

PRESTONGRANGE INDUSTRIAL HERITAGE MUSEUM
Morrison's Haven, Prestonpans,
East Lothian
Tel: 0131 653 2904

STENTON GALLERY
Main Street, Stenton, East
Lothian EH42 1TE
Tel: 01368 850256
Regular programme of exhibitions.

EDINBURGH

CALTON GALLERY
10 Royal Terrace, Edinburgh
EH7 5AB
Tel: 0131 556 1010
Fax: 0131 558 1150
*Specialising in art from 1750 to
1940, the Gallery displays
paintings, watercolours and
sculptures by Scottish and European
artists.*

COLLECTIVE GALLERY
22–28 Cockburn Street,
Edinburgh EH1 1NY
Tel: 0131 220 1260
*Supporting new and emerging
contemporary art and artists, the
gallery encourages diversity and
experimentation through its
programme of installation, painting,
performing arts, sculpture and video.*

THE DEAN GALLERY
Administration Offices, 13
Heriot Row, Edinburgh
EH3 6HP
Tel: 0131 624 6200
Fax: 0131 343 3250
*First new gallery dedicated to the
whole of the 20thC modern and
contemporary art to open since
1984. Includes parkland and
sculpture garden.*
For further details see page 91

EDINBURGH CITY ART CENTRE
Market Street, Edinburgh
EH1 1DE
Tel: 0131 529 3993

EDINBURGH PRINTMAKERS WORKSHOP & GALLERY
23 Union Street, Edinburgh
EH1 3LR
Tel: 0131 557 2479
Fax: 0131 558 8418
*Watch artists at work and see the
huge range of contemporary etchings,
lithographs, screenprints, and prints
for sale.*

EDINBURGH UNIVERSITY COLLECTION OF HISTORIC MUSICAL INSTRUMENTS
Reid Concert Hall, Bristo
Square, Teviot Place, Edinburgh
EH8 9AH
Tel: 0131 650 2423/4367
Fax: 0131 650 2425
*Two thousand musical instruments
exemplifying the history of folk and
domestic music, band music and the
orchestra over the last 400 years.*

FRUITMARKET GALLERY
45 Market Street, Edinburgh
EH1 1DF
Tel: 0131 225 2383
Fax: 0131 220 3130
*Contemporary art gallery with a
busy schedule of diverse
mixed-media exhibitions.*

HUNTLY HOUSE MUSEUM
142 Canongate, Edinburgh
EH8 8DD
Tel: 0131 529 4143
Fax: 0131 557 3346
*Local history and topography;
important collections of Edinburgh
silver, glass and Scottish pottery;
reconstruction of an old Scots
kitchen.*

THE LEITH GALLERY
65 The Shore, Leith, Edinburgh
Tel: 0131 553 5255
Fax: 0131 553 5655

MUSEUM OF CHILDHOOD
42 High Street, Royal Mile,
Edinburgh EH1 1TG
Tel: 0131 529 4142
Fax: 0131 558 3103
*Vast collection of toys, dolls, games,
costume, etc – still the noisiest
museum in the world!*

MUSEUM OF FIRE
Lothian & Borders Fire Brigade,
Brigade Headquarters, Lauriston
Place, Edinburgh EH3 9DE
Tel: 0131 228 2401

MUSEUM OF SCOTLAND
Chambers Street, Edinburgh
EH1 1JF
Tel: 0131 225 7534
*New museum tracing Scotland's
history from its geological beginnings
to the present day – due to open
November 1998.*

NATIONAL GALLERY OF SCOTLAND
Administration Offices, 13
Heriot Row, Edinburgh,
Edinburgh EH3 6HP
Tel: 0131 624 6200
Fax: 0131 343 3250
*An outstanding collection of
paintings, drawings and prints by
major artists from the Renaissance
to Post Impressionism.*
For further details see page 91

NEWHAVEN HERITAGE MUSEUM
24 Pier Place, Newhaven
Harbour, Edinburgh EH6 4LP
Tel: 0131 551 4165
*New museum telling about the
fishing village of Newhaven and its
people.*

THE PEOPLE'S STORY
Canongate Tolbooth, 163
Canongate, Edinburgh
EH8 8BN
Tel: 01315 294057
*Housed in the 16thC Tolbooth, this
exciting museum tells the story of the
life and work of Edinburgh's people
over the past 200 years.*

QUEENSFERRY MUSEUM
53 High Street, South
Queensferry, Edinburgh
EH30 9HP
Tel: 0131 331 5545
Fax: 0131 557 3346
*Tells the story of South Queensferry
and its people, and the building of
the great rail and road bridges
spanning the Forth.*

ROYAL MUSEUM OF SCOTLAND
Chambers Street, Edinburgh
EH1 1JF
Tel: 0131 225 7534
Fax: 0131 220 4819
*Houses the national collections of
decorative arts of the world,
ethnography, natural history,
geology, technology and science.*
**For further details see pages 40
& 90**

ROYAL SCOTS REGIMENTAL MUSEUM
Edinburgh Castle, Edinburgh
EH1 2YT
Tel: 0131 310 5014
Fax: 0131 310 5019
*The museum of the oldest regiment
in the British Army, housed in
Edinburgh Castle.*

ROYAL SCOTTISH ACADEMY
National Galleries of Scotland,
The Mound, Edinburgh
EH2 2EL
Tel: 0131 225 6671
Fax: 0131 225 2349

RUSSELL COLLECTION
St Cecilia's Hall, Niddry Street,
Edinburgh EH1 1LJ
Tel: 0131 650 1000
*Russell collection of early keyboard
instruments. Fifty keyboard
instruments, including harpsichord,
clavichords, fortepianos, spinets,
virginals and chamber organs.*

SCOTTISH AGRICULTURAL MUSEUM
Ingliston, Newbridge,
Edinburgh EH28 8NB
Tel: 0131 333 2674
*Illustrates the history of
agriculture in Scotland with room
settings, crafts, animal husbandry,
etc.*
For further details see page 90

THE SCOTTISH NATIONAL GALLERY OF MODERN ART
Administration Officer, 13
Heriot Row, Edinburgh,
Edinburgh EH3 6HP
Tel: 0131 624 6000
Fax: 0131 343 3250
*Scotland's finest collection of
20thC painting, sculpture and
graphic art, including Dada and
Surrealist masterpieces, French art
and German Expressionism.*
For further details see page 91

SCOTTISH NATIONAL PORTRAIT GALLERY
Administration Offices, 13
Heriot Row, Edinburgh,
Edinburgh EH3 6HP
Tel: 0131 624 6200
Fax: 0131 343 3250
*Visual history of Scotland told
through portraits, including those
of Mary, Queen of Scots and
Robert Burns right up to Sean
Connery.*
For further details see page 91

SCOTTISH TARTANS MUSEUM
39-41 Princes Street, Edinburgh
EH2 2BY
Tel: 0131 556 1252
Fax: 0131 556 9529
*Over 600 examples illustrate the
history of tartan from 325 AD to
the present day.*

SCOTTISH UNITED SERVICES MUSEUM
Edinburgh Castle, Edinburgh
EH1 2NG
Tel: 0131 225 7534
*Collection of material connected
with Scottish armed forces from
17th–20thC.*
For further details see page 90

TALBOT RICE GALLERY
University of Edinburgh, Old
College, South Bridge,
Edinburgh EH8 9YL
Tel: 0131 650 2211
Fax: 0131 650 2213
*Georgian gallery showing Edinburgh
University's collection of Old Master
paintings and bronze, with a
contemporary space showing up to
seven exhibitions a year.*

WRITERS' MUSEUM
Lady Stair's House, Lady Stair's
Close, Lawnmarket (Royal
Mile), Edinburgh EH1 2PA
Tel: 0131 529 4901
Fax: 0131 557 3346
*A reconstructed town house dating
from 1622 with exhibits connected
with Robert Burns, Sir Walter Scott
and R L Stevenson.*

FALKIRK

BIRKHILL CLAY MINE
Bo'ness Development Trust,
17–19 North Street, Bo'ness,
West Lothian EH51 0AQ
Tel: 01506 825855
Fax: 01506 828766
*A former fire-clay mine, where
experienced guides are at hand to
help visitors explore, that opens to
the public in conjunction with the
Bo'ness and Kinneil railway (which
operates for approximately 100 days
of the year).*

GRANGEMOUTH MUSEUM
Public Library, Bo'ness Road,
Grangemouth FK3 8AG
Tel: 01324 504699
*Tells the story of one of Scotland's
earliest planned industrial towns.*

SCOTTISH RAILWAY PRESERVATION SOCIETY
The Station, Union Street,
Bo'ness EH51 9AQ
Tel: 01506 822298
*Visitors can ride on a working steam
engine, travelling along a 3 1/2
mile standard gauge railway, and
view a static display of locomotives,
carriages and wagons.*

FIFE

ABBOT HOUSE
Dunfermline Heritage Trust,
Maygate, Dunfermline, Fife
KY12 7NE
Tel: 0138 373 3266
Fax: 0138 362 4908
*Museum opened in 1995 depicting
the history of Dunfermline, ancient
capital of Scotland, in a medieval
building.*

ANDREW CARNEGIE BIRTHPLACE MUSEUM
Moodie Street, Dunfermline,
Fife KY12 7PL
Tel: 01383 724302
Fax: 01383 729002
*Born in a humble weaver's cottage,
Andrew Carnegie became the
greatest steelmaster in 19thC
America – and gave away $350
million.*

BRITISH GOLF MUSEUM
Bruce Embankment,
St Andrews, Fife KY16 9AB
Tel: 01334 478880
*The museum tells the story of
British golf from the Middle Ages to
present day, and follows British
influence abroad.*

BUCKHAVEN MUSEUM
College Street, Buckhaven, Fife
Tel: 01592 412860
Fax: 01592 412870

BURNTISLAND EDWARDIAN FAIR MUSEUM
102 High Street, Burntisland,
Fife KY3 9AS
Tel: 01592 412860
Fax: 01592 412870
*New displays bring back the fun,
colour and noise of an Edwardian
fairground.*

CRAIL MUSEUM
Museum & Heritage Centre,
62–64 Marketgate, Crail, Fife
KY10 3TL
Tel: 01333 450869

CRAWFORD ARTS CENTRE
93 North Street, St Andrews,
Fife KY16 9AL
Tel: 01334 474610
*The centre provides exhibitions of all
kinds of visual art from sculpture
and painting to photography, design
and architecture.*

DUNFERMLINE MUSEUM
Viewfield Terrace, Dunfermline,
Fife KY12 7HY
Tel: 01383 721814
*Local history and natural history of
the district.*

INVERKEITHING MUSEUM
Fife Council Museums West,
The Friary, Queen Anne Street,
Inverkeithing KY11 1LS
Tel: 01383 313595
*Local museum about the Royal
Burgh of Inverkeithing and nearby
Rosyth. Memorabilia on Sir Samuel
Greig, father of the modern Russian
navy and son of Inverkeithing.*

**KIRKCALDY MUSEUM & ART
GALLERY**
War Memorial Gardens,
Kirkcaldy, Fife KY1 1YG
Tel: 01592 412860
Fax: 01592 412870
*Unique collection of paintings
including works by the Scottish
Colourists, the Camden Town
Group and contemporary artists with
fascinating historical displays and a
lively exhibition programme.*

LAING MUSEUM
120 High Street, Newburgh,
Fife KY14 6DX
Tel: 01337 840223
*Attractions include a replica
Victorian study and a varied
schedule of local-interest exhibitions.*

MCDOUALL STUART MUSEUM
Rectory Lane, Dysart, Fife
KY1 2TP
Tel: 01592 412860

**PITTENCRIEFF HOUSE
MUSEUM**
Pittencrieff Park, Dunfermline,
Fife KY12 8QG
Tel: 01383 722935
*History of Pittencrieff House and
Park, costume displays, temporary
paintings and photographic
exhibitions.*

ST ANDREWS MUSEUM
Kinburn Park, Doubledykes
Road, St Andrews, Fife
KY16 9DP
Tel: 01334 412690

**ST ANDREWS PRESERVATION
TRUST MUSEUM**
12 North Street, St Andrews,
Fife KY16 9PW
Tel: 01334 477629
*Small, local-history museum set in
an 18thC merchant's house.*

SCOTLAND'S SECRET BUNKER
Underground Nuclear
Command Centre, Crown
Buildings, Troywood, nr
St Andrews, Fife KY16 8QH
Tel: 01333 310301
Fax: 01333 312040
*Visitors can explore sections of this
underground labyrinth, which was
built in 1951 to protect central
government and military command
from a nuclear holocaust.*

**SCOTTISH FISHERIES
MUSEUM TRUST LTD**
St Ayles, Harbourhead,
Anstruther, Fife KY10 3AB
Tel: 01333 310628
*16th–19thC buildings housing
fishing and ships' gear, model and
actual fishing boats, period
fisher-home interior, reference library
and boat yard.*

GLASGOW

THE ANNAN GALLERY
T & R Annan & Sons Ltd, 164
Woodlands Road, Glasgow
G3 6LL
Tel: 0141 332 0028
Fax: 0141 332 0028
*Selection of paintings and
photographs including some of
Charles Rennie Macintosh.*

ART EXPOSURE GALLERY
19 Parnie Street, Glasgow
G1 5RJ
Tel: 0141 552 7779
*Exhibitions featuring the work of
local artists, jewellers and
ceramicists.*

THE ART GALLERY & MUSEUM
Helvingrave, Argyle Street,
Glasgow G3 8AG
Tel: 0141 221 2600
*Enjoy a fabulous range of European
painting and fascinating displays on
natural history, archaeology and
ethnography in Glasgow's principle
art gallery and museum.*

**BARCLAY LENNIE FINE ART
LTD**
Regent House, 113 West
Regent Street, Glasgow
G2 2RU
Tel: 0141 226 5413
*A permanent display of early 20thC
Scottish art, with an additional
programme of contemporary touring
exhibitions.*

THE BURRELL COLLECTION
2060 Pollockshaws Road,
Glasgow G43 1AT
Tel: 0141 649 7151
Fax: 0141 636 0086
*Sir William Burrell's
world-famous collection of
beautiful art objects housed in a
specially designed, award-winning
building.*
For further details see page 92

**CENTRE FOR
CONTEMPORARY ARTS**
350 Sauchiehall Street, Glasgow
G2 3JD
Tel: 0141 332 0522
Fax: 0141 332 3226
*One of the UK's leading venues for
new art, offering a programme of
exhibitions, performances, talks and
events by artists from Scotland and
abroad.*

COLLINS GALLERY
University of Strathclyde, 22
Richmond Street, Glasgow
G1 1XQ
Tel: 0141 552 4400 ext 2558
*Busy schedule of touring exhibitions
featuring contemporary work by
Scottish artists.*

COMPASS GALLERY
178 West Regent Street,
Glasgow G2 4RL
Tel: 0141 221 6370
*Diverse range of monthly exhibitions
showing work by emerging and
established artists.*

CYRIL GERBER FINE ART
148 West Regent Street,
Glasgow G2 2RQ
Tel: 0141 221 3095/204 0276
Fax: 0141 248 1322
*Busy schedule of exhibitions by
British artists displaying work from
1880 to the present.*

DUNCAN R MILLER FINE ARTS
144 West Regent's Street,
Glasgow G2 2RQ
Tel: 0141 204 0708
*An extensive collection of modern
British art.*

FOSSIL GROVE
Victoria Park, Glasgow
G14 1BN
Tel: 0141 950 1448
*Fossilised trees and rocks which
are 330 million years old. It is
the only preserved forest of its
kind in the world. Open summer
season only.*
For further details see page 92

**THE GALLERY OF MODERN
ART**
Queen Street, Glasgow
G1 3AZ
Tel: 0141 229 1996
*Set in a re-furbished, neo-classical
building in the heart of Glasgow,
this Gallery has 4 floors of
display space housing a collection
of post-war art and design.*
For further details see page 92

THE GATEHOUSE GALLERY
Rouken Glen Road, Giffnock,
Glasgow G46 7UG
Tel: 0141 620 0235
*Schedule of monthly displays
exhibiting contemporary work by
Scottish artists.*

**GLASGOW PRINT STUDIO
GALLERY**
1st Floor, 22 King Street,
Glasgow G1 5QP
Tel: 0141 552 0704
Fax: 0141 552 2919
*Ongoing programme of monthly
exhibitions, predominantly featuring
contemporary work by emerging
Scottish artists.*

GLASGOW SCHOOL OF ART
167 Renfrew Street, Glasgow
G3 6RQ
Tel: 0141 353 4500
Fax: 0141 353 4746

HEATHERBANK MUSEUM
Caledonian University, Park
Campus, 1 Park Drive, Glasgow
G3 6LB
Tel: 0141 337 4402
Fax: 0141 337 4500
*A unique museum on the history of
social work with outreach
exhibitions, a reference library of
over 2,000 books and a picture
library.*

HOUSE FOR AN ART LOVER
Bellahouston Park, Dumbreck
Road, Glasgow G41 5BW
Tel: 0141 353 4770
Fax: 0141 353 4771
*Permanent Macintosh exhibition
rooms in recently constructed Charles
Rennie Macintosh building,
designed for a competition in 1901.*

HUNTERIAN ART GALLERY
82 Hillhead Street, Glasgow
G12 8QQ
Tel: 0141 330 5434
Fax: 0141 330 3618
*Unrivalled collections of C R
Mackintosh, including reconstructed
interiors of the architect's house and
of J A M Whistler.*

HUNTERIAN MUSEUM
University Avenue, Glasgow
G12 8QQ
Tel: 0141 330 4221
Fax: 0141 330 3617
*The oldest museum in Scotland.
Houses displays of archaeology,
ethnography and geology.*

**KELVINGROVE ART
GALLERY & MUSEUM**
Glasgow G3 8AG
Tel: 0141 287 2699
*The Gallery and Museum house
a wide variety of permanent and
temporary exhibitions.*
For further details see page 92

MCLELLAN GALLERIES
270 Sauchiehall Street,
Glasgow G2 3EH
Tel: 0141 331 1854
*The largest touring display venue
in Britain outside London, these
galleries house temporary
exhibitions from around the
world.*
For further details see page 92

MUSEUM OF TRANSPORT
Kelvin Hall, 1 Bunhouse
Road, Glasgow G3 8DP
Tel: 0141 287 2720
Fax: 0141 287 2692
*A new and considerably enlarged
museum of the history of
transport, including a reproduction
of a typical 1938 Glasgow street.*
For further details see page 92

THE NS GALLERY
53 Cresswell Street, Glasgow
G12 9AE
Tel: 0141 334 4240
Fax: 0141 334 4240
*An ongoing programme of temporary
exhibitions showing contemporary
work by a variety of guest artists.*

THE ORIGINAL PRINT SHOP
22 & 25 King Street, Glasgow
G1 5QZ
Tel: 0141 552 1394
Fax: 0141 552 2919
*An ongoing programme of monthly
displays showing innovative work by
up and coming and established
printmakers.*

PEOPLE'S PALACE
Glasgow Green, Glasgow
G40 1AT
Tel: 0141 554 0223
Fax: 0141 550 0892
*Museum of Glasgow's history
from 1175 to the present day
with collections which cover early
Glasgow, the rise of tobacco in the
18thC and domestic, social and
political life in the 19th and
20thC.*
For further details see page 92

THE PIPING MUSEUM
The Piping Centre, 30–34
McPhater Street,
Cowcaddens, Glasgow
G4 0HW
Tel: 0141 353 0220
Fax: 0141 353 1570
*An outstanding collection of
bagpipes and piping artefacts that
introduce the visitor to the
mysteries of bagpiping, its history
and origins.*
For further details see page 90

POLLOK HOUSE MUSEUM
2060 Pollockshaws Road,
Glasgow G43 1AT
Tel: 0141 649 7151
*House built c1750 in Palladian
style with Edwardian additions,
containing the Stirling Maxwell
Collection of paintings.*
For further details see page 92

THE PRACTICE GALLERY
200 Bath Street, Glasgow
G2 4HG
Tel: 0141 331 0722
Fax: 0141 331 0733
*Monthly programme of exhibitions
by Scottish, British and European
artists.*

PROJECT ABILITY
Centre for Developmental Arts,
18 Albion Street, Glasgow
G1 1LH
Tel: 0141 552 2822
Fax: 0141 552 3490
*Busy schedule of shows by local and
visiting artists displaying a wide
range of work.*

PROVAND'S LORDSHIP
3 Castle Street, Glasgow
Tel: 0141 552 8819
Fax: 0141 552 4744
*This is the oldest house in
Glasgow set in the heart of the
most ancient part of the city.
Dating from 1471, it was
originally built as the Manse for
St Nicholas Hospital and shows
period displays, including a sweet
shop on the ground floor.*
For further details see page 92

ROGER BILLCLIFFE FINE ART
134 Blythswood Street, Glasgow
G2 4EL
Tel: 0141 332 4027
Fax: 0141 332 6573
*Three floors of contemporary
painting and applied art which
predominantly features work by
Scottish artists.*

ROYAL HIGHLAND FUSILIERS
Regimental Headquarters, 518
Sauchiehall Street, Glasgow
G2 3LW
Tel: 0141 332 5639
Regimental museum.

ST MUNGO MUSEUM OF RELIGIOUS LIFE & ART
2 Castle Street, Cathedral Precinct, Glasgow G4 0RH
Tel: 0141 553 2557
Opened in 1993, this unique museum explores the universal themes of life and death and the hereafter through beautiful and evocative art objects associated with different religious faiths.
For further details see page 92

SCOTLAND STREET SCHOOL MUSEUM
225 Scotland Street, Glasgow G5 8QB
Tel: 0141 429 1202
Fax: 0141 420 3292
Designed in 1904 by Charles Rennie Macintosh the displays tell the story of education in Scotland from 1872 to 1972 with Victorian, Second World War, 1950s and 60s classrooms and an Edwardian cookery room.
For further details see page 92

SPRINGBURN MUSEUM
Atlas Square, Ayr Street, Glasgow G21 4BW
Tel: 0141 557 1405
Changing exhibitions about the past and present of an area which was once the greatest centre of steam locomotive manufacture in Europe.

STREET LEVEL PHOTOWORKS
26 King Street, Glasgow G1 5QP
Tel: 0141 552 2151
Fax: 0141 552 2323
Houses a diverse programme of photographic and lens-based multimedia exhibitions from local, national and international sources with the gallery providing a platform for high-profile displays and an outlet for emerging and innovative work.

TRAMWAY
25 Albert Drive, Glasgow G41 2PE
Tel: 0141 422 2023
Fax: 0141 422 2021
Presents a varied, innovative and international programme of work in the visual and performing arts.

TRANSMISSION GALLERY
28 King Street, Glasgow G1 5QP
Tel: 0141 552 4813
Fax: 0141 552 1577
A broad programme of exhibitions and events by local and international artists.

HIGHLAND

CHILDHOOD MEMORIES (THE TOY MUSEUM)
Coylumbridge, by Aviemore, Inverness-shire PH22 1RD
Tel: 01479 812022
Home to over 2500 toys, dolls, teddy bears and working trains sets.

CLAN CAMERON MUSEUM
Achnacarry, Spean Bridge, Inverness-shire PH34 4EJ
Tel: 01397 712480
Museum of the clan, its involvement in the 1745 uprising, displays about the Queen's Own Cameron Highlanders and the commandos.

CLAN GUNN HERITAGE CENTRE & MUSEUM
Latheron, Caithness, Highland KW5 6DG
Tel: 01595 721325

CLAN MACPHERSON MUSEUM
Clan Macpherson House & Museum, Main Street, Newtonmore, Inverness-shire PH20 1DE
Tel: 01540 673332
Displays historical relics of the Clan MacPherson and traces its relationship with neighbouring clans.

COLBOST FOLK MUSEUM
by Dunvegan, Isle of Skye IV55 8ZT
Tel: 01470 521296
Features an exhibition illustrating what it was like living in the Scottish Highlands during the 19thC.

CROMARTY COURTHOUSE
Church Street, Cromarty, Ross & Cromarty IV11 8XA
Tel: 01381 600418
18thC courthouse in well-preserved 18thC town, reconstructed trial with animated figures, video, exhibition, tape-tour of town, school pack.

DINGWALL MUSEUM
Town House, High Street, Dingwall, Ross & Cromarty IV15 9RY
Tel: 01349 862116
Collection of objects, militaria and photographs relating to the Dingwell area with temporary exhibitions throughout the season.

FORT GEORGE
By Ardersier, Inverness-shire
Tel: 01667 462777
Built following the Battle of Culloden, Fort George is one of Europe's finest examples of late artillery fortifications.

GAIRLOCH HERITAGE MUSEUM
Achtercairn, Gairloch, Ross-shire IV21 2BJ
Tel: 01445 712287
Local history museum illustrating all aspects of past life in a West Highland parish. Events and hands-on activities.

GIANT ANGUS MACASKILL MUSEUM
Dunvegan, Isle of Skye IV55 8WA
Tel: 01470 521296
Has lifesize model of the tallest "true" giant with stories of his feats of strength.

GLENCOE & NORTH LORN FOLK MUSEUM
Glencoe, Argyll PA39 4HS
Thatched restored 'Cruck' cottage in Glencoe village with exhibits including domestic bygones, costume, weapons, Jacobite relics, agricultural implements and natural history.

GLENFINNAN STATION MUSEUM
Station Cottage, Glenfinnan, Inverness-shire PH37 4LT
Tel: 01397 722295
Fax: 01397 722363
Housed in converted buildings at a working station, this exhibition traces the history of the West Highland railway line.

GROAM HOUSE MUSEUM
High Street, Rosemarkie, Ross-shire IV10 8UF
Tel: 01381 620961/621730
Fax: 01381 621730
An award-winning Pictish centre for Ross & Cromarty with original sculptured stones, video displays, temporary exhibitions, activities, Picto/Celtic shop.

HIGHLAND FOLK MUSEUM
Duke Street, Kingussie, Inverness-shire PH21 1JG
Tel: 01540 661307
Fax: 01540 661631
A comprehensive collection of old Highland artefacts including examples of craftwork, tools, household plenishings and tartans.

HIGHLAND MUSEUM OF CHILDHOOD
The Old Station, Strathpeffer, Ross-shire IV14 9DH
Tel: 01997 421031
Displays bring to life the story of childhood in the Highlands with quizzes, toys and a dressing-up box for children.

INVERNESS MUSEUM & ART GALLERY
Castle Wynd, Inverness IV2 3ED
Tel: 01463 237114
Fax: 01463 225293
Interprets the human and natural history of the Highlands, with displays of Highland weapons, musical instruments, costume and Jacobite memorabilia.

THE LAST HOUSE MUSEUM
John O'Groats, Caithness KW1 4YR
Tel: 01955 611250
Set in a restored 18thC house, this local-history museum has several displays, including an exhibition of photographs and artefacts from the once inhabited island of Stroma.

LHAIDHAY CROFT MUSEUM
Dunbeath, Caithness KW6 6EH
Tel: 01593 731244
Typical Caithness longhouse and cruck barn. Rush thatched. Appropriate furnishings and implements.

LYTH ARTS CENTRE
Lyth, by Wick, Caithness, Highland KW1
Tel: 01955 641270
Fax: 01955 641414
Annual programme of contemporary music, drama and visual art.

NAIRN FISHERTOWN MUSEUM
Laing Hall, King Street, Nairn IV12
Tel: 01667 453331
Featuring model ships, photographs and artefacts associated with the town's fishing industry and community, from the 18thC to the present.

QUEEN'S OWN HIGHLANDERS REGIMENTAL MUSEUM
Fort George, Ardersier, Inverness, Inverness-shire IV1 2TD
Tel: 01463 224380

SKYE MUSEUM OF ISLAND LIFE
Kilmuir, Isle of Skye IV51 9LE
Tel: 01470 552206
Fax: 01470 552206
Group of seven thatched cottages.

STRATHNAVER MUSEUM
Clachan, Bettyhill (by Thurso), Sutherland
Tel: 01641 521418/330
The main theme of the museum is the Strathnaver Clearances of the early 19th century. The displayed collection includes references to both the domestic and working life of the local people.
For further details see page 93

TAIN THROUGH TIME
Tower Street, Tain, Ross & Cromarty IV19 1DY
Tel: 01862 894089
Museum, visitor centre and medieval church with audiovisual, CD tour and children's activities.

THURSO HERITAGE CENTRE
Town Hall, High Street, Thurso, Caithness KW14 8AG

TOY MUSEUM
Glendale, Isle of Skye IV55 8WS
Tel: 01470 511240
A hands-on experience with plenty of toys, games and dolls for visitors to play with. Talisker quality award winner.

TREASURES OF THE EARTH
A830 Mallaig Road, Corpach, Fort William, Inverness-shire PH33 7JL
Tel: 01397 772283
Display of crystals, precious stones, gold and silver in their natural state, also fossils, books and toys.

ULLAPOOL MUSEUM & VISITOR CENTRE
7/8 West Argyle Street, Ullapool, Ross & Cromarty IV26 2TV
Tel: 01854 612987
Award-winning museum housed in historic former church. Interactive displays; audio visual; archives; social and natural history.

WEST HIGHLAND MUSEUM
Cameron Square, Fort William, Inverness-shire PH33 6AJ
Tel: 01397 702169
Historical, natural history and folk exhibits including displays of Prince Charles Edward Stuart and the 1745 Rising, items of local interest from pre-history to modern industry and tartans.

INVERCLYDE

CUSTOMS & EXCISE MUSEUM
Greenock Custom House, Greenock PA16
Tel: 01475 726331
The museum shows the diverse and colourful history of the organisation and highlights the great variety of work currently done by the department

MCLEAN MUSEUM & ART GALLERY
15 Kelly Street, Greenock PA16 8JX
Tel: 01475 723741
Fax: 01475 731347
Displays include local history, ethnography, maritime history, natural history and fine art. Temporary exhibitions. Licensed café and shop.

MIDLOTHIAN

SCOTTISH MINING MUSEUM
Lady Victoria Colliery, Newtongrange, Midlothian EH22 4QN
Tel: 0131 663 7519
Fax: 0131 654 1618
Scotland's national coal mining museum at the historic Lady Victoria Colliery.

MORAY

BARNYARD STUDIOS
Connagedale, Garmouth, Grampian IV32 7LX
Tel: 01343 870599
Working studio with gallery/exhibition of artists/craftsmens work.

DUFFTOWN MUSEUM
The Tower, The Square, Dufftown, Moray AB55 4AD
Tel: 01309 673701
Fax: 01309 675863
Local history, Mortlach Kirk, temporary exhibitions.

ELGIN MUSEUM
Moray Society, 1 High Street, Elgin, Moray IV30 1EQ
Tel: 01343 543675
Fax: 01343 543675
Award-winning museum with fossil, fish and reptiles, Pictish stones and archaeology, and general displays. Activities throughout the season.

FALCONER MUSEUM
Tolbooth Street, Forres, Morayshire IV36 0PH
Tel: 01309 673701/676688
Fax: 01309 675863
Local history, natural history, exhibits on Hugh Falconer and other prominent local people and temporary exhibitions.

FOCHABERS FOLK MUSEUM
High Street, Fochabers, Morayshire IV32 7EP
Tel: 01343 821204
Set in a converted church, this large display of local-interest artefacts includes a collection of horse-drawn vehicles and a replica Victorian parlour.

LOGIE STEADING
Logie, Forres, Grampian IV36 0QN
Tel: 01309 611378
Attractively converted farm steading. Workshops with professional craftsmen at work.

LOSSIEMOUTH FISHERIES & COMMUNITY MUSEUM
Fitgaveny Street, Lossiemouth, Morayshire
Tel: 01343 813772

MORAY MOTOR MUSEUM
Bridge Street, Elgin, Moray IV30 2DE
Tel: 01343 544933
Unique collection of veteran, vintage and classic cars and motor bikes housed in an old mill building.

THE LANTERN GALLERY OF FINE ART
18 South Guildry Street, Elgin, Morayshire IV30 1QN
Tel: 01343 546864
Wide selection of water colours, oils, paintings by local artists and wood sculptures.

TOMINTOUL MUSEUM
The Square, Tomintoul, Moray
AB37 9ET
Tel: 01309 673701
Fax: 01309 675863
Features displays on local wildlife, the local skiing industry and the history of Tomintoul.

TUGNET ICE HOUSE
Spey Bay, Fochabers, Moray
Tel: 01309 673701
Fax: 01309 675863
Visitors to this industrial ice house can view exhibitions presenting the story of shipbuilding and salmon fishing on the Spey.

NORTH AYRSHIRE

CHRISTIAN HERITAGE CENTRE
5 Mackerston Place, Largs,
Ayrshire KA30 8BY
Tel: 01475 687320

DALGARVEN MILL
Museum of Ayrshire Country
Life, Dalry Road, Kilwinning,
Ayrshire KA13 6PN
Tel: 01294 552448
Water-driven flour mill, with a three-storey grain store converted into a museum of Ayrshire country life.

ISLE OF ARRAN HERITAGE MUSEUM
Rosaburn, Brodick, Isle Of
Arran KA27 8DP
Tel: 01770 302636

LARGS MUSEUM
Manse Court, Largs, Ayrshire
KA30 8AW
Tel: 01475 687081
Small independent museum. Member of Museums Council Edinburgh.

NORTH AYRSHIRE MUSEUM
Manse Street, Saltcoats, North
Ayrshire KA21 5AA
Tel: 01294 464174
Fax: 01294 462234
Traces the history of North Ayrshire with displays on archaeology, costume, transport and popular culture. The museum also includes a section showing the maritime history of the port of Ardrossan and a reconstruction of an Ayrshire cottage interior. Accompanied children can play in the children's activity area.
For further details see page 93

SCOTTISH MARITIME MUSEUM
Laird Forge, Gottries Road,
Irvine, North Ayrshire
KA12 8QE
Tel: 01294 278283
Fax: 01294 313211
Full-size ships, a boat shed special exhibition gallery with a new maritime theme display every year, an educational centre and a restored tenement flat.
For further details see page 93

NORTH LANARKSHIRE

SUMMERLEE HERITAGE PARK
Heritage Way, Coatbridge,
Lanarkshire ML5 1QD
Tel: 01236 431261
Fax: 01236 440429
Museum of social and industrial history with indoor and open-air exhibits including a working tramway, belt-driven machinery and a 19thC coal mine.

THE WEAVERS' COTTAGES MUSEUM
23–27 Wellwynd, Airdrie
ML6 0BN
Tel: 01236 747712
Attractive 18thC craftsman's house containing traditional weaving and domestic exhibits.

ORKNEY ISLANDS

ORKNEY WIRELESS MUSEUM
Viewfield, Church Road,
St Margarets Hope, Orkney
KW17 2SR
Tel: 01856 871400

PIER ART CENTRE
Victoria Street, Stromness,
Orkney Islands KW16 3AA
Tel: 01856 850209
Permanent collection of 20thC British art; also a programme of changing exhibitions.
For further details see page 93

STROMNESS MUSEUM
Orkney Natural History Society,
52 Alfred Street, Stromness,
Orkney KW16 3DF
Tel: 01856 850025
Orkney maritime museum displays include fishing, shipping, whaling, the Hudson's Bay Company and the German fleet in Scapa flow.

TANKERNESS HOUSE MUSEUM
Broad Street, Kirkwall, Orkney
Islands KW15 1DH
Tel: 01856 873191
Fax: 01856 871560
Two restored farmsteads illustrating tradition and change in island life.

PERTH AND KINROSS

ALYTH MUSEUM
Perth Museum, George Street,
Perth PH1 5LB
Tel: 01738 632488
Fax: 01738 443505
Displays of local history and agriculture. Seasonal opening.

ATHOLL COUNTRY COLLECTION
Old School, Blair Atholl,
Perthshire PH18 5SP
Tel: 01796 481232
A unique and lively Highland museum with innovative displays of village and glen life from the good old days.

BLACKWATCH MUSEUM
Balhousie Castle, Hay Street,
Perth PH1 5HR
Tel: 0131 310 8530
Fax: 01738 643245
The regimental museum of the Black Watch. 250 years of military history, paintings, medals, weapons and uniforms.

BLAIR CASTLE
Blair Atholl, Pitlochry, Perth
and Kinross PH18 5TL
Tel: 01796 481207
Fax: 01796 481487
Traditional home of the Dukes of Atholl, and their unique private army, the Atholl Highlanders. Blair Castle today boasts a 32 room exhibition of infinite variety, painting a stirring picture of Scottish life from the 16th Century to the present day. The Castle is set in extensive grounds. Entry charge.
For further details see page 94

BYGONES MUSEUM & BALQUHIDDER VISITOR CENTRE
Stronvar House, Balquhidder,
Perthshire FK19 8PD
Tel: 01877 384688

CHILDHOOD HERITAGE CENTRE & TOY MUSEUM
Cuil-an-Daraich, Logierat, by
Pitlochry, Perthshire PH9 0LL
Tel: 01796 482535
Eighteen display rooms covering all aspects of 1920s and 1930s childhood.

CLAN DONNACHAIDH MUSEUM
Clan Centre, Bruar, Pitlochry,
Perthshire PH18 5TW
Tel: 01796 483264
History and artefacts from the 14thC to the present day.

DUNBLANE CATHEDRAL MUSEUM
The Cross, Dunblane, Perth and
Kinross FK15 0AQ
Tel: 01786 823440
Artefacts which illustrate the life of the Cathedral. Collection of communion tokens.

FERGUSSON GALLERY
Marshall Place, Perth, Perth and
Kinross PH2 8NN
Tel: 01738 441944
Housing the largest collection of work by the Scottish colourist painter, John Duncan Fergusson.

GLENLYON GALLERY
The Studio, Bridge of Balgie,
Glen Lyon, Aberlady, Perth and
Kinross PH15 2PP
Tel: 01887 866260
Original wildlife paintings, prints and sculpture by Alan Hayman.

MEIGLE MUSEUM
Dundee Road, Meigle,
Perthshire PH12 8SB
Tel: 0131 668 8800
Notable collection of 27 Pictish sculptured stones from the early Christian period.

PERTH MUSEUM & ART GALLERY
George Street, Perth PH1 5LB
Tel: 01738 632488
Fax: 01738 443505
Displays of local and natural history, fine and applied art. Changing exhibition programmes.

SCOTTISH HORSE REGIMENTAL MUSEUM
The Cross, Dunkeld, Perth and
Kinross
Tel: 01350 727688

RENFREWSHIRE

BARRHEAD COMMUNITY MUSEUM
128 Main Street, Barrhead,
Renfrewshire G78 1SG
Tel: 0141 876 1994
Museum with artefacts depicting the history of Barrhead.

LOCHWINNOCH COMMUNITY MUSEUM
Craw Place, Lochwinnoch,
Renfrewshire PA12
Tel: 01505 842615
A series of changing exhibitions reflecting the historic background of local agriculture, industry and village life.

PAISLEY MUSEUM & ART GALLERIES
High Street, Paisley,
Renfrewshire PA1 2BA
Tel: 0141 889 3151
Fax: 0141 889 9240
A world famous collection of Paisley shawls; the collections illustrate the local, industrial and natural history of the town and district.

SHETLAND ISLANDS

BOD OF GREMISTAR
The Shetland Mills, Lower
Hellhead, Lerwick, Shetland
ZE1 0EL
Tel: 01595 695057
Fax: 01595 696729
This renovated 18thC fishing booth is famous for being the birthplace of Arthur Andersen, a co-founder of the P&O shipping company.

SHETLAND CROFT HOUSE MUSEUM
South Voe, Donrossness,
Shetland
Tel: 01595 695057
Fax: 01595 696729
Typical Shetland thatched crofthouse, refurbished in the style of the late 19thC.

SHETLAND MUSEUM
Lower Hillhead, Lerwick,
Shetland ZE1 0EL
Tel: 01595 695057
Fax: 01595 696729
The main museum of the Shetland Islands houses general-interest exhibitions including geology, archaeology, fishing, agriculture and domestic life.

TINGWALL AGRICULTURAL MUSEUM
2 Veensgarth, Gott, Shetland
ZE2 9SB
Tel: 01595 840344
Fax: 01595 840344

SOUTH AYRSHIRE

BURNS COTTAGE & MUSEUM
Burns National Heritage Park,
Alloway Village, Alloway,
Ayrshire KA7 4PY
Tel: 01292 441215
Fax: 01292 441750
The birthplace of Robert Burns (1759) this thatched cottage houses a museum of Burns' relics.

ROZELLE HOUSE GALLERY
Rozelle Park, Monument
Road, Ayr, South Ayrshire
KA7 4NQ
Tel: 01292 445447
Fax: 01292 442065
A gallery for art and museum exhibits.
For further details see page 94

TAM O'SHANTER EXPERIENCE
Burns National Heritage Park,
Alloway, Ayrshire KA7 4PQ
Tel: 01292 443700
Fax: 01292 441750
An audio-visual presentation depicting Burns' famous poem.

SOUTH LANARKSHIRE

BIGGAR GASWORKS MUSEUM
Biggar, South Lanarkshire
Tel: 01899 221050
Museum of the gas industry with a selection of gas lights and domestic appliances on display and working steam engines on some Sundays in mid-season.

DISCOVER CARMICHAEL
Visitor Centre, Warringhill
Farm, Carmichael Estate, Biggar,
South Lanarkshire ML12 6PG
Tel: 01899 308336
Fax: 01899 308481
Historical wax-work displays, including famous Scottish heroes and villains, wind turbine renewable energy exhibition, deer farm and agricultural displays.

GLADSTONE COURT STREET MUSEUM
Biggar Museum Trust, Moat
Park, Biggar, South Lanarkshire
ML12 6DT
Tel: 01899 221050
Small indoor street of shops, workshops, a bank, telephone exchange and village library.

HUNTER HOUSE MUSEUM
Maxwellton Road, Calderwood,
East Kilbride, South Lanarkshire
G74 3LU
Tel: 01355 261261
Life at the cutting edge.

LEADHILLS MINERS' LIBRARY
Main Street, Leadhills,
Lanarkshire
Tel: 01659 74326
The lead miners' subscription library established in 1741. Rare books, mining documents, and local records and history.

LOW PARKS MUSEUM
129 Muir Street, Hamilton,
Lanarkshire ML3 6BJ
Tel: 01698 283981
The Cameronians (Scottish Rifles) Regimental Museum has been merged with the Hamilton District Museum on Muir Street.

MUSEUM OF LEADMINING
Wanlockhead, by Biggar,
Lanarkshire ML12 6UT
Tel: 01659 74387
Fax: 01659 74481
Set in Scotland's highest village in the beautiful Lowther Hills.

NEW LANARK VISITOR CENTRE
New Lanark Mills, Lanark, South Lanarkshire ML11 9DB
Tel: 01555 661345
Set in a 200-year-old conservation village, this visitor centre houses exhibitions illustrating the history of the village.
For further details see page 94

THE THIMBLE MUSEUM
100 High Street, Biggar, Lanarkshire ML12 6DH
Tel: 01899 221581
Display of collectable items, including thimbles, toby jugs and teapots.

STIRLING

ARGYLL & SUTHERLAND HIGHLANDERS REGIMENTAL MUSEUM
Stirling Castle, Stirling FK8 1EH
Tel: 01786 475 165
Displays on the history of the Regiment. Features weapons, uniforms, silver, medals, colours, pictures.

DOUNE MOTOR MUSEUM
Doune, Perthshire FK16 6HD
Tel: 01786 841203
Fax: 01786 842070

SMITH ART GALLERY & MUSEUM
Dumbarton Road, Stirling, Stirling FK8 2RQ
Tel: 01786 471917
Fax: 01786 449523
Founded in 1874, the Gallery houses a collection of Scottish paintings, with the Museum displaying natural and cultural Scottish artefacts.

STIRLING OLD TOWN JAIL
St John Street, Stirling
Tel: 01786 450050
A 150 year old Victorian Gothic jail, once a military and a civil establishment.

WEST DUNBARTONSHIRE

CLYDEBANK DISTRICT MUSEUM
Old Town Hall, Dumbarton Road, Clydebank, West Dunbartonshire G81 1XQ
Museum on local and industrial history. Displays of sewing machines and a small collection on the story of ship building and engineering.

DENNY TANK
Scottish Maritime Museum, Castle Street, Dumbarton G82 1QS
Tel: 01389 763444
The oldest surviving model ship experiment tank in the world giving an insight into Victorian processes for testing the design of hulls.

WEST LOTHIAN

BENNIE MUSEUM
9–11 Mansfield Street, Bathgate, West Lothian EH48 4HU
Tel: 01506 634944

WESTERN ISLES

BERNERA MUSEUM
Bernera, Isle of Lewis, Western Isles HS2 9LT
Tel: 01851 612331
Local Museum.

SHAWBOST SCHOOL MUSEUM
Shawbost, Isle Of Lewis PA86
Tel: 01851 710213
Created under the Highland Village Competition in 1970, the museum shows the old way of life in Lewis.

WALES

BRIDGEND

SOUTH WALES POLICE MUSEUM
Cowbridge Road, Bridgend CF31 3SU
Tel: 01656 869315
Fax: 01656 869399
Two exciting galleries chronicle the story of policing in Glamorgan from the Celts to the present day.

CAERPHILLY

DRENEWYDD MUSEUM
26 & 27 Lower Row, Butetown, Rhymney, Caerphilly
Tel: 01685 383704
Fax: 01685 383704
Museum comprising an iron worker's cottage including original cellar dwelling restored to 1870s period.

CARDIFF

1ST THE QUEEN'S DRAGOON GUARDS REGIMENTAL MUSEUM
Cardiff Castle, Cardiff CF1 2RB
Tel: 01222 222253 ext 8232
Collection includes KDG Mounted Officer tableau.

CARDIFF CASTLE
Castle Street, Cardiff CF1 2RB
Tel: 01222 878100
Fax: 01222 231417
Castle with Roman and Norman remains.

DE MORGAN FOUNDATION
Cardiff Castle, Cardiff CF1 2RB
Tel: 01222 878100
Fax: 01222 231417
A dedicated room in the Castle contains an important part of the Foundation's collection of William De Morgan tiles and ceramics.

MUSEUM OF WELSH LIFE
St Fagans, Cardiff, Cardiff CF5 6XB
Tel: 01222 573500
Fax: 01222 573491
One of Europe's foremost open-air museums, the Museum of Welsh Life features everything from a castle to the humble moorland cottage of a slate quarry worker among its unique collection of furnished re-erected buildings. Fifty years 1948–1998.
For further details see page 94

THE NATIONAL MUSEUM & GALLERY CARDIFF
Cathays Park, Cardiff, Cardiff CF1 3NP
Tel: 01222 397951
Fax: 01222 573321
A dazzling range of displays on art, natural history and science. Come and be dazzled.
For further details see page 94

TECHNIQUEST
Stuart Street, Cardiff CF1 6BW
Tel: 01222 475475
Fax: 01222 482517
A science discovery centre with 160 interactive exhibits, a planetarium, a discovery room and a hi-tech science theatre.

THE WELCH REGIMENT MUSEUM
Cardiff Castle, Cardiff CF1 2RB
Tel: 01222 229367
Colours, uniform and appointments of the 41st and 69th Foot, later 1st and 2nd Battalions.

WELSH INDUSTRIAL & MARITIME MUSEUM
Bute Street, Cardiff Bay CF1 6AN
Tel: 01222 481919
Fax: 01222 487252
These fascinating exhibits give an insight into the way industry, coal, road, rail and sea, combined to make Cardiff one of the world's premier ports and formed the basis for the rich and varied heritage it enjoys today.

CARDIGANSHIRE

ABERYSTWYTH ARTS CENTRE
Penglais Hill, Aberystwyth, Cardiganshire SY23 3DE
Tel: 01970 622888
Fax: 01970 622883
Situated on the university campus with views over Cardigan Bay.
For further details see page 95

CERAMICS GALLERY
Aberystwyth Arts Centre, The University of Wales, Aberystwyth, Aberystwyth, Cardiganshire SY23 3DE
Tel: 01970 622460
Collection of 20thC pioneer studio and contemporary ceramics and a changing programme of exhibitions.

CEREDIGION MUSEUM & COLISEUM GALLERY
Main Building, Coliseum, Terrace Road, Aberystwyth, Cardiganshire SY23 2AQ
Tel: 01970 633088
Fax: 01970 633084
Local history museum housed in a restored Edwardian theatre.

LLYWERNOG SILVER-LEAD MINING MUSEUM
Ponterwyd, Aberystwyth, Cardiganshire
Tel: 01970 890620
An award-winning restoration of a Victorian water-powered metal-mine which captures the spirit and atmosphere of the 'boom-days'.

THE NATIONAL LIBRARY OF WALES
Aberystwyth, Cardiganshire SY23 3BU
Tel: 01970 623816
Fax: 01970 615709
Legal deposit Library with Exhibition Galleries.

THE SCHOOL OF ART GALLERY AND MUSEUM
University of Wales, Aberystwyth, Cardiganshire SY23 1NE
Tel: 01970 622460
Fax: 01970 622461
Permanent collection of graphic art from 15th–20thC particularly 1860s illustration, 1920s/30s and contemporary prints, 20thC Italian and British photography.

CARMARTHENSHIRE

THE CARMARTHENSHIRE COUNTY MUSEUM
Abergwili, Carmarthenshire SA31 2JG
Tel: 01267 231691
Fax: 01267 223830
Situated in the former Palace of the Bishop of St David's, the museum is surrounded by seven acres of beautiful parkland.

KIDWELLY INDUSTRIAL MUSEUM
Broadford, Kidwelly, Carmarthenshire SA17 4LW
Tel: 01554 891078

MUSEUM OF THE WELSH WOOLLEN INDUSTRY
Dre-fach Felindre, Llandysul, Carmarthenshire SA44 5UP
Tel: 01559 370929
Fax: 01559 371592
The Museum of the Welsh Woollen Industry is located at Dre-fach Felindre which was once the most important wool producing area in Wales and supplied flannel to the mining communities of the South Wales Valleys.
For further details see page 94

NEVILL GALLERY
Vaughan Street, Llanelli, Carmarthenshire SA15 3AS
Tel: 01554 773538
Fax: 01554 750125
Collection of the works of local artists, travelling and other exhibitions.

PARC HOWARD MANSION MUSEUM & ART GALLERY
Llanelli, Carmarthenshire SA15 3AS
Tel: 01554 773538
Fax: 01554 750125
Collection of Llanelli pottery.

CONWY

LLANDUDNO MUSEUM
17–19 Gloddaeth Street, Llandudno, Conwy LL30 2DD
Tel: 01492 876517
Fax: 01492 876517
Features a local history exhibition with artefacts dating from prehistoric times to the Second World War.

ORIEL MOSTYN MUSEUM
12 Vaughan Street, Llandudno LL30 1AB
Tel: 01492 879201

DENBIGHSHIRE

BODELWYDDAN CASTLE
Bodelwyddan, St Asaph, Denbighshire LL18 5YA
Tel: 01745 584060
Fax: 01745 584563
Bodelwyddan Castle has been authentically restored as a Victorian country house and contains a major collection of portraits and photography on permanent loan from the National Portrait Gallery.

MOTOR MUSEUM
Pentrefelin, Llangollen LL20 8EE
Tel: 01978 860324

PLAS NEWYDD
Hill Street, Llangollen, Denbighshire
Tel: 01978 861314
Home of the Ladies of Llangollen. A Gothic cottage with intriguing oak carving, collections, displays, open Easter to the end of October.

RHYL LIBRARY
Museum & Arts Centre, Church
Street, Rhyl, Denbighshire
LL18 3AA
Tel: 01745 353814
Fax: 01745 331438
*Changing programme of temporary
exhibitions featuring a wide variety
of art work and artefacts.*

RUTHIN CRAFT CENTRE
Park Road, Ruthin,
Denbighshire LL15 1BB
Tel: 01824 704774
Fax: 01824 702060
*A Crafts Council selected gallery
housed within a purpose-built
craft centre in the picturesque Vale
of Clwyd. The gallery shows the
best of fine crafts by contemporary
designer-makers from all over the
British Isles. The Centre also
houses a restaurant and 10
independent Craft Studios where
Designer Craftsmen make a wide
range of artefacts ranging from fine
art prints, designer jewellery and
bench glass blowing to folk art and
domestic ceramics.*
For further details see page 95

FLINTSHIRE

GREENFIELD VALLEY
Basingwerk House
Administration Centre,
Greenfield, Holywell, Flintshire
CH8 7RB
Tel: 01352 714172
Fax: 01352 714791
*Museum of buildings and farm set in
70 acres of country park.*

GWYNEDD

BANGOR MUSEUM
Fforddgwynedd, Bangor,
Gwynedd LL57 1DT
Tel: 01248 353368
Fax: 01248 370149
*Country exhibition featuring Welsh
furniture and artefacts with an art
gallery displaying contemporary
work.*

**CAERNARFON MARITIME
MUSEUM**
Victoria Dock, Caernarfon
Tel: 01248 752083
*Discover the maritime past of
Caernarfon and its area.*

**THE CHAPEL OF ART – CAPEL
CELFYDDYD**
8 Marine Crescent, Criccieth,
Gwynedd LL52 0EA
Tel: 01766 523570
*A small art centre, situated opposite
Criccieth Castle, in a restored
19thC chapel, exhibiting high
quality contemporary fine arts and
craft.*

FFESTINIOG RAILWAY
Harbour Station, Porthmadog,
Gwynedd LL49 9NF
Tel: 01766 512340
Fax: 01766 514576
*Museum in part of former goods
shed illustrating the railway's history
from the 1830s to the present day.*

LLECHWEDD SLATE CAVERNS
Blaenau Ffestiniog, Gwynedd
Tel: 01766 830306
Fax: 01766 831260
*Preserved section of a slate mine
offering mine tours to visitors.*

THE LLOYD GEORGE MUSEUM
Llanystumdwy, Criccieth,
Gwynedd LL52 0SH
Tel: 01766 522071
*The museum outlines the life and
times of the statesman and
Highgate, his boyhood home.*

**ORIEL PLAS GLYN-Y-WEDDW
GALLERY**
Llanbedrog, Pwllheli, Gwynedd
LL53 7TT
Tel: 01758 740763
*Mixed exhibitions of contemporary
Welsh and worldwide artists.*

PENRHYN CASTLE
Bangor, Gwynedd LL57 4HN
Tel: 01248 353084
Fax: 01248 371281
*Penrhyn is a gigantic neo-Norman
fantasy Castle by Thomas Hopper
who also designed the magnificent
interior decoration and much of the
furniture.*

**PORTHMADOG MARITIME
MUSEUM**
Porthmadog, Gwynedd
LL49 9LU
Tel: 01766 513736/512864
*Situated on one of the old wharves
of Porthmadog harbour, the last
remaining slate shed houses a
display on the maritime history of
Porthmadog and district.*

SNOWDONIA MUSEUM
Llanberis, Gwynedd LL55 4UR
Tel: 01286 870636
Fax: 01286 871331
*The Snowdonia Museum is the
National Museum of Wales' main
centre in North Wales and is located
in Llanberis in an attractive setting
overlooking Lake Padarn at the foot
of Snowdon.*

SYGUN COPPER MINE
Beddgelert, Gwynedd
LL55 4NE
Tel: 01766 510100
Fax: 01766 510102
*A Prince of Wales and British
Tourist Authority award-winning
family attraction in the heart of the
stunning Snowdonia National Park.*

WELSH SLATE MUSEUM
Llanberis, Gwynedd
LL55 4TY
Tel: 01286 870630
Fax: 01286 871906
*When the extensive Dinorwig
quarry at Llanberis, was closed in
1969 the workshops, most of the
machinery and plant were
preserved and the Welsh Slate
Museum was established.*
For further details see page 94

ISLE OF ANGLESEY

**BEAUMARIS GAOL AND
COURTHOUSE**
Beaumaris, Isle of Anglesey
Tel: 01248 810921
Fax: 01248 790382
*Built in 1829 the Gaol is a grim
reminder of the harshness of justice
in Victorian Britain.*

HAULFRE STABLES
Llangoed, Nr Beaumaris,
Llangoed, Isle of Anglesey
Tel: 01248 724444/490709
*The Stables represent the landed
gentry's way of life in the last
century.*

MUSEUM OF CHILDHOOD
1 Castle Street, Beaumaris, Isle
of Anglesey LL58 8AP
Tel: 01248 712498
*The museum is housed in nine
rooms of a Georgian building
opposite Beaumaris Castle, with
over 2000 items on display it brings
back nostalgic childhood memories.*

ORIEL YNYS MON
Llangefni, Anglesey LL77 7TQ
Tel: 01248 724444
Fax: 01248 750282
*Museum with displays tracing the
history of Anglesey history. Art
gallery with changing programme of
exhibitions. Shop, café. Fully
accessible to the disabled.*

PLAS NEWYDD
Llanfairpwllgwyngyll, Anglesey
LL61 6DQ
Tel: 01248 714795
Fax: 01248 713673
*18thC house by James Wyatt in
stunning location. Houses Rex
Whistler exhibition, his largest
painting. Military museum with
relics from the Battle of Waterloo.*

MERTHYR TYDFIL

**CYFARTHFA CASTLE MUSEUM
AND ART GALLERY**
Brecon Road, Merthyr Tydfil
CF47 8RE
Tel: 01685 723112
Fax: 01685 723112/72
*This Gothic mansion was built in
1824. A museum since 1910, it
now contains fine ceramics, art and
social history collections.*

**JOSEPH PARRY'S
BIRTHPLACE**
4 Chapel Row, Georgetown,
Merthyr Tydfil CF48 1BN
Tel: 01685 721858
Fax: 01685 721858
*Ground floor set in 1840s period as
in childhood of Dr Joseph Parry,
composer.*

**MERTHYR TYDFIL HERITAGE
TRUST**
Ynysfach Road, Merthyr Tydfil
CF48 1AG
Tel: 01685 721858
Fax: 01685 721858
*Award-winning Ynysfach Iron
Heritage Centre, museum of the
iron industry and Joseph Parry's
cottage a restored 1840s
ironworker's cottage.*

MONMOUTHSHIRE

**ABERGAVENNY MUSEUM &
CASTLE**
The Castle, Castle Street,
Abergavenny, Monmouthshire
NP7 5EE
Tel: 01873 854282
*Archaeological exhibits and a social
history of Abergavenny and district.*

CALDICOT CASTLE
Church Road, Caldicot,
Monmouthshire NP6 4HU
Tel: 01291 420241
*A medieval castle with pleasant
gardens surrounded by a wooded
country park.*

**CASTLE AND REGIMENTAL
MUSEUM, MONMOUTH**
The Castle, Monmouth,
Monmouthshire NP5 3BS
Tel: 01600 772175
Fax: 01600 712935
*Historical record of the Royal
Monmouth Engineers (militia), and
the earlier defences of Monmouth.*

CHEPSTOW MUSEUM
Gwy House, Bridge Street,
Chepstow, Monmouthshire
NP6 5EZ
Tel: 01291 625981
Fax: 01291 625983
*Recently moved to this elegant late
18thC town house, the museum's
collections illustrate the history and
development of Chepstow and the
surrounding area.*

GWENT RURAL LIFE MUSEUM
The Malt Barn, New Market
Street, Usk, Monmouthshire
NP5 1AU
Tel: 01291 673777
*Agricultural and craft tools, wagons,
vintage machinery, farmhouse,
kitchen, laundry and dairy.*

MONMOUTH MUSEUM
Priory Street, Monmouth,
Monmouthshire NP5 3XA
Tel: 01600 713519
*Monmouth Nelson Museum and
Local History Centre houses a rich
collection of personal and
commemorative objects associated
with the famous admiral as well as
dealing with the past of this Wye
valley town.*

NEATH AND PORT TALBOT

**CEFN COED COLLIERY
MUSEUM**
Crynant, Neath Road, Neath,
Neath and Port Talbot
SA10 8SN
Tel: 01639 750556
Fax: 01639 750556
*The museum vividly portrays the
story of men and machines involved
in the mining of coal at the former
Cefn Coed Colliery.*

**MARGAM ABBEY STONES
MUSEUM**
Margam, Port Talbot
Tel: 01639 871184

NEATH MUSEUM
4 Church Place, Neath
SA11 3LL
Tel: 01639 645741

NEWPORT

**NEWPORT MUSEUM & ART
GALLERY**
John Frost Square, Newport
NP9 1PA
Tel: 01633 840064
Fax: 01633 222615
*Natural science displays including
geology; fine and applied art,
specialising in early English
watercolours, teapots and
contemporary crafts; Prehistoric finds
from Gwent and Romano-British
remains from Caerwent; local history
including the Chartist movement.*

**ROMAN LEGIONARY
MUSEUM**
High Street, Caerleon,
Newport NP6 1AE
Tel: 01633 423134
Fax: 01633 422869
*The history of Roman Caerleon
and the daily life of its garrison
are featured in the displays of
exciting finds from the area.*
For further details see page 94

**TREDEGAR HOUSE &
PARKNEWPORT NP1 9YP**
Tel: 01633 815880
Fax: 01633 815895
*A guided tour of the house gives
visitors an insight into the life of the
Lords Tredegar and their servants.*

PEMBROKESHIRE

**HAVERFORDWEST CASTLE
MUSEUM AND ART GALLERY**
The Castle, Haverfordwest,
Pembrokeshire
Tel: 01437 763087

MILFORD HAVEN MUSEUM
The Old Custom House, The
Docks, Milford Haven,
Pembrokeshire SA73 3AF
Tel: 01646 694496
*The story of a historic waterway and
a new town's struggle to fulfil its
potential, whales, fishing and oil.*

PENRHOS COTTAGE
Llanycefn, near Meanclochog,
Haverfordwest, Pembrokeshire
Tel: 01437 731328
*A traditionally furnished Welsh
cottage near Preseli Hills that can be
viewed by appointment.*

SCOLTON MANOR MUSEUM
Spittal, Haverfordwest,
Pembrokeshire SA62 5QL
Tel: 01437 731328
*A museum about Pembrokeshire set
in a 60 acre country park.
Countryside Centre, woodland
nature trail, picnic sites.*

**TENBY MUSEUM & ART
GALLERY**
Castle Hill, Tenby,
Pembrokeshire SA70 7BP
Tel: 01834 842809
Fax: 01834 842809
*An outstanding display of the
geology, archaeology, natural and
maritime history of Pembrokeshire.*

TUDOR MERCHANT'S HOUSE
Quay Hill, Tenby SA70 7BX
Tel: 01834 842279

**THE WILSON MUSEUM OF
NARBERTH**
13 Market Square, Narberth,
Pembrokeshire SA67 7AU
Tel: 01834 861719
*A rich collection of objects and
photographs illustrating the life of
Narberth's people and surrounding
villages.*

POWYS

BRECKNOCK MUSEUM
Captain's Walk, Brecon, Powys
LD3 7DW
Tel: 01874 624121
Fax: 01874 611281
*Collections illustrating the local and
natural history of Brecknock.
Including art gallery featuring
contemporary Welsh art.*

CELTICA
Y Plas, Aberystwyth Road,
Machynlleth SY20 8ER
Tel: 01654 702702
Fax: 01654 703604

LLANIDLOES MUSEUM
Temple Street, Llandrindod
Wells, Powys LD1 5DL
Tel: 01597 824513
Social and industrial history of the town. A treasure-chest of exhibits.

OLD BELL MUSEUM & EXHIBITION CENTRE
Arthur Street, Montgomery,
Powys SY15 6RH
Tel: 01686 668313
A 16thC building has been converted into a local history museum by the Montgomery Civic Society, winning a Prince of Wales Award.

POWIS CASTLE
Welshpool, Powys SY21 8RF
Tel: 01938 554336
Fax: 01938 554336
Castle, museum and gardens are all open to the public.

POWYSLAND MUSEUM & MONTGOMERY CANAL CENTRE
The Canal Wharf, Welshpool,
Powys SY21 7AQ
Tel: 01938 554656
The museum displays archaeological collections, the history of the railways and the canal, agricultural development and social history material.

RADNORSHIRE MUSEUM
Temple Street, Llandrindod
Wells, Powys LD1 5DL
Tel: 01597 824513
The social and archaeological history of the old mid-Wales county of Radnor and the growth of Landrindod Wells as a country spa resort.

ROBERT OWEN MEMORIAL MUSEUM
The Cross, Newtown, Powys
SY16 2BB
Tel: 01686 626345
Robert Owen (1771–1858), model employer, social reformer, co-operator.

THE SOUTH WALES BORDERERS AND MONMOUTHSHIRE REGIMENTAL MUSEUM
The Barracks, Brecon, Powys
LD3 7EB
Tel: 01874 613310
Fax: 01874 613275
The museum portrays the history of the 24th Regiment (The South Wales Borderers), as well as associated militia and volunteer units, from 1689–1969.

W H SMITH MUSEUM
24 High Street, Newtown,
Powys SY16 2NP
Tel: 01686 626280
The small museum is on the first floor of the Newtown branch of W H Smith.
For further details see page 95

RHONDDA CYNON TAFF

CYNON VALLEY MUSEUM
Depot Road, Gadlys, Aberdare
CF44 8DL
Tel: 01685 886729
New social history museum looking at the lives of people in the valley over the last 200 years – due to open winter 1998.

MODEL HOUSE CRAFT CENTRE
Bull Ring, Llantrisant, Rhondda
Cynon Taff CF72 8EB
Tel: 01443 237758
Fax: 01443 224718
Visitor centre displaying craft exhibitions and history displays Group talks, craft demonstrations and hands-on activities.

PONTYPRIDD HISTORICAL & CULTURAL CENTRE
Bridge Street, Pontypridd,
Rhondda Cynon Taff CS37 4PE
Tel: 01443 409512
Social history museum with working models, photographs, artefacts and audio-visual displays.

SWANSEA

CERI RICHARDS GALLERY
Taliesin Arts Centre, University
of Wales, Swansea SA2 8PZ
Tel: 01792 295492
Fax: 01792 295899

GLYNN VIVIAN ART GALLERY
Alexandra Road, Swansea
SA1 5DZ
Tel: 01792 655006
Fax: 01792 651713
Pictures, sculpture, glass and Swansea pottery and porcelain.

SWANSEA MARITIME & INDUSTRIAL MUSEUM
Museum Square, Maritime
Quarter, Swansea SA1 1SN
Tel: 01792 650351
Fax: 01792 654200
See the working woollen mill; transport, maritime and industrial displays. Programme of touring and temporary exhibitions.

SWANSEA MUSEUM
Victoria Road, Maritime
Quarter, Swansea SA1 1SN
Tel: 01792 653763
Fax: 01792 652585
Social history, archaeology, natural history, ceramics, costume, archives, photography, topography, local history library.

TORFAEN

BIG PIT MINING MUSEUM
Blaenavon, Torfaen NP4 9XP
Tel: 01495 790311
Fax: 01495 792618
A former working colliery offering unique underground tours 300ft below the surface plus original colliery buildings, workshops, exhibitions and displays.

LLANTARNAM GRANGE ARTS CENTRE
St Davids Road, Cwmbran,
Torfaen NP44 1TD
Tel: 01633 483321
Early Victorian farmhouse with warm, gracious atmosphere.

LLANYRAFON FARM
Llanyrafon, Cwmbran, Torfaen
Tel: 01495 752036
Fax: 01495 752043
Display of agricultural machinery.

THE VALLEY INHERITANCE
Park Building, Pontypool,
Torfaen NP4 6JH
Tel: 01495 752036
Fax: 01495 752043
Museum telling the story of the eastern valley of Gwent.

VALE OF GLAMORGAN

TURNER HOUSE
Plymouth Road, Penarth, Vale
of Glamorgan CF64 1DM
Tel: 01222 708870
A small gallery holding temporary exhibitions of pictures and objets d'art from the National Museums & Galleries of Wales and other sources.
For further details see page 94

WREXHAM

BERSHAM HERITAGE CENTRE
Bersham, Wrexham LL14 4HT
Tel: 01978 261529
Fax: 01978 361703
Remains of John Wilkinson's 18thC ironworks plus archaeological artefacts.

CHIRK CASTLE
Chirk, Wrexham LL14 5AF
Tel: 01691 777701
Fax: 01691 774706
The castle is an outstanding example of a Marcher fortress, built 1295–1310, and is still inhabited.

ERDDIG HALL
Wrexham LL13 0YT
Tel: 01978 355314
Fax: 01978 313333
A late 17thC house with 18thC additions containing much of the original furniture.

KING'S MILL VISITOR CENTRE
King's Mill Road, Wrexham
LL13 0NT
Tel: 01978 362967
Restored mill housing 'The Miller's Tale' – what it was like to live and work in an 18thC mill.

MINERA LEAD MINES
Wern Road, Minera, Wrexham
LL11 3DU
Tel: 01978 753400
Surface remains of a 19thC lead mine including a beam engine house and interpretative displays set in a country park.

WREXHAM COUNTY BOROUGH MUSEUM
County Buildings, Regent
Street, Wrexham LL11 1RB
Tel: 01978 358916
Fax: 01978 353882
Collection includes social history, archaeology and mining exhibits plus hands-on exhibition 'Mechanical Mayhem'.

THEMATIC INDEX

HERITAGE CENTRES

INTERIOR DECORATING

SPORT

TRANSPORT

ALPHABETICAL INDEX

ADVERTISERS' INDEX

Editor:	Rachel Collins
Projects manager (ETB):	Alison Foyle
Production manager:	Steve Capes
Database editorial manager:	Jayne Murphy
Advertisement controller:	Becky Wieczorek
Sales manager:	Leyla Bozdogan
Senior sales executive:	Craig Sher
Publisher:	Natalie Mudd
Editorial production director:	Jayne Forbes
Publishing director:	David Harrington
Managing director:	Chris Letcher

Front cover photos courtesy of: The British Library; Gainsborough's House Society; Imperial War Museum Duxford; National Museum of Photography, Film and Television; National Museums of Scotland; The Natural History Museum

Back cover photos courtesy of: Donington Grand Prix Collection; John M Capes; V&A/George Hoyningen-Huene

Published by Hobsons Publishing PLC, Bateman Street, Cambridge CB2 1LZ

ISBN: 1 86017 457 4

Ref: F661/ELZ/8/E/D/JI

Printed in England by: The Burlington Press (Cambridge) Ltd